EARLY CHILDHOOD EDUCATION

Special Problems, Special Solutions

Contributors

Ted R. Ruggles

Wilma J. Holt

Betty Hart

Judith M. LeBlanc

Mary H. Aangeenbrug

E. Elizabeth Stella

Alita York Cooper

Mildred E. Copeland

Trudylee G. Rowbury

Barbara C. Etzel

Annabelle L. Nelson-Burford

Susan A. Fowler

Note: Preparation of this book was supported in part by the Kansas Research Institute for the Early Childhood Education for the Handicapped Grant from the Office of Education (USOE 300-77-0308).

EARLY CHILDHOOD EDUCATION

Special Problems, Special Solutions

K. Eileen Allen

Elizabeth M. Goetz

University of Kansas
Lawrence, Kansas

AN ASPEN PUBLICATION®
Aspen Systems Corporation
Rockville, Maryland
London
1982

Library of Congress Cataloging in Publication Data

Allen, K. Eileen.
Early childhood education.

Includes bibliographies and index.
1. Child development. 2. Education of children.
I. Goetz, Elizabeth M.   II. Title.
LB1115.A419   372   82-4029
ISBN: 0-89443-657-0   AACR2

Publisher: John Marozsan
Editorial Director: R. Curtis Whitesel
Managing Editor: Margot Raphael
Editorial Services: Jane Coyle
Printing and Manufacturing: Debbie Swarr

Printed in the United States of America

1 2 3 4 5

To the memory of

Florence R. Harris,

friend of children and parents, outspoken critic of *laissez-faire* educational practices, and pioneer researcher in experimental preschool programs. It was she who modeled ways to incorporate successfully the rigor of the experimentalist and the tender, informed understanding of the early childhood teacher into practices that inspired all of us, directly or indirectly.

K. EILEEN ALLEN
ELIZABETH M. GOETZ

9947

Table of Contents

Foreword

From the New Frontier and Great Society programs of the 1960s to the present, there has been a sharply increased awareness in America of the value of early childhood education to children, families, and society as a whole. The development of organized day care for infants and toddlers, and the proliferation of programs for preschoolers have made terms such as "preacademic curriculum," "school readiness," and even "Montessori School" household words, along with "Headstart" and *Sesame Street*. The adaption of these potential benefits for atypical children, whether physically or mentally handicapped, developmentally delayed, learning disabled, retarded, emotionally troubled, or indeed gifted has been an important natural extension of the development of early childhood programs. Child care needs of families in which both parents or the only parent works outside the home, public awareness and acceptance of group care programs of high quality, and the enthusiasm of children for such programs have all contributed to their success, growth, and apparent permanence on the American scene.

In scientific child psychology during these two decades, there has been rapid growth of certain subfields, while others have dwindled and now appear outmoded. Like the growth of early childhood education, the development and application of behavioral technology, though often controversial, do not represent the whimsical trendiness of fads and fashions. Rather they exemplify the systematic and practical application of basic advances in science to the solution of human problems. Their recent growth is not dissimilar to that in electronics, pharmacy, computing, and communications.

There is in psychology, however, a curious split between the radical behaviorists (sometimes called Skinnerians, operant psychologists, behavior analysts, or behavior modifiers) and the rest of the discipline. The split is an unfortunate consequence of the encounter between the conservatism of established science and the brashness of a new approach that threatens the complacency and exclusiveness of the older orthodoxy. As often happens in such conflicts between impatient iconoclastic "presumptors" on the one hand and a status quo-oriented establishment on the other, the radicals tend to overstate their case, often throw away hard-won lessons in their haste to break away from traditional assumptions, and even appear contemptuous of much that is worth retaining of earlier wisdom. This, in turn, prompts an unnecessarily hostile and defensive response from the traditionalists. The innovators are scorned for failure to follow established methods, for reinventing the wheel out of necessity and a lack of background information, and, above all, for teaching that the established truths may be nothing more than foolish myths, inconsequential facts, or empty rituals.

All this would be little more than a tempest in an academic teapot, however, if it were not for two facts. First, the radical behaviorists have frequently turned out to be more practical and effective as engineers and problem solvers than as basic scientists. Second, in the domains where their techniques are most successful, they have acquired a deep sensitivity to the basic human issues in society that often transcends the self-styled humanistic psychologists.

No one in traditional psychology was surprised when the best opportunities for the application of operant psychology turned out to be in situations where the behavior of dependent people could be manipulated "for their own benefit" by an individual who was charged with responsibility for their welfare and empowered to arrange their environments to those ends. After all, the prototype of radical behaviorism is the demonstration of behavioral control by psychologists over laboratory animals. However, few traditional psychologists adequately credit the behaviorists for their deep warmth, respect, concern, and affection for their clients; it is easier to invoke repugnant images of brain-washing and exploitative control of one group over another than it is to discover how much caring and sensitivity can result from the rational application of empirical science. The authors of this volume share that discovery.

Nuclei of sufficient numbers of applied behavior analysts have developed in a few universities so that they are liberated from a need to proclaim, defend, and proselytize. Behaviorists in such enclaves have been free to see how far their once-radical ideas could take them. One such "protected" center of activity has been the large and unique group of behaviorists interested in children that flourishes at the University of Kansas and its affiliated facilities. While not a behaviorist, and a member of the loyal opposition, the author of this Foreword is proud of this tradition at Kansas and of the authors of this volume, all of whom share it.

In the 1960s, a far-sighted chairperson of the Department of Human Development and Family Life, Frances Degen Horowitz, a leading mainstream developmental psychologist, brought to Kansas an outstanding group of behavioristically-oriented child psychologists, many of them disaffected faculty and staff members from the University of Washington. They included third-, fourth-, and fifth-generation students of B. F.Skinner, founder of operant psychology and behavior analysis. Horowitz encouraged their commitment to solving real problems of children (and adults) through the application of behavioral principles, but she also helped maintain the involvement of many of them with the parent science of psychology, and in particular, developmental and child psychology. The result of that breadth of application and commonality of methods has been an extraordinarily successful program of applied research and training that has made the University of Kansas a mecca for child behaviorists.

In addition to psychologists, professionals in such diverse fields as pediatrics, speech and hearing, law, special education, linguistics, human biology, primary education, gerontology, communication research, juvenile delinquency, higher education, community development, mental retardation, nutrition, parent education, and law enforcement have become involved. The Bureau of Child Research, the three-campus University Affiliated Facility, the John T. Stewart Children's Center, the Center for Mental Retardation and Human Development, the Living Environments Group, the Achievement Place Project, the Behavior Analysis Follow Through Model, and the Research Institute for the Early Education of the Handicapped are but a few of the enterprises spawned by this group at Kansas. Indeed one recent university publication boasts that over half of the world's published literature on language delay or disability and its remediation in children has resulted from reseach conducted at this university. In short, the authors of this volume indeed have a supportive environment and what is fast becoming a tradition of excellence behind them.

The key to the success of these applied behavior analysts in working with young children and their developmental anomalies is not that behavior modification is the only way or even the best way to solve all developmental problems. The key does not lie in the support they receive from the large number of like-minded colleagues in the same place working with other problems in other populations, though that support is immensely helpful. The key to their success lies in two fundamental, shared, and transcendent axioms adopted by the applied behavior analysts who work with children, presumptions that are in a sense two sides of the same coin. First, children are always right; that is, their behavior is a lawful consequence of the environmental events that have shaped that behavior. Therefore, second, if the children are not doing what parents, teachers, or caregivers believe they should be doing, then the fault and the remedy lie with those same adults who have some control over their environment.

The first of these leads to a deep respect and affection for young children, no matter how exasperating and apparently self-defeating current behavior may seem. The second lends hope, persistence, and creative energy to those involved in the enterprise of helping them. When student practitioners see the immediate and objectively verifiable results of their first disciplined efforts at modifying a child's change-worthy behavior, there is a surge of optimism and excitement, and the feelings of strangeness, contempt, or aloofness that atypical children so readily arouse are replaced by an individualized caring and commitment. The child-helper is reinforced by the child's progress, which in turn is supported by the helper's involvement in positive behavioral change.

Because behavioral procedures are developed specifically to establish and demonstrate experimental control over the behavior in question (note that this is *environmental* control, not *experimenter* control), and because the criteria by which such control is measured are public, objective, and easily subject to replication or disconfirmation by others, the intervention procedures are what is to be evaluated. This means that allegiance to charismatic individuals, rhetorical postures, fashionable constructs, or embattled theory camps are eschewed in favor of getting on with helping the children. This means that syndrome naming and history blaming become irrelevant in early intervention with developmentally "different" children. It also means that the common enterprise is demystified; it is as accessible to the student as it is to the established and experienced expert. Finally, this approach means that the dependency of the child on the professional helper does not serve to bolster the ego of the therapist. ("See how critical my role is to the well being of this child!") Rather that natural dependency becomes a behavior to be modified. ("See how these children have learned to take control of their own behavior!")

The openness of behavioral techniques to adoption by anyone—parents, caregivers, peers, and especially the child—makes this kind of book both possible and practical. There are no holy mysteries that only the professional may know. Everyone is involved in the treatment program, and the criterion of what works is the graph of behavior from day to day.

In summary, the contributors to this wise, practical, and immensely useful volume share something more than professional expertise and love of children. What they offer is a demonstrably effective way to avoid uncertainty and disputes over what advice and whose advice to follow in a field overburdened with prescriptions. The final arbiter is the child.

JOHN C. WRIGHT
Professor
Department of Human Development and
Family Life and Department of Psychology
University of Kansas
Lawrence, Kansas

Preface

The intent of this book is to weave together the many threads of research related to a behavioral analysis of early identification and intervention of developmental problems in young handicapped, normal, and at-risk children. While this approach has been undergoing research at various centers around the nation, it is the work of many of the authors in this text (and a succeeding text soon to be published) that sets the stage for an experimental analysis of children's behavior in the naturalistic environments of the preschool, day care, home, and clinic. With the exception of the historical perspective of the first chapter, this text is an unfolding of the efforts of the staff at the Edna A. Hill Child Development Laboratory Preschools to find more effective ways of working with young children in need of special help.

The work of this group of researchers is noteworthy, and their research is unique in that each is first and foremost an early childhood teacher, a practitioner, a "hands-on" person. Each is expertly familiar with children and developmental processes; each is attuned to the influence of the family and home on the developing child; each is cognizant of the impact of school and day-care experience in determining major aspects of learning in young children; and, most importantly, each believes that *every* child can learn, and that *every* child can develop more optimally in a learning environment in which there are caring, facilitative adults. It is these early childhood specialists, supervising classroom work with children and training teachers of young children, while at the same time conducting research, who are the contributing authors of this text. Their research takes them in many directions, such as social, language, motor, and cognitive development with varying emphases, including assessment, instructional control, and children's transitions to public school settings.

Authors contributing to this text illustrate colleagueship at its best. They have supported each other in pursuing their individual interests within the framework of a behavioral approach to early chilhood education. Much of the research cited shows two, three, or more individuals working together on behalf of the same child. These same individuals have shared their concern for all types of children even further by joining together to produce this book designed to present an intergrated picture of a behavioral approach to working with the special problems of young children. The *esprit de corps* evident in working together on this project has been a particularly gratifying result for all. We, the editors, thank the authors for sharing their expertise in this group effort to tell the story of ongoing behavioral research in the Edna A. Hill Child Development Laboratory Preschools in the Department of Human Development and Family Life at the University of Kansas.

This book begins with the story of the early development of an applied behavioral analysis approach to early childhood education at the University of Washington. Then, as each chapter unfolds, the book goes on to show how the behavior analysis approach has been effectively expanded and elaborated upon in working with young children over the ensuing years. As the text indicates, the approach has been documented as successful over and over again. As individuals deeply committed to the well-being of young children and their families, we believe that this volume will prove useful in helping all teachers work more sensitively and successfully with all types of children displaying all types of developmental problems.

K. EILEEN ALLEN
ELIZABETH M. GOETZ

Chapter 1

Applied Behavior Analysis and Early Intervention: In the Beginning

K. Eileen Allen

This chapter is written in a story format. If it seems like a sentimental journey into the past, that's because, in many ways, it is. The teachers and the psychologists who are a part of the story are special people who worked with young children and their families to conduct ground-breaking and precedent-setting research in the experimental analysis of the behavior of children in the naturalistic environment of the preschool and the home. Though the story in many ways is a personal account, the research episodes are well documented and are available in numerous technical and popular books, journals, and magazines.

THE PRESCHOOL AS A RESEARCH SETTING

The setting for the initial research studies was originally called the Bailey-Gatzert Institute of Child Development (ICD) on the campus of the University of Washington in Seattle. The physical plant was a two-story, four-square frame building built in 1905 as a temporary exhibit hall for the Alaska-Yukon Exposition. The building still stands and is in daily use. It houses classrooms for young gifted children. The program, conceived by the late Hal Robinson, continues under the directorship of Nancy Robinson. (The Robinsons have long been noted for their work with exceptional children and are the authors of a classic text on mental retardation [Robinson & Robinson, 1976].)

During the late 1940s, after having undergone several remodelings and having served the university in various capacities over the years, the building was once again renovated to become a laboratory nursery school named the Bailey-Gatzert Institute of Child Development. The ICD had one classroom for three year olds and one for four year olds. The facilities were spacious, nicely designed, and furnished with many windows at child height

1

that looked out onto large play yards bordered by trees and green grass. Indoors and out, the classrooms were well furnished with materials and equipment selected for their appropriateness to the age and skill levels of the three- and four-year-old children who were served in the particular classrooms.

In 1960, under the leadership of Sydney W. Bijou, the ICD was reorganized and renamed the Developmental Psychology Laboratory (DPL). Bijou, who had come to the University of Washington in 1948, was a psychologist with a long-term interest in investigating the principles of operant conditioning as derived from B.F. Skinner's work at Harvard. Bijou's goal was to gain a better understanding of developmental processes in young children. In the course of his early work, he became a recognized leader in research related to the effects of various schedules of reinforcement and various types of reinforcers on both retarded and normal children in laboratory settings. In 1957, Donald M. Baer, who had done his graduate work at the University of Chicago with Jacob L. Gewirtz, joined Bijou at the University of Washington and began his own laboratory research on social development. It was at this time that Bijou and Baer commenced their long continuing collaboration on extending learning principles to developmental psychology (Bijou & Baer, 1961).

THE STUDY OF CHILDREN IN A NATURAL SETTING

As in all university-based laboratory preschools, the children served as subjects for the laboratory studies conducted by faculty and graduate students. The studies were carried out in several small experimental rooms on the first floor of the building. As is customary in most laboratory school settings, children were checked in and out of the preschool for brief periods each day to participate in a variety of research studies conducted in small, experimental cubicles.

Soon, however, a new and important dimension was added to the research program: the experimental analyses of child behavior in the naturalistic environment of the preschool classroom itself. The opening of classroom doors to onsite experimental research, the first of its kind to be conducted on the sacrosanct ground of a traditional nursery school, can be attributed primarily to Florence R. Harris. Harris, a traditional child developmentalist, was a nursery school teacher for many years and a college professor of outstanding talent. When Bijou reorganized the child development laboratory, he asked Harris to assume the directorship of the school, which had been renamed the DPL. Harris was a brilliant and farsighted woman who, in her infinite sensitivity and commitment to children and their families, had begun to question the effectiveness of early childhood educators' traditional ways of working with young children, particularly those who were developmentally delayed or deviant.

She voiced her discomfort about the deterministic aspects of child development as espoused by Gesell's genetic maturationist approach; she was also uncomfortable with the use of the then-popular psychodynamic-pathological-Freudian base for attempting to understand developmental problems in children.

Essentially, the genetic and psychodynamic approaches were all that were available as theoretical bases for understanding and teaching about how children grow and develop. All child development programs across the country, with few exceptions, subscribed to a theoretical base that was a combination of genetic and psychodynamic principles. The nursery school staff at the University of Washington was no exception; all were staunch purveyors of an "ages and stages" approach to working with children, for these were the days of genetic supremacy dominated by such concepts as the fixed intelligence quotient (IQ) and maturational "unfolding." J. McV. Hunt's research (1961) on the relationship of intellectual development to experience was information not yet in the popular domain. A change was in store, however. Serendipity was at work; Montrose M. Wolf joined the DPL research team in 1962.

TRAINING TEACHERS IN EXPERIMENTAL ANALYSES OF CHILD BEHAVIORS

Wolf had worked on reading research with A. W. Staats at Arizona State University. There he and his colleagues had demonstrated the utility of token reinforcement in working with individual children. When Wolf came to the University of Washington, he, in collaboration with Jay Birnbrauer, designed a token system for use in an experimental classroom that Bijou had set up at Rainier School, a residential institution for retarded children. More important, however, in terms of this story is Wolf's work with the nursery school teachers in the DPL preschool. It all began with a seminar he held for the preschool staff. Wolf assigned readings on the analysis of behavior which were read, discussed, argued, and hotly contested in the light of the staff's traditional training. Little by little, however, under Wolf's tutelage and Harris' catalystic prompting, prodding, and encouraging, the staff members began to understand operant language and its processes. The seminars were not a one-way exchange however; throughout this period Wolf assured the staff members how much *he* was learning about young children from them.

The next step in the metamorphosis was to work with a laboratory rat. To the traditional early childhood teachers, resistance to the idea was extreme. Disdain, as evidenced in such questions as "Who could learn anything about teaching children from working with a rat?," was matched at the end of the training sessions only by tremendous enthusiasm for what had been learned.

Following is an account of this training based on an early paper by Harris (1967). In this paper, Harris recounts how each teacher, following Michael's manual (1963), trained a subject, a naive rat, to perform a number of complex behaviors:

> Each teacher learned to record the initial or baseline rate of the targeted complex behavior (a nonexistent behavior in the beginning, it might be noted).

> Each teacher learned to specify one goal behavior at a time, to define it precisely, to record its occurrence, and to shape the subject's responses through carefully graded steps toward the goal (with ample allowance for individual differences in getting there).

> Each teacher learned to begin with behavior that the subject already had in its repertoire; to wait for the subject to emit a closer approach to the desired behavior; and then immediately to give reinforcement (in this case, pellets of food).

> Each teacher learned that if the subject's behavior was not shaping up, [he or] she, the teacher, needed to examine [his or] her own behaviors and to correct these, rather than to waste time and energy calling [his or] her subject rat "retarded," "brain-damaged," "negative," "immature," "passive-resistant," "oppositional," or "non-compliant" (terms so popular in those days to explain learning and developmental problems in children).

> Each teacher learned that if [he or] she moved too fast in [his or] her training, [his or] her subject's behavior deteriorated quickly. Thus, the teacher learned to go back to earlier, easier behaviors and start again, progressing more slowly or in a slightly different fashion the second time.

During the seminars that were held in conjunction with this training, there was ample opportunity to discuss, compare notes, argue, engage at times in heated battle, and consider reinforcement principles from all points of view. Experience proved that discussion of all these issues could be kept much more objective, rational, and analytical when it focused on rats as subjects rather than children. After watching many subsequent teachers learn about reinforcement principles in the above fashion, the staff concluded that any complete program of teacher training should combine a study of learning theory with experiences in training a laboratory animal. With such training a teacher would never blame either the handicapped or the normally developing child for failing to learn; instead, the teacher would reexamine and redesign his or her own instructional format to meet the needs of the child.

Acquiring specific skills in observing child behavior in its immediate environmental context was the next step in the training. Bijou and Baer's (1961) *Child Development* was the text, and efforts were focused on the observation and recording of the behaviors of children in the laboratory preschool. Staff members learned to observe and describe behavior in terms of what the child actually said and did, recording both the behavior and events that were immediately contiguous, before and after. They learned to define behaviors functionally and to avoid speculation that went beyond the data. Thus they learned to say, not "an insecure child," but a child who "engaged in thumb-sucking 70 percent of free-play time." They learned to code and record data on one or two selected behaviors, to analyze these behaviors and their consequences in reinforcement terms, and to graph their data. The emphasis in this course was on collecting evidence, that is, empirical data as a basis for planning appropriate intervention procedures.

THE FIRST STUDIES

The course and the laboratory work were Wolf's way of providing short, successful steps (successive approximations) toward a final goal behavior: the actual use of reinforcement principles in working with children. The teachers were now prepared to conduct a study of their own, under supervision. In retrospect, completing a simple study was the best way for teachers to gain for themselves convincing evidence that a reinforcement approach to teaching young children was more effective, faster and therefore less wasteful of "living time" (both the child's and the adult's), and not damaging, but instead beneficial to children and to the total learning environment.

Because the staff members were in an experimental setting, they did have trained observers to help in collecting data. Certainly, paid observers are good to have, but are not absolutely necessary in conducting classroom studies. There are many kinds of data that teachers themselves can collect, such as how many times a child cries, hits out, or smiles. Data of these kinds can be collected readily with pocket counters or pad and pencil while teachers are carrying out regular supervisory duties.

The point is that the staff learned that objective data *must* be collected. Only quantifiable daily records can communicate to everyone concerned the precise ways in which contingencies are being met and behavior changes are taking place in relation to a particular child. The kinds of skills and learning that accrued to the teaching staff can perhaps be illustrated best by describing briefly a few studies selected from a long series of case studies. Certainly it was not easy in the beginning for teachers traditionally trained not to experience some qualms (and not to make some errors).

Regressed Crawling in a Young Child

Harris took the lead in conducting the first classroom study (Harris, Johnston, Kelley, & Wolf, 1964). The child was a physically intact, three-year-old girl who had regressed to almost continuous crawling or crouching. This study taught the staff members a major lesson on the necessity for securing objective data. Beyond a half-hour of anecdotal records of the child's behavior, they had only subjective verbal descriptions—"hearsay" evidence—that the child spent more than 80 percent of each school session in off-feet positions and that teachers had begun giving this regressively infantile behavior a good deal of attention to "build her security" and to compensate for the new baby in the home. Though the staff members had no data to support the intensive increase in their nurturing efforts, a month of such solicitous attention had not improved the child's behavior. In other words, no solid data of any kind demonstrating the ineffectiveness of the traditional nurturing approach to ameliorating the problem had been recorded.

At the time, the staff members were unaware of their error and went ahead with their newly learned social reinforcement procedures, that is, giving adult attention to the child only when she was on her feet, starting with such close approximations as when she pulled herself partially to her feet to hang her sweater on a hook. When crouched or crawling, the child was not to receive teacher attention. One teacher, assigned to see that reinforcement contingencies were precisely met, found it exceedingly difficult to change her own behaviors in accordance with the child's behavior. In fact, for the first half of the first morning of the new procedures, Harris sat by the teacher's side shaking her head and frowning to keep the teacher from approaching the crouching child, then nodding and smiling whenever it was appropriate for the teacher to attend to the child. Fortunately, the child almost immediately began shifting to on-feet activities. Concurrently, the child began to talk and then to laugh with the reinforcer teacher. Within three days, the child's behavior was gratifyingly normal. The staff was amazed and delighted. Sadly enough though, they had secured no data—no concrete evidence—to support their enthusiastic descriptions of what had happened.

At that point in the first study, the staff members naively thought their work was completed because the child was behaving in a more appropriate fashion. It took much persuasion and discussion with Wolf to convince the staff that they had actually proved nothing about the true cause of the behavior change. It might easily have been coincidental, a change in the weather or the child's new shoes. Wolf finally convinced the staff members that a reversal of procedures was mandatory, that is, that teachers must return to their former responsiveness to the child's infantile motor patterns. If off-feet behavior returned, then it was highly probable that teacher attention was indeed the variable responsible for the child behaving more appropriately in the intervention phase of the study. With much trepidation, the staff members performed this step (and concurrently began to record voluminous data). They agreed in advance, however, to stop the procedures at once if any signs of strain on the child were observed. To their amazement, not only did off-feet behavior return promptly, but the child continued to talk, to laugh with adults and children, and to enter all activities that did not require that she be on her feet.

The only person in the classroom who showed signs of being upset over the procedure was the reinforcer teacher. Again, Harris had to sit at one side, this time warning her away whenever the child got to her feet, but cueing the teacher to attend as soon as the child dropped to the floor. At the end of the first morning of the reversal of procedures, after all of the children had left, the reinforcer teacher burst into tears. The strain was excessive on all the adults, although there were no signs of it being detrimental to the child.

This study and many subsequent ones using reversals led the staff members to believe that this experimentally necessary procedure is not only harmless, but may actually benefit a child. Following a reversal, staff members noted for example, that desirable behaviors often returned in even greater strength than before. They also collected evidence that a reversal may help the child to generalize the desirable behaviors. In the study just described, the child, during the reversal period, began to interact with all of the teachers instead of solely with the reinforcing teacher. The child maintained this generalized responsiveness from then on.

The Isolate Child

The next study that was undertaken dealt with a four-year-old girl in her second year of nursery school who rarely played or interacted with other children in the group (Allen, Hart, Buell, Harris, & Wolf, 1964). This four year old was the type of child typically described as shy, withdrawn, insecure, and overly-dependent on adults. This time, the teaching staff knew that it was necessary to collect data before starting an intervention. Systematic observations during baseline indicated that the child spent a large portion of her playtime at school in solitary play or in monopolizing an adult. Little of her time was spent interacting with children. The baseline data indicated further that when she did play with children, teachers seldom interacted with her.

Acting on the hypothesis that play with children (deemed by most early childhood teachers as necessary for optimum social adjustment) could be strengthened if it received the appropriate kind of attention from teachers, a program was planned and put into operation. The teachers agreed that they would not attend to the child when she played alone or when she attempted to interact with them when no peers were present. On the other hand, they would give her continuous attention whenever she interacted with other children. While this seemed to be a good plan in terms of the earlier experience, it had to be revised almost immediately. Daily records showed that the child would immediately turn away from children and the play activity to focus on the teacher delivering the approving statement. Thus, the strategy was reexamined and approving statements were revamped to include the group: "Susie and Ann (the subject child) and Marla, you are making beautiful sand towers. I am going to watch *the three of you* playing together." The isolate child seemed to learn quickly that if she stopped playing with children, the teacher would leave the situation and become engaged in other supervisory tasks. Within a few days, after the isolate child began receiving teacher attention for interacting with children (of course, mere approach and proximity to children received attention in the beginning), social interaction rose from about 15 percent of her total playtime to well over 50 percent. At the same time, her exclusive interactions with teachers, to which teachers were responding minimally, were reduced by half.

On the twelfth day of the study, the consequences of isolate and nonisolate play were reversed. It was immediately evident that the teachers' attention had been the deciding factor. Play with children dropped to a former low, while the child's focus on adults went back up to its earlier high level. After five reversal days, teachers resumed their intervention program, that is, attending to the child's play with children while giving little attention for solitary play or for monopoly of a teacher. Again, the amount of time spent with peers increased markedly. After several weeks the teachers gradually reduced the amount of their attention to the point where the child was receiving no more attention than any other child in the group who was playing sociably. The increased social behavior held up and appeared to be largely self-maintaining, although, of course, the child was now receiving a great deal of attention (reinforcement) from the children with whom she was playing. Post-checks, taken at random throughout the remainder of the school year, indicated a stable maintenance of the appropriate social behavior. What the data did not show was an active, smiling child who seemed to be enjoying her preschool experience to the fullest, much to the delight of her parents and her teachers.

The Operant Cryer

Another early study of a behavior that always seems to interest preschool teachers had to do with two five-year-old boys who did far more crying than any other children in the group (Hart, Allen, Buell, Harris, & Wolf, 1964). The child to be discussed was a sturdy, handsome, capable four year old. Morning after morning, however, he had more crying episodes than any other child in the group. The first few weeks of school passed with no decrease in the child's screams and tears; if anything, there was an increase. After several weeks of dashing to "save" the child or to comfort him, teachers noted the following: (1) the crying was usually set off by some minor bump or frustration; (2) the child rarely got hurt and it was never serious; (3) the child often cast a quick glance around before emitting his piercing cries; (4) the volume increased if no one came at once; and (5) at least one teacher, sometimes all three, hurried to "rescue" him from the current disaster, with one staying to wipe his tears and comfort him. In other words, this child's crying was netting him a great deal of adult attention.

Before starting the intervention procedures, teachers used pocket counters to determine the rate of crying episodes. Over a period of ten days they found that the child averaged about eight all-out crying spells each morning. Once again, the intervention plan that teachers put into effect was straightforward and simple; they would not go to the child when he burst into screams or tears; instead they would remain busy elsewhere until the crying had completely ceased. Concurrently, whenever the child made the slightest effort to resolve his own problem, either verbally or physically, a teacher would go to him immediately and give appreciative attention. Were he actually to hurt himself, one teacher would go immediately to the child.

Positive results came about almost at once. Within five days, the number of crying episodes per day had dwindled to one; during all of the next five days there was only one crying episode. Again, a test procedure had to be put in to make sure that the change in teachers' patterns of responding to the child had brought about the changes. Now teachers paid little heed to the child's noncrying efforts to solve problems with children or materials. Since there was practically no crying to attend to, the teachers, in order to effect a reversal, had to watch for times when the child frowned or grimaced over a bump or mishap. Crying episodes for the next few days showed a steady increase. Having thus proven to themselves by this experimentally rigorous procedure that it was indeed their attention and not some other variable such as maturation that had affected the child's rate of crying, teachers returned to delivering their attention to the child when he was not crying. Crying episodes again became infrequent.

Parents, as always, were kept informed of the progress of the study. As with the isolate child's parents, these parents were also pleased with the changes, and they began to follow, at least to some extent, the same procedures at home.

Building Motor Skills in a Preschool Child

A study undertaken soon after the crying study focused on promoting gross motor skills. The child was a frail, passive, extremely slow-moving three year old who joined in none of the active play experiences that his peers engaged in so vigorously and spontaneously (Johnston, Kelley, Harris, & Wolf, 1966). The child's extreme passivity also seemed to hamper his development of skills in other areas of growth, that is, social, intellectual, and physical. Despite teachers' traditional efforts to stimulate and encourage the child into activities, the records kept toward the end of winter quarter showed that the boy's lethargic and aimless play behaviors were not diminishing; indeed, they were increasing. The records also showed that this sedentary behavior, while repelling or failing to hold playmates, was drawing a good deal of teacher attention. It was decided, therefore, to undertake a study to determine if the child could be helped to become more vigorous and thus better able to participate in the group's activities.

Becoming more vigorous is not a state of being that is easy to define objectively. Teachers agreed, however, that using the tall climbing frame in the play yard required physical behaviors; furthermore, its use could be readily observed and reliably recorded. Therefore, increased activity on the climbing frame was designated as the goal behavior for the child.

Initial records showed that the child's use of this piece of equipment was essentially nonexistent. Therefore, the following program was put into effect. Teacher attention was to be given to the child as soon as (and for as long as) he was in contact with the climbing frame. Since there was practically no climbing frame behavior to attend to, it had to be developed out of a behavior the child already emitted, that is, an occasional lacka-daisical wandering down a nearby cement walk. Stationing herself beside the climbing frame, the teacher in charge of the study busied herself until the child drifted down the walk to a point closest to the frame. Then the teacher turned, spoke, and remained smilingly attentive to the child as long as he paused in that spot or came closer. When he moved away, the teacher immediately turned back to her work with other things. It was not long (actually the first day of procedures) before the child came closer and paused longer. At that point, the teacher, according to plan, began to expect more of the child. Soon he actually touched the frame and next, put his foot tentatively on the lowest rung. By the end of the first day, the child had begun some tentative climbing. By the third day, climbing be-havior had markedly increased. On the ninth day, the child spent more than 60 percent of the play period using the climbing frame. Although the data cannot show the actual vigor of his play, teachers reported that the child was in almost constant motion on the seventeenth and eighteenth days. Teachers, of course, gave continuous social reinforcement as long as this formerly lethargic child remained on the climbing frame.

In order to determine if the new behavior was indeed a result of the shift in adult attention, teachers withheld their attention for a few days when the child was on the climbing frame. He was, however, given im-mediate attention for engaging in any other activity. For two days the child spent frequent, though brief, periods on the climbing frame. Then climbing frame activity dropped to zero and remained at a near zero rate for the rest of the reversal period. The child did, however, engage actively in many other forms of outdoor play, including use of other climbers, the easel painting facilities, and the large hollow blocks. While participating in these activities the child, of course, received ample amounts of adult attention. On the twenty-fourth day of the study, adult attention to climbing frame behavior was reinstituted. The child's climbing on that particular piece of equipment returned quickly and remained high on a day-after-day basis. The teacher decided therefore that the objective for the child had been achieved: he was now a vigorous climber!

Postchecks made the following year showed that the child maintained his vigorous play behavior, spending about half of his outdoor playtime in spontaneous and skilled use of the various pieces of climbing apparatus while in the company of other children. Presumably, vigorous physical social activity had become pleasurable for this child. His parents were certainly pleased, especially at his increased appetite, better sleeping patterns, and healthier color. Teachers were delighted, too, with his zest for all types of activities, including preacademic, music, and rhythms.

When reporting these early studies at various professional meetings, teachers and program directors often questioned the brief periods of withholding of teacher attention following a successful intervention. They were concerned that the procedure, even though necessary for rigorous experimental research, might be detrimental in some way to the child. The staff members had the same questions and anxieties in the earliest studies and had watched closely for any signs in a subject-child's behavior that the procedure might be detrimental in any way. Not one such sign was ever in evidence. Indeed, the teachers began to believe that the procedure was often of actual benefit to a child. They noted, for example, that children often seemed to generalize and expand the more desirable behaviors to other situations. In the climbing frame study, for example, the child, during the reversal period, began to use such materials as outdoor easel paint, finger paint, and hollow blocks actively and purposefully for the first time.

In the course of the climbing frame study and others, it was also noted that, while teacher efforts were concentrated on the modification of one behavior, other behaviors also changed. Again, using the climbing frame study as an example, the child played and talked with children who came to join in the fun. Thus, social and verbal behaviors increased along with the motor behavior, suggesting that classes of behaviors may be reciprocal and developmentally responsive to teacher attention.

Developing Attention Span in a Five Year Old

What to do with a child who always appeared to be in constant motion was another question for study during those early years. The child in this study (Allen, Henke, Harris, Baer, & Reynolds, 1967) was close to his fifth birthday and was scheduled to go to kindergarten in the fall. He appeared to have a well-developed repertoire of physical, social, and verbal skills, yet he rarely settled down to any sustained activity; in other words, he displayed all of the behavioral symptoms of the classic hyperactive. During the initial daily recording period, the child was observed flitting from activity to activity, as much as 82 times during a 50-minute session of free playtime. The overall average for this pretreatment period was 56 activity changes per 50-minute session with an average stay of only 55 seconds per activity. Analysis of the data revealed that the child's flitting from one thing to another consistently produced consequences from the teachers as they attempted to encourage, suggest, or structure more lasting activities for him.

Satisfied on the basis of the daily records that a serious problem did in fact exist, the following program was put into effect: (1) all teacher attention was to be withheld until the child had remained with an activity for one continuous minute; (2) at that moment, a teacher was to go to the child and give interested attention and support to him and his activity, whatever it might be; (3) the teacher was to stay with the child for the duration of that activity, but to turn to other supervisory tasks the moment he left; (4) the teacher was to keep busy with other things until the child again engaged in an activity for one continuous minute; and (5) a teacher was never to attempt to reengage the child in an activity when he was leaving or was on the move.

In this study an observer was used not only to record precise time intervals, but also to cue the teachers as to when it was appropriate for them to attend to the child in terms of the length of time he had been engaged in an activity. The observer signaled the teachers by moving into an upright position a bright red card attached to her clipboard. There the card remained, in conspicuous view, for the duration of the child's stay at that activity. The remainder of the time the observer kept the red cue card out of sight, indicating that teacher attention was to be concentrated elsewhere.

The one-minute criterion mentioned earlier as a part of the intervention plan was chosen as a first approximation to increased span of attention, since the initial data indicated that the child occasionally held on an activity for that length of time. As in preceding cases, when a behavior is virtually nonexistent or exhibited infrequently, effective teaching must focus on attention to small steps in the appropriate direction. Thus, many "successes" are assured the child as he or she moves incrementally toward the goal.

In this particular case study, the plan, starting with only one minute of participation in an acitivity, resulted in an immediate decrease in the actual number of activity changes. The average number of activity changes following the change in procedure was 27 per session for an average duration of one minute 51 seconds per activity, twice that of the initially recorded period.

Two particular days during the course of the study deserve special attention. On one day the child's mother was present for her regularly scheduled once-a-month visit (such visits were an involvement built into the program for all parents). The mother, a highly voluble individual, interacted with her child freely by commenting, suggesting, directing, and questioning him at frequent intervals. This class session with the mother in attendance represented the greatest number of activity changes for this stage of the program. Looking back into the preintervention data, it was interesting to note, too, a peak day that was also one of the mother's earlier visiting days. It became the obvious conclusion that the attention of the child's mother was of far greater value to the child than the attention of the teachers. What is also interesting is that the mother was attending to behaviors, that is, frequent activity changes, that were incompatible with what teachers were giving their attention to, that is, infrequent activity changes. These two unusual data points only strengthened the evidence that the child's short attention span was in large part a function of the attention of significant adults.

By the end of the school year, the child was often spending 15, 20, or 25 minutes in one activity. The mother reported that he was more settled at home, too, although no data were collected there. Both the parents and teachers considered the child eminently more ready to meet the expectations of public school than he would have been if left to mature and settle in naturally.

The Terrible Twosome

One of the early studies that continuously strikes a responsive note with teachers focused on a "terrible twosome" (Allen, Henke, Harris, Baer, & Reynolds, 1967). The two boys, both almost five years old, roamed the playground and schoolroom with what seemed to be one purpose: creating havoc by taunting other children, interfering with ongoing play projects, racing about aimlessly and destructively, and defying teachers. In addition, they had an extensive array of bathroom words and behaviors that was continually expanding through their mutual efforts. When apart, each child exhibited a perfectly normal range of social behaviors with children and adults. The major problem was that they were seldom apart unless they had quarrelled or vowed never to play with the other again as long as they both should live. That vow was seldom kept longer than ten minutes, as is typical of all young children.

The teaching staff agreed midway through the fall semester that if the other children were to be protected from harrassment and if the boys themselves were to profit from the preschool experience, the boys' time together must be reduced. Thus, a number of traditional guidance procedures had been tried (for example, redirection, provision of a punching bag, and the arranging of special projects). None had had more than a limited effect on the problem behaviors. A drastic alteration in the teaching strategy was needed; therefore, a behavior management program was designed and implemented.

Two teachers were assigned to the children as a part of their regular supervisory responsibilities; one teacher was to be responsible for one boy, and the other teacher for the other boy. Never was a teacher to attend to either boy as long as they were together. The moment they separated, however, no matter how briefly or for what reason, each teacher was to go to her particular child, giving him warm, undivided attention. If at all possible, she was also to steer him subtly into the activities of the nearest group of children, unless his cohort was among the children in that group. The moment the boys teamed up again, both teachers were to move away, busying themselves elsewhere.

While these plans sounded practical, the staff had strong doubts that their attention would be powerful enough to compete with the reciprocally reinforcing qualities that the boys seemed to hold for each other. Such doubts were soon dispelled. Between days 15 and 27 of the study, the boys were spending less than 15 percent of their playtime together and approximately 75 percent of it with other children.

The usual reversal was invoked, at the end of which the teachers redoubled their efforts to give attention to the boys' purposeful activities with other children so that each boy might acquire an extensive set of alternate playmates. Postchecks taken at random throughout the remaining months indicated that such a goal had been achieved. Each boy was spending 58 percent to 77 percent of his time with other children, only 13 percent to 21 percent with his former "best friend." Teacher attention was now at a rate commensurate with the amount received by other children and was presented to the two boys noncontingently with one exception: if they engaged in one of their former disruptive acts together, the teacher withdrew. Postchecks during the remainder of the semester showed that the two boys continued to play with a range of other children and with each other, though infrequently as an exclusive pair.

During this period of the early and mid-1960s, the staff members worked with a variety of other problem behaviors in young children, problems typical of those concerning teachers in all types of early childhood settings, because the problems were seen as contributing factors in promoting developmental delays or deviations in children. They demonstrated, for example, how children's verbal skills could be improved in terms of both quantity and quality (Allen, Hart, Buell, Harris, & Wolf, 1967). They demonstrated the decrease of negative, hostile behaviors in a four-year-old girl so that she became more acceptable to her peer group (Hart, Reynolds, Baer, Brawley, & Harris, 1968). They also examined the reciprocity effects of improving outdoor play skills on the social development of a three-year-old girl (Buell, Stoddard, Harris, & Baer, 1968).

This early work was exciting. The studies taught the staff members that young children's behavior was directly responsive to a variety of factors in the environment. The most important (and powerful) environmental factor, however, was the attention of significant adults. In the preschool, of course, this meant the teachers and how they responded to the children. The long series of experimental studies conducted during this period demonstrated that quite ordinary forms of social responsiveness on the part of teachers—looking toward, smiling at, talking to, and assisting children and providing them with interesting materials, self-motivating play activities, and challenging learning experiences—functioned in one way or another as positive reinforcers for the child in the group. The staff members learned that by controlling the timing of these various forms of social responsiveness, teachers were able to change quickly and dramatically those behaviors in a child that seemed to be interfering with his or her ability to make full use of the learning opportunities available in the preschool.

Baer (1967) summarized the procedure well in describing appropriate responsiveness on the part of the teachers:

> A teacher may reinforce a behavior then by turning toward it in [his or] her usual way; when the behavior ceases or is replaced by an undesirable behavior, the teacher may keep the effects of [his or] her reinforcement consistent simply by turning away. Turning away is not an act of punishment in this application: the teacher turns away not in anger, disapproval, or spite; [he or] she simply turns away, as [he or] she does many times from every child in the group during any normal session. For the teacher, then, [his or] her technique of reinforcement is simple: what [he or] she turns toward will increase, what [he or] she does not turn toward, or turns away from will not increase. (p. 4)

WORKING WITH AUTISTIC CHILDREN

The experimental work just described generated a tremendous amount of interest both locally and far afield. The staff members were invited to travel to various clinical and institutional settings to consult about children in severe trouble. One of these early studies, done in a children's residential hospital setting, is of particular interest because of the dramatic demonstration of the efficacy of early intervention. The series of interventions with this child resulted in several data-based and widely disseminated studies that have served as exemplars in college courses and for personnel training programs around the country throughout the intervening years. Following is a brief case history and synopsis of the studies.

The Story of Dicky

Dicky, as he is called in the published research papers (Nedelman & Sulzbacher, 1972; Wolf, Risley, Johnston, Harris, & Allen, 1967; Wolf, Risley, & Mees, 1964) was just past three years of age when the intervention program was undertaken. From the child's clinical records it appeared that he had progressed normally until nine months of age when cataracts were discovered in the lenses of both eyes. At that time severe temper tantrums and sleeping problems began to develop. During his second year, Dicky had a series of eye operations that culminated in the removal of the occluded lenses in both eyes, making it mandatory that he wear glasses. Year-long efforts by his parents failed to establish glasses wearing. During this time Dicky was seen by a variety of specialists who diagnosed him, variously, as profoundly mentally retarded, diffuse and locally brain-damaged, and psychotic. One specialist recommended that he be placed in an institution for the retarded since his prognosis appeared to be so poor.

Dicky did, in fact, have many problems. He did not eat normally, and he lacked normal social and verbal repertoires. He also had severe tantrums, which included self-destructive behaviors such as head banging, self slapping, hair pulling, and face scratching. His mother reported that after a severe tantrum, "He was a mess, all black and blue and bleeding." In addition, he did not sleep much at night, forcing one or both parents to remain by his bed. Sedatives, tranquilizers, and restraints were tried, without notable success.

At the age of three Dicky was admitted to a children's mental hospital with the diagnosis of childhood schizophrenia. A few months later the ophthalmologist predicted that unless Dicky began wearing glasses within the next six months he would lose his macular vision permanently. At that point, Montrose Wolf and Todd Risley of the DPL staff were invited by the hospital staff to serve as consultants in training Dicky to wear his glasses. First, however, before the child could be trained to wear his glasses, it was necessary to reduce the frequency and severity of the child's problem behaviors, for it was these that made training sessions in wearing glasses impossible to conduct.

The tantrums were dealt with by a combination of extinction and mild punishment. At the onset of a tantrum, the hospital attendant sent Dicky immediately to "his room" (a hospital room containing a bed, chair, table, and window). The door was kept closed until the tantrum behavior subsided. The initial tantrums were violent, one lasting more than 45 minutes. Even so, the procedure was adhered to and, by the end of the 2½ months, the more severe self-destructive behaviors such as head banging, face scratching, and hair pulling, had almost completely disappeared; crying, screaming, and face slapping were almost nonexistent after about 5½ months.

The bedtime problems were handled in a similar manner. Dicky was prepared for bed, cuddled, and tucked in with the door left open. If he got out of bed, he was told to return to bed, or his door would be shut. This procedure produced a series of tantrums for five consecutive nights. On the sixth night, Dicky was tucked in and soon went to sleep without making a scene. Bedtime was seldom a problem again.

Glasses wearing was brought about through a process often referred to as *shaping*. The glasses were first held in front of Dicky, then moved closer and closer until they were placed in contact with his face for a brief moment, trial after successive trial. Bites of meals were used as reinforcers. Later, as the child came under social control, other rewards or reinforcers, such as walks, rides, play, snacks, and toys, were used to shape and maintain glasses wearing. Once shaped, glasses wearing increased gradually from only a few minutes a day to about 12 hours a day.

The procedure used for generating verbal language was similar to that used to teach glasses wearing. Dicky's verbal behavior was originally limited to occasional echolalic responses and the rote singing of certain songs. Again, using bites of his meals as reinforcers, the attendant first reinforced Dicky for imitating her verbally as she named a series of five pictures, one at a time. After several days the attendant gradually omitted saying the word first, with the result that Dicky would usually say the word without a prompt. In three weeks he was making appropriate labeling responses to ten pictures. He then progressed to picture books, common objects, and finally to naming various objects not in immediate view.

After almost seven months in the hospital under this kind of systematic programming, Dicky's case was reviewed. Since he was wearing his glasses all day long, was having almost no tantrums or bedtime problems, and was developing a rudimentary verbal and social repertoire, Wolf and Risley reasoned that the hospital environment seemed less beneficial than his home might be. Dicky was discharged from the hospital. Prior to sending him home, however, his parents were trained to deal with the problems described earlier in case they should arise again. Telephone interviews held soon after Dicky's release indicated that all was well and that Dicky was continuing to make progress.

In later interviews the parents continued to report no recurrence of the severe problem behaviors. In fact, they appeared to be quite content with their little boy who was now almost five years old. However, the child was neither toilet trained nor did he appear to be making progress in social, language, or self-help development. The father explained that attempts to instruct Dicky in these areas often led to the child becoming "fussy," a condition that had preceded the temper tantrums before his hospitalization. When left to his own devices there was no difficulty, but when it was firmly suggested that he learn something new or out of the ordinary, he showed the preliminary stages of his old tantrum behavior. This "fussiness" had been effective in suppressing his parents' attempts to establish further self-help and play skills. Thus, it was recommended that Dicky be enrolled in the laboratory preschool where the teaching staff had had a wide range of experiences in working effectively with many types of problem behaviors.

Dicky attended preschool regularly each weekday morning for two years. In the beginning Dicky showed many of the same behaviors that his father had described. He spent most of his time lying on the floor, repetitively twirling a small object in his hand or wandering aimlessly about the room or play yard. Left alone he was no problem. However, when the teachers began guiding him firmly through activities or offering him play objects, he began to whine. When the teachers persisted, Dicky reacted more vigorously. In a few days, he began crying and slapping himself, a return to his old temper tantrum pattern. The teachers attempted to disregard the outbursts. At the same time, they tried *not* to let the outbursts terminate the instruction period, since it was felt that termination would only serve to maintain the tantrums. However, the loud and self-destructive tantrums were difficult to ignore; in addition, during their occurrence it was impossible to engage him in an instructional activity or game. After several days it seemed apparent that the tantrums and slapping behavior were not going to diminish as a result of the ignoring condition; in fact, they appeared to be increasing in severity. The tantrum problem had been dealt with in the hospital by sending Dicky to "his room" contingent upon each tantrum. It was decided to arrange a room in the nursery school for Dicky where he would be taken when he began to have tantrums. In the hospital, approximately 100 trips to "his room" had been necessary to eliminate tantrums. It took only three trips to eliminate them at school.

Dicky had received no systematic toilet training and wore diapers on a regular basis. As noted earlier, Dicky's parents were hesitant to pursue any training that provoked reactions similar to the earlier severe tantrum behavior; toilet training was no exception. The teachers, therefore, set about teaching Dicky to use the toilet. First, the child was familiarized with the bathroom itself and what the children did there. Soon Dicky learned to take his clothing down and stand up to the toilet, although he never did make the crucial response. Then, during the fourth week of school, Dicky was taken alone to the bathroom and placed in front of the toilet. The teacher had a small bag of M & Ms in her hand which she showed to Dicky as she instructed him. This time he did produce a trace and was given an M & M. (M & Ms were a popular reinforcer in the early days). That day after school another attempt was made, and again Dicky produced a trace and received an M & M. This time, the teachers kept him at the toilet a little longer. Soon he gave a slightly larger trace and received another M & M. After an additional period of waiting, a short stream occurred; a few minutes later another short stream. He then appeared to relax and voided completely. Each response had resulted in a bite of an M & M. The complete series had taken about 25 minutes.

The following day Dicky urinated twice at school when taken to the toilet. On these occasions he was able to perform fairly soon after being placed at the toilet. That same afternoon he urinated in the toilet at home for the first time. For a few days, he was given M & Ms both at home and at school for each use of the toilet. By the end of the first week, these were discontinued. However, a successful urination continued to evoke warm praise from teachers and parents. The parents reported only a few further instances of wet pants at home; there were no more at school. After appropriate urination in the toilet was strongly established, bowel training was begun. It, too, was accomplished readily, this time within a few days.

Dicky had several bizarre behaviors of the type frequently called autisms. One was a rhythmic twisting of the head and shoulders; another, which the staff called "fiddling," involved a rapid flexing of his fingers and hands, often while touching toys, objects, or people. Through systematic programming the staff members were able to teach the child to use play materials without these repetitive maladaptive responses and eventually to engage in play activities with other children. The daily records indicated that as the rate of constructive activities increased, the rate of autistic-type behaviors reciprocally decreased. Remnants of the fiddling did persist, however. One film that was made during the latter half of his second school year shows Dicky painting at an easel with great absorption. At one point, as he put his paint brush back into the paint cup before selecting another color, he flipped his fingers against his leg a couple of times. This behavior no longer appeared bizarre, however, for the episode was so brief and was obviously in the context of great concentration on an appropriate task. (Actually, all people have small nervous mannerisms that they display at times. Dicky's mannerisms by this time were appearing quite normal.)

During the two years in the preschool, the staff also worked intensively on Dicky's verbal and prereading skills. Much of this work was planned by Baer and carried out in one-to-one training sessions as well as in the naturalistic environment of the preschool. The following autumn (by this time Dicky was seven years old) he was enrolled in a special education public classroom in his own community. His adjustment went smoothly and well. During his primary years, Dicky reached grade level in all subject areas.

Several years ago when Dicky was about 13 years of age, a videotape was made (Neldeman & Sulzbacher, 1972). A major part of the tape focuses on a conversation between Dicky and one of his former nursery school teachers. At this point Dicky was in a regular junior high school where he was at grade level or above in all academic areas. He was apparently comfortable and content with his social life and was engaging in a number of recreational activities that seemed to be satisfying to him.

As far as peculiar mannerisms were concerned, a review of the videotape indicated that Dicky had no more than the teacher had. Dicky occasionally flipped the corner of his collar, the teacher rolled and rerolled the ends of a ribbon tie that she wore. Dicky shot his fingers forward and back once in awhile, she twisted her rings back and forth. Dicky turned his head aside frequently to escape the glare of the studio lights on his heavy lensed glasses, the teacher often closed her eyes momentarily. The teacher and the youth were pretty well matched; they looked equally normal or equally peculiar, depending on the viewer's perspective. What was obvious was that both were enjoying reminiscing about Dicky's years in the preschool. Obvious, too, was the fact that Dicky's memory was considerably better than the teacher's about several earlier events.

Brian

As the initial successes with Dicky became known, various clinics and hospitals called on the staff for consultations on other severely disturbed children. The case study of Brian (Dodge, Harris, & Allen, 1967) was typical of several conducted during this period. The child, a seven-year-old boy labeled as autistic, was in his second year of residential treatment in the children's psychiatric ward of a medical center. Never had Brian been seen to smile, laugh, cry, or look directly at another individual, although he did engage in frequent screaming episodes. Brian passed his days looking at the wall, fiddling with pieces of string, or watching the water as it ran out of the faucet and down the washbasin drain. The attention of others, adults or children, appeared neither to be of interest to him nor to hold any reinforcing value. Therefore, the experimental teacher, who was able to go into the ward for only one hour a day, began intervention by pairing herself with the child's lunch. She fed him his meal, making each bite contingent upon some bit of behavior that eventually would be part of a more complex social response. The teacher/experimenter began by training a rudimentary but necessary requisite to social behavior, that is, simply trying to get eye contact. Even this was too great a step for this child, however. Therefore, bit by bit and bite by bite, holding the spoon at successively higher levels near her face and moving up gradually from her chin to her eyes, the teacher got Brian to visually follow the travels of the food-laden spoon, thus bringing his head up to where eye contact was almost impossible to avoid. When eye contact was well established and the child engaged in it spontaneously, the teacher moved to attempting to get Brian to smile and laugh; in other words, hand shaping those basic social responses, that are established almost automatically in most infants by two or three months of age. Once the child was showing basic social responsiveness, the teacher moved to the shaping of receptive language, that is, simple direction following and imitation responses, such as "Touch your nose," "Open your mouth," and "Clap your hands." The next step was teaching interactions with play materials, such as blocks, simple puzzles, jumping boards, and water play toys.

So rapid was Brian's improvement that by the end of five weeks (about 28 hours of work with the child), staff members began to bring him to the laboratory preschool for one hour each morning so that he might be exposed to a more normal social milieu. At first he withdrew completely into many of his former autistic behaviors. After he was judged to be well adapted and comfortable in the new situation, the experimental teacher began to respond differentially. That is, she gave Brian attention for all activities *except* the detrimental wall gazing, string fiddling, and water watching. When he did engage in any of the latter behaviors, she turned away. The maladjustive behaviors dropped out quickly under this procedure, while appropriate episodes of play with materials increased rapidly.

The change, however, was evident *only* during his one hour each day at the laboratory preschool. On the ward, Brian continued to be the same severely impaired child that he had always been. Explaining the reason for such differences in the child's behavior was not difficult. The daily treatment program on the ward was based on concentrated one-to-one interactions between therapist and child throughout much of the day. The staff person exercised no contingencies, supplying instead continuous loving care and total "acceptance" of all of the child's ward behaviors (which, as described earlier, were almost entirely bizarre). The pictures of the child in the two milieus were in sharp contrast, verging almost on the eerie. It was as if there were two different boys encased in the same skin, the one a thorough-going autistic, the other an active, smiling, vocalizing child who was almost ready to take the next step in the socialization process, that of interacting with other children. It was not the amount of adult attention that led to this child acquiring a beginning set of more appropriate social behaviors; rather it was the type of behaviors to which important adults were responding that determined which behaviors would predominate in which environment.

Charles

Another study (Brawley, Harris, Allen, Fleming, & Peterson, 1969), also conducted on a children's psychiatric ward, further illustrates the role of differential adult attention in shaping either appropriate or inappropriate behavior patterns in young children. This child, Charles, was a seven-year-old boy who was also diagnosed as autistic and was nearing the end of two years of psychiatric treatment. The staff felt that institutionalization was the next step, as the child had shown little improvement over the two years of intensive treatment. The baseline data that the experimental teacher gathered showed that Charles spent more than half his time on the ward engaged in severely maladaptive behaviors, for example, hitting himself about the face and head, or being almost immobilized and staring off into space, vocalizing incomprehensibly, and engaging in catastrophic outbursts and severe temper tantrums. Only about one fourth of the child's time was spent in appropriate speech or interaction with materials. The data indicated that caregiving adults on the ward devoted the preponderance of their attention to the child's outbursts, such as the self-hitting episodes, temper tantrums, and screaming spells.

To get a start on changing Charles' severely maladaptive behaviors, the teacher-experimenter again employed food; this time, she used potato chips, a favorite food for this child. She also introduced into the treatment-experimental sessions a variety of play and academic materials with which she hoped to shape appropriate play and work skills. The intervention plan called for the presentation of a piece of potato chip whenever Charles made any attempt to interact with or verbalize appropriately about the material being presented. Adult attention in the form of smiles, nods, and approving words was paired with the bits of potato chip. Soon, adult attention became a strong reinforcer for this child, and the potato chips needed to be used only infrequently.

Appropriate use of materials began to increase almost immediately after the start of intervention, although appropriate verbalizations, which had been almost nonexistent during baseline, rose only slightly. Soon, however, verbalizations began to increase too, as did appropriate use of materials. The child was so responsive to treatment procedures that it was decided to involve his mother in the intervention program at this point. The teacher-experimenter taught the mother the techniques that were being used in the daily training sessions while the physician who was working with the preschool staff on this experimental intervention project worked with the family at home, helping all members of the family to respond differentially to Charles. That the training (both on the ward and at home) was effective can be seen from the physician's report of the following episode that he witnessed in the home.

It was dinner time, and the family (mother, father, and five children) were all at the table when Charles began a string of bizarre verbalizations and self-hitting behaviors. As one person, every member of the family turned away, chatting among themselves while not so much as looking in Charles' direction. When he stopped the maladaptive behaviors, as one person, the family turned and resumed their interactions with him for as long as he maintained appropriate behaviors.

AN EARLY STUDY OF PARENT-CHILD INTERACTION

As the staff worked with children like the ones just described, it became increasingly evident, as Bronfenbrenner (1976) noted much later, in discussing early intervention, that the only truly effective programs are those that involve the parents. One of the early, more dramatic parent involvement intervention programs (Allen & Harris, 1966) was centered on a five-year-old girl who, according to the mother, had engaged in mutilative self-scratching for more than a year. The scratching had resulted in unsightly scabs and sores on the child's nose, forehead, left cheek, and neck, as well as up and down the child's left leg and arm. When the mother brought the child to the DPL for an initial visit, the child was indeed unsightly.

Her parents had sought medical help for many months and from several sources, but no amelioration of the problem had been effected. The most recent professional advice had been that the child's arms be placed in pneumatic splints to restrain her self-scratching. The mother was reluctant to use such drastic measures, but she could see no alternative if the child was not to be permanently disfigured. During the initial visit additional difficulties were also revealed by the mother. The parents apparently had tried various disciplinary approaches in their efforts to stop the child's scratching. Often the father spanked the child severely when her scratching reopened partially-healed sores. The spankings disturbed the mother, as did the husband's constant berating of what he considered the mother's inept handling of the child's scratching.

In addition, the mother, who was expecting another child soon, said that she was so repelled by the little girl's appearance that she had come to have an intense dislike for her. Often, said the mother, she had even wondered if the child and the marriage would not be better off if the child were placed outside the natural home. The case was certainly a difficult one; the teacher-experimenters were not sure they could help, but said they would be willing to try if the mother felt that she and her husband could participate in an intensive home intervention program. The mother replied that the father would not become involved in direct therapy, but he would probably become involved, at least to some extent, in the home program.

A first step in designing an intervention program was to schedule observations of mother-child interactions in the playroom at the laboratory preschool. Two important conditions were noted: (1) the child was basically an attractive little girl with a well-developed repertoire of social, verbal, cognitive, and physical skills; and (2) the mother interacted in an almost entirely negative fashion with the child by scolding, criticizing, redirecting, and instructing her to behave differently. The observation led staff members to believe that the child could "do no right" in her mother's eyes.

A treatment plan with three basic components was designed. The first recommendation was that the mother try to discontinue her constant correction and criticism of the child's behavior, and especially the self-scratching, which was to be completely ignored regardless of the number of new or reopened lesions. The staff members advised the mother that their experience with many children by this time had demonstrated that maladaptive behaviors, targeted for amelioration, almost always increased before they were reduced. It was as if children had to test the limits to the extreme to see if they could still evoke adult attention by exhibiting even greater excesses of undesirable behaviors. The second part of the program was to introduce a token system. A token system was decided on in this instance because of the severity of the problem and because it appeared to be nearly impossible for this mother to respond to her child in a positive fashion. Because most young children find gold stars pleasing, a plan was worked out in which the mother went to the child at 20 or 30 minute intervals; if there was no evidence that the child had scratched herself during that period, the mother was to make as approving a statement as she could muster and give the child a gold star to paste in a little booklet. Occasionally the mother was also to offer a bit of food or drink that the child particularly liked, perhaps a small cookie and a glass of juice. The third part of the procedure was that at midday the gold stars were to be counted. If several had been accumulated, the mother was to give the child an inexpensive trinket of some kind. The same procedure was to be followed in the early evening.

For the next several weeks staff members saw the mother on a weekly basis, revamping the program as needed. Improvement was slow at first with several set-backs that were most disheartening for everyone. The mother did stick with the program, however, and did institute the program changes that were suggested as well as she could. Eventually the child stopped the self-scratching. At the end of six weeks, every sore was completely healed, although there were several bright red scar-type areas visible, particularly on the cheek and chin. Four months later when staff members visited with the child and the mother (and the new baby) in the home in order to conduct a postcheck on the effectiveness of the procedures, the scars had faded to a pale pink and were barely discernible.

THE RESEARCH TEAM AND NEW LOCATIONS

In the mid-1960s the various researchers left the University of Washington. The experimental analysis of child behavior was, for the most part, phased out at the DPL. Soon, however, a somewhat different line of experimental studies of child behavior was instituted in the Experimental Education Unit (EEU), one of four components of the new Child Developmental and Mental Retardation Center at the University of Washington. This research was under the leadership of Norris Haring and Alice Hayden. K. Eileen Allen, one of the teacher-experimenters in the studies described in this chapter and senior editor of this text, joined the EEU as coordinator of early childhood education and research and continued, with Haring and Hayden, the analyses of children's learning and developmental problems.

Interventions with Head Start Children

The first major studies conducted by this group were in conjunction with Head Start, helping to relieve the pressures created by severely deviant children in the various Head Start classrooms throughout the city. The EEU team provided a special management classroom for those children who exhibited severe behavior problems or developmental deviations (Allen, Turner, & Everett, 1970; Haring, Hayden & Allen, 1971). This special management classroom was designed to be a short-term diagnostic and remedial placement for those Head Start children who were referred for various developmental deviations. Disruptive, hyperactive, incontinent, communication-disordered, echolalic, brain damaged, and schizoid are but a few examples of the referral labels that were attached to the children.

The ideal program for each child contained four phases:

1. observation (and data collection) of the child and the child's teachers in the community classroom prior to enrollment in the special management classroom;

2. enrollment in the special management class for a period of time deemed adequate for diagnosing and ameliorating the child's problems (data collection was continued throughout the entire intervention program);
3. involvement of the child's community classroom teacher in an inservice training program and the opportunity to engage in first-hand teaching experiences in the special management classroom;
4. return of the child to the original community classroom when improvement in the child's behavior was stable, and the provision of follow-up support services to the classroom staff. (Follow-up data were collected at regular intervals.)

Once again, in this series of studies, it was demonstrated most convincingly that a teacher's responsiveness, when offered differentially, was crucial in determining what and how children learned. These were the days of planned variation following Head Start (whereby communities decided which one of several theoretical curriculum models would be employed in their center). Regardless of which education model was in effect in the child's own classroom, marked improvement in each referred child's problems was documented. Again it was apparent that the teacher's behavior was the deciding factor (Allen, Turner, & Everett, 1970). Later this was demonstrated again by Weikart (1971), who made the same finding in his comparisons of curriculum models.

The Experimental Integration of Handicapped Children

Almost concurrent with the work with Head Start, the Handicapped Children's Early Education Assistance Act (HCEEA, 1968) was enacted. The First Chance Network, as this program soon came to be called, provided the research and demonstration funds (administered by Bureau of the Education for the Handicapped) that led to even greater research productivity by the EEU team of experimentalists. The behavioral analysis studies, which were far too numerous to even attempt to recap here, resulted in a publication that contained 50 selected early intervention studies (Hayden, Haring, Allen, Dmitriev, & Rieke, 1972).

Many of the interventions were carried out in conjunction with the interdisciplinary team of the Clinical Training Unit (CTU), also a part of the Child Development and Mental Retardation Center at the University of Washington. Children with a variety of severely handicapping conditions were provided with effective individualized classroom programs in collaboration with such disciplines as nursing, medicine, physical therapy, psychology, nutrition, speech therapy, audiology, and social work. (For a full review of many of these interdisciplinary studies, see Allen, Holm, & Schiefelbusch, 1978).

At about the same time as these interdisciplinary experimental interventions with handicapped children, what was probably the first research- and service-oriented preschool mainstreaming effort in the country was designed and implemented. This mainstreaming project was undertaken long before the terms "mainstreaming" and "least restrictive environment" had infiltrated the educational scene. One key study (Allen, Benning, & Drummond, 1972) from this era has the distinction of being the first mainstreaming study of its kind. In fact, for several years it was the only early education study documenting the potential efficacy of intergrating handicapped and nonhandicapped children. Following is a brief account of that study.

The child had just turned four when she was enrolled in the integrated preschool classroom at the EEU. Her treatment placement during the preceding year had been in a psychiatric preschool in the children's hospital in the area. The child's voluminous clinical records revealed a number of problems and the assignment of a variety of labels, such as the following: mentally retarded; emotionally disturbed; neurologically involved; language disordered; and developmentally disabled. In addition, the child was unusually small for her age, with poorly developed large motor skills and infantile speech patterns. There were, however, no untoward medical signs except arrested hydrocephalus, a condition that had been treated in early infancy. Further medical evaluation at the time of enrollment indicated no signs of physical or neurological impairment.

Most conspicuous was the child's extensive display of inappropriate and maladaptive social behaviors. Baseline data showed that on the fifth day in the EEU school setting her physical attacks on children—hitting, biting, gouging, hair pulling, and knocking down—numbered 70 in a two-hour period. Drastic measures had to be taken in order to protect the other children. Thus, it was decided that the first prong of the intervention program must be to remove her from contact with children or play activities immediately following each and every physical attack. The teachers were simply to turn away from the remainder of her maladaptive behaviors when they occurred, or, in cases of the child's tantrums, teachers were to remove quietly the other children from the vicinity and provide them with interesting activities elsewhere. In between attacks and tantrums, teachers were to attempt to respond to any approximation the child made to behaving appropriately, even if it was simply standing quietly and watching other children's play activities. Because the child appeared to have few ideas about the use of play materials, the teachers actually taught her how to play. Once she acquired a minimal set of play responses, they required that she select a place to play in order to decrease her disruptive and disastrous wanderings. As the physical attacks on children dropped to a near zero rate, which happened soon after the start of the intervention program, teachers also began to teach the child how to play with children and materials.

The results of the intervention were dramatic and lasting. Within three months, the child was barely distinguishable from her classmates in appropriate participation in all classroom activities. In fact, on the last segments of the videotapes that were made throughout the study, naive judges who did not know the child were unable to identify the "disturbed" child. Because of her small stature and the additional "catch-up" time needed for motor and language development, the child was kept in the preschool an extra year. When she did enter public school kindergarten at age six, she had acquired an extensive array of appropriate developmental skills.

CONCLUSION

Concurrent with this work, many of the researchers who had been collaborators in the early DPL research reassembled at the invitation of Frances D. Horowitz and Donald M. Baer at the University of Kansas in the Department of Human Development and Family Life. Their research during the ensuing years has reached into the analysis of behavior at every level and in many settings. The remainder of this text has to do with the diversified work that has been going on in one of those settings, the Edna A. Hill Child Development Laboratory. These chapters report the elaborate and increasingly sophisticated application of behavioral principles to early childhood special education for both typical and atypical children.

REFERENCES

Allen, K.E., Benning, P.M., & Drummond, W.T. Integration of normal and handicapped children in a behavior modification preschool: A case study. In G. Semb (Ed.), *Behavior analysis and education, 1972*. Lawrence, Kan.: Printing Services, 1972.

Allen, K.E., & Harris, F.R. Elimination of a child's excessive scratching by training the mother in reinforcement procedures. *Behavior Research and Therapy*, 1966, *4*, 79–84.

Allen, K.E., Hart, B., Buell, J.S., Harris, F.R., & Wolf, M.M. Effects of social reinforcement on isolate behavior of a nursery school child. *Child Development*, 1964, *35*, 55–58.

Allen, K.E., Henke, L.B., Harris, F.R., Baer, D.M., & Reynolds, N.J. Control of hyperactivity by social reinforcement of attending behavior. *Journal of Educational Psychology*, 1967, *58*, 231–237.

Allen, K.E., Holm, V.A., & Schiefelbusch, R.L. *Early intervention—A team approach*. Baltimore, Md.: University Park Press, 1978.

Allen, K.E., Turner, K.D., & Everett, P.M. A behavior modification classroom for Head Start children with problem behaviors. *Exceptional Children*, 1970, *37*:2, 119–129.

Baer, D.M. Recent examples of behavior modification in preschool settings. Paper presented at the Ninth Annual Institute for Clinical Psychology, University of Kansas, Lawrence, April 1967.

Bijou, S.W., & Baer, D.M. *Child Development, Volume I*. New York: Appleton-Century-Crofts, 1961.

Buell, J.S., Stoddard, P., Harris, F., and Baer, E.M. Collateral social development accompanying reinforcement of outdoor play in a preschool child. *Journal of Applied Behavior Analysis*, 1968, *1*, 167–174.

Haring, N.G., Harden, A.H., & Allen, K.E. Programs and projects: Intervention in early childhood. *Educational Technology*, 1971, *11*:2, 52–60.

Harris, F.R. This is the training that produces the practices. Paper presented at the 45th annual convention of the Council for Exceptional Children, St. Louis, 1967.

Harris, F.R., Johnston, M.K., Kelley, C., & Wolf, M.M. Effects of positive social reinforcement on regressed crawling in a preschool child. *Journal of Educational Psychology*, 1964, *55*, 35–41.

Hart, B.M., Allen, K.E., Buell, J.S., Harris, F.R., & Wolf, M.M. Effects of social reinforcement on operant crying. *Journal of Exceptional Child Psychology*, 1964, *1*, 145–153.

Hart, B.M., Reynolds, N.J., Baer, D.M., Brawley, R., & Harris, F.R. Effects of contingent and non-contingent social reinforcement on the cooperative play of a preschool child. *Journal of Applied Behavior Analysis*, 1968, *1*, 73–78.

Hayden, A.H., Haring, N.G., Allen, K.A., Dmitriev, V., & Rieke, J. *Selected case studies: Compilation for Bureau of Education for the Handicapped* (OEG–09570–309–4549 [619] and P.M. 83–313, Title I ESEA). 1972.

Hunt, J. McV. *Intelligence and experience*. New York: Ronald, 1961.

Johnston, M.K., Kelley, C.S., Harris, F.R., & Wolf, M.M. An application of reinforcement principles to development of motor skills of a young child. *Child Development*, 1966, *37*, 379–387.

Michael, J. *Laboratory Studies in Operant Behavior*. New York: McGraw-Hill, 1963.

Nedelman, D., & Sulzbacher, I. Dicky at 13 years of age: A long term success following early application of operant conditioning procedures. In G. Semb (Ed.), *Behavior analysis and education, 1972*. Lawrence, Kan.: University of Kansas Printing Press, 1972, 3–10.

Robinson, N., & Robinson, H.B. *The mentally retarded child* (2nd ed.). New York: McGraw-Hill, 1976.

Weikart, D. Relationship of curriculum teaching and learning in preschool education. In J. Stanley (Ed.) *Preschool programs for the disadvantaged*. Baltimore, Md.: The Johns Hopkins Press, 1971.

Wolf, M.M., Risley, T.R., Johnston, M.K., Harris, F.R., & Allen, K.E. Application of operant conditioning procedures to the behavior problems of an autistic child: A follow-up and extension. *Behavioral Research and Therapy*, 1967, *5*, 103–111.

Wolf, M.M., Risley, T.R., & Mees, H. Application of operant conditioning procedures to the behavior problems of an autistic child. *Behavioral Research and Therapy*, 1964, *1*, 305–312.

Chapter 2

Behavior Principles and Techniques

Elizabeth M. Goetz

WHAT ARE BEHAVIORAL PRINCIPLES?

Davy was a bright three-year-old boy with quadriplegia resulting from severe spinal cord damage that occurred either *in utero* or at the time of birth. His motor skills were markedly impaired, although he did have some use of his shoulders, arms, and hands. However, his language and preacademic skills were quite advanced, he showed a great deal of curiosity about his environment, and he was most responsive to adult attention (Mock, 1977).

Davy was enrolled in a preschool that integrated handicapped and non-handicapped children. His father had constructed a number of devices that allowed Davy to sit, stand, and scoot himself about. Playing blocks was one of Davy's favorite activities at school. In the beginning, however, he was somewhat reluctant to put his blocks back on the shelf when he had finished with them. The teachers knew, however, that there must be no double standard; handicapped and nonhandicapped children alike were expected to put their blocks back on the shelves so that all could experience the satisfaction of independence and task completion. Thus, teachers insisted (and helped) Davy to put away his blocks, thanking him and praising him for his efforts throughout the process. Soon Davy was putting his blocks away as independently as any other child.

Most teachers naturally thank and praise a child who does something appropriate, such as picking up blocks or putting away toys. This may simply be an expression of gratitude or good manners, but it usually has a more important effect, if not a conscious objective: it encourages the child to repeat the rewarded conduct, as in the case of Davy and the blocks. This commonly-observed characteristic of human behavior—that conduct that is rewarded is likely to be repeated—is one of the behavioral principles discussed in this chapter. Like some other behavioral principles, this may

31

seem like common sense; after all, years ago, parents raised their children using this same approach. Unfortunately, however, common sense alone does not guide people to all behavioral precepts.

Behavioral principles are natural laws of behavior based on objective data. They provide fundamental truths about human conduct. The application of behavioral principles to understand and solve human problems has become an area of research known as applied behavior analysis. Developmental, child, and educational psychologists have been applying these principles to numerous problems, such as the following, that teachers encounter while working with both typical and atypical children: motivation (Kadzin, 1977; O'Leary, 1971); sharing (Rheingold, 1977); aggression (McNamara, 1970); self-regulation (Bolstad & Johnson, 1972); social interaction (Allen, Hart, Buell, Harris, & Wolf, 1964); tattling (Wright & Hawkins, 1970); autism (Lovaas, 1973); eating (Ireton & Guthrie, 1972); toilet training (Madsen, Hoffman, Thomas, Koropsak, & Madsen, 1975); language (Hart & Risley, 1975); motor skills (Johnston, Kelley, Harris, & Wolf, 1966); imitation (Gelfand, Hartmann, Mahan, & Lamb, 1975); reading (Statts, Finley, Minke, & Wolf, 1964; Whitehurst, Domash, & DiGennaro, 1976); writing (Hopkins, Schutte, & Garron, 1971); arithmetic (Resnick, Wang, & Kaplan, 1973); creativity (Holman, Goetz, & Baer, 1977); curriculum objectives (Vargas, 1972); organization (LeLaurin & Risley, 1972); peer tutoring (Harris, Sherman, Henderson, & Harris, 1972); and teacher training (Sulzer & Mayer, 1972; Thomson, Holmberg, & Baer, 1978).

Though teaching techniques based on behavioral principles may be used with both typical and atypical children, they are especially functional for working with atypical or exceptional children. Because of their developmental delays and disabilities, these children are faced with learning tasks that are more difficult for them to master than for normal children. Consequently, atypical children are less apt to learn by trial and error, and, when they do, it is often a slow and tedious method. Therefore, both physically and mentally handicapped children need to be motivated and have the necessary prerequisite behaviors strengthened in the areas of their deficits. Reinforcement, and shaping techniques are invaluable for stimulating and increasing these behaviors in handicapped children as has been demonstrated repeatedly in the experimental literature. When a child who could only crawl across the floor before a behavior management program is able to walk, and when a three year old who neither smiled nor made eye contact with anyone—even his or her mother—reaches out and touches her face and smiles at her, that is convincing evidence of the effectiveness of behavioral techniques in working with young severely handicapped children (O'Neil, McLaughlin, & Knapp, 1977).

One advantage of behavioral principles is that teachers find them easy to understand because they are stated in objective, clearcut terms. Consequently, teachers feel confident in discussing young handicapped and nonhandicapped children with other teachers and with parents, since all involved will be speaking in the strictly factual behavioral terms.

HOW ARE BEHAVIORAL PRINCIPLES DETERMINED?

Behavioral principles are based on an analysis of observable behavior, not unseen mental processes or feelings. This does not mean that behaviorists deny the existence of so-called mental processes or feelings, but that they explain them in observable terms. For example, rather than saying that a child *knows* the alphabet, it might be said that a child labels the letters upon their presentation, or rather than saying that a child *feels* aggressive, it might be said that a child strikes several peers a day. All aspects of human behavior are analyzed in this sense to formulate behavioral principles.

Behaviorists reject theories that go beyond objective data, such as Freud's psychoanalytic theory of personality development, Piaget's theory of cognitive development, Chomsky's theory of language development, and the Hull-Spence theory of learning (Hawkins, 1977). Developmental theories focus on innate, sequential unfolding development rather than on how learning takes place according to the natural laws of behavior. These theories usually examine what normally happens without training, not what *could* happen with training. Of course, physiological, genetic, and biochemical variables are recognized as possible determinants of behavior, but not overly so (Hawkins, 1977). Behaviorists are not negative thinkers when it comes to coping with such problems as retardation, learning disabilities, and developmental delays.

For example, Baer (1981) has declared that he will proceed as if all exceptional children are capable of learning under instruction, since he has succeeded often enough in teaching them by trying something different. He then states that the set of behavioral techniques available to teach these children are not fully tried and not fully invented; therefore, special educators are still learning about teaching techniques and the nature of behavioral prerequisites to behavior change. Thus, efforts to help these children must be continued because it has not been proven that they cannot be helped. These efforts, he continues, make it manifest that this society intends to do its best even for the least of its children, that it is good for the society's ethos and therefore all its children, even if *these* children progress only one response toward better self-help in their whole lives.

Numerous research studies are needed to prove the validity of behavioral principles. Research replications with different subjects in different locales and in different settings within a single locale show that a precise manipulation of environmental conditions to which a person has been exposed will bring about a definite behavioral result. This is referred to as the *external* validity of a behavioral principle.

Internal validity must also be convincing. Internal validity means the relationship between the experimental procedure using the behavioral principle(s) and the observed behavior change. For example, was the out-of-seat behavior of Terry, an eight-year-old Downs syndrome child, actually eliminated by the teacher's ignoring out-of-seat behavior and praising in-seat behavior, or was some other variable perhaps the cause?

Admittedly, research that verifies behavioral principles and the related techniques for employing these principles can become somewhat complicated; precise characteristics of responses and related stimuli must be defined, observed, counted, graphed, and analyzed, and experimental control must be demonstrated. However, the extent to which this experimental analysis of behavior needs to be refined is determined by the purpose of the analysis. The important point is that observable responses and their related observable stimuli become the data base for formulating natural laws or principles of behavior. Since this book is not designed to present such research itself, needless difficulties in understanding the complexities of research and experimental designs will be avoided. However, the principles and techniques presented do have a solid data base and are not mere theoretical speculations.

HOW CAN BEHAVIORAL PRINCIPLES BE TEACHER-HELPERS?

If it is true that behavioral principles may sometimes be detected by common sense and are easy to understand, why then are some teachers plagued with behavior, learning, and management problems? Why do some teachers feel they are capable of handling the typical child, but not the atypical child? This is because—as research has shown—to make effective use of behavioral principles for the betterment of each child, they must be implemented in a systematic, consistent, and precise manner with due regard for individual differences. Furthermore, behavioral principles should always be used within a framework of sound developmental guidelines; it would be futile to try to teach children skills without a base of appropriate physical and cognitive development. However, teaching technologies based on the *proper* use of *all* principles can help preschool practitioners with everyday problems. Behavioral principles can be teacher-helpers and can enable teachers to help children in trouble.

BEHAVIORAL PRINCIPLES AND TECHNIQUES

Reinforcement

Reinforcement is a basic behavioral principle. It involves the application of an event (a stimulus) after some action (a response) so that the application will cause that action to be repeated. To be effective, the stimulus should be applied immediately after the action. Otherwise, the essential contingency between the reinforcement and the desired behavior will be lost on the child. A stimulus can be considered reinforcing only in terms of its effect, rather than its extrinsic physical properties or verbal content. In other words, if a particular contingency increases a behavior, it is a reinforcer, regardless of what it may otherwise be. What is reinforcing to a given child in a particular situation is determined by that child in that situation, not by a teacher.

The principle of reinforcement can be illustrated with an example familiar to many teachers. Assume that Mary, a retarded child being mainstreamed in the preschool, seldom smiles. Mrs. Smith, the head teacher, has noticed this lack of smiling for several days and is concerned that Mary may be unhappy. Not only does Mrs. Smith feel that lack of smiling may indicate unhappiness, but she also speculates that the more Mary smiles, the more friends she will attract, and the happier she will become. Therefore, Mrs. Smith decides to count Mary's smiles during a portion of the day—snacktime—to verify that indeed she is correct that Mary seldom smiles. After this counting confirms her original speculation, Mrs. Smith tries to catch Mary when she is slightly smiling during snacktime and then tell her each time that she has a beautiful smile, that it's nice to see her smiling, or just to smile back at her. Over time, Mary's smiling increases because Mrs. Smith has applied the stimulus of a compliment or smile immediately after the action of Mary's smiling. The compliment or returned smile is a reinforcer because it has increased Mary's smiling. A graph of this example of reinforcement is depicted in Figure 2-1.

Reinforcement techniques can be grouped into the following two broad categories: (1) social reinforcement and (2) tangible reinforcement. Social reinforcement can be subdivided into the following: (1) attention; (2) general praise; and (3) descriptive praise. Tangible reinforcement can be subdivided into the following: (1) food reinforcers; (2) trinket reinforcers; and (3) token reinforcers.

Figure 2–1 Reinforcement Example

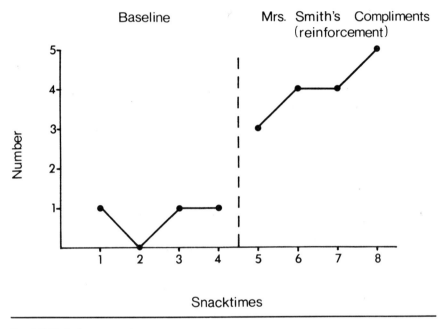

Mary's Smiles

Social Reinforcement

Social reinforcers may be either general attention or specific attention directed toward particular aspects of a response. More specifically, social reinforcers may be nonverbal (such as a smile) or verbal (such as a compliment). They may be delivered directly to the child or indirectly (that is, to a group of which the child is a member). Of course, if a child happens to dislike a teacher, the smile or compliment is unlikely to have much effect. Social reinforcement is easily accepted since it depends on a positive interpersonal relationship between child and teacher—a highly valued human situation.

Attention.   The key characteristic in attention is its lack of specification of the particular behavior it follows or consequates. On the nonverbal level, attention may be a smile, a pat on the head, or just the teacher's presence after a desired response. On the verbal level, it may be a comment after the desired response that is unrelated to it. For example, while a child is engaged in the desired response of working diligently on a puzzle, a teacher might say, "It's a beautiful day today, isn't it, Mikey?"

General attention alone may or may not change behavior, however. Early research did not investigate the effect of general attention alone as contrasted to praise and/or descriptive praise, but rather combined these three types of social reinforcers under the label of general attention. For example, Allen et al. (1964) successfully used this type of general attention to change the isolate behavior of a severely withdrawn four-year-old child. The isolated pattern of social behavior was changed when adult's attention became contingent upon the child's play with peers instead of isolated play.

On the negative side, too much teacher nonverbal and verbal general attention in children's group activities can lead to decreased child-child interactions (Hatfield & Goetz, 1975; Rintoul, Cooper, Schilmoeller, & LeBlanc, 1975). When using contingent attention, a teacher should therefore take note of the ratio of child-child interactions to teacher-child interactions. If the ratio seems undesirable, contingent attention should then be discontinued in favor of some alternative technique.

General Praise. General praise is verbal communication for a child's being good or doing the right thing, but that does not specifically describe what is good or right. "You are such a good girl, Sally," or "You are working so hard, David," are typical examples.

Goetz and Salmonson (1972) investigated the effects of general praise as opposed to descriptive praise, when children were painting different forms at an easel. The general praise consisted of comments such as "That's good," and "That's nice." Descriptive praise defined the particular form in addition to praising it, for example, "That's a very fine circle you made, it goes all the way around." It was found that for three preschool children in the study, general praise increased form diversity, but descriptive praise increased it even more, and more rapidly.

Descriptive Praise. As can be seen from the Goetz and Salmonson study, descriptive praise specifies the particular behavior being reinforced. Sally, a cerebral palsied child, might be told she is a good girl because she is sitting with her legs stretched out rather than in a W position, which, according to her physical therapist, is detrimental to her motor development. David, another cerebral palsied child, might be told he is working hard at trying to feed himself with a spoon. Descriptive praise must be given in words the child can understand.

Several other studies have demonstrated the utility of descriptive praise for increasing children's creativity, as measured by their production of diverse forms or shapes in block building, easel painting, Lego building, and felt pen drawing (Fallon & Goetz, 1975; Goetz & Baer, 1973; Goetz,

Jones, & Weamer, 1974; Holman et al., 1977). In this research, descriptive praise, contingent upon each form created within the single product, acknowledged the nature and novelty of the form (for example, "That zigzag line goes up and down. You haven't done that before. It looks great!").

All types of social reinforcement (general attention, general praise, and descriptive praise) may be used with children as direct or indirect reinforcement. When social reinforcement is delivered directly to a child by facial orientation or use of the child's name, it is termed direct reinforcement. On the other hand, if it is delivered to a group of children with the facial orientation to the group or use of the group's name (for example, "all of you"), it is termed indirect reinforcement. Goetz, Thomson, and Etzel (1975) found that indirect reinforcement combined with indirect primes can be more effective than direct reinforcement combined with direct primes in increasing peer interaction for an adult-oriented child. While the direct approach increased peer interaction somewhat, it tended to start a chain of adult-child interaction that interfered with peer interaction. This is a good example of the child rather than the teacher determining what is the most effective reinforcer for that child.

Tangible Reinforcement

For some children, especially those labeled aphasic or autistic, social reinforcement may not be effective. These children may have been raised in an environment that has not relied on social reinforcement to shape and change behavior or for some unknown reason they may not be sensitive to it. For such children, a teacher might have to resort to tangible rewards, at least initially. The tangible reward can be paired with social reinforcement, but, over time, the teacher should gradually shift from the combined use of tangible and social reinforcement to social reinforcement alone, which is considered to be more desirable by both teachers and parents.

Since tangible rewards are not what children encounter in usual learning environments, learning based on tangible rewards might be expected to deteriorate when children enter the "real world." Nevertheless, LeBlanc, Etzel, and Domash (1978) have identified the following three situations that may justify the use of tangible rewards: (1) when a child does not learn under the usual conditions of teacher attention and feedback, and it is critical that the child progress on the specified task in order to enhance overall development; (2) when a child is just beginning to learn a difficult and complex task, and a source of extrinsic motivation is needed to maintain the child's efforts until intrinsic reinforcers for performing the task become evident; and (3) when a child's behavior is frequently disrupting the classroom, and an immediately effective program of behavior change is needed to maintain the learning environment for the child and peers. Whenever any one of these three situations exists, which can be fairly often in classes that contain children with learning problems and developmental delays, a teacher should consider the use of tangible reinforcement, but it should never be used without parental permission. Some parents oppose such a reward system for philosophical reasons.

Food Reinforcers. For young or handicapped children, preferred foods or beverages following desired responses can be powerful reinforcers. Of course, food used as a reinforcer should be healthful, with low sugar and fat content. Certain cereals, frozen yogurt, dried fruits, juices, or raw vegetables are good options. A bowl with a mixture of food bits from which a child may choose is often appealing. In planning the use of food, it should be remembered that a child's hunger will have an effect on food as a reinforcer. Commonly, food reinforcers are paired with social reinforcers and, as soon as feasible (when the child is under instructional control), food should be replaced gradually with other reinforcers.

To illustrate, Hopkins (1968) used candy as a reinforcer to increase smiling in two retarded boys; the candy was gradually eliminated, but the smiling was maintained, apparently reinforced by natural social interactions. Cunningham, Cooper, Schilmoeller, and LeBlanc (1975) used small bits of a favorite food with a child who was not learning under typical conditions of teacher instructions for preacademic tasks. The food initially helped teach the child to follow simple teacher instructions and to act appropriately in the learning situation. Later, the child was shifted to a motivational system that involved teacher attention and the provision of a plastic chip for correct responding on the preacademic tasks. In this case, the chips were only to provide feedback for correct responding and were not exchanged for any tangible reinforcer.

Trinket Reinforcers. Most children enjoy trinkets, which, like food, may be used as reinforcers after desired responses. A "whole" trinket might be given after a desired response that need not occur often, such as going to bed on time at night. A part of a trinket (for example, one pop bead from a set of pop beads) might be given after a desired response that occurs fairly often, such as toileting. Allowing a child to choose a trinket from several available ones seems to improve motivation. Trinkets that do not fall apart easily prove more attractive in the long run and are safer. Sharp edges and anything small enough for a child to swallow must be carefully avoided. Finally, the use of trinkets should be faded because a child with too many trinkets probably will lose interest in them, and they will no longer serve as reinforcers.

Redd, Ullmann, and Roesch (1979) used trinkets as reinforcers to improve the academic performance of underachieving first-grade children. A polaroid picture was used by Romero, Holt, Stella, Baer, and Etzel (1978) to promote a creative product of the colored cube designs of a preschool child. A picture was taken of the child with the completed design each time the child worked with the cubes. In this case, it was enough just to show the picture to the child. (It was saved as the experimental measure.)

Token Reinforcers. A third type of tangible reinforcer is a token. Any stimulus consistently associated with a reinforcer itself takes on reinforcing properties for the person who experiences that association. This phenomenon, called "conditioned reinforcement," underlies the development of token reinforcement. Tokens themselves become reinforcing because they can be exchanged for a reinforcer.

A token is customarily used as an immediate reinforcer for a response. To avoid "sloppy" responding, a token should be given only when the child is correct the first time. The tokens can be saved for a period of time or during a behavioral chain. Later, they can be traded for a reinforcer, such as food, a trinket, or a special classroom privilege.

Tokens may take the form of poker chips, tickets, stars, points on a tally sheet or counter, checkmarks, punched holes on cards, currency or coins individually designed for the program, foreign coins, plastic credit cards, computer cards, and so on (Kadzin, 1977). Items used as tokens may have to meet specific requirements depending on the setting, population, and in some cases, special problems (for example, counterfeiting) that arise. The primary requirement for selecting the token is that it be easy for the teacher to deliver and the child to save before trading it in. One of the early model demonstrations of an effective token system with institutionalized mentally retarded children was carried out by Birnbrauer, Bijou, Wolf, and Kidder (1965) at the Rainier School.

Despite their being somewhat controversial, tokens do have unique advantages over food and trinket reinforcers. Children may become satiated with food or bored with a surplus of trinkets. Yet tokens are especially valuable in allowing a sequence of responses (for example, dressing oneself) to be reinforced without interruption. The number of tokens can easily be reduced once learning is underway. In any event, a token system in a classroom allows individual class members to work for different reinforcers. Rowbury, Baer, and Baer (1976), working with children with behavior problems and learning disabilities, utilized this advantage by giving all children in a class tokens for personally prescribed preacademic behaviors. These tokens allowed the children to enter a free-play area where they could select from a variety of activities.

The question is sometimes raised whether the use of tangible rewards with individual children in a classroom may have adverse effects on peer observers. Christy (1975) addressed this question in a remedial program for preschoolers with behavior problems (for example, hyperactivity, withdrawal, oppositional behavior, and speech disorders). Two groups of children with low baseline rates of in-seat behavior in a consecutive procedure received a verbal contingency and food rewards for sitting, while their peers (with either low or high rates of in-seat behavior) received neither food nor teacher attention for sitting. This procedure neither decreased the in-seat behavior of peer observers nor increased their aggressive or disruptive behavior. On the other hand, verbal and food contingency did increase in-seat behavior for the target children. All children exhibited improved sitting by the end of the study. Christy concluded that the class improvement in sitting behavior and the absence of negative effects on observers may have been partially due to the high frequency of attention the teacher maintained for other desired behavior and the lack of attention to children's complaints. In any event, use of individual tangible reward systems (food, trinkets, or tokens) within a classroom seems to be effective.

Punishment

Punishment, another basic behavioral principle, is the application of an event (a stimulus) after some action (a response), which causes that action to decrease. As an alternative, it is the removal of some positive event after an action; a removal that causes that action to decrease. As in the case of reinforcement, a stimulus is defined as punishing in terms of its effect rather than its physical properties or verbal content. Also, as in reinforcement, the child's own behavior, not the teacher, determines what may be punishing for that child. Thus, punishment need not entail pain or physical coercion, or serve as a retribution for misbehaving. Still, for ethical reasons, all punishment techniques must be carefully evaluated for any possible psychological and physical discomfort. These techniques definitely should not be used unless reasonably predictable benefits justify the means. Of course, parents should be consulted for permission before any punishment is used.

The use of punishment is illustrated here using Mary, the retarded preschool child mentioned earlier who seldom smiled, as an example. The head teacher, Mrs. Smith, increased Mary's smiling during snacktime by positively responding to her each time she smiled. Suppose that Mrs. Smith becomes ill and asks a substitute to take her place and to continue to tally the number of times that Mary smiles. If the first time that Mary smiles the substitute tells her she has a "funny" little smile, and the second time the substitute makes the same comment, and if Mary dislikes this comment, Mary probably will not smile during snacktime for the next several days. The substitute has applied the "funny" comment stimulus immediately after the action of Mary's smiles. This is a punishing stimulus because it decreased smiling. Of course, when Mrs. Smith returns, Mary's smiling quite likely will increase because of Mrs. Smith's positive attention to that behavior. A graph of this example of punishment, in conjunction with the previous example of reinforcement, would take the form depicted in Figure 2-2.

The following three punishment techniques will be discussed: (1) aversive stimulus; (2) time-out; and (3) response cost. In addition, the technique of reinforcing incompatible behavior will be explained, not as a punishment technique, but as a means for preempting undesirable behavior.

Aversive Stimulus

An aversive stimulus, such as spanking, involves some pain or discomfort. Obviously, unless a teacher is working with severe deviant behavior, there is no justification for even considering such an aversive stimulus. Even then, before using an aversive stimulus as a punisher, other milder forms of punishment and reinforcement for incompatible behavior should be tried first. Yet, when dealing with severely deviant behavior, such as the prolonged screaming episodes in certain psychotic disorders, the discomfort in using this technique may well be less for both the teacher and child than the discomfort involved in allowing that behavior to continue.

Time-Out

One useful, yet mild punishment technique for young children is "time-out." Before it can be used, the rule on which it is based must be explained to the child. In time-out, a child is reminded unemotionally that a rule has been broken, then the child is told to sit on a chair for one to three minutes, separated from others, before being allowed to return to the former activity. In this way the child will experience the removal of a positive event after an undesirable behavior. Of course, time-out will not be effective if the child does not like the situation from which he or she is removed. Also, liking a situation depends not only on the nature of the activity itself, but also the amount of positive attention received from peers and teachers while in that activity (Plummer, Baer, & LeBlanc, 1977).

A milder version of time-out may be used in a teacher-directed preacademic task with a child while both are seated. When a child makes an undesirable response, the teacher can simply avoid eye contact and discontinue the task and the interaction for a few seconds until the child

Figure 2-2 Punishment Example

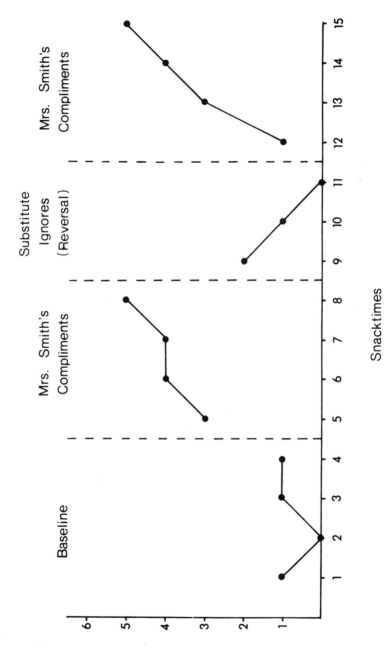

appears ready to work. This version has proven successful with even severely disturbed children of the type described in Chapter 1.

Luiselli, Helfen, and Colozzi (1977) have utilized time-out in a classroom to eliminate screaming behavior in special education students. Porterfield, Herbert-Jackson, and Risley (1976) used a combination of time-out and instructions to reduce disruptive behavior of one- and two-year-old children in a day-care center. Hanley, Perelman, and Holman (1979) trained parents to apply a combination of time-out and reinforcement of incompatible behavior to reduce their child's self-stimulatory behavior. As shown in these last two studies, time-out can be used in a combination procedure.

Response Cost

Response cost is a punishment technique that can be applied only to a token system of the type described earlier under the principle of reinforcement. As indicated, tokens are presented to a child initially for correct or desirable responses. Later the saved tokens are traded for a back-up reinforcer. In a response cost, one or several of the saved tokens can be withdrawn after an undesirable response. As with time-out, this accomplishes the removal of a positive stimulus after an undesirable response.

To use a response cost, there must be tokens to remove. Therefore, at the beginning of each session or day the child needs to have or be given sufficient tokens to allow for some removals. A teacher may therefore give a child tokens for relatively incidental, yet desirable, behaviors, such as sitting up straight, paying attention, or being helpful. A teacher might even give a child a supply before the earning of tokens begins.

Chiang, Iwata, and Dorsey (1979) eliminated disruptive bus-riding behavior of a retarded child in this way. The bus driver administered a token reinforcement system using a hand counter on the dashboard. The route was divided into intervals according to geographic landmarks. Points were awarded, withheld, or taken away at each of the intervals via the hand counter depending on the "quality" of the bus-riding behavior during an interval.

Reinforcing Incompatible Behavior

If a child's desirable behavior is reinforced and therefore increases, this tends to preclude opportunities to engage in undesirable behavior. Being good and being bad are usually incompatible; ordinarily a child cannot be both at the same time. Yet, if two teachers in a classroom endorse opposing objectives (for example, the child speaking versus the child being quiet), a child can appear to engage in good and bad behavior at the same time. This is confusing to a child and should not be allowed to occur. Which conduct is compatible and which is incompatible should be clearly established for the teachers and the child.

The reinforcement of the incompatible behavior does not punish undesirable behavior but rather preempts it. Goetz, Holmberg, and LeBlanc (1975) reinforced a child's compliant behavior to teacher instructions, which resulted in decreasing an abnormal amount of noncompliant behavior without punishing it. There simply was not time left to be noncompliant. Such techniques are common in applied behavior analysis, which stresses a positive approach rather than the negative.

Extinction

The behavioral principle of extinction does not involve presenting or withdrawing events in the usual sense. Instead, this principle refers to discontinuing an event that previously was delivered following a behavior. The theory is that behavior strengthened and maintained through reinforcement will weaken if the reinforcing consequence simply stops occurring. Just as a reinforcing stimulus after a behavior increases it and a punishing stimulus after a behavior decreases it, the withholding of a stimulus after a behavior that has been previously reinforced will decrease or extinguish it. Thus, extinction may be thought of as ignoring a behavior previously reinforced by tangible or social reinforcement.

This principle of extinction may be clarified by another example with which teachers are well acquainted. Suppose the children in a special preschool classroom have been accustomed to being praised by their head teacher while they quickly pick up their toys after a free-play period; then a substitute teacher does not praise them for picking up quickly. The amount of time used to pick up the room might well increase because there is no reinforcing stimulus after the fast pick-up behavior previously reinforced. Since the fast pick-up behavior is ignored, it begins to extinguish. Figure 2-3 depicts this incident of extinction.

Pinkston, Reese, LeBlanc, and Baer (1973) reduced a child's aggressive behavior in preschool by ignoring the aggressive behavior that previously had received attention. In addition to ignoring the aggressor, part of the technique was to attend to the child against whom the aggression had occurred. Thus, the aggressor not only did not receive attention, but also observed the recipient of the aggressor's attack receiving lavish teacher attention. Observing this attention seemed to be punishing for the aggressor.

Schedules of Reinforcement

Reinforcement schedules involve the systematic occurrence of reinforcing consequences following behavior. Such scheduling of reinforcement is

Figure 2–3 Extinction Example

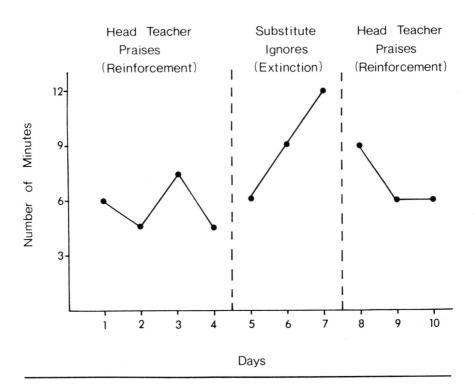

shown in the following set of behavioral principles: (1) continuous reinforcement; (2) intermittent reinforcement; and (3) delayed reinforcement.

Continuous Reinforcement

Continuous reinforcement is the occurrence of a reinforcer for every
occurrence of a particular response. Though it takes constant surveillance,
many consider this technique worthwhile because it usually produces a
more rapid change in behavior than other schedules. For example, Hall
and Holmberg (1974) taught two-year-old children to taste all foods on
their plates by praising each bite of a different food. In addition, the
children were instructed to try different foods and were allowed dessert
only if all foods were tasted. Continuous verbal reinforcement was used
along with instructions and a delayed tangible reinforcer of dessert.

Intermittent Reinforcement

Intermittent reinforcement may be delivered on a fixed ratio (for example, every third time a response occurs) or on a variable ratio (for example, the first, second, third, or fourth time with an overall average of three). Studies have shown that variable ratio schedules maintain a desired behavior better than a fixed ratio. Intermittent reinforcement may also be delivered on a fixed time interval (for example, every ten minutes) or a variable interval (for example, after five, ten, or fifteen minutes with the overall average of ten). A fixed interval schedule has been found to produce a marked pause in the occurrence of a behavior at the beginning of each interval, whereas a variable interval does not. As a practical matter, in the natural setting of a school, intermittent reinforcement usually is delivered "every now and then" without any ratio or interval schedule because it is difficult to be completely systematic and to teach at the same time.

Even though intermittent reinforcement does not change behavior as rapidly as continuous reinforcement, it usually maintains behavior and makes it more resistant to extinction. Therefore, a teacher might be well advised to arrange for continuous reinforcement until responding becomes reliable and then shift to a leaner and leaner schedule of reinforcement, which will maintain the behavior while conserving teacher time, energy, and other resources. Of course, if the behavior weakens, the teacher should return to continuous or at least less intermittent reinforcement.

Saudargas, Madsen, and Scott (1977) found that elementary school students completed more assignments, and Van Houten and Nau (1980) observed that deaf children were more attentive in class, on variable ratio schedules rather than on fixed. Goetz, Ayala, Hatfield, Baer, and Etzel (1974) used interval reinforcement to reinforce appropriate behavior by using a tape with recorded intervals to cue a preschool teacher to look for appropriate behavior in the classroom and to reinforce it. Similarly, Goetz, Holmberg, and LeBlanc (1975) increased a preschool child's compliance with continuous reinforcement and later maintained it with "every now and then" intermittent reinforcement.

Delayed Reinforcement

Though reinforcement is usually thought of in terms of immediacy after a response, sometimes it may be delayed and still be effective. Such delayed reinforcement does not increase behavior as rapidly as continuous immediate reinforcement, but it does promote generalization of the behavior. Rogers-Warren and Baer (1976) reinforced normal preschool children for reports of sharing during previous ten-minute work periods with art materials. This delayed reinforcement increased sharing whether the reports were true or not. Fowler and Baer (1981), using both normal and behavior problem preschool children found "Late" as compared to "Early" delayed reinforcement more effective in increasing good social behaviors and study habits.

Shaping

Reinforcement techniques obviously can be applied only when the desired behavior occurs. But what if it never occurs? The solution is related to the technique called "shaping." Shaping may either teach a totally new behavior step-by-step or extend existing behavior that is an approximation to the desired behavior. Shaping is particularly useful with young and/or handicapped children whose skills are largely undeveloped and must be mastered one small step at a time. In shaping, the terminal behavior may be achieved in one of the following two ways: (1) reinforcing small steps toward the final response; and (2) reinforcing approximations toward the final response.

Reinforcing Small Steps

Any task that can be broken down into small steps may be shaped. For example, handwriting may be shaped by first teaching a child how to hold a pencil, then to make different types of strokes, and finally to combine these strokes into letters, and letters into words. Self-help skills, such as toileting, handwashing, and eating, are other good examples. Using this technique, O'Brien, Bugle, and Azrin (1972) taught a retarded child proper eating in the following step-by-step procedure: (1) picking up the spoon; (2) dipping the spoon into the food; (3) lifting the spoon close to the mouth; (4)opening the mouth; (5) putting the spoon into the mouth; and (6) moving the spoon upward and outward with the food being removed from the spoon by the child's upper teeth or lips.

Reinforcing Approximations

Often a child may exhibit an approximation to a desired response. For instance, a child may work on a puzzle for a minute or two but not continue to completion. In this case, the teacher may reinforce longer and longer occurrences of working on the puzzle, thereby increasing the child's "attention span."

Certain motor skills may be approximations to sought-after terminal behaviors. Thus, a child may be reinforced for throwing a large ball and then throwing smaller and smaller balls. A child may also be reinforced for riding a kiddy-car, a trike, and then a two-wheeler. A child may be reinforced for approximations to climbing. Knapp, O'Neil, and Allen (1977), for example, taught Suzi, a four year old with severe orthopedic problems to crawl, stand, crutch walk, walk independently, and finally climb to the top of a six-foot jungle gym. Social and token reinforcers were used in each successive phase in this motor development program. A note of caution must be inserted here, however. Teachers must not program for any physical or medical problems except in conjunction with the appropriate clinical consultation and supervision. In the case of Suzi, the program, while carried out in the preschool classroom, was under the continuous supervision of an orthopedic nurse. Jackson and Wallace (1974) reinforced approximations to shape a disturbed girl's normal voice loudness; higher and higher decibles were systematically reinforced. Appleman, Allen, and Turner (1975) shaped speech sounds in a retarded nonverbal child.

Stimulus Control

While a reinforcing or punishing stimulus following the response will have an effect on it, a stimulus may also *precede* a response and similarly control it. This stimulus is technically called a "discriminative stimulus," and it may be visual, auditory, or in the form of a teacher's tactile (manual) guidance or modeling. The control of the discriminative stimulus over the following response involves the behavioral principle of stimulus control. Stimulus control is measured by some value(s) of the preceding stimulus and the strength or predictability of a certain following response. In stimulus control learning, discrimination is necessary because the stimulus that causes a certain response must be singled out.

An everyday example illustrates this principle. Assume that a toddler has learned to say "cat" in the presence of that animal. First comes the discriminative stimulus of the cat itself, and then comes the response of the word "cat," which the child has been reinforced for saying. The stimulus causing this response, however, may be the four legs, the fur, or the meow. It is not always clear which of these elements is controlling the child's verbal response of "cat," but if that child were to say "cat" when a dog walks by, then a person could surmise it was not the meow but probably the four legs or fur.

Of course, in addition to stimulus control, both reinforcement after the correct response and repetition are important conditions for learning at this level. In fact, reinforcement after the correct response alerts the child to the particular discrimination to be singled out. The child might wonder, "Hey, I was right that time. Now what cued me to do it right?" To help children think about "being right" on some basis, the results of a study by

Marholin and Steinman (1977) can be applied. They found that children came under the appropriate stimulus control of academic materials more readily when academic accuracy and rate were reinforced instead of simply reinforcing on-task (attending to materials) behavior. Thus, telling a child, "Good, you are working very nicely," is not as effective as saying, "Good, two and two are four."

The principle of stimulus control reminds the teacher to attend to the design and complexity of learning materials or the learning steps presented to children, not just the response made while children interact with these materials or perform these steps. Learning materials and learning steps for the handicapped, for example, often need to be simplified in ways relating to the children's handicaps. They need to be easy enough to enable the child to make the discrimination: one matching-shape problem on a page or a single instruction probably would best start a successful stimulus–response relationship for a visual, hearing, or learning disabled handicapped child.

Errorless Stimulus Control

Errorless stimulus control programs, which have as their goal the reduction of errors, are a rather new and exciting behavioral technology for difficult-to-teach children (Etzel & LeBlanc, 1979). Though sometimes time consuming and complex, it is worth the effort to teach such children concepts they otherwise might not acquire. In errorless programs, the discrimination (recognition) of the preceding stimulus that controls the correct response is made so easy that children make few, if any, errors. The initial discrimination is always one the child can already make. As the program progresses, this discrimination of the correct stimulus (or the incorrect stimulus distractors) is slowly manipulated to the final (criterion level) discrimination being taught in the program. The six basic errorless stimulus control procedures identified in the literature (Etzel, LeBlanc, Schilmoeller & Stella, 1981) are the following: (1) stimulus fading; (2) stimulus shaping; (3) superimposition; (4) superimposition and fading; (5) superimposition and shaping; and (6) delayed instructions. Additional verbal and motor responses and criterion-related or noncriterion-related cues will also be discussed.

Stimulus Fading. Fading involves a change across some stimulus dimension, such as size, color, intensity, or distance, with the objective of gradually shifting stimulus control from one dimension to the final (criterion) dimension. For example, a teacher may want a child to learn differences between different shades of a color or to order a set of color cards from dark to light. Teaching this task to children who have trouble learning is possible by using a procedure developed by Schlosberg and Solomon (1943). Starting with dark red and white, a child can be taught to always point to the darker (or lighter) color. In succeeding steps, the dark red is gradually faded to lighter red, and the white is gradually faded to darker red. The child's task is to compare the two color sets and choose the darker as the color difference between them becomes less. In this manner children learn to make finer discriminations between shades of a color than if they had not started with extreme differences.

Stimulus Shaping. Stimulus shaping makes use of graduated change in the overall stimulus configuration or topography, such as the gradual shaping of a square into a circle (Sidman & Stoddard, 1966). Figure 2-4 compares the two procedures of fading and shaping. When the large circle is faded to a small circle, the overall configuration remains the same, but when the square is shaped to a circle, the topography of the initial square is quite different at the final discrimination between circle and oval. Fading is appropriate to use under some circumstances and shaping under others (Etzel & LeBlanc, 1979; Etzel et al., 1981).

Superimposition and Fading or Shaping. In superimposition a discriminated stimulus may be superimposed on a "neutral" stimulus, and then faded or shaped slowly across time. The neutral stimulus then takes over control of the response, and the faded or shaped stimulus is removed. A stimulus may be "highlighted" by adding a cue to a stimulus element within the stimulus compound. As an example, Guralnick (1975), using handicapped children, reported by their teachers to have poor discrimination skills, superimposed the "known" color red on the black diagonal line, which then slowly turned black as the red was faded out, leaving only the presence or absence of the diagonal line in control of the response.

Delayed Instructions. Delayed instructions may involve a visual, motor, or verbal cue denoting the correct criterion behavior according to a progressively delayed schedule (Etzel et al., 1981; Touchette, 1971). For example, a teacher may present a discrimination task to a child and immediately tell the child the correct answer. Then, over time, the visual, motor, or verbal cue the teacher is using (telling the child the answer) is progressively delayed but is still given if the child does not respond before the cue. In this way the child can always imitate and give the correct answer while learning, and the teacher will know when the child begins to solve the problem independently, since the child will answer before the teacher cues.

Additional Verbal and Motor Responses. In addition to specially designed materials for children with learning problems, a teacher can also

Figure 2–4 Stimulus Fading and Stimulus Shaping

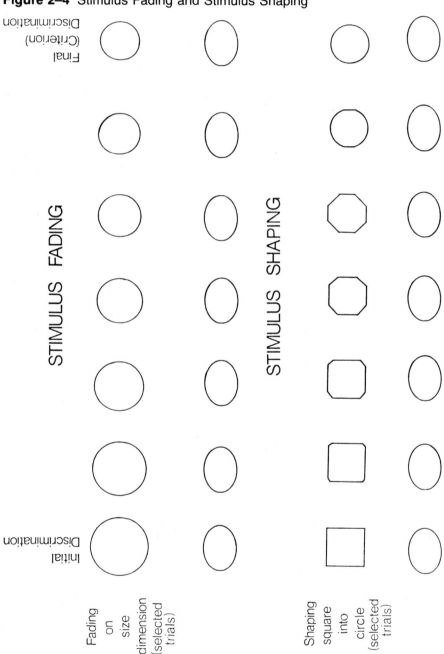

have the child engage in extra verbal or motor responses while solving the task. Such extra responses must be easy to learn and must serve as cues to the child for the correct (final) answer. One illustration (Miller, Kolb, Baer, & Etzel, 1975) was a left-right program for teaching the lower case "p" as distinguished from the lower case "q". Superimposed over the "p" was a picture of a person (called "peter p") who liked to fish. The story accompanying the program showed peter with wide open eyes looking toward the *right* at a big worm he was about to use for fishing. The "q" had a different person superimposed on the letter (called "ooo q"), who had eyes tightly closed and a head rotated in the opposite (or *left*) direction, away from the worm. The children were required on each trial either to close their eyes tightly (like ooo q) or to open them up wide (like peter p), while at the same time turning their heads in the appropriate direction and saying the name of the character (peter p or ooo q). One set (left or right) of these responses always preceded the final response of pointing to either "p" or "q". The superimposed figures were then slowly faded (and shaped) out of the letters while the children continued to engage in the extra responses. Once these extra responses are given without external stimuli to cue them, the child has learned the discrimination and probably will eliminate the unnecessary responses.

Successful Cuing: Criterion-Related versus Noncriterion-Related. When teachers feel a child needs extra help in solving a problem, they often give a cue, either verbally or physically, by pointing out some aspect of the stimulus. They hope the cue will not only help the child solve the problem at that moment, but that the cue will also help the child learn why the response is the correct one. For example, coloring the letter "i" red in the word "dig," which is to be discriminated from the word "dog," probably would result in the child reading "dig" as "dig," as long as the "i" is red. If the red were changed to black to match the coloring of the other lettering, however, the child probably would not continue to be correct. This can be predicted because the child learned that the red color means say "dig" rather than that "i" means say "dig." This use of the red color on the "i" is an example of a noncriterion-related cue, because the cue will not be present under criterion or the final condition; books are not written with the "i" in "dig" printed in red.

On the other hand, the teacher might tell the child the "i" in dig looks something like a long shovel and because a person digs with a shovel, the "i" can remind the child that the word is "dig" not "dog." This would be a criterion-related cue, which points out to the child an element of the stimulus that can be used at the criterion or final level to make a correct response.

The procedure of stimulus shaping could also be applied to this example. The teacher could draw a small shovel in place of the "i" between the "d" and "g" to cue the child for reading "dig" instead of "dog." Then across time and sentences the shovel could be changed slowly into an "i." Research by Schilmoeller and Etzel (1977) has shown that similar elements of a stimulus that will be present at the final or criterion level can be used for making a discrimination. This is done by shaping the element from some initial (and meaningful-to-the-child) level to the to-be-learned-level. In this way the initial element becomes the criterion-level cue for correct responding and is carried out (shaped) so that the child is controlled by the cue both during and after learning.

Prompting

Prompting is a form of stimulus control because the stimulus of the prompt precedes the response and influences it. Prompts may be gestures, cues, instructions, directions, suggestions, examples, or models to initiate a response. They may be nonverbal or verbal, or possibly a combination of both. Moreover, they may be explicit or subtle, direct or indirect. (As noted under social reinforcement techniques, the distinction between direct and indirect is whether the stimulus is presented directly to the child by facial orientation or by use of the child's name, or indirectly to the child in a group with facial orientation to the group or use of the group's name.)

When a prompt results in a desired response, it can be reinforced. When a prompt initiates a behavior that is reinforced, that prompt eventually becomes a signal to the child that the correct behavior will be reinforced. The prompt, therefore, serves two purposes: (1) it hints or tells the child what to do; and (2) it serves as an indication that reinforcement will follow the correct response. For example, if a parent asks a child to wipe a runny nose with a tissue and when the child does so the parent is delighted, in the future the child will consider that particular request a sign that wiping nose behavior will be reinforced.

Prompting techniques will be discussed in the following two broad categories: (1) nonverbal prompts; and (2) verbal prompts. Nonverbal prompts will be subdivided into the following: (1) manual guidance; (2) modeling; (3) pictorial prompts; (4) color prompts; and (5) eyeing. Verbal prompts will be subdivided into the following: (1) modeling; (2) suggestions; (3) instructions; and (4) written prompts.

Nonverbal Prompts. Physically guiding a child through a task such as putting a puzzle together, turning pages in a book, or cutting with scissors represents *manual guidance*. If the child is guided through each step of the entire task, the guidance is explicit. For example, O'Brien et al. (1972)

used explicit manual guidance in teaching a retarded child the steps of proper eating. On the other hand, if manual guidance is used only at a few key points, it may be considered more subtle. For instance, a teacher may only help the child with the first puzzle piece, lift the corner of a page to be turned, or readjust the child's hold on paper to be cut.

An extremely effective nonverbal explicit prompt is the full *modeling* of a nonverbal task to be trained. A teacher might put a six-piece puzzle together and then ask the child to do it, or the teacher might be more subtle by putting only two pieces together and asking the child to finish. Stromer (1975) modeled with writing of correct and incorrect reversals of letters and numerals as part of his procedure to train elementary pupils to print them.

Peer modeling should not be overlooked. Apolloni and Tremblay (1978) found that children as young as two years will imitate novel use of materials that has been previously modeled by a peer. Atwood, Ruebush, and Everett (1978) found that grade school children delay gratification behavior after such delay is modeled by peers. The reinforcement for imitating these modeled behaviors may come from the peer in the form of friendship based on liking someone who does what you do. Accordingly, a teaching technique may be to pair a child with a peer who exhibits a desired behavior. Handicapped children modeling the behavior of normal peers is, of course, one of the assumptions underlying the mainstreaming movement (Guralnick, 1978).

Pictorial prompts are useful in teaching reading and other skills. A child learning to read the word "apple" can be shown a picture of an apple beside or superimposed on the word. Corey and Shamow (1972) used superimposed related pictures to prompt the learning of sight words. A variation of a pictorial prompt would be a sequence of pictures, such as handwashing steps placed above the bathroom sink to prompt correct handwashing.

Color prompts are sometimes used to teach difficult discriminations or organizational strategies. For instance, the right/left discrimination that is needed to put on the correct glove may be cued by a blue dot on the right hand and the right glove. Mendoza, Holt, and Jackson (1978) used color coding to prompt the discrimination involved in holding a pencil for writing; various parts of the pencil and fingers were color coded for the correct three-finger grip. An organizational strategy of storing all puzzles on the top shelf and all math materials on the bottom shelf may be prompted by a red dot on the top shelf and on all the puzzles, and by a blue dot on the bottom shelf and on all the math materials. In all cases, color coding can be faded by simply making the dots smaller or lighter until they disappear.

A teacher's glance, or *eyeing,* at a correct choice amid distractors can cue the child to point correctly. For instance, if a teacher asks the child to point to the circle amid square and triangle distractors and glances at the circle only, this eyeing of the correct stimulus may cue the correct response. Although research is not available to substantiate the effectiveness of this technique, common experience tends to support it.

Verbal Prompts. The oral *modeling* of a verbal task provides a clear example to the child. It is helpful for children to hear the exact verbal response, particularly in teaching language. For instance, telling a child to say "please" when asking for something not only requests a response, but tells the child exactly what the response is. A teacher might say, "What shape is this?" Say, "This is a circle." Modeling of an oral answer prompts the words as well as intonation and pace. Oral modeling by a peer as well as by a teacher may be effective.

Oral modeling may be limited to an example of the desired behavior. Such was the case when Haskett and Lenfestey (1974) successfully used oral exemplars to initiate and increase reading-related behavior in an open preschool classroom. When tutors read aloud in the reading area, reading-related activity with books other than the tutor's increased compared to a condition in which the tutors did not read aloud. In this study, the tutors did not encourage the children to sit and read with them, but merely modeled reading behavior.

A mere *suggestion* to a child can be successful, at least for some tasks. Saying to a child, "Why don't you play with the blocks?" or "How about painting at the easel?" or "Would you like to give the writing table a try?" may be effective in getting that behavior started. Effective suggestions may even be as subtle as, "Look at all the fun they're having with the blocks," or "Nobody is using the easel," or "There's an empty chair at the writing table." Hardiman, Goetz, Reuter and LeBlanc (1975) successfully used similar suggestions to prompt a young child, who was medically diagnosed as having cerebral palsy, to use large-muscle equipment outdoors.

Unlike suggestions, *instructions* tell a child exactly what to do or sometimes what not to do. For instance: "I'm going to ask a question. If you know the answer, raise your hand. Do not tell me the answer until I call on you." There are several important considerations to bear in mind when delivering instructions. The words should be ones the child understands, and there should not be too many component parts to remember. Instructions should not be given to a child who is "messing around"; the teacher should wait until the child settles down. Also, adequate time should be allowed for a child to comply with the instruction.

Price, Buchman, Toburen, and Goetz (1979) used detailed instructions as part of a procedure to train an aide for a preschool classroom. The aide was given instructions, in lay language, for teaching (for example, attending, instructing, and correcting) children in a preacademic group. Data collected on the aide's behavior and graphs of the behavior shown to the aide proved to be part of a successful combination procedure of which instructions were a vital component.

Verbal prompts may be either oral or written. Since young children usually do not read, *written prompts* are of limited use for them, but simple written prompts may be used to induce beginning reading. This was the case in the Brenner and Goetz (1980) study in which common objects (for example, eraser, book, or table) in the preschool were labeled as written prompts to initiate beginning reading of these words. Although each written prompt was one word, it suggested, "Read me. I am what I am attached to." Some children learned some of the words with the written prompt alone, but more children learned more words when the written prompt was combined with simple daily instructions to look at the words and try to read them. Under both conditions, the children were reinforced if they read the words.

In all of these nonverbal and verbal techniques, if the prompt is explicit, the teacher should try over time to make the prompt less explicit in order to shift the child to correct performance without help. The child's learning acquisition will determine the rate of fading from explicit to subtle or possibly no prompts at all. Prompts should only be temporary stimulus support for correct responding.

Chaining

When a learner sequences two or more stimulus-response situations to perform a task, this is called "chaining." A chain is composed of a series of responses joined together by stimuli that serve both as a reinforcer after the previous response and a discriminative stimulus before the next response. A link in a chain is the discrimination stimulus, the response, and the reinforcer. Chaining may occur at the motor level, such as walking or tying a shoe, or at the verbal level, such as naming numbers in order or telling a story. A child's following of a preschool schedule that required both motor and verbal responses may be considered a long complex chain made up of smaller chains, such as cleaning up materials after an activity, performing a finger play, and getting ready to go home.

Actually, most behavior is a part of a chain rather than an isolated response. A child engages in chaining when putting on a sweater. The empty right sleeve is the discriminative stimulus for the response of putting the right arm in the right sleeve. The child puts the right arm in the right sleeve, an action that is reinforced by the fit of the sleeve. This fitted sleeve now signals that a person must look to the left for an empty sleeve. This look is reinforced because indeed the left sleeve is empty. Now the left sleeve becomes the discriminative stimulus for putting the left arm in the left sleeve. And so it goes with each accomplishment of a step becoming a reinforcer on one hand, and yet on the other hand a discriminative stimulus for the next step. Put simply, each step leads into the next.

A skilled teacher breaks a behavioral chain into small steps and teaches them in sequence. This may be considered a type of shaping procedure as described earlier. Such teachers have an invaluable technique for teaching young or handicapped children, since the smaller the step, the easier it is for the child to learn. These small steps may be taught as forward chaining or backward chaining. Chaining is considered by some to be a separate basic behavioral principle.

Forward Chaining

Chaining is sometimes taught forward. For example, a child may be taught the first step of tying a shoe (crossing the laces), then the second step (one lace under and over), and so on (Cooper, LeBlanc, & Etzel, 1968). Many chains can only be taught forward because competence in or completion of the preceding step is a prerequisite for the next one. Thus, the chain of walking can only be learned forward with the child learning to get on feet first, then to balance and stand, and finally to place one foot in front of the other. In forward chaining the child is taught to produce by the child's own actions, that is, discriminative stimuli that in turn evoke other behaviors to follow. Mahoney, Van Wagenen, and Meyerson (1971) taught the forward chain of toileting to normal and retarded children as (1) walking to the commode; (2) removing clothes; (3) sitting down or standing up in front of the commode; (4) replacing clothes; and (5) returning to play.

Backward Chaining

In backward chaining, the last step is taught first, then the next-to-last-step, and so on. Jacobson (1970) taught shoe tying backwards; the pulling of the bow was taught first with the teacher performing the previous steps, then, the next to last step of putting part of the bow under for tying was taught, after which the child continued the chain of pulling the bow, and so on. Shoe tying is an example of a chain that can be taught either forward or backward because the steps are at the same relative skill level and one step does not depend on mastered competence in the previous step. Some teachers prefer backward chaining whenever possible because it provides whatever possible intrinsic reinforcement may flow from completing a task.

Generalization

When behavior change occurs, whether through reinforcement, punishment, extinction, shaping, stimulus control, prompting, or chaining, it is possible that the change may not occur under different nontraining conditions (that is, across subjects, settings, persons, behaviors, and/or time). In that event, the behavior change did not generalize. To illustrate, some members of a preschool class may pick up playground toys more quickly to earn the privilege of being leaders when the group walks back to the classroom, while other members continue to clean up in slow motion. (No generalization across subjects.) A child may be trained to interact socially with other children while in the classroom, but that child may still not interact with them on the playground. (No generalization across settings.) A child may learn to follow the teacher's instructions, but then fail to follow parents' instruction. (No generalization across persons.) A child may learn to be courteous in saying "please" when asking for something, and yet not say "thank you" after the request is granted. (No generalization across related behaviors.) Finally, a child may be in training for compliance at the beginning of the school day and show improvement, but at the end of the day again be noncompliant. (No generalization across time.)

Generalization is another behavioral principle (Kazdin, 1977, Ch. 7; Wildman & Wildman, 1975) that is not only desirable but necessary for children to develop their full potential in all situations. Generalization occurs when a behavior is not tightly controlled by the stimuli and responses involved in training that behavior. Retarded children tend to be overselective in attending to specific stimuli and responses, and thus they have difficulty generalizing from the training setting to the natural environment. When a teacher trains a desirable behavior in a child, then the teacher should plan generalization of the behavior to different nontraining conditions for the training to be effective in the child's total life experiences. Stokes and Baer (1977) have suggested the following nine techniques as the current skeleton of a technology of generalization: (1) train and hope; (2) sequential modification; (3) introduce to natural maintaining contingencies; (4) train sufficient exemplars; (5) train loosely; (6) use indiscriminable contingencies; (7) program common stimuli; (8) mediate generalization; and (9) train to generalize.

Train and Hope

This title is self-explanatory; the teacher trains a child's behavior in one situation in the hope that it will generalize to other relevant situations. For example, DeVoe and Sherman (1978) trained children's prosocial behavior in school using a microtechnology of models on videotape, subjects on videotape, discussion, and confrontation. Sharing generalized over time in school (that is, one week after the training sessions), but it was not feasible to assess or train sharing in other situations in the home or community. It could only be hoped that training would generalize. Sharing is a productive social behavior that would justify a program of generalization, but research resources sometimes may not allow it.

Sequential Modification

This technique systematically trains a behavior in each situation where it is desired. Sequential modification may require cooperation between parents at home and teachers in school, or among different teachers in various settings in school. Since teamwork may be the key to this method of programming generalized behavior change, teachers should recruit and nurture "team" members. Wahler (1969) controlled oppositional and disruptive behavior of two children, who were referred to an outpatient clinic for psychological problems, in their homes by using time-out and differential attention (that is, attending to appropriate behavior but not attending to inappropriate behavior). When generalization to the children's school behavior was not evidenced, similar contingency operations were employed to accomplish changes in the school settings as well.

Introduce to Natural Maintaining Contingencies

This procedure reduces the number of primes, reinforcers, or whatever is used during training, to the natural level occurring in the nontraining situation. Introducing children to natural maintaining contingencies should be done gradually. The point should never be reached where a desirable behavior is completely ignored over a period of days; classrooms in which desirable behavior is completely ignored should not be considered the natural state of affairs.

Romero et al. (1978) trained preschool children to make triangles and parallelograms with colored cubes by using contingent descriptive praise. This resulted in increased complexity of colored-cube designs. Eventually, praise was decreased but was used intermittently to a level that was thought to approximate the natural number of praise statements that might be given to a single child by a busy teacher attending to an entire class. The making of complex designs generalized to this natural reinforcement condition.

Train Sufficient Exemplars

The training of sufficient exemplars may be thought of in terms of training a behavior in various settings and with various persons until the child engages in the behavior in an untrained setting or with an untrained person. The teacher using this method should continue to model various examples of the generalizable lesson until the child is engaging in generalized behavior related to the specific trained examples. The number of exemplars found to be sufficient for a desirable level and durability for generalization probably is determined by the nature of the task and the child's prior skills.

Parsonson and Baer (1978) used exemplars to train children to improvise with different objects that could be used for a specific task. For example, the teacher provided an example of a rock, a shoe, and a stick, each of which could be used as a hammer to pound a nail, in order to help a child improvise independently for hammers.

Train Loosely

So-called "loose" teaching is conducted with relatively little control over the stimuli presented or the correct response allowed. An example has been the training of vocal imitation skills of retarded children using two methods: (1) emphasizing tight serial (that is, progressive steps) training; and (2) a greater or loose range of vocal imitations (Schroeder and Baer, 1972). Greater generalization occurred to the as-yet-untaught vocal imitations using the loose techniques. In planning lessons for children, it might be wise for generalization purposes to include some variety along with the systematic building of knowledge step-by-step.

Use Indiscriminable Contingencies

As noted under scheduling, the delivery of reinforcers may be "now-and-then" as well as everytime a certain behavior occurs. Under a now-and-then schedule, the child cannot be certain whether a particular behavior will be reinforced, although if the child has previously been through an everytime schedule, the child may sense what is likely to happen for engaging in certain behavior. Goetz, Holmberg, and LeBlanc (1975) trained a noncompliant child to comply with teachers' requests by priming compliance and reinforcing it immediately everytime it occurred. After compliance became consistent, reinforcement on a now-and-then basis maintained it. Compliance had generalized to instances in which there was no reinforcement.

Another indiscriminable contingency that may be used to help generalization is varying discriminative stimuli that signal the forthcoming reinforcement. To this end, Schwarz and Hawkins (1970) videotaped a child's behavior during math and spelling classes. Later, after each school day, the child was shown the math tape and was reinforced for good posture, absence of face touching, and appropriate voice loudness, which were seen and heard on the tape. Although reinforcers were given only on the basis of behavior displayed in the math class, behaviors in the spelling class improved as well. It may be that taping both the math and spelling classes made it difficult for the child to discriminate in which class the behaviors were critical for reinforcement. Perhaps uncertainty helps generalization.

Program Common Stimuli

As one way to promote generalization, sufficient stimuli should be used in the training setting that will also be present in the generalization setting. Common stimuli in training and generalization settings need not be limited to inanimate objects; they may include persons, such as a child's peer or parents. A peer tutor who is also a member of the child's class might help generalize to the classroom skills taught in a private session. Parent aides in the classroom may also be the common stimuli to generalize academic skills from the school to home.

Handleman (1979) taught four autistic boys responses to common questions (for example, "Where do you take a bath? What color is snow?") during training in a cubicle at school, but there was little generalization of this behavior to the kitchen in the home setting. When training was taught in multiple natural settings in school (for example, classroom, lounge, coat cubbies, bathrooms, front door, and office), however, the behavior generalized to multiple natural settings in the home (for example, bedroom, television room, bathroom, front door, and kitchen). The multiple natural school and home settings had common physical stimuli that seemed to facilitate transfer of training.

Mediate Generalization

This technique requires establishing as part of the new learning a mediating response that is likely to be utilized in other problems as well and that will provide sufficient commonality between the original learning and the new problem to result in generalization. One such common mediator is language.

Brady, Brenner, Fjellstrom, Rawson, and Goetz (1980) trained two preschool "buddies" to interact with other peers, rather than exclusively with each other, by using a technique that included language mediation. These two buddies were taught to set their own timers for ten-minute periods during indoor free play and to say for alternate ten-minute periods, "Now I will help others," or "Now I may play with my friend." In fact, these children did say the instructions and followed them. Use of the timers was faded, but the children were asked to continue with the self-instructions. Without the timers, these two children continued to play with many different classmates in the classroom and anecdotally generalized the behavior to the playground. The language mediation, which had elements of self-control, helped generalize the behavior across time when the timers were not used, as well as across settings to the outdoors.

Train To Generalize

The generalization of a behavior may itself be reinforced and thereby be trained as well as the original behavior. Using this approach, Goetz and Baer (1973) trained the generalization of making different forms in block-building. Descriptive social reinforcement was offered for every different form a child built in a single construction (that is, contingent on every first appearance of any blockbuilding form within a session, but not for every subsequent appearance of that form). In this way, the child was rewarded for moving along the generalization gradient underlying block-form inventions and never for staying at one point. In general, this technique succeeded in that the children steadily invented new block forms while this contingency was in use. In cases where no generalization occurs for the teacher to reinforce, the teacher may consider telling the child of generalization possibilities and asking for it.

Self-Control

In the preceding discussion of behavioral principles, a person other than the one with the problem implemented the technique to change the behavior. That is, the teacher attempted to influence the child's behavior. But, sometimes children can control their own behavior. This is known as self-control.

Self-control is highly desirable. A self-controlled child does not need constant supervision. In addition, children who control their own behavior may experience more durable behavior change in many situations. Finally, the education of children is typically geared toward independence, for which self-control is indispensable.

Children can use a variety of self-control techniques, either alone or in varying combinations. A combined use is usually more effective, but for clarity, individual use will be discussed under the following headings: (1) self-instruction; (2) self-recording; (3) self-contract; (4) self-reinforcement; and (5) self-punishment. Ideally, the teacher can help the child understand the behavioral principles on a child's level and suit the techniques to the child and the behavior.

Self-Instruction

Self-instruction may be aloud (overt) or to oneself (covert). Overt instruction seems more effective than covert, but this may be because when instructions are covert, there is no objective evidence they were given at all, and comparison may not be possible. The desired focus of the instruction should be considered. Should the child instruct what to do (e.g., work with the nesting kegs) or what not to do (e.g., pester a friend)? If one focus is not effective, another may be tried. Although self-instruction may be used alone, it seems to be more successful if the natural environment (which includes oneself) provides some reinforcement for the self-instructed response.

Bornstein and Quevillon (1976), working with disruptive preschool children, introduced a self-instructional training procedure to help these children increase their on-task preacademic behavior with such tasks as figure drawing and story reading. In individual sessions, each child watched and listened to the teacher give instructions while working on the task. The child then gave instructions aloud, in a whisper, and finally in private speech. The instructions consisted of such statements as, "What does the teacher want me to do?" and "Oh, that's right, I'm supposed to copy the picture," and "OK, first I draw a line here," and "How about that, I really did that well." Each step of the procedure included self-reinforcement, initially paired with food reinforcement. On-task behavior increased substantially and was maintained for many weeks.

Self-Recording

Knowledge of performance, sometimes combined with other procedures, may produce and maintain a change in behavior. If that knowledge is provided by self-recording, the result is self-control. A person can record with pencil and paper, fingers, or various counting devices, such as golf and bead counters. The change may be either an increase in desirable behavior or a decrease in undesirable behavior.

When self-recording, children may assess both the quantity and quality of their own behavior. Teachers may be helpful in providing clear behavior definitions and examples. The effectiveness of the procedure may depend on accuracy of the assessment and the difficulty of the task, but precise accuracy and an easy task do not seem imperative for successful change.

Self-recording does not seem to effect significant changes in the behaviors of children with severe deviancies, but it is very effective with children who have already demonstrated a fair amount of appropriate behavior. In cases where self-recording cannot change a behavior initially, however, it may help maintain a behavior achieved by some other technique. When self-recording is effective, is seems to be because it elicits self-reinforcing or self-punishing responses.

Attending and academic behaviors lend themselves to self-recording. Reiber, Schilmoeller, and LeBlanc (1976) asked preschool children to use their fingers to self-count disruptive behavior during the daily large group activity. Children were signaled approximately every two minutes during a ten-minute period to assess whether or not they had been disruptive during that time interval. At the end of large group, they counted their fingers and told the teacher how many times, if any, they had been disruptive. The teacher confirmed or gently corrected their reports, and praised or encouraged them to try harder. This self-recording with fingers was successful; disruptive behavior decreased. Similarly, Priestley and Kratochwill (1977) asked a girl (who had referred herself to the school psychologist) in elementary school to self-assess her correct performance on daily math and spelling assignments. Reinforcement with "fun" activities was self-administered, according to a self-determined criterion. Correct performance in math and spelling increased.

Self-Contract

Even a young child may "write" and sign a simple contract specifying the procedure to be used to change a behavior with a teacher's help. The contract should define the target behavior and provide the criterion for the contingency of the reinforcer or possibly punishers. For example, a contract may read, "I may take a sticker and put it on my card if I share toys and do not hit others during recess. I may have a small toy for three stickers." Picture or sign language may be used to enable a nonreader to "read" the contract. The teacher should negotiate criteria that seem reasonable and conducive to change. More stringent standards will produce greater performance than lenient ones, but too stringent standards may invite cheating or self-delusion. Realistically, adult supervision of a child's self-contract is probably needed for strict adherence, especially so if the child is retarded or very young. Even so, the self-contract serves as a reminder or prompt for correct behavior and the child's responsibility for that behavior. In addition, being able to choose one's own contingencies may function as a response facilitator.

White-Blackburn, Semb, and Semb (1977) negotiated good behavior contracts of this type with sixth-grade students. The contracts defined good conduct, disruptive behavior, and assignment completion goals, and specified a list of rewards and penalties that made use of existing facilities and classroom privileges. These contracts improved classroom behavior.

Self-Reinforcement

In some instances, it may be possible to teach children to reinforce themselves for desirable behavior. For young children, teacher assistance is necessary and appropriate. First, the child must learn to note that a response that meets an established criterion has occurred; this involves judgment and possibly simple recording. Then the child must select a reinforcer that is personally potent and manipulatable. Using the example explained under self-contracts, the child would have to judge whether toys were shared and other children were not hit before applying the sticker reinforcer to the card that serves as a simple recording device. The final self-reinforcement would be trading each card with three stickers for a personal choice of a trinket from an assortment.

Self-reinforcement could be tangible, as in the case of the sticker or trinket, or overt/covert verbal behavior, such as "Good, I did that right," or a "feeling" of satisfaction. The self-administration of reinforcement seems reinforcing in itself. How often children say, "I want to do it myself." When properly used with young children, self-reinforcement should be effective alone or incremental when added to other procedures, and equal to or better than external reinforcement alone.

Applied research on this technique with young children is difficult to find. On a more advanced level, Glynn (1970) demonstrated that secondary school students performed equally well with self-determined reinforcement or experimenter-determined reinforcement in history and geography classes. Also, Ballard and Glynn (1975) demonstrated that self-reinforcement with points exchanged for classroom privileges, added to self-recording of writing skills, significantly improved story writing.

Self-Punishment

Another possible technique by which children may control their own behavior is self-punishment. Obviously, a teacher would not train a child to use any sort of physical punishment, but self-criticism or token loss might be considered for some children. As with self-reinforcement, teacher assistance is necessary and appropriate. For instance, a child learning to write a numeral and checking the attempt with a clear plastic overlay of an enlarged outline of the numeral, when incorrect, might be taught to say, "That isn't right. I must do it again." This child might instead be taught to take a token for a correct form and remove a token for an incorrect form. To be "fair" and allow for some token reinforcement, the overlay outline could be quite large. For some children, self-punishment seems to be as effective as self-reinforcement or works as well in combination with it, either to change behavior initially or to maintain it.

Humphrey, Karoly, and Kirschenbaum (1978) used a self-administered token system for reward or response cost with a normal second-grade reading class. All children self-evaluated their workbook performance. Students in the self-reward group were instructed to reinforce themselves for accurate academic performance. Students in the self-imposed response-cost group were given the maximum number of tokens that could be earned on a particular day and were instructed to fine themselves for inaccurate academic performance or failure to complete the daily assignment of reading papers. Both procedures increased the number of pages completed, with self-reward proving slightly more effective. No adverse effects of the response-cost procedure were noted.

EXPERIMENTAL DESIGNS

Experimental designs are used to demonstrate that the independent variable of the stimulus before or after the response is actually causing the observed change in the dependent variable of the response. Acquaintance with experimental designs helps a person understand how a behavioral principle has been verified in research. Practitioners, of course, do not have to conduct research, but they may want to use these designs in some way to assure themselves that their teaching and caring for children are effective. The following three types of individual analysis designs are commonly used: (1) pretest/training/posttest; (2)reversal; and (3) multiple baseline.

Pretest/Training/Posttest

The pretest/training/posttest design is often used when dealing with pre-academic tasks, such as color, shape, and numeral discrimination, or motor tasks, such as riding a trike or walking downstairs. For example, first the child is pretested to assess whether the child knows colors. Then the child is trained by some means, such as matching, pointing to, and labeling colors. Finally, the child is posttested to determine whether the training was successful. If the child performed poorly on the pretest and well on the posttest, it may be assumed that the training caused the change. Of course, it is possible that events outside of training may have changed the behavior.

Reversal

A reversal design can be used when the behavior might easily reverse or revert to its original pattern when treatment is withdrawn. For example, a child's social interaction may decrease or reverse when the treatment of prompting the child into social interaction is withdrawn. On the other hand, discrimination of colors probably would not reverse since once a child learns to discriminate colors, the child usually continues to do so. A reversal may take the form of an increase or decrease. If a low-rate behavior is increased with treatment, the reversal would be a decrease in that behavior. If a high-rate behavior is decreased with treatment, then the reversal would be an increase in that behavior.

In a reversal design, the normal or baseline rate of a behavior is measured before any attempt is made to change it. For instance, if a teacher wished to help a child develop social interaction skills, occurrences of social interaction would be measured over a short period of time for several days before treatment began. Such a baseline measure would be taken until the behavior appeared stable. During treatment by means of prompts to play with others, social interaction would continue to be measured. If social interaction increased for several days of treatment, the treatment then would be discontinued temporarily to find whether the treatment was indeed the cause of the increase. If the treatment were withdrawn and the social interaction decreased or reversed toward the baseline rate, this would demonstrate that the treatment was the cause of the behavior change. For ethical reasons, the next step would be to reinstate the treatment that had been proved effective in increasing a desirable behavior.

The previously-discussed case of Mary's smiling may be used to illustrate a reversal design. Initially, Mrs. Smith tallied the number of times Mary smiled during snacktime to assure herself that she was correct that Mary was seldom smiling. Then for several days Mrs. Smith complimented Mary each time she smiled, and the smiling increased. Mrs. Smith became ill, and a substitute, who did not compliment Mary for smiling, took her place. Smiling decreased. Finally, Mrs. Smith returned to school, again complimented Mary for smiling, and smiling increased. Mary's smiling reversed when Mrs. Smith was ill and reversed yet another time when Mrs. Smith returned. Figure 2-5 shows an example of this reversal design.

Multiple Baseline

The multiple baseline design is used when teaching a behavior that is not expected to reverse (for example, using outdoor play equipment) or one that is not deemed desirable to reverse (for example, aggression). In this design, baseline or normal rates of behavior must be established for the following: (1) two or more similar behaviors for the same child; (2) the same behavior for the same child in two or more settings; or (3) the same behavior for two or more different children in the same setting. The

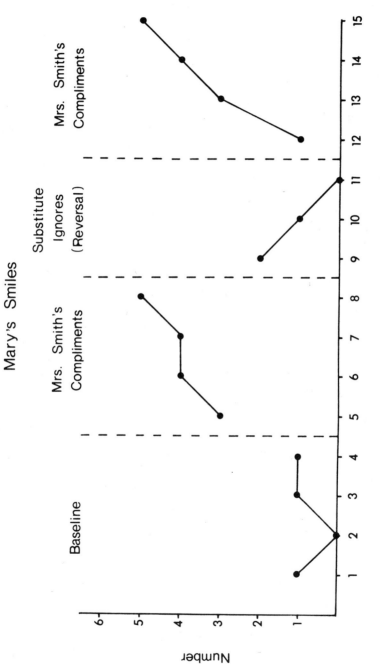

Figure 2-5 Reversal Design Example

second, third, and so on behavior, setting, or child provides experimental control against the possibility of coincidence having been the explanation for any change in the first behavior, setting, or child. After a definite effect has been observed for the first treatment, the second is introduced, and so on, as effects are observed in each. Each succeeding manipulation serves as a replication of the effects of the previous treatment. The more replications, the stronger the experimental control.

A simple example may clarify the use of a multiple baseline design. Consider a young handicapped child who does not interact socially with other children in a preschool during both indoor free-play time and outdoor recess. The teacher observes the child's normal rate of social interaction both indoors and out. After the baseline rate of social interaction has been determined and stabilized in both settings, the teacher begins to prompt the child to play with others only during the indoor free-play time. Indoor social interaction increases, while outdoor social interaction remains low. Now the teacher begins to prompt the child to play with others outdoors as well as indoors. At this time, outdoor social interaction also increases, and indoor social interaction continues at the higher rate. Thus, prompts increased social interaction successively—not at the same time—in two different settings. It would not seem that social interaction increased coincidentally indoors since the outdoor social interaction remained low when treatment took place only indoors. Additionally, the subsequent outdoor treatment replicated the results of the indoor treatment. For these reasons, experimental control was demonstrated.

CONCLUSION

A wide variety of behavioral principles and techniques are available and offer individualized guidance for both typical and atypical children who need help in learning physical and academic skills or in maturing in socially productive and creative ways. These principles and techniques can be highly effective teacher-helpers in working with children, if used properly, consistently, and individually. Though a few of the techniques presented do not yet have a strong data base to verify their effectiveness, they too should be considered so that teachers themselves may assess their validity or demonstrate their imperfections.

In learning to use behavioral principles and techniques, teachers should think in terms of shaping themselves and should learn to use them one or two at a time, as the occasion suggests. Prompting, reinforcement, and scheduling of reinforcement will probably be the first ones used. When comfortable with these, a teacher might think of overcoming any teaching difficulties by means of shaping, stimulus control, chaining, generalization, and self-control solutions. Practice with such procedures as delivering continuous or intermittent reinforcement and general or descriptive reinforcement will tend to make using them seem easy and natural. When problems persist, the teaching may be at fault, not the child. Each time a child fails to learn or change a behavior, that child is telling the teacher that the learning environment is not arranged properly. Furthermore, the more handicapped, delayed, or retarded a child is, the more important it is for the teacher to find ways to rearrange the learning environment and the teacher's responsiveness to the child in such a way that the child does learn.

While other programs have successfully used the behavioral approach for both typical and atypical children, and much of their research has been cited, the following chapters will update the behavioral approach used at the University of Kansas. This behavioral approach will be shown as an accommodating system, not a technological one, with the emphasis on helping all types of children rather than on perfecting techniques. Behavior analysis will be seen as a positive and carefully considered approach. Reinforcement rather than punishment techniques are used whenever possible. Social reinforcement is always considered before tangible reinforcement. The child's welfare is the prime concern. Behavior analysis is not only a teacher-helper—it is also a child-helper.

REFERENCES

Allen, K.E., Hart, B., Buell, J.S., Harris, F.R., & Wolf, M.M. Effects of social reinforcement on isolate behavior of a nursery school child. *Child Development*, 1964, *35*, 511–518.

Apolloni, T., & Tremblay, A. Peer modeling between toddlers. *Child Study Journal*, 1978, *8*, 243–253.

Appleman, K., Allen, K.E., & Turner, K.D. The conditioning of language in a nonverbal child conducted in a special education classroom. *Journal of Speech and Hearing Disorders*, 1975, *40*, 3–12.

Atwood, M.D., Ruebush, B.K., & Everett, F.L. The effects of modeling and role playing on children's delay of gratification behavior. *Child Study Journal*, 1978, *8*, 149–163.

Baer, D.M. A hung jury and a Scottish verdict: "Not Proven." *Analysis and Intervention in Developmental Disabilities*, 1981, *1*, 91–97.

Ballard, K.D., & Glynn, T. Behavioral self-management in story writing with elementary school children. *Journal of Applied Behavior Analysis*, 1975, *8*, 387–397.

Birnbrauer, J.S., Bijou, S.W., Wolf, M.M., & Kidder, J.D. Programmed instruction in the classroom. In L.P. Ullman & L. Krasner (Eds.), *Case studies in behavior modification*. New York: Holt, Rinehart & Winston, Inc., 1965, 358–363.

Bolstad, O.D., & Johnson, S.M. Self-regulation in the modification of disruptive behavior. *Journal of Applied Behavior Analysis*, 1972, *5*, 443–454.

Bornstein, P.H., & Quevillon, R.P. The effects of a self-instructional package on overactive preschool boys. *Journal of Applied Behavior Analysis*, 1976, *9*, 179–188.

Brady, M.E., Brenner, E.P., Fjellstrom, G.G., Rawson, R.M., & Goetz, E.M. The "buddy" study: Increasing the rate of social interaction through the use of timers. Paper presented at the Association for Applied Behavior Analysis, Dearborn, Michigan, May 1980.

Brenner, E.P., & Goetz, E.M. Incidental learning: The acquisition of "sight-word" labels in a preschool classroom. Unpublished manuscript, University of Kansas, 1980.

Chiang, S.J., Iwata, B.A., & Dorsey, M.F. Elimination of disruptive bus riding behavior via token reinforcement on a "distance-based" schedule. *Education and Treatment of Children*, 1979, *2*, 101–110.

Christy, P.R. Does use of tangible rewards with individual children affect peer observers? *Journal of Applied Behavior Analysis*, 1975, *8*, 187–196.

Cooper, M.L., LeBlanc, J.M., & Etzel, B.C. A shoe is to tie (16mm color 10-minute film depicting a programmed sequence for teaching shoe tying to preschool children). Edna A. Hill Child Development Laboratory, Department of Human Development, University of Kansas, January 1968.

Corey, J.R., & Shamow, J. The effects of fading on the acquisition and retention of oral reading. *Journal of Applied Behavior Analysis*, 1972, *5*, 311–315.

Cunningham, P.J., Cooper, A.Y., Schilmoeller, K.J., & LeBlanc, J.M. Procedures for obtaining instructional control of an "oppositional" child. Paper presented at the Society for Research in Child Development, Denver, Colorado, April, 1975.

DeVoe, M.W., & Sherman, T.M. A microtechnology for teaching prosocial behavior to children. *Child Study Journal*, 1978, *8*, 83–92.

Etzel, B.C., & LeBlanc, J.M. The simplest treatment alternative: The law of parsimony applied to choosing appropriate instructional control and errorless-learning procedures for the difficult-to-teach child. *Journal of Autism and Developmental Disorders*, 1979, *9*, 361–382.

Etzel, B.C., LeBlanc, J.M., Schilmoeller, K.J., & Stella, M.E. Stimulus control procedures in the education of young children. In S.W. Bijou and R. Ruez (Eds.), *Contributions of behavior modification to education*. Hillsdale, N.J.: Lawrence Erlbaum Associates, in press.

Fallon, M.P., & Goetz, E.M. The creative teacher: The effects of descriptive social reinforcement upon the drawing behavior of three preschool children. *School Applications of Learning Theory*, 1975, *7* (2), 27–45.

Fowler, S.A., & Baer, D.M. Do I have to be good today? The timing of delayed reinforcement as a factor in generalization. *Journal of Applied Behavior Analysis*, 1981, *14*, 13–24.

Gelfand, D.M., Hartmann, D.P., Mahan, M.A., & Lamb, A. Children's imitation of adult behavior control techniques. In D.M. Gelfand (Ed.), *Social learning in childhood: Readings in theory and application* (2nd ed.). Monterey, Cal.: Brooks/Cole, 1975.

Glynn, E.L. Classroom applications of self-determined reinforcement. *Journal of Applied Behavior Analysis*, 1970, *3*, 123–132.

Goetz, E.M., Ayala, J.M., Hatfield, V.L., Baer, A.M., & Etzel, B.C. An auditory stimulus as a conditioned reinforcer and/or discriminative stimulus for preschoolers. Paper presented at the American Psychological Association, New Orleans, Louisiana, September, 1974.

Goetz, E.M., & Baer, D.M. Social control of form diversity and the emergence of new forms. *Journal of Applied Behavior Analysis*, 1973, *6*, 209–217.

Goetz, E.M., Holmberg, M.C., & LeBlanc, J.M. Differential reinforcement of other behavior and noncontingent reinforcement as control procedures during the modification of a preschooler's compliance. *Journal of Applied Behavior Analysis*, 1975, *8*, 77–82.

Goetz, E.M., Jones, K., & Weamer, K. The generalization of creativity "training" in easel painting to blockbuilding. Abstracted in *Research in Education* (Document No. Ed. 086 324). Urbana: University of Illinois, Educational Resources Information Center/Early Childhood Education, May 1974.

Goetz, E.M., & Salmonson, M.M. The effect of general and descriptive reinforcement on "creativity" in easel painting. In G.B. Semb (Ed.), *Behavior analysis in education, 1972*. Lawrence, Kan.: University of Kansas Support and Development Center for Follow Through, 1972, 53–61.

Goetz, E.M., Thomson, C.L., & Etzel, B.C. An analysis of direct and indirect teacher attention and primes in the modification of child social behavior: A case study. *Merrill-Palmer Quarterly*, 1975, *21*, 55–65.

Guralnick, M.J. Effects of distinctive-feature training and instructional technique on letter and form discrimination. *American Journal of Mental Deficiency*, 1975, *80*, 202–207.

Guralnick, M.J. Integrated preschools as educational and therapeutic environments: Concepts, design and analysis. In M.J. Guralnick (Ed.), *Early intervention and the integration of handicapped and nonhandicapped children*. Baltimore, Md.: University Park Press, 1978, 115–146.

Hall, J.S., & Holmberg, M.C. The effect of teacher behaviors and food serving arrangements on young children's eating in a day care center. *Child Care Quarterly*, 1974, *3*, 97–108.

Handleman, J.G. Generalization by autistic-type children of verbal responses across settings. *Journal of Applied Behavior Analysis*, 1979, *12*, 273–284.

Hanley, E.M., Perelman, P.F., & Holman, C.I. Parental management of a child's self-stimulation behavior through the use of time-out and DRO. *Education and Treatment of Children*, 1979, *2*, 305–310.

Hardiman, S.A., Goetz, E.M., Reuter, K.E., & LeBlanc, J.M. Contingent attention, primes, and training: A comparison of the effects on a child's motor behavior. *Journal of Applied Behavior Analysis*, 1975, *8*, 399–409.

Harris, F.R., Sherman, J.A., Henderson, D.G., & Harris, M.S. Effects of peer tutoring on the spelling performance of elementary classroom students. In G.B. Semb (Ed.), *Behavior analysis and education, 1972*. Lawrence, Kan.: University of Kansas Support and Development Center for Follow Through, 1972.

Hart, B.M., & Risley, T.R. Incidental teaching of language in the preschool. *Journal of Applied Behavior Analysis*, 1975, *8*, 411–420.

Haskett, G.J., & Lenfestey, W. Reading-related behavior in an open classroom. Effects of novelty and modeling on preschoolers. *Journal of Applied Behavior Analysis*, 1974, *7*, 233–242.

Hatfield, V.L., & Goetz, E.M. The effect of teacher absence or presence on peer interaction during snack time. *School Applications of Learning Theory*, 1975, *8*, 34–42.

Hawkins, R.P. Behavior analysis and early childhood education: Engineering children's learning. *Psychological processes in early education*. New York: Academic Press, Inc., 1977, 99–131.

Holman, J., Goetz, E.M., & Baer, D.M. The training of creativity as an operant and an examination of its generalization characteristics. In B.C. Etzel, J.M. LeBlanc, & D.M. Baer (Eds), *New developments in behavioral research theory, methods, and application. In honor of Sidney W. Bijou*. Hillsdale, N.J.: Lawrence Erlbaum Associates, 1977, 441–472.

Hopkins, B.L. Effects of candy and social reinforcement, instructions and reinforcement schedule learning on the modification and maintenance of smiling. *Journal of Applied Behavior Analysis*, 1968, *1*, 121–130.

Hopkins, B.L., Schutte, R.C., & Garron, K.L. The effects of access to a playroom on the rate and quality of printing and writing of first- and second-grade students. *Journal of Applied Behavior Analysis,* 1971, *4,* 77–88.

Humphrey, L.L., Karoly, P., & Kirschenbaum, D.S. Self-management in the classroom: Self-imposed response cost versus self-reward. *Behavior Therapy,* 1978, *9,* 592–601.

Ireton, C.L., & Guthrie, H.A. Modification of vegetable eating behavior in preschool children. *Journal of Nutrition Education,* 1972, *4,* 100–103.

Jackson, D.A., & Wallace, R.F. The modification and generalization of voice loudness in a fifteen-year-old retarded girl. *Journal of Applied Behavior Analysis,* 1974, *7,* 461–472.

Jacobson, B. Teaching children to tie their shoes. *School Applications of Learning Theory,* 1970, *3,* 47–48.

Johnston, M.K., Kelley, C.S., Harris, F.L., & Wolf, M.M. An application of reinforcement principles to development of motor skills of a young child. *Child Development,* 1966, *37,* 379–387.

Kazdin, A.E. *The token economy.* New York: Plenum Press, 1977.

Knapp, M.B., O'Neil, S.M., & Allen, K.E. Teaching Suzi to walk. In S.M. O'Neil, B.N. McLaughlin, & M.B. Knapp (Eds.), *Behavioral approaches to children with developmental delays.* St. Louis: C.B. Mosby, 1977, 105–114.

LeBlanc, J.M., Etzel, B.C., & Domash, M.A. A functional curriculum for early intervention. In K.E. Allen, V.A. Holm, & R.L. Schiefelbusch (Eds), *Early intervention: A team approach.* Baltimore, Md.: University Park Press, 1978, 331–382.

LeLaurin, K., & Risley, T.R. The organization of day care environments: "Zone" versus "man-to-man" staff assignments. *Journal of Applied Behavior Analysis,* 1972, *5,* 225–232.

Lovaas, O.I. *Behavioral treatment of autistic children.* Morristown, N.J.: General Learning Press, 1973.

Luiselli, J.K., Helfen, C.S., & Colozzi, G. Teachers' use of reinforcement and time-out procedures to modify disruptive classroom behavior of special education students. *School Applications of Learning Theory,* 1977, *9* (4), 49–64.

Madsen, Jr., C.H., Hoffman, M., Thomas, D.R., Koropsak, E., & Masden, C.K. Comparison of toilet training techniques. In D.M. Gelfand (Ed.), *Social learning in childhood: Readings in theory and application.* Monterey, Cal.: Brooks/Cole, 1975, 104–112.

Mahoney, K., Van Wagenen, K., & Meyerson, L. Toilet training of normal and retarded children. *Journal of Applied Behavior Analysis,* 1971, *4,* 173–181.

Marholin II, D., & Steinman, W.M. Stimulus control in the classroom as a function of the behavior reinforced. *Journal of Applied Behavior Analysis,* 1977, *10,* 465–478.

McNamara, J.R. The broad based application of social learning theory to treat aggression in preschool children. *Journal of Clinical Psychology,* 1970, *26,* 245–247.

Mendoza, M., Holt, W.J., & Jackson, D.A. Circles and tape: An easy teacher implemented way to teach fundamental writing skills. *Teaching Exceptional Child,* Winter 1978, 48–50.

Miller, B.J., Kolb, D., Baer, D.M., & Etzel, B.C. Effects of interpolated errors on errorless discrimination learning in preschoolers. Paper presented at the American Psychological Association, Chicago, August 1975.

Mock, L. Dave learns to dress himself. In S.M. O'Neil, B.N. McLaughlin, & M.B. Knapp (Eds.), *Behavioral approaches to children with developmental delays* St. Louis: C.V. Mosby, Co., 1977, 62.

O'Brien, F., Bugle, C., & Azrin, N.H. Training and maintaining a retarded child's proper eating. *Journal of Applied Behavior Analysis,* 1972, *5,* 67–72.

O'Leary, K.D., & Drabman, R. Token reinforcement programs in the classroom. *Psychological Bulletin,* 1971, *75,* 379–398.

O'Neil, S.M., McLaughlin, B.N., & Knapp, M.B. *Behavioral approaches to children with developmental delays.* St. Louis: C.V. Mosby, Co., 1977.

Parsonson, B.S., & Baer, D.M. Training generalized improvisation of tools by preschool children. *Journal of Applied Behavior Analysis,* 1978, *11,* 363–380.

Pinkston, E.M., Reese, N., LeBlanc, J.M., & Baer, D.M. Independent control of aggression and peer interaction by contingent teacher attention. *Journal of Applied Behavior Analysis,* 1973, *6,* 115–124.

Plummer, S., Baer, D.M., & LeBlanc, J.M. Functional considerations in the use of time out and an effective alternative. *Journal of Applied Behavior Analysis,* 1977, *10,* 689–705.

Porterfield, J.K., Herbert-Jackson, E., & Risley, T.R. Contingent observation: An effective and acceptable procedure for reducing disruptive behavior of young children in a group setting. *Journal of Applied Behavior Analysis,* 1976, *9,* 55–64.

Price, L., Buchman, B., Toburen, C.S., & Goetz, E.M. A case study of the training of a classroom aide by an undergraduate student in a child development laboratory preschool setting. *Education and Treatment of Children,* 1979, *2,* 202–220.

Priestley, M., & Kratochwill, T.R. Self-management of academic behavior: A case report. *School Applications of Learning Theory,* 1977, *9* (3), 56–72.

Redd, W.H., Ullmann, R.K., & Roesch, P. A classroom incentive program instituted by tutors after school. *Education and Treatment of Children,* 1979, *2,* 169–176.

Reiber, J.L., Schilmoeller, G.L., & LeBlanc, J.M. The use of self-control to maintain attending of preschool children after self-counting procedures. In T.A. Brigham, R.R. Hawkins, J. Scott, and T.F. McLaughlin (Eds.), *Behavior analysis in education* (Vol. V). Dubuque, Iowa: Kendall-Hunt, 1976, 32–38.

Resnick, L.B., Wang, M.C., & Kaplan, J. Task analysis on curriculum design: A hierarchically sequenced introductory mathematics curriculum. *Journal of Applied Behavior Analysis,* 1973, *6,* 679–709.

Rheingold, H.L. Sharing at an early age. In B.C. Etzel, J. M. LeBlanc, & D.M. Baer (Eds.),*New Developments in behavioral research: Theory, method and application. In honor of Sidney W. Bijou.* Hillsdale, N.J.: Lawrence Erlbaum Associates, 1977, 489–502.

Rintoul, B., Cooper A.Y., Schilmoeller, K.J., & LeBlanc, J.M. The effects of decreased teacher interaction and social primes of verbal peer interaction in a small group of preschool children. *Child Study Journal,* 1975, *5,* 115–124.

Rogers-Warren, A., & Baer, D.M. Correspondence between saying and doing: Teaching children to share and praise. *Journal of Applied Behavior Analysis,* 1976, *9,* 335–354.

Romero, P.N., Holt, W.J., Stella, M.E., Baer, D.M., & Etzel, B.C. Training preschool children to make complex and creative color cube designs. Paper presented at the American Psychological Association, Toronto, August 1978.

Rowbury, T.G. , Baer, A.M., & Baer, D.M. Interactions between teacher guidance and contingent access to play in developing preacademic skills of deviant preschool children. *Journal of Applied Behavior Analysis,* 1976, *9,* 85–104.

Saudargas, R.W., Madsen, Jr., C.H., & Scott, J.W. Differential effects of fixed and variable-time feedback on production rates of elementary school children. *Journal of Applied Behavior Analysis,* 1977, *10,* 637–678.

Schilmoeller, K.J., & Etzel, B.C. An experimental analysis of criterion-related and noncriterion-related cues in "errorless" stimulus control procedures. In B.C. Etzel, J.M. LeBlanc,

& D.M. Baer (Eds.), *New developments in behavioral research: Theory, method and application. In honor of Sidney W. Bijou.* Hillsdale, N.J.: Lawrence Erlbaum Associates, 1977, 317–348.

Schlosberg, H., & Solomon, R.L. Latency of response in a choice discrimination. *Journal of Experimental Psychology,* 1943, *33,* 27–39.

Schroeder, G.L., & Baer, D.M. Effects of concurrent and serial training on generalized vocal imitation in retarded children. *Developmental Psychology,* 1972, *6,* 293–301.

Schwarz, M.L., & Hawkins, R.P. Application of delayed reinforcement procedures to the behavior of an elementary school child. *Journal of Applied Behavior Analysis,* 1970, *3,* 85–96.

Sidman, M., & Stoddard, L.T. Programming perception and learning for retarded children. In N.R. Ellis (Ed.), *International review of research in mental retardation* Vol. II. New York: Academic Press, 1966, 151–208.

Staats, A.W., Finley, J.R., Minke, K.A., & Wolf, M.M. Reinforcement variables in the control of unit reading responses. *Journal of Experimental Analysis of Behavior,* 1964, *7,* 139–149.

Stokes, T.F., & Baer, D.M. An implicit technology of generalization. *Journal of Applied Behavior Analysis,* 1977, *10,* 349–368.

Stromer, R. Modifying letter and number reversals in elementary school children. *Journal of Applied Behavior Analysis,* 1975, *8,* 211.

Sulzer, B., & Mayer, G.R. *Behavior modification procedures for school personnel.* Hinsdale, Ill.: Dryden, 1972.

Thomson, C.L., Holmberg, M.C., & Baer, D.M. An experimental analysis of some procedures to teach priming skills to preschool teachers. *Monographs of the Society for Research in Child Development,* 1978, *43* (4 Serial No. 176).

Touchette, P.E. Transfer of stimulus control: Measuring the moment of transfer. *Journal of the Experimental Analysis of Behavior,* 1971, *15,* 347–354.

Van Houten, R., & Nau, P.A. A comparison of fixed and variable ratio schedules of reinforcement on the behavior of deaf children. *Journal of Applied Behavior Analysis,* 1980, *13,* 13–21.

Vargas, J.S. *Writing worthwhile behavioral objectives.* New York: Harper and Row, 1972.

Wahler, R.G. Setting generality: Some specific and general effects of child behavior therapy. *Journal of Applied Behavior Analysis,* 1969, *2,* 239–246.

White-Blackburn, G., Semb, S., & Semb, G. The effects of a good behavior contract on the classroom behaviors of sixth-grade students. *Journal of Applied Behavior Analysis,* 1977, *10,* 312.

Whitehurst, C., Domash, M., & DiGennaro, C. The effect of storybook design on attention and story relevant verbalizations in preschool children. In T.A. Brigham et al. (Eds.). *Behavior analysis in education: Self-control and reading.* Dubuque, Iowa: Kendall-Hunt, 1976, 145–150.

Wildman, II, R.W., & Wildman, R.W. The generalization of behavior modification procedures: A review—with special emphasis on classroom applications. *Psychology in the schools,* 1975, *12,* 432–448.

Wright, J.H., & Hawkins, R.P. The elimination of tattling behavior through the use of an operant conditioning technique. *School Applications of Learning Theory,* 1970, *2,* 9–13.

Chapter 3

Some Considerations in the Use of Teacher Implemented Observation Procedures

Ted R. Ruggles

Any statement of the conditions that are necessary for effective teaching would almost certainly include educational planning based on some form of periodic assessment of children's performance. In many cases, the assessment that occurs within a classroom consists of the teacher's casual observation and comparison of a child's performance with that of other children in the setting or in the teacher's past experience. Often, however, the need arises for some more formal assessment or documentation of children's behavior. The options available for such formalized measurement are broadly varied. Included within these options are behavioral observation techniques.

Although in themselves diverse, behavioral observation techniques share some common characteristics. Perhaps foremost among these is that behavioral observation procedures concentrate on those aspects of children's behavior that are overt. A behavioral assessment of a child's social skills, for example, would not be concerned with the child's or teacher's subjective impressions of interpersonal relationships, but would concentrate instead on such observable aspects as the amount of time the child spent in physical proximity to children or adults or the frequency with which the child directed verbalizations toward other people. A related characteristic of behavioral observation is an emphasis on objective descriptions of behavior. In this respect the contrast between the information collected through behavioral observation and that collected through more traditional methods is marked. While procedures using information from verbal report, standardized assessment techniques, rating scales, and so forth rely heavily on the observer's interpretation of behavioral occurrences, behavioral observation stresses the avoidance of such judgments. Heynes and Lipsitt (1954) in fact have likened the behavioral observer to a "thermometer" or "an instrument for measuring the stimulus situation" (p. 370). This statement points out that behavioral observation is ideally a process in which a noninterpretative translation of behavior into quantitative record occurs.

An additional characteristic of behavioral observation procedures is that they typically result in ordinal information regarding behavior. Perhaps more simply stated, behavioral observation procedures generally go beyond noting the presence or absence of a behavior and yield information regarding the degree or frequency with which a behavior occurs. Such information allows an assessment of change in a particular child's behavior over time (perhaps, for example, as an educational intervention progresses) or an assessment of the level of a child's behavior relative to that of the child's peers.

Among the situations in which behavioral observation and quantification of children's behavior may be desirable are examinations of the level of a particular child's (or group's) behavior relative to that of other children in the classroom or some larger population. By gathering information about the behavior of a particular child for comparison to composite characterization of the behavior of other children within a setting, the behavioral dimensions responsible for subjective impressions may be identified. Educational interventions aimed at remediating a global problem, such as deficient social interaction, can be much more precise and efficient once the observable subcomponents of the behavior (for example, initiating peer interaction, verbalizing when initiated to, and so on) where the child varies from other children are identified. Since behavioral observation techniques identify the behaviors that it may be desirable to change, such procedures serve prescriptive as well as diagnostic functions. Once it has been established that a particular behavior by a particular child occurs at a level that is different from that which is expected or characteristic of other children, the behavior that may need to be changed is readily apparent. The composite characterization or "normative" information gathered in this fashion also yields guidelines as to the level to which a child's behavior should be changed. Thus, for example, if a particular child is found to initiate fewer interactions than most other children in the setting, a remediation procedure might have as its goal increasing the target child's initiations to a level approximating that exhibited by the child's classmates. While the preceding characteristics may seem quite apparent, they are not common across all behavior assessment strategies.

Once a teaching strategy aimed at a particular behavioral outcome has been implemented, an ongoing assessment of the behavior addressed by this strategy allows an assessment of the effectiveness of the technique. On many occasions such ongoing evaluation has demonstrated the need for adjustments of the technique. These adjustments have often resulted in the ultimate effectiveness of the procedure; success that would not otherwise have been realized.

Finally, behavioral observation serves a communicative function. Educational records are often used to document a child's progress or lack of progress through an educational program. Such records should communicate to other professionals information regarding aspects of the child's behavior that may be valuable in establishing educational procedures for the child. Another aspect of the communicative function is documentation. The effectiveness of particular teaching strategies for addressing educational problems may be documented through the presentation of information about the patterns of child behavior preceding, during, and after implementation of a particular teaching strategy. The communication of information about a child's performance or the effectiveness of a particular teaching procedure is facilitated through the type of objective description that is characteristic of most behavioral observation procedures.

FACTORS INFLUENCING THE SELECTION OF BEHAVIORAL OBSERVATION PROCEDURES

The Economics of the Setting

The process through which a particular observation procedure is selected for use in a given situation involves consideration of a number of interactive factors. Perhaps the considerations that present themselves most immediately are those that involve the economics of the setting in which the observation is desirable. Since, in most instances, teachers are expected or required to maintain their full teaching duties while gathering behavioral information, the amount of time any teacher can contribute toward observing is generally limited. It must be determined whether there are times during which a teacher might be freed from teaching for short periods so that observation might be accomplished or whether observation must be carried on while teaching duties continue. A related consideration is whether all or only some of the classroom personnel should be involved in the observation or whether people from outside of the classroom should be recruited to help in the observation process. In many cases, high school or college students have acted in this capacity in return for receiving training in behavioral intervention. On rare occasions, older children have also acted as observers. Recently, however, this practice has been criticized on the basis that it provides few educational benefits for the observer and so is not a justifiable expenditure of the observer's time.

The Type or Amount of Information That Is Necessary

Interacting closely with the consideration of which personnel might be available for conducting observations are questions about the type or amount of information that is necessary. Careful preliminary attention to the types of decisions that may be based on the information obtained from the planned observations may aid in avoiding either of two common problems. First, it is economically unwise to collect more information than is necessary for the decisions that are to be made (Scott & Goetz, 1980). Second, such preliminary considerations may help to avoid situations in which the data collected are not sufficient to provide the basis for the necessary decisions. In many instances, even with careful planning, it is impossible to avoid both of these problems. Where this is the case, it seems most teachers prefer to err on the side of collecting slightly more information than may be necessary initially.

One such issue is the number of subjects that should be observed. It is important to consider whether the situation that is to be addressed by the observation problem pertains to one child, a few children, or all of the children in the classroom. When information is desired for more than one child, the teacher must decide whether information is needed on each separate member of the group or whether a composite of the behavior of a number of children would be suitable. Thus, one option available to a teacher interested in decreasing the occurrence of classroom noise would be to attempt to measure the amount of noise made by each child. As can be imagined, this data-gathering procedure would require much more observer time and attention than other options in which teachers or observers simply record the occurrence of noise without respect to which child produced it. In situations in which the only goal of the intervention is to limit the amount of classroom noise, the latter procedure would be considered more economical since it would produce only that information that is necessary to the goals of the program. If, on the other hand, the goals of the program are not only to reduce classroom noise but to assess the results of the procedure on individual class members, procedures providing individualized information would be necessary.

A related issue is the number of separate observations that are necessary. Since levels of behavior often fluctuate from day to day, it is seldom advisable to rely on information obtained from a single observation. An observation conducted on a given day may reflect a "good" or a "bad" day in which the level of the child's behavior, although within the range of normal variability, is not characteristic of the child's performance. For that reason decisions should be based on enough observations to reflect the range of the child's performance in the given situation. To some extent, the range of behavioral levels may reflect the variety that is possible in the setting in which the behavior occurs. Thus, with such "academic" behaviors as letter writing or numeral recognition, the range of situations in which the behavior would be expected to occur is relatively limited (that is, the child would generally be expected to produce these behaviors only in "academic" situations, such as when the teacher asks for a numeral or asks the child to produce a letter). Social behaviors, on the other hand, may be affected by such variables as the nature of the play equipment that is present or the number of children or adults present. Sufficient observations should always be conducted to reflect the range of the behavior across the various situations in which the behavior is relevant.

When information is desired about the behavior of several individuals, it is important to consider whether it is necessary or preferable to collect that information simultaneously or whether information on the behavior of individuals may be gathered at different times. If, for example, the goal of the observation is to collect information that would allow a comparison of the behavior of several children in the same setting, then some arrangement in which observations of the behavior of several children during the same time period would be preferable (since, in this manner, differences attributable to variations in time, activities, or additional learning could be eliminated). If simultaneous information is not necessary, it may be advisable (and perhaps more feasible) to arrange to collect information for different children successively.

Decisions regarding the distribution of observations interact with the availability of personnel and the characteristics of the observation systems that are utilized. When simultaneous observations are required and limited personnel are available, data collection systems that allow observers to record behavior for more than one subject during the same observation period are necessary. When successive observations are suitable, a single observer could record the behavior of only one child at a time.

The Characteristics of the Behavior

Along with considerations of the economics of the setting and the information that is necessary for the decisions to be made, are the characteristics of the behavior itself. One such issue is the extent to which the behavior that is of interest tends to occur in predictable situations. If, for example, a behavior occurs only at specific times (for example, during transition times, lunch, or recess), then observations might be limited to those situations in which the behavior occurs. In many instances a few days of anecdotal observation in which the teacher simply notes when and where a behavior occurs has resulted in considerable savings in observation time.

A second issue concerning behavioral characteristics is whether the behavior results in some physical evidence that remains after the behavior occurs. Academic tasks, such as writing assignments and mathematics worksheets, result in "permanent products"—the written letters or problem solutions—that may be evaluated after the behavior has occurred. When permanent products exist, the task of observation is made much easier since the observer may evaluate these products at a time that is convenient. Although academic tasks are the most obvious situation in which permanent products exist, these are not the only behaviors for which such procedures have been used. Littering (by measuring the weight of the trash left in a given area), whether or not children took materials home to parents (by counting the number of articles in the child's locker before and after school), and many other behaviors have been measured in this fashion.

In addition to the environmental circumstances in which behavior occurs and whether a behavior results in permanent products, the choice of an observation procedure may also be affected by the physical (topographical) characteristics of the behavior. One such factor is the speed with which the behavior is repeated. When repetitions of a behavior occur in rapid succession (for example, finger tapping), physical limitations, such as the observer's ability to count each occurrence of the behavior, may exist. In addition, it is important to note that the total number of behaviors that a single observer is charged with recording is the product of the number of times each child emits the behavior and the number of children observed. Thus, a behavior that each child in a setting emits fairly infrequently may prove to be an observation problem if a single observer is charged with counting occurrences of the behavior across several children.

The length of each behavioral occurrence may also influence the choice of observation tactics. Some observation procedures, for example, capture only those behaviors that are of more than momentary duration, while others adequately measure both momentary and longer duration behaviors. Procedures that are adequate for recording a behavior, such as engagement in block play, may not always be adequate for recording more discrete behaviors, such as hitting a peer. Another aspect of this same consideration is the extent to which the duration of behavioral episodes varies over time. When considerable variability in the length of behavioral episodes occurs, some behavioral observation techniques produce information that reflects this change, while others are insensitive to it. Thus, when it is necessary that durational differences that occur across time or across children in the classroom be revealed, consideration must be given to the adequacy with which a given procedure will reflect such changes. This consideration involves not only attention to existing behavioral characteristics, but demands some forethought with respect to the qualitative changes that may occur as the result of planned interventions. With isolate children, for example, interactions before treatment may consist of short duration contacts between the child and adults or other children. An observation procedure that adequately characterizes and isolates a child's behavior before treatment may not reflect the changes toward longer duration interactions that would result from an intervention procedure.

A final physical characteristic of behavior that is important is the extent to which the beginning and end points of each behavioral episode are discriminable. Observers generally have little difficulty in agreeing when a behavior such as rock throwing begins and ends. For other behaviors, for example, "conversation," the discrimination is much more difficult. Since observation procedures vary greatly with respect to whether discrimination of the beginning and end points of behavior is necessary, consideration of this characteristic is necessary in the process of matching observation procedure to behavior.

THE CHARACTERISTICS OF BEHAVIOR OBSERVATION STRATEGIES

Interacting with the economics of the setting, the nature of the information needed, and the characteristics of the behavior to be observed are characteristics of the various observation procedures that may be used.

Narrative Recording

Some of the earliest methods for accumulating information about the behavior of children took the form of narrative recordings in which developmental progress, usually of a single child, was noted. Often such records, referred to as diaries (Irwin & Bushnell, 1980) consisted of the collection and synthesis of notes about the development of the diarist's own children. As early as 1774, for example, Pestalozzi documented the development of his children in *A Father's Diary* (De Guimps, 1906). Charles Darwin (1877) similarly kept and later published notes on the development of his infant son, William. Diaries generally traced or noted the development of children over relatively extended periods of time and provided perhaps the first documentation of developmental sequences.

While diaries were generally concerned with documenting the emergence of *new* behaviors, other procedures evolved to record the occurrence of *existing* behaviors across numerous environmental situations. One such tactic, the anecdotal record, consists of brief descriptions of various incidents involving children's behavior. Anecdotal records were initially viewed as beneficial in training teachers to observe children (Irwin & Bushnell, 1980). Currently, anecdotal records may be useful as preliminaries to more highly structured observational strategies. Such records may, for example, provide information as to which children, settings, or behaviors may merit more thorough study. Such preliminary observations, conducted on an informal basis, often result in considerable time savings in later analyses.

When more detailed information regarding specific behavioral incidents is desired, "running records" or "specimen records" have been used. The purpose of the running record is to record behavioral incidents in sufficient detail so as to allow later analysis. The specimen record is much like the running record, but it requires even more detail, generally uses predetermined criteria for noting occurrence of specific behaviors, and requires that the observer be unoccupied in the setting except for recording (Irwin & Bushnell, 1980).

Perhaps the largest disadvantage in the use of running and specimen records is the expense involved in collecting such information. Not only is the recording time that is required quite extensive, but an equal or greater amount of time is required for the transcription (generally from audiotape) and analysis of these records. Another issue with such records is that, despite efforts to the contrary, different observers may concentrate on slightly different aspects of behavior. When this occurs, the impressions gained of the behavior of a specific child may vary, not as a function of changes in the child's behavior, but as a function of differences in observers' interpretation of the behavior.

A final problem with both running records and specimen records is the problem of data reduction. In order to be useful in providing normative data, in providing information about the effects of a specific teaching procedure, or in communicating information across professionals, information provided by running or specimen records must be summarized into some easily interpretable form. With running and specimen records, such summarization involves developing methods of coding the narrative accounts, and counting or otherwise summarizing the occurrence of particular behaviors.

Nonnarrative Recording (Closed Systems)

The process of data reduction associated with narrative recording techniques is a side effect of the emphasis on preserving as much of the context of behavior as is possible. Another set of procedures, which might be referred to as nonnarrative or closed systems, circumvents a large portion of the data reduction process by recording only the occurrence of a limited number of preselected behaviors. While such procedures are generally much more economical, it is sometimes pointed out that nonnarrative records do not preserve the richness in detail available from narrative records. The purpose of these records is not, however, to allow a later reconstruction of the "flow" of behavior, but rather to characterize the occurrence of specific behavioral subcomponents. The use of observation systems that focus on particular behaviors demands that considerable forethought be given to the determination of exactly which behaviors are to be quantified. This preliminary investment generally includes the specification of the characteristics of the behavior to be recorded and consideration of those practical issues described earlier.

Frequency Recording

Frequency recording systems provide information about the number of times a particular behavior occurs. Most frequency measurement consists of incrementing a count whenever an occurrence of a behavior is detected. Since mental notations may easily be disrupted when other matters, such as teaching or redirecting, distract the teacher's attention, it is desirable to make some permanent record of each behavioral occurrence. The means by which such records are made vary. The notation systems may be as simple as accumulation of hatch marks on paper or may involve the use of mechanical devices, such as golf counters or bead counters. If it is desirable to record multiple behaviors or the behavior of more than one child, recording sheets or devices that provide for separately tallying each behavior or the behavior of each child must be used. Exhibit 3–1 presents an example of a data sheet designed for recording and summarizing the frequency of a behavior by each of several children.

In order to be meaningful, counts of a behavior must be interpreted in terms of the opportunity for the behavior's occurrence. Interpretation of the information that a child initiated ten interactions with peers, for example, would be different if the observation took place over a ten-minute period than if the child had been observed for one week. Thus, when frequency recording is used, some statement of the opportunity for the behavior's occurrence must always be included. When counts are made of the number of times a behavior occurs, the most common reference is the amount of time over which the observation took place. The combination of this information yields an occurrence per unit of time (or rate) measure. Another such reference is the number of responses that were possible. Thus, for example, a teacher may count the number of correct mathematics problems that a child completed and relate this number to the number of problems on the worksheet to obtain a percent correct figure. When, as

Exhibit 3–1 Sample Data Sheet for Recording and Summarizing the Frequency of Children's Behaviors

Date _____

Observer _____

Time Observation Began _____

Time Observation Ended _____

Total Minutes of Observation _____

$$\text{Summary Rate} = \frac{\text{number of instances}}{\text{minutes of observation}}$$

Child Name	Talley Behavior			Total	Summary Rate

with many worksheet formats, the number of items on which the child responds is constant, there may be no need to note this number specifically; it is nonetheless taken into account when evaluation of these data occurs.

The collection of information about the frequency of behavior may be greatly facilitated when physical evidence of the behavior (permanent products) exist. The evaluation of worksheet performance is perhaps the most common instance in which permanent product information is used, but, as noted earlier, the occurrence of many other classroom behaviors has been documented in this fashion.

Frequency recording systems lend themselves well to behaviors that have easily discriminable beginning and end points. In order to count a behavior as occurring and to separate individual occurrences of the behavior, an observer must be able to tell when a behavior begins and when it ends. Behaviors such as throwing a rock or calling the teacher's name are usually easily recorded with frequency recording systems. Behaviors such as conversation and crying, on the other hand, are not so easy to record in this manner since the observer may have difficulty in determining when to record the occurrence of each "incident" of the behavior.

As mentioned earlier, frequency recording may prove difficult when behavior occurs at a high rate. This problem may be encountered when occurrences of the behavior of a single child occur in rapid succession or when it is necessary to record the behavior of several subjects at the same time. It is also important to note that frequency recording systems are not sensitive to changes in behavioral duration that occur over time. It is conceivable, for example, that a teacher could count the same number of occurrences of a child leaving his or her seat before and after implementing an intervention aimed at eliminating this problem. Based on the data from these observations, a person would be forced to conclude that the intervention had no effect on the child's behavior. It is possible, however, that each occurrence of out-of-seat before the intervention might have lasted one-half hour while those instances that occurred after the intervention were of only momentary duration. Frequency data alone would not reveal changes in the amount of time each behavioral instance took, but would only allow the statement that the same number of incidents of behavior occurred before and after treatment.

Duration Measures

A second major type of information that may be derived from behavioral observation procedures is information about the duration of behavior. This information may take the form of the duration of specific instances of the behavior or may be combined to yield information about the total amount or proportion of time that a behavior occupies. Duration records may be obtained by starting and stopping a stopwatch corresponding with the beginning and end of behavioral episodes. Thus, if a teacher wanted to gather information about the total amount or proportion of time that a child spent out of his or her seat, the teacher could simply start a stopwatch whenever the child's behavior met the teacher's definition for out-of-seat and stop the watch when the child returned to the seat. If information about the length of each occurrence of out-of-seat was desired, the teacher could record that information following each occurrence and reset the stopwatch to be ready for timing the next occurrence. If, on the other hand, the teacher was only interested in obtaining information about the *total* amount or proportion of time that the child spent out-of-seat (within a day, for example), then the teacher could simply stop, but not reset, the stopwatch between occurrences of the behavior. Like frequency measures, measures of the duration of any behavior are not meaningful without some referent that defines the total amount of time over which these observations were conducted. By dividing total duration of the behavior of interest by the total time observed (multiplying by 100 if a percentage is desired), a figure representing the proportion of the total observation period that the behavior occupied may be acquired.

Behaviors that may be recorded by using duration measures include those that, like those that may be recorded with frequency systems, have discriminable beginning and end points. Unlike frequency recording, however, duration measures are particularly well suited to those instances in which the duration of behavior changes with time. Perhaps the largest disadvantage in the use of duration measures is that, since the observer must specifically note the beginning *as well as* the end of each behavior, the amount of teacher attention reqired to record duration information is generally much greater than that required to record frequency information. Perhaps for this reason duration measurement procedures have seldom been used in situations where it is desirable or necessary to record more than one behavior for a single subject or the behavior of more than one subject simultaneously. Also, because of the effort involved, it may not be economically prudent to record the occurrence of those behaviors that *do not* vary in duration across time since these behaviors may be recorded much more easily and just as accurately by using frequency recording systems.

Duration measures need not always involve the use of a stopwatch. For many behaviors, reference to the position of the hands on a wall clock or the numerals on a digital clock may be useful. Thus, if a teacher wished to measure the amount of time a child needed to finish lunch, the teacher could simply note the time when the child started and finished eating.

Similarly, the times at which a paper was fastened to and removed from an easel might be noted on the back of the paper. By comparing these two time notations, an indication of the amount of time a child spent painting at the easel might be acquired.

In some cases teachers have greatly facilitated the collection of duration information for a number of children through the design of the data recording sheet. Pulliam-Ruble, Plummer, and Huske (1977), for example, were interested in finding out how much time each of several children spent in a particular free-play area. Their solution was to design a data sheet that contained two columns of small clock faces drawn with the numbers but without hands. One column of clock faces was marked "in," and the other marked "out." To the left of the columns of clock faces, the children's names were placed in a column so that each child's name corresponded to one clock face marked "in" and one marked "out." The teachers then simply marked in the position of the wall clock's hands on the "in" clock's face when the child entered the free-play area and marked the hand positions on the "out" clock when the child left the area. After the class, the teachers went back through the data sheet and calculated (from the clock faces) how much time each child spent in each area. This system, although requiring relatively little teacher time, yielded an impressive amount of information about each child's activity preference and area use, as well as the patterns of area use by the class as a whole.

Interval Recording

Thus far, the observation systems that have been described have involved recording all behavioral occurrences within a designated observation period. Other systems involve recording only a portion of the behavioral occurrences. In one of these systems, generally referred to as interval recording, the observation period is divided into smaller time units, and presence or absence of the behavior within each of these smaller units is noted. A teacher might, for example, divide a 30-minute period during which observation takes place into "intervals" of ten seconds each. The teacher would then start a stopwatch and watch the subject(s) of the observation. If the behavior occurred within the first ten-second interval, the teacher would mark the data sheet to indicate the behavior's occurrence and wait for the end of the interval. If the interval ended and no occurrence of the behavior was noted, the interval would be marked to indicate the behavior's absence. Scoring then moves to the next interval, and again the presence or absence of the behavior within the interval would be noted. This procedure continues for the duration of the observation period.

To summarize this observation, the total number of intervals in which the behavior was recorded as occurring would be divided by the number of intervals during which observation took place, and this figure would be multiplied by 100 to yield a "percent of intervals" figure. Exhibit 3–2 presents an example of a data sheet that could be used to record and summarize interval observations of a single child for several minutes.

Several points should be made about the procedural aspects of interval recording. The observer's task in interval recording is to note only the presence or absence of a particular behavior within each interval. Thus, regardless of the *number* of discrete occurrences that might have been observed, the observer would score only once per interval. This characteristic is the basis of one of the major advantages of these systems; with interval recording, the observer need not determine when the behavior begins and ends, or how often the behavior is repeated within a particular

Exhibit 3–2 Sample Data Sheet for Recording and Summarizing Interval Observations of a Single Child

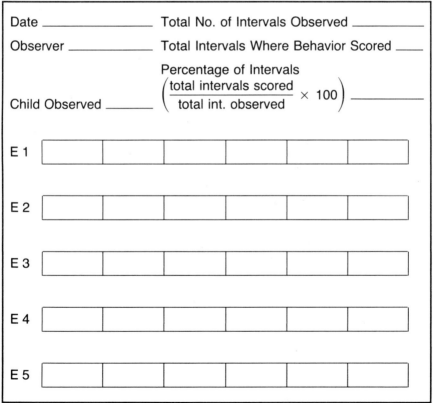

interval, but only whether the behavior is present at all during the interval. The second point that should be made is that the length of the interval chosen for a particular project may be adjusted according to the situation. An interval length of ten seconds, for example, has often been used in behavioral research because it provides the needed sensitivity while being a length that most observers can adjust to readily. In addition, however, intervals of one minute, five minutes, ten minutes, and longer have often been utilized. Intervals of longer duration may be less sensitive to changes in behavioral frequency than intervals of shorter duration. Thus, for example, if a behavior occurred about once every ten seconds and decreased over time to once every twenty seconds, a ten-second interval system would reflect this change as a decrease from the occurrence in 100 percent of the intervals to occurrence in 50 percent of the intervals. If, on the other hand, an interval length of one minute was used, no change, based on the interval data, would be seen since the behavior would always occur in 100 percent of the intervals. When interval systems are to be used, a decision as to the interval length should be made on the basis of observer skill, characteristics of the behavior (most commonly length of each occurrence of the behavior), and the degree of sensitivity that is necessary for the data-based decisions to be made.

Another major advantage of interval recording systems is that they allow the recording of more than one behavior at a time. If a teacher were interested in a child's social interaction and contact with classroom materials, for example, the presence of either or both of these behaviors could be noted during an interval. The percentage of intervals in which each behavior occurred could then be calculated separately when the observation was completed.

Variations of interval recording procedures, usually referred to as scanning systems, have often been used to gather information on the behavior of several children during the same observation period. With scanning systems, the observation intervals are distributed across the children for whom the information is desired. If, for example, the behaviors of several different children in the classroom were to be observed, the teacher might use an interval system in which the behavior of one child was observed in the first interval, another child was observed in the second interval, another in the third interval, and so forth. Although the amount of information that is gathered about the behavior of each child is diminished when scanning procedures are used, they have proven useful in situations in which a relatively small amount of information is desired about the behavior of each of a number of children.

Time Sampling

The amount and variety of information that may be collected by using interval observation systems is substantial. Often, however, these procedures may prove impractical in applied settings, since they require considerable attention by the observer. For that reason, interval observation systems are not often used in situations in which the observer has other responsibilities, such as teaching. In these situations, variations of these procedures, in which periods of observation and recording alternate with periods in which no observation takes place, are often useful. In one such procedure, which is referred to as time sampling, brief observation intervals are interspersed with longer periods in which observation does not take place. These intervals usually occur according to some preestablished periodic or aperiodic schedule. Thus, for example, a teacher might watch a child during a ten-second period that occurs once per minute and record whether or not a particular behavior occurs during this time period. The beginning of each observation interval is often signaled by a stopwatch or a wall clock. In other instances, in which it has not been possible for a teacher to attend to a clock while continuing teaching duties, some auditory signal has been used to designate the observation interval. One fairly common method of providing this signal is to tape-record the signal at the desired regular or irregular interval, and then allow the tape to playback during the time observations are to be made.

Perhaps the largest disadvantage associated with the use of time sampling procedures is that, depending on how often observations are conducted, considerable time may be required to gather sufficient information to characterize a child's behavior adequately. In addition, short duration time samples (that is, those in which the observation interval is relatively short) may prove problematic when the behavior of interest is of short duration and occurs infrequently. It is quite unlikely, for example, that a ten-second time sample would ever result in the observer recording the occurrence of a behavior such as a rock toss that occurred only once or twice per day (that is, there is little chance that the child would ever happen to throw the rock at the time that an observation interval was scheduled).

Varieties of time sampling, in addition to the one in which periodic observation intervals occur, are potentially quite useful and therefore worth mentioning. The first of these has become known as the "snapshot" technique. This procedure differs from the procedure described earlier in that the periodic interval during which the observer watches the child is much briefer. With this procedure, the teacher remains engaged in ongoing activities until a signal (usually auditory) occurs. At the instant at which the signal is detected (or sometimes as soon afterward as is possible), the teacher *glances* at the child, records what the child was doing at the instant that observation took place, and immediately returns to teaching. Such procedures require a minimum of teacher attention. As with the longer time samples, it is extremely unlikely that behaviors of short duration would be recorded by using this procedure.

A second variation of time-sampling procedures, generally referred to as "mapping," has also proven useful in specific instances. Mapping has often been used where information about children's interactions with other children or areas of the classroom has been desired. The data sheet used with mapping is a diagram of the area to be observed, which includes the location of specific play area and equipment. Figure 3–1 presents a data sheet that might be used to record behavior in a playground setting.

At periodic intervals, the teacher using a mapping technique would look at one or more of the areas defined within the map and record the initials of those children who are within each area. At some later time, information about each child's use of classroom areas, as well as information about peer relationships and other information, may be summarized from the scored recording sheets.

A third variation, developed by Risley and his colleagues, is referred to as the Planned Activity Check (Pla-Check©) procedure (Doke & Risley, 1972). With this procedure, a periodic count of the number of children present within an area is followed immediately by a count of the number of children engaged in a specific behavior within the area. Such systems, could, for example, yield information about the proportion of children who manipulate materials within each of several free-play areas. To obtain this information, an observer would periodically count the number of children present in the area and then immediately count the number of children within the same area who meet the definition for "manipulation of materials."

WRITING BEHAVIORAL DEFINITIONS

At the basis of any observation system are the definitions that specify the characteristics of the behavior that is to be measured. In general terms, the process of developing behavioral definitions involves changing global, sometimes inexact descriptions of behavior into components that are observable and measurable. Thus, for example, it is not possible to measure a complex behavior such as social interaction until some decisions and specifications are made with respect to the exact observable aspects of the complex behavior that are of interest. The first step in developing behavioral definitions is to determine which aspects or subcomponents of the

Figure 3–1 Sample Data Sheet for Recording Behavior in a Playground Setting

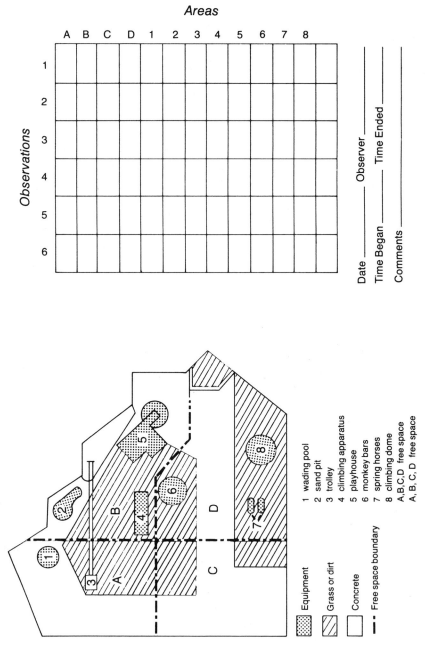

Areas

	A	B	C	D	1	2	3	4	5	6	7	8
1												
2												
3												
4												
5												
6												

Observations

Date _____ Observer _____

Time Began _____ Time Ended _____

Comments _____

Equipment

Grass or dirt

Concrete

Free space boundary

1 wading pool
2 sand pit
3 trolley
4 climbing apparatus
5 playhouse
6 monkey bars
7 spring horses
8 climbing dome
A,B,C,D free space
A, B, C, D free space

behavior are observable and meaningful to the question to be addressed. Bell and Low (1977) have suggested that two characteristics of observable subcomponents are that they describe a single behavior and that they describe movement of some kind. The observable subcomponents of "social interaction," for example, might include being within three feet of another child, directing verbal statements to other people, or sharing certain types of play equipment. In the same manner, "aggression" might consist of hitting, biting, or pushing others. Behavioral subcomponents may sometimes be defined in terms of observable products or effects. The components of academic productivity, for example, might include completed worksheets and so on.

A second step in developing behavioral definitions is the description of the criterion to be used in scoring behavioral occurrences. Hawkins and Dobes (1973) have described this procedure as one that involves describing the boundaries of what is to be included and excluded in scoring the behavior. Thus, it is necessary to describe those aspects of the behavior that indicate the presence of the behavior and, in many cases, when the behavioral occurrence begins and ends. In most cases, specific examples of behavioral occurrences that should be scored and those behavioral approximations that are *not* to be scored should be included since these simplify scoring and limit the need for interpretation of the definition. Table 3–1 presents examples of behavioral descriptions that would not allow quantification of behavior and behavioral definitions that might be used to observe and record these behaviors reliably.

In the process of writing behavioral definitions, it is often advisable to attempt to anticipate changes in the topography of the behavior that may occur, as a function of maturation of some intervention that is anticipated. Aggressive behaviors, for example, often change from obvious to covert or vary in magnitude as an intervention progresses. Decisions should be made about whether such anticipated topographical changes should be included in existing categories, recorded as "new" categories, or ignored when they occur. Although it is seldom possible to anticipate all such changes of this nature, many dilemmas may be avoided if these possibilities are considered and the appropriate modifications made in behavioral definitions before an observation project begins.

ASSESSING THE RELIABILITY OF OBSERVATION SYSTEMS

Perhaps the most important criterion in evaluating the adequacy of an observation procedure is that the system yield characterizations of behavior that are both consistent and valid. With behavioral observation procedures,

Table 3–1 Descriptions of Behavior and Behavioral Definitions That Might Be Used To Quantify These Behaviors

Nonobservable Description	Behavioral Definitions of Observable Components of the Behavior Described
"___doesn't interact with other children."	*Verbal interaction*—spoken initiations or responses to either a single child or a group.
	Nonverbal interaction—any physical behavior (movement or direct touch) directed toward another child or a group of children. This includes handing objects to or taking objects from another child, and gesturing or responding to gestures.
"___is abusive to other children."	*Physical aggression to peers*—hitting, punching, pinching, kicking, slapping, throwing materials at another person, pulling hair, striking or knocking down another child's structure or materials, or striking another child with an object.
	Verbal aggression—verbal behavior that threatens, forbids access to an activity, or indicates a negative judgment about another child.
"___doesn't follow teacher directions."	*Compliance to teacher instructions*—recorded when, within 15 seconds of the teacher's instruction, the child does or begins to do what the teacher directed the child to do.

the most common method of estimating this consistency involves comparisons of the records of two or more independent observers who simultaneously use the same observation procedure to record the same behavior by the same subject. These comparisons, referred to as measures of interobserver reliability, provide estimates of the extent to which differences in the data collected across children and/or time are attributable to differences in behavior and not to variations in the scoring criteria. When the characterization of behavior is consistent across observers, then the observers are probably using the same scoring criteria. If, on the other hand, the characterization of behavior is not similar (that is, reliability levels are low), then it could be assumed that the observers used different scoring criteria.

In most cases, when reliability estimates indicate low levels of interobserver agreement, some problem exists with the structure or the use of the behavioral definitions. Reliability estimates are thus routinely used as estimates of the adequacy of observation systems. The methods that may be used to estimate interobserver reliability are many and varied. Perhaps the most straightforward, and probably for that reason the most common, methods are percent agreement methods. These methods, which vary somewhat according to the type of observation system used, yield percentage figures (0–100) that estimate the extent to which the scoring criteria or behavioral characterizations are consistent across independent observers.

With frequency measures, in which the observer simply counts the number of times a behavior occurs, the interobserver reliability may be estimated by comparing the number of occurrences of behavior that were scored by each of the observers. This comparison is accomplished through the use of the formula:

$$\frac{\text{smaller number of behavioral occurrences scored}}{\text{larger number of behavioral occurrences scored}} \times 100.$$

Thus, for example, if one of the two observers recorded the occurrence of an aggressive behavior 15 times, while another observer, watching the same child at the same time, scored 20 instances of the behavior, the reliability estimate could be arrived at through the following computation:

$$\frac{15}{20} \times 100 = 75\%.$$

A variation of this formula may be used to calculate percent agreement for duration information:

$$\frac{\text{shorter total duration}}{\text{longer total duration}} \times 100.$$

The reliability estimates that may be used with recording procedures in which the observation period is broken into small units (interval and time-sampling procedures) are somewhat more varied. The simplest procedure is one that is similar to that used for frequency and duration data:

$$\frac{\text{smallest number of intervals scored}}{\text{largest number of intervals scored}} \times 100.$$

While this calculation is sufficient to compare *characterizations* of behavior that each of two observers obtained, it is sometimes argued that there is no indication that the observers scored instances of the behavior at the same time (in other words, observers may never have agreed as to exactly when the behavior occurred, but only that the behavior occurred approximately the same number of times during the observation period). For that reason, "point-by-point" calculations that evaluate the extent to which observers agree on the scoring of individual instances of behavior have often been used with interval and time-sampling recording procedures. With point-by-point reliability estimates, the scoring by independent observers is compared within each interval, and a count of those intervals in which the two observers' scoring was in agreement is compared to the total number of intervals during which the two observers recorded. Thus, if in the first interval of scoring both observers recorded a behavioral occurrence, that interval would be counted as an "agreement." Similarly, an agreement would be counted when neither observer scored the behavior. When one observer scored the behavior as occurring and the other said that the behavior did not occur, that interval would be counted as a disagreement. After each interval has been compared in this fashion, a count is made of the total number of agreements and disagreements. These figures are then used in the following formula:

$$\frac{\text{number of agreements}}{\text{number of agreements} + \text{number of disagreements}} \times 100.$$

This formula produces a percent agreement figure that indicates the proportion of intervals in which the two observers were in agreement. Although other, more complex percent agreement calculations are often used to overcome problems of overestimation of reliability that arise with particularly high or low rate behaviors, those procedures will not be described in the present context.*

The interpretation of obtained percent agreement levels varies greatly with the type of behavior, the setting, the nature of the reliability calculation used, and the teacher's or researcher's own criteria. Certain guidelines, however, may be suggested. In general, percent agreement levels of 85–90 percent or higher are considered to indicate that the observation system is adequate. When reliability is consistently below 60–70 percent, on the other hand, some further analysis and modification of the observation procedure may be indicated.

---

* The following articles provide excellent discussions of the use of occurrence, nonoccurrence, and chance reliability calculations: Bijou, S.W., Peterson, R.F., Harris, F.R., Allen, K.E., & Johnston, M.S. Methodology for experimental studies of young children in natural settings. *The Psychological Record*, 1969, *19*, 177–210; and Hopkins, B.L., & Hermann, J.A. Evaluating interobserver reliability of interval data. *Journal of Applied Behavior Analysis*, 1977, *10*, 121–126.

RECOMMENDATIONS: CHOOSING APPROPRIATE OBSERVATION PROCEDURES

The purpose of the review presented to this point has been to provide basic information regarding aspects of consideration in conducting behavioral observations. If it were possible to provide information about which observation procedure to use in each specific situation, this sometimes general, sometimes overly technical information would not be necessary. However, no two instances in which behavioral observation is conducted are ever the same; thus a certain amount of tailoring of observational tactics to individual situations is almost always necessary. Although each observation situation is different, there are a number of rather specific recommendations that can be made about matching observation techniques to problems.

Recording Social Behaviors

Children's social interactions may be divided into two major types: (1) those that involve adults; and (2) those that involve other children. Some aspects of child-child interactions can be measured by using frequency observation systems. It is conceivable, for example, that teachers could count the number of times a child initiated interactions with peers or the number of times that a child's peers initiated interaction. Recording in this manner could be accomplished by using a hand counter, golf counter, or a simple paper and pencil tally. Collecting such information would be greatly facilitated if the children were contained within a small area (so that the teacher would be able to see all the children at all times) and if the total number of children in the setting was small. Some aspects of child-child interaction, including most aggressive acts, are fairly obvious and thus easy to record in a group setting. Recording other, more subtle, behaviors may be more difficult.

Perhaps the most common problem encountered in recording the frequency of child-child interactions is that the concentration required may disrupt the teacher's other supervising and teaching responsibilities. This is especially true if the observation is conducted where children are likely to move over a fairly large area. These observations may often be facilitated by structuring a setting or opportunity for these behaviors to occur and observing only this restricted setting. Thus, if the teacher were interested in observing a child's reaction to peer initiations, a peer could be prompted to initiate to the subject ("James, why don't you go over and ask Johnny what he's doing"), and the subject's response to this initiation could be noted. Such structured situations often yield essentially the same information as would be available from more "naturalistic" settings while requiring substantially *less* teacher time.

Often it is not necessary to observe *each* initiation or response in an unrestricted environment in order to ascertain the level of a child's interaction abilities. It may be much more economical, for example, to use a sampling procedure to obtain estimates of the amount of time a child spends in different types of social interaction. Time-sampling systems often allow teachers to conduct their normal classroom activities while collecting useful data. A teacher might, for example, visually locate a child at periodic intervals and make note of whether that child was alone, in proximity to, or verbally interacting with another child. With such systems, it is often possible for a single teacher to collect information simultaneously on the social behavior of more than one child. The parameters of time-sampling procedures may easily be arranged to fit a variety of situations. Thus, the amount of time between observations may be increased or decreased according to the demands of the observer's teaching responsibilities. In addition, time-sampling procedures may be sequenced to allow the observation and recording of the behavior of a number of children within the same observation period. Hickey and Allen (1980), for example, reported the use of a time-sampling procedure to record the location and behavior of four to nine children during a free-play period. These investigators reported that the recording procedure detracted little from the teachers' attention to their other responsibilities and produced data that compared quite favorably to data collected concurrently with a continuous observation system.

Perhaps the most common problem encountered in the use of time sampling procedures is that short duration behaviors, such as aggressive acts, are not likely to coincide with observation intervals. Thus, these discrete behaviors may seldom or never be recorded. Such short duration behaviors may be recorded by using a type of frequency count, but longer duration behaviors, such as most of the social categories described earlier, should be recorded using a sampling system

When information is desired about the frequency of particular types of social interaction that occur within the classroom, and it is not necessary to characterize the interaction of *individual* children, some variation of Doke and Risley's Planned Activity Check (1972) may be useful. Thus, for example, if a teacher wanted information about the portion of the children in the classroom who engaged in isolate play, the teacher could, at periodic intervals, count the number of children present in the classroom and then immediately count the number of children who met a preestablished definition for isolate play. By dividing the number of "isolates" by the total number of children present, the desired proportion could be attained.

A variety of information about interactions between children and teachers may be collected by having teachers record aspects of their own interactions with children. Thus, for example, teachers might use golf or bead counters to tally the number of times a child initiates or the number of prompts or praise statements the teacher makes to the child. Such recording takes little time, does not usually divert attentions from ongoing activities, and, when several adults simultaneously collect such data, yields a surprising amount of information.

Recording Behavior in Free Choice Situations

In many instances, it is desirable to obtain information about children's contact with the activities or areas that are structured within the classroom. In addition, *qualitative* information about the behavior of children within these settings may be necessary in making various educational decisions. A number of existing strategies allow teachers to record such information with minimal impact on ongoing activities. The strategy used by Pulliam-Ruble, Plummer, and Huske (1977) is useful in this context. This procedure, which is described earlier, involves marking blank clock faces with the position of a wall clock's hands to indicate the time at which children entered and left a *particular* free-play area. Analyses of such information would allow an assessment of the duration of time children spent in a particular area. By analyzing such data *across* areas, children's movements from area to area might be assessed.

Mapping, another strategy described earlier, is also useful for tracking children's contact with various classroom areas. Mapping strategies may be enhanced to include information about the quality of a child's interaction with the area as well as that the child was located within the area when the observation was made. Thus, in addition to marking a child as present in an area, the teacher might include a code to indicate whether the child was interacting appropriately or inappropriately, was sharing materials with another child, or working alone. In addition to information regarding which areas a child contacted and the quality of the child's interactions within each area, information such as whether the child chose activities in which a number of children were involved or about how long a child spent in a particular area might be summarized from such observations.

In many instances, children's contact with classroom activities has been summarized by using procedures that allow "after the fact" assessment. In some instances, for example, children have been given "tickets" that they give to the teacher in an area in order to be admitted to the area's activity.

If these "tickets" are marked with the child's name, they provide a permanent record of the child's visit to that area. In a variation of this procedure, the children present small cards to the teacher upon entering the area. These cards may be marked with colored stickers or colored pens to indicate the areas in which a child has been involved. In some cases, these cards are placed into slots on a board and returned to the child when the child leaves. This procedure not only provides a permanent record of each child's participation in free-play areas, but, if a limited number of slots are placed on the entry board, it controls the number of children congregated in an area at any one time.

Recording Academic and Preacademic Behaviors

Perhaps the characteristics of preacademic and academic behaviors that most readily separate them from social behaviors is that they tend to occur in somewhat more restricted settings. Thus, hopefully, teachers who record behaviors in preacademic settings are not faced with the necessity of following the child's movements around the classroom.

In many cases, the information that is desired from preacademic settings consists of a record of how a child responds to the tasks that are presented in this format. A carefully designed scoring sheet may serve not only to provide the format for recording these behaviors, but may serve as a cue for and a permanent record of what tasks were presented. These scoring sheets should provide the following for each "trial" for each child in the setting: (1) some notation of the task that is to be presented (for example, "point to the dog"); (2) an indication of how the child responded (ideally, exactly what the child's response was rather than simply "correct or incorrect"); and (3) some indication of whether the teacher praised the child, asked the child to repeat the response, corrected an incorrect response, and so on. In addition, it is often helpful to provide a place to record the occurrence of "other" behaviors, such as disruptions or questions.

After the teaching session is completed, relevant information, such as percent correct, proportion of responses on which the child received feedback, and so on, may be summarized. If exact responses on each trial have been recorded, it is often possible to analyze a child's errors to obtain information about the nature of the errors made. Such information is often valuable to the design of intervention strategies.

In many cases, recording preacademic or academic behaviors may be facilitated by analysis of permanent products. Thus, with writing tasks or arithmetic worksheets, the child's performance during the training session may be analyzed after the session is completed.

CONCLUSION

The preceding discussion has focused on some of the considerations involved in establishing observation procedures for use by teachers in classroom settings. The advantages inherent in utilizing assessment procedures that quantify observable behavior are numerous. These include, but are not limited to, such factors as general ease of interpretation, the direct relationship between observable behavioral deficits and remedial procedures, and flexibility with respect to the variety of situations in which such procedures are useful. The primary intent of the present discussion, however, has not been to argue in favor of these quantification strategies; such arguments have been developed in a number of previous discussions (Arrington, 1943; Heynes & Lippitt, 1954; Johnson & Bolstad, 1973). It has thus been assumed that a discussion of how behavioral observation strategies are matched to particular problems would be more useful than a discussion of why these strategies are useful.

Also, an attempt has been made to explain those issues that determine how well a given observation tactic matches a particular problem. The variety of setting and behavioral variables that typically interact in any classroom are numerous. Some understanding of the nature of the interactions between these variables is an absolute necessity in designing practical observation strategies.

A considerable emphasis has been placed on preliminary considerations. The reason for this is simple: most cases in which attempted behavioral observation proves insufficient or discouraging are attributable to some lack of planning. In general, any initial investment in consideration of factors is more than repaid by a program that runs smoothly and yields the quality of information that is desirable.

REFERENCE NOTE

1. Pulliam-Ruble, S., Plummer, S.E., & Huske, D. Using clocks to tell where, when, and with whom children play during free time. In G. Schilmoeller, (Chair.), *Data collection systems with no outside observations: Let children and staff collect data for you.* Symposium presented at the meeting of the Midwest Association for Applied Behavior Analysis, Chicago, Ill., May 1977.

REFERENCES

Arrington, R.E. Time sampling in studies of social behavior: A critical review of technique and results with research suggestions. *Psychological Bulletin,* 1943, *40,* 81–124.

Bell, D.R., & Low, R.M. *Observing and recording children's behavior.* Richland, Wash.: Performance Associates, 1977.

Darwin, C. A biographical sketch of an infant. *Mind,* 1877, *2,* 285–294.

De Guimps, R. *Pestalozzi, his life and work*. New York: Appleton, 1906.

Doke, L.A., & Risley, T.R. The organization of daycare environments: Required vs. optional activities. *Journal of Applied Behavior Analysis*, 1972, *5*, 405–420.

Hawkins, R.P., & Dobes, R.W. Behavioral definitions in applied behavior analysis: Explicit or implicit. In B.C. Etzel, J.M. LeBlanc, & D.M. Baer (Eds.), *New developments in behavioral research: Theory, methods and application. In honor of Sidney W. Bijou*. Hillsdale, N.J.: Lawrence Earlbaum and Associates, 1977.

Heynes, R.W., & Lipsitt, R. Systematic observational techniques. In G. Lindsey (Ed.), *Handbook of social psychology* (Vol. 1). Cambridge, Mass.: Addison-Wesley, 1954.

Hickey, D., & Allen, K.E. A teacher-analysis of preschool children's free choice preferences. Paper presented at the annual meeting of the National Association for the Education of Young Children, San Francisco, 1980.

Irwin, D.M., & Bushnell, M.M. *Observational strategies for child study*. New York: Holt, Rinehart and Winston, 1980.

Johnson, S.M. & Bolstad, O.D. Methodological issues in naturalistic observations: Some problems and solutions in field research. In L.A. Handy & E.J. Marsh (Eds.), *Behavior change: Methodology, concepts and practice*. Champaign, Ill.: Research Press, 1973, 7–67.

Scott, C.L., & Goetz, E.M. Pros and cons of teachers collecting their own data. *Education and Treatment of Children*, 1980, *3* (1), 65–72.

Chapter 4

Development of Social Skills and the Management of Common Problems

Alita York Cooper and Wilma J. Holt

Social development begins in infancy and is one of the major areas of skill acquisition in the young child. Included in the general heading of social development are such areas as emotional growth, moral development, development of self-concept, sex role interpretation, self-help skill development, and cultural identification. Through interactions with others, the developing child defines his or her own character and learns what others expect.

Until recently, most studies of social behavior were directed toward school-age and older children. Some studies, however, have shown that by the time infants are 18 months old, they are more interested in playing with other children than with their own mothers (Eckerman, Whatley, & Kutz, 1975; Rubenstein & Howes, 1976). Cooper, Schillmoeller, & Le-Blanc (1975) have found that two-and-a-half-year-old children are just as sociable as many older pre-schoolers. Hartup (1970), in one of his many studies on play behavior, found four- and five-year-old children often went to their peers for attention in preference to adults. Thus, preschool is not too early to begin studying social behavior and encouraging the development of positive social skills. In fact, Halverson and Waldrop (1970) found a positive relationship between a child's social participation and level of social activity at two years and the same child's level of social ability at age seven, indicating that sociability is a trait that is established early and is maintained by the child's social environments.

The importance of social development to overall adjustment and competence cannot be overestimated. Children who are sociable and friendly tend to be emotionally well adjusted throughout childhood, to have high self-esteem, and to be more assertive than children whose social competence is less well developed (Hartup, 1970). Socially isolated children are less likely than their more social counterparts to finish school and are more likely to become delinquent adolescents and suffer mental health problems as adults (Asher, Gottman, & Oden, 1977).

Given the importance of social skill development, many early childhood specialists, among them Cartledge and Milburn (1980), believe that social behaviors should be specifically taught to children. They propose that instruction is necessary for social competence, just as it is for the acquisition of academic skills. These authors see early childhood environments as ideal settings in which to teach specific social behaviors to children.

HOW CHILDREN LEARN SOCIAL SKILLS

Children develop socially through interaction with their environment, the cultural environment, the family environment, and the play environment. Each makes a unique and long-lasting contribution to the child's development.

The Influence of Society

Culture is defined as the social heritage individuals receive from the social group to which they belong, the system through which humans learn and share behavior in adapting to their environment. Culture is society's way of life, its customs, knowledge, beliefs, and morals (Horton & Hunter, 1964; Rogers, 1977). The word *culture* is also used to refer to the behavior patterns of smaller populations of people within a larger society. These smaller populations, often referred to as subcultures or ethnic groups, may be based on religion, economic class, or geographical area of origin. Before children reach the stage of abstract thinking, they adopt patterns of behavior characteristic of the society and subculture in which they live. They learn how to behave from contacts with family, friends, neighbors, and teachers (Longstreet, 1978).

With increasing maturity, children may choose to modify or drop certain ethnically learned behaviors; however, the early patterns are often resistant to change. Generally, the cultural group also exerts pressure against behavior change. As long as economic factors restrict an individual's ability to establish residence outside the ethnic group, that person will be expected to behave according to the standards of the culture. When an individual does move into a different subculture, he or she often experiences difficulty in adapting to the new social patterns. For example, an urban teenager may commonly respond to authoritative commands with aggression, because in the center city subculture an aggressive act is respected. If the same teenager moves to suburbia, he or she will be expected to respond differently to authority, and his or her aggression will not meet with success.

A younger child whose cultural experience has been unlike others in a preschool may appear to have "problems" in play. In fact, the child may have acquired a set of social skills through observation and direct participation in activities with others in his or her ethnic environment. These skills, though appropriate at home, may be overly sophisticated (for example, play is for little kids; my job is earning some money), and the child may not want to participate in play. Encouraging such children to participate in well-planned, supervised social activities will help them come in contact with positive aspects of the school environment. As play with peers becomes more pleasant, the child will begin to seek opportunities to play with other children, thereby practicing and continuing to acquire appropriate social skills.

Some minority children may appear to teachers to be more interested in material items than in verbal praise and approval. This, too, may be preceived as a "problem." However, the child may have never become accustomed to positive adult attention that is directly related to his or her behavior. Instead, the child may have been given material objects whether he or she had been "good" or not, and he or she may never have been verbally praised at home. A child who has rarely had the experience of receiving a new toy may also respond to such a gift with excessive excitement and joy.

Children's ethnic background must be considered before their behavior is labeled a problem. Often, the only problem may be that the teacher is judging the child by an inappropriate cultural standard. For example, learning to behave in a respectful and courteous manner toward adults is an important aspect of the childhood socialization process in all cultures. In the dominant American culture, it is demanded of children that they make eye contact with an adult who speaks to them. However, in the Mexican-American, Native American, and Puerto Rican cultures, children demonstrate respect for elders by *not* making eye contact and by remaining silent when reprimanded (Goodman, 1978). Thus, a child who has been taught to behave politely will be seen as rude and lacking in social skills.

Because culturally transmitted behavior patterns are generally learned early in life, they sometimes seem instinctive. Knowledge of other cultures and subcultures helps teach persons that all social behaviors are learned and represent an adaptation of the individual to a cultural environment.

The Influence of Television

One marked characteristic of American culture is the almost constant exposure to mass communication that provides common experience for vast numbers of persons. Of the various forms of mass media, television is perhaps the universal medium, in that most American homes have at least one TV set. With television so readily available to a large number of children, many parents, educators, social scientists, child psychologists, and pediatricians have become concerned about the impact of TV on young children.

That television is a major socializing agent of young children cannot be overlooked. Many children spend a high proportion of their time viewing television. Children may imitate the models they see on TV and may be equally influenced by the *absence* on TV of people from certain cultural or social groups. Television programming tends to focus on males who are for the most part Caucasian, middle class, and in a position of power. Minorities, as a whole, and women not only appear less often in TV programming, but are depicted in lesser positions with less power than Caucasian males (McGhee & Fruch, 1980). Thus television offers poor children, most minority children, and girls few successful or respected models. Their absence may lower a child's self-concept and in turn affect the development of positive social skills.

Gender role stereotyping on television and in the culture is interrelated with socialization (Block, 1973). Early "sex-typing" may restrict a child's involvement in play activities that encourage the development of a broad range of social, cognitive, and motor skills, and may also restrict the exploration of alternative role responsibilities that the child may need to assume later in life. Teachers of young children representing different cultures should be aware of differences in the children's experiences regarding gender role behavior. Such awareness will help to avoid conflicts between cultural socialization and the teacher's expectations of a child's behavior.

Television provides an abundance of models for aggression. There is evidence that the viewing of violent acts on TV by young children who are heavy viewers may increase their expression of aggression in interpersonal interactions. It also appears that the more realistic the acts of aggression are, the more children are inclined to imitate the model (Bandura & Walters, 1963). In general, the "cartharsis" theory, which proposed that viewing aggression would provide a "drainage" or "release" valve, has not been upheld. Instead, children who watch aggressive acts on TV become more aggressive in their play and tend to view aggression as a technique to be used in settling differences with others.

Most children watch TV at home where parents have the option of monitoring what they watch. If parents exercise this option, they can explain and discuss program content. Such shared viewing and discussion helps children learn from the more positive aspects of television, particularly when adults help children interpret motivation and recognize consequences of behavior.

Research currently in progress suggests that high quality children's programming may have positive effects on at least two areas of children's development: intellectual and social. Fast-oriented programs, such as *Sesame Street* and *Electric Company* seem to contribute to the development of cognitive skills, whereas slower, more people-oriented programs, such as *Fat Albert* and *Mister Rogers' Neighborhood* seem to help children develop social skills, such as cooperation and sharing (Coats, Pusser, & Goodman, 1976; Fox & Huston-Stein, 1977).

Further research is required to delineate the processes involved in children's learning from TV. In the meantime, television exerts a considerable influence on the socialization of most children in the United States today.

The Influence of the Family

The family acts as the culture's agent in teaching social behavior to children. This process begins in infancy, as even young babies have considerable social repertoires. Many theorists view social experiences in early infancy as critical to later development. Of special importance are early attachment bonds between babies and the adults who care for them.

Attachment bonds are characterized by smiling, touching, cuddling, and talking. Some research suggests that a sense of trust arising from early attachment is important to later social development (Marion, 1981). Gardner (1978) suggests that a child forms feelings, memories, wishes, expectations, and intentions from original attachments, and these influence subsequent experiences with others.

White and Watts (1973) have proposed that during the period from about ten months to three years, the child's social and cognitive development is strongly related to parental child-rearing practices. These researchers suggest that in the environment of a highly competent child, the parents are likely to be "responsive," that is, sensitive to the child's needs and interested in what the child does.

Parents and other caregivers should understand that being responsive and building attachment bonds are not one-way processes. Some infants with handicaps, particularly those that are not easily detected at birth, such as hearing impairment, may be quite unresponsive to the stimuli and people around them. When such an infant fails to respond, adults may feel inept or rejected, and they therefore may decrease the amount of time they spend with the baby. Early detection of physical handicaps is important in order to reassure parents that they were not at fault and to help them provide a stimulating environment for their baby.

The family environment continues to be important throughout childhood. Stressful family situations brought on by unemployment, divorce, and long-term illness tend to affect child behavior adversely (Kempe & Helfer, 1972). Because stressful situations are often accompanied by family disorganization, it is not unusual for children to feel rejected or uncared for. Under these conditions, children may appear to be functioning well in most areas, but they may have behavior disorders that interfere with normal development. A child may become afraid of school, withdraw from peers, or act aggressively. Teacher awareness of family problems is necessary if the child is to be handled patiently and effectively.

The family is the source of children's learning about themselves and their relationships with others. To many children the family is the emotional base from which they gain the ability to explore the physical and social world. In this regard the family functions both as an extension of the larger socializing environment, "the culture," and also as a separate unit that may be more or less effective in preparing the child to live in society.

The Influence of Play

Beyond cultural and familial influences, social skill development occurs predominantly through play. While numerous definitions—some bordering on poetry—have been proposed for play, LeFrancois (1977) has offered one of the most basic. In his view, play is a fundamental and necessary part of a child's activities, and almost everything a young child does is play; therefore, play must be important for every aspect of a child's development.

Piaget (1932) and Parten (1932) were among the earliest psychologists to examine play behavior. Piaget believed that by understanding a child's play, what the child knows or thinks about the world could be understood. Parten categorized play by level of social interaction and described children as moving in their development from solitary play in infancy to parallel, associative, and, finally, cooperative play. Parten's definitions of play behavior and research on social interaction in young children, though conducted 50 years ago, remain viable today.

Every normally developing child plays from the earliest weeks of infancy, (wriggling and watching fingers and toes; experimenting with sounds), through childhood, and into adulthood with sequentially more complex materials or activities. Play is typically a voluntary act, an enjoyable experience in which a person becomes actively involved. Through play of all types, young children develop an understanding and mastery of their environment. When other people join in play, they also provide opportunities for the development of language, verbal interaction skills, and social skills.

To be able to play appropriately with others is critical if a child is to develop acceptable social skills. Play is a natural setting for spontaneous social interaction. It is in play with peers that children begin to understand themselves and each other, learn ownership (mine and yours), and become respectful of the rights of others. In the context of play, children interact on a nonverbal and verbal basis, share, make and follow rules, "live around" each other, and become accepted group members.

Dramatic play opportunities are a major facilitator of peer interaction. Through taking various roles in play, children learn to see the world from other eyes and thus gain an appreciation for other points of view. By stepping out of their own personalities, if only briefly, young children may have a chance to "try out" new behaviors and see their consequences.

By observing children's play, parents and teachers can evaluate the progress of social skill development. Children at play may be identified as immature, shy, fearful, dominating, or aggressive. On the other hand, observation can give clues to the happy, well-adjusted child as well.

It is neither expected nor desirable that children interact with others all day. A child must learn not to crave and demand constant adult supervision and attention, or the constant presence of other children; instead, all children need to learn to enjoy being alone and playing independently for at least some portion of each day. A learning environment must offer ample opportunities for the child to develop independence and autonomy, as well as social and interactive skills.

CHARACTERISTICS OF NORMAL SOCIAL DEVELOPMENT

In any area of child development, a basic understanding of normal growth processes and what they mean is crucial. So is an appreciation for individual differences that may result in different behavior patterns among normally developing children. In general, normal social development is characterized by:

- interacting appropriately with both adults and children;

- sharing materials, time, and space;

- respecting the property of others;

- adopting the moral values of the family and community;

- acquiring a conscience (learning right from wrong and acting upon the knowledge);

- becoming courteous and considerate;

- understanding feelings in self and others;
- having a positive self-concept and sense of self-worth;
- initiating and asserting self, as well as accepting the lead of others.

The acquisition of a set of basic social skills is vital if a child is to be accepted, respected, and well liked. Yet social skill development does not occur independently of other areas of development. In fact, children who are competent socially also tend to be developing well in motor skills, cognition, and language. Similarly, a child who lacks the motor, cognitive, or language skills to become involved in play with other children will be socially handicapped.

In some cases, children may be developing quite normally in some areas and at the same time be delayed or handicapped in others. A child with a serious orthopedic problem may not be able to run, ride a trike, or climb, yet that same child may be advanced in language and conceptual skills. Such deficits certainly affect the social interactions of young children. Adults working with children need to be aware of the influence delayed development in one area may have on other areas.

Motor Development

Motor development affects social development because children who are skillful and can do things well are sought after as desirable playmates. By contrast, children who are seriously delayed motorically, who cannot run fast, climb, or put a block on a structure without knocking it down, are not as apt to be included in a play group. In fact, these children are quite likely to be *excluded*. Therefore, helping a handicapped child to develop reasonable approximations to at least one of the motor areas is valuable in setting the stage for cooperative play.

Cognition

As with physical adeptness, a child who is developing well in conceptual skills and has the ability to use them in play is more desirable to be with, can be more of a leader, and is typically more social. It is easy to see the plight of the handicapped child who cannot hand someone the "red block" when asked or who does not know how to play the role of doctor or nurse in a dramatic play situation. A child with such cognitive deficits will not be sought after as a playmate.

Marzollo and Lloyd (1972) sum up importance of play to cognitive development in this way: "The early childhood years are exciting and powerful years for building the foundations of intelligence. The act of play is the extraordinary process by which [intelligence] happens" (p. 2). The impact for the handicapped child who has not yet acquired basic cognitive skills is obvious.

Language Development

One of the most dramatic and remarkable accomplishments of a child's first year is the acquisition of language. Early patterns of mother-child interaction suggest that from birth onward the child makes every effort to engage in communicative interchanges with others in the environment (Brazelton & Tronick, 1980). These exchanges occur nonverbally at first, through focused attention and gesture, and later through vocal and verbal exchanges (Bates, 1976). It is in the context of these early social interchanges that much linguistic and conceptual information is acquired by the child (Moerk, 1974; Schacter, 1979). Between the ages of eighteen months and three years, most children master the basic structure of language and can communicate with others more or less effectively.

A preschool child who does not have basic communication skills will be severely handicapped in social activities. Because play is a vehicle for learning and for observing peer models who are exhibiting appropriate behaviors, a child who has difficulty interacting with others will tend to fall further and further behind. Generalization of newly learned language (or language in the process of being acquired) occurs most readily when there are regular opportunities for the child to engage in verbal interactions (Warren & Rogers-Warren, 1980). Thus it is important for teachers of language delayed children to provide frequent opportunities for social interchanges with peers in order for the handicapped child to use communication skills and experience pleasant interactions with other children. In addition, social interaction provides the opportunity for the child to use new skills in the appropriate context and to learn communication forms that are socially and specifically relevant to the setting. In other words, as Hart and Risley (1980) point out, the child must learn from the environment that language "works", that it will get the child whatever it is that he or she wants from the situation, be it play materials, snack, or attention.

Milestones in Social Development

It is important for teachers of all children—normal, at risk, and handicapped—to be knowledgeable and familiar with the milestones of social development. This information helps teachers determine whether a child is outside the developmental norms in terms of appropriate social skills.

There appears to be fairly consistent agreement on the developmental sequence of social growth for normal children. However, it is not known if the same sequence describes the developmentally delayed or handicapped child. At this time, until more data are available, teachers must use the normative data and adapt it for use with the developmentally different child.

Exhibit 4–1 provides a key to important social behaviors acquired by children in the first six years. Although this material is arranged by age for convenience and ready reference, skill development in this area, as others, tends to be sequential and dependent on experience rather than age alone.

Identifying Problems

Not all children acquire adequate social skills simply from the "developing process." Delayed and handicapped children will tend to have more than their share of problems in social development, but some children who seem normal in other areas may be viewed as poorly adjusted socially. The failure to develop normal social skills is often identified in one of the following ways:

- *Separation problems.* A child beyond age two who continues to have extreme difficulty when away from mother may not be developing normally. Also, younger children whose response to mother's return following separation is not happy but rejecting, turning away, and crying may be showing signs of a poor relationship with mother.

- *Severe shyness.* There are many degrees of shyness, and certainly most children show some timidity around strangers or in unfamiliar environments where there are a lot of other people. In some children, however, shyness may become a problem if it prevents them from taking part in normal activities or if the child becomes withdrawn and rarely plays with others.

- *Inability to pay attention.* A child who moves constantly from one task or play activity to another, never settling down to complete something, may have social problems.

- *Inability to follow instructions.* Children who consistently fail to follow instructions may not hear them, or they may be refusing to comply. In either case, such children need attention from teachers and parents.

- *Difficulty understanding language or talking to others.* Delays in language development naturally influence social skill development. A

Exhibit 4–1 Milestones in Social Development

Birth to 3 Months
1. Smiles socially.
2. Visually recognizes mother.
3. Responds to voices by turning head.
4. Fixes eyes on another's face.

3 to 6 Months
1. Vocalizes when spoken to.
2. Laughs aloud.
3. Smiles at own image in mirror.
4. Reaches for familiar persons (fathers, siblings).

6 to 12 Months
1. Appears anxious with strangers.
2. Likes being played with, talked to, held.
3. Likes watching other people.
4. Enjoys simple games like peek-a-boo or pat-a-cake.
5. Repeats activities that receive attention, and is responsive to social approval.
6. Waves bye-bye.

12 to 18 Months
1. Learns to walk (making the "world" more accessible).
2. Understands more language than is able to produce.
3. Possesses toys rather than sharing them.
4. Explores the environment, discovers, and becomes creative, providing the environment encourages creativity.
5. Tries to cooperate in dressing self.
6. Begins to follow suggestions.
7. Tries out new situations, tests limits.
8. Is less shy toward strangers.

18 to 24 Months
1. Shows interest in interacting with other children.
2. Begins to understand personal ownership of things.
3. Helps with some household chores.
4. Likes to imitate what adults or older children do.
5. Calls self by name.

24 to 30 Months
1. When around other children, watches them intently.
2. Plays in proximity to other children and uses same toys, but seldom interacts (parallel play).

Exhibit 4–1 continued

24 to 30 Months (continued)
3. Occasionally acts aggressively toward others.
4. Objects to sharing own toys.
5. Can play simple make-believe games.

30 to 36 Months
1. Takes toys from others, but refuses to share own toys.
2. Alternates between insisting on "doing it by self" and refusing to help himself or herself even when he or she can do the task.
3. With other children, play tends to involve physical interaction (handing toys back and forth, or building together) but not verbal interaction.

36 to 42 Months
1. Increasingly becomes involved in social play.
2. Has a special friend, and often can be persuaded to do something if a friend is doing it.
3. Shares more willingly, and learns to take turns.
4. Can fully understand language and express self verbally.

42 to 48 Months
1. Seems to try deliberately to annoy adults by whining, excessive questioning, complaining, and taunting. ("Don't look at me!")
2. Becomes involved in more imaginative play.
3. Can separate from mother without crying.
4. Sometimes shows off.
5. Becomes more affectionate, especially toward younger brothers and sisters.

4 to 5 Years
1. Plays more cooperatively with others.
2. Enjoys friends, and is willing to share with them.
3. Participates in more dramatic play, and can assume a variety of roles.
4. Asks many questions, and truly seems interested in the answers.
5. Finds other children's behavior "contagious": as one child starts to spin in a circle, others join in, and soon they will fall to the floor in glee; one starts to rhyme words, and others add more rhymes, often silly ones.
6. Boasts, and likes to have the "biggest" or "best".
7. Sometimes defies adult instructions, tests limits.

Exhibit 4–1 continued

4 to 5 Years (continued)
8. Tells really tall tales at times; seems unaware of the fine line between fact and fiction.
9. Uses profanity and "bathroom talk" (sometimes for fun, sometimes in anger).

5 to 6 Years
1. Becomes more stable and predictable.
2. Tends to be calm, friendly, less demanding in relationships with others.
3. Follows instructions well, and usually asks adult permission in doing things.
4. Seeks out friends who share common interests or enjoy the same activities.
5. Enjoys dramatic play, and has a good command of language.
6. Experiments and explores constantly, keeping busy most of the time.
7. Appears to be eager and excited to learn new things.

By 6 Years (beginning first grade)
1. Becomes more self-assertive, more aggressive.
2. Is more competitive than previously and sometimes boastful.
3. Joins a group of children rather than playing alone or staying with adults.
4. Shows more interest in stereotypically masculine or feminine activities.
5. Acts more mature outside the home than with the family.
6. Considers special friends very important.

child who cannot initiate interaction with others or who responds inappropriately to what others say will have difficulty behaving socially.

- *Disruption.* A child who is overly aggressive with the children around him or her, who uses materials inappropriately, who constantly grabs toys from others, and who tantrums frequently cannot gain positive social experiences.

- *Inability to take turns or share.* Once past toddlerhood, all children should begin to understand the concept of sharing and of taking turns. A child who simply refuses may be showing signs of delayed social skill development.

- *Demanding adult attention.* Children who make excessive demands on adults, by asking innumerable questions, whining, crying, asking to be held, or following adults around may be having difficulty interacting with agemates.

None of these behaviors alone is cause for alarm; neither is the occasional occurrence of any of them. Instead, a repeated pattern of behavior that is maladaptive is a danger signal that merits adult attention and carefully planned intervention (Allen, Rieke, Dmitriev, & Hayden, 1972).

MANAGING PROBLEMS IN SOCIAL DEVELOPMENT

Some successful techniques are available for teachers to use with young children who seem to indicate some delay in social skill development. The behavioral techniques described in this section have been demonstrated to be useful in changing behavior that is interfering with children's social development (Cooper, Ruggles, & LeBlanc, 1979).

Rearranging the Classroom

Teachers can arrange classrooms so that children are encouraged to interact with peers. The materials the teacher chooses and their arrangement in the classroom are important in increasing the opportunity—or setting the stage—for cooperation (Cooper, 1972). Certain types of activities and toys tend to promote particular types of play.

For example, a worktable set up with four dishes of glue, four sheets of paper, and some precut pictures lying beside each dish of glue sets the stage for parallel play. This environmental arrangement suggests that the children each produce an independent product. However, a table with one large sheet of paper, one or two glue dishes, several brushes, and a single pile of pictures that must be shared suggests that the children cooperatively produce a group collage. This environmental arrangement encourages team effort.

Some materials lend themselves more easily to one kind of play than another. Equipment that is most naturally used in solitary and parallel play situations includes many of the manipulative toys, such as beads, Legos, puzzles, Tinkertoys, shape sorters, and pegboards. Woodworking and science are examples of activities that are typically solitary or parallel. Other activities and pieces of equipment lend themselves to interaction and working toward a common goal. Examples of these materials include large motor equipment designed for two or more (rocking boat, see-saw, climbing frame), large peg trays, floor puzzles, blocks, and simple games. Perhaps the most obvious kind of interactive equipment is found in housekeeping areas and other dramatic environments.

With some kinds of materials and equipment, the type of play depends on how the materials are set out. Cooperation in such activities as music and movement experiences, art, and cooking can be encouraged or discouraged through specific environmental arrangements or teacher input.

Younger children, almost without fail, will begin interactions on a non-verbal basis. The things they do together do not need verbal exchange; they rock in a boat together, hand things back and forth during a tea party, or paint on the same piece of paper. As language and cognitive skills develop, children become more sophisticated or "complex" in their inter-actions. Preschool children, being the great imitators they are and having some past history with which to relate, are able to place themselves in the roles involved in running hospitals, restaurants, gas stations, grocery stores, and, of course, the all-time favorite, playing house and dress up.

A teacher who wishes to increase positive social interactions and co-operative play in the classroom can change the environment by adding more opportunities for cooperative interaction. This approach may be referred to as an enhanced environment (Cooper, 1972). A teacher who enhances the classroom by providing opportunities for cooperative activities in several areas should see an effect on the play behavior of the whole group (Cooper, 1980). A comparison of an enhanced environment with a more typical preschool setting is shown in Exhibit 4–2. It is easy to see that a child's chance of becoming involved with peers is increased in the

Exhibit 4–2 Comparison of an Enhanced Environment with a Typical Preschool Setting

Free Play	
Typical Environment	*Enhanced Environment*
Painting individual pictures	Painting a group mural
Hospital (dramatic play setting)	Hospital (dramatic play setting)
Unit blocks with four 18″ × 18″ pieces of masonite set out on which to build	Unit blocks with little cars and traffic signs
Science corner with items to examine with magnifying glass	Cooking project—making vegetable soup

enhanced environment. A large part of promoting cooperative peer inter-actions is simply setting the stage.

Providing more structure in the play environment is another way of encouraging positive social behavior, because it reduces the opportunities for disruption. By specifying rules, limiting the number of children in an area, and restricting the variety of activities available, the teacher effec-tively increases supervision and reduces aggressive and "acting out" be-havior (Safford, 1978). Such arrangements seem to be particularly helpful for children who display behavior problems and/or are aggressive (Gardner, 1978). Too many choices and too many children in one place increases these children's disruptiveness and unproductive play. When more struc-ture is provided, more teacher time is needed to monitor free play and provide teacher attention to children who are behaving appropriately.

Praising Positive Social Interaction

Most children respond to and enjoy teacher attention. To promote social interaction, it is important to provide attention to children when they are playing together, sharing, and interacting in a positive way. This can be done without interfering with the children's play, as by saying, "It's great to see Audrey and Tom building such a *big* tower. You got it that high by taking turns, didn't you?" or "David, you and Sarah have really enjoyed yourselves playing with clay today. I heard you laughing and telling jokes together."

Many parents and teachers have an alarmingly low rate of paying atten-tion to and praising children who are playing appropriately (Embry, in press; Goetz, Domash, & Allen, 1976). Some adults fear breaking up a good play situation, while others seem to feel that they should not interfere with a pleasant atmosphere. A number of empirical studies have clearly shown, however, that praising children for appropriate social interaction does indeed increase positive social play (Allen, Hart, Buell, Harris, & Wolf, 1964; Buell, Stoddard, Harris, & Baer, 1968; Goetz, Thomson, & Etzel, 1975).

Ignoring Inappropriate Social Interaction

Attention to any behavior—whether the attention is positive or nega-tive—will increase that behavior (Pinkston, Reese, LeBlanc, & Baer, 1973). Consequently, teachers may fall into the trap of giving children attention at the wrong time, unwittingly reinforcing or increasing grabbing, hitting, or verbal taunts. Children will do many things to get adult attention, and this includes participating in undesirable social interactions. Yet if no adults pay attention to disruptions, the behavior will occur less frequently and finally disappear. Inappropriate peer interaction can also be reduced if the teacher ignores the aggressor and lavishes attention on the recipient of the attack (Pinkston et al., 1973).

Individual Training Sessions

With some children, whose social development is seriously delayed or with whom rapid behavior change is needed, individualized training in the use of materials or in peer interaction while using materials will be more effective than the methods described earlier. In particular, this seems to be the case with children with severe handicaps (Fallows, Cooper, Ruggles, & LeBlanc, 1980), many of whom may have had little opportunity for group interaction. When individualized training sessions are used, the teacher should plan for generalization of training effects to the natural environment and not assume that skills taught in training sessions will be used in the classroom. Such techniques as training in several different situations and providing the same or similar materials in both the training and natural situation are helpful. (Generalization techniques are described in Goetz's Chapter 2.) For example, if a dollhouse with people and furniture is used for training, these same materials should be set up and available to the child in free play.

In another special training procedure that has been found effective, children look at pictures or slides of others engaged in cooperative play and then practice making positive praise statements to other children (Ayala, Holt, & LeBlanc, 1973; McClure-Porteous, Cooper, Plummer, & LeBlanc, 1976). Whenever a social partner is provided for practice in social skills, that child should be a special friend if possible.

Tangible Reinforcers

Children who do not respond to social reinforcement or social skills training may be able to work for tangible reward, such as a small toy, stickers on a chart, or special activities, contingent on appropriate social behavior. Such a child should be given a simple explanation of what he or she must do to earn the reward, such as follow a certain rule, use play materials the way they are intended to be used, or play with friends calmly and gently. The child's behavior must be observed and recorded so the teacher and child both know when the child has met the criterion response (Cooper, Ruggles, & LeBlanc, 1979).

Time Out

When aggressive acts occur during social interaction, having a child take a brief time out from the social activity is an effective means of reducing undesirable behavior. (Procedures for using time out in the classroom are described in Chapter 2.)

PROMOTING SOCIAL DEVELOPMENT OF HANDICAPPED CHILDREN

Mainstreaming—the placement of handicapped children in classrooms with nonhandicapped children—has the goal of offering handicapped youngsters the same kinds of opportunities for social, cognitive, and motor development that are available to other children. To ensure normal social skill development, all children must have access to a diversity of play materials and activities, and, most especially, to other children. Handicapped children can learn a great deal about social behavior by watching nonhandicapped children and imitating their play behavior.

Early intervention has been shown to be one of the keys to success in most areas of development (Darlington, Royce, Snipper, Murray, & Lazar, 1980), and there is no reason to believe that social development should be different. The early years are optimal learning years for both handicapped and nonhandicapped children. Society has commited itself to making the lives of handicapped people more complete and less different; by beginning in early childhood, society may have the best opportunity for success.

The earlier the intervention, the most likely improvement will occur in social skills in the least amount of time (Bronfenbrenner, 1974; Safford, 1978). Thus, at-risk and handicapped children should be provided opportunities to develop social skills at as early an age as possible. A good preschool setting or well-run play group in the home can be most helpful to handicapped children. The younger the children, the smaller and less obvious are the differences in competencies between handicapped and nonhandicapped children. Furthermore, many of the activities and much of the equipment used with preschoolers require minimum skills levels, making it possible for handicapped children to take an active part in play. Finally, interactions among young children naturally occur at different degrees of sophistication; there is generally as much nonverbal as verbal interaction, and the handicapped child is therefore at less of a disadvantage.

However, simply mixing handicapped and nonhandicapped children in a classroom does not necessarily result in positive experiences for children. There are many possible stumbling blocks to mainstreaming at the preschool level. Teachers may have negative attitudes or lack confidence in working with handicapped children. Physical plants may not be designed to accommodate children with physical handicaps. In many instances, not enough teachers may be available to meet the teacher-child ratios, and the money may not be available to provide extra staff, materials, and special equipment. Furthermore, attitudes of both nonhandicapped and handicapped children—excessive shyness, feelings of inadequacy, or fear—may hinder their social interaction.

In general, research indicates that social interaction is more difficult for handicapped children than it is for their nonhandicapped counterparts (Cooper, Ruggles, & LeBlanc, 1980). Handicapped children frequently have verbal or motoric difficulties or delays that impede communication (Guralnick, 1980). These deficiencies do not necessarily preclude interaction with peers in preschool settings, however. Activities can be made available that require a minimum of skilled behavior, and within these activities, interactions can occur at a variety of levels. Of course, the degree of interaction difficulty is correlated with the severity of the handicapping condition. Research indicates that the more severely handicapped the child, the fewer the peer interactions (Allen, 1980).

Some researchers have proposed that systematic instruction in the use of leisure time is necessary for handicapped children (and adults) if they are to learn to play appropriately (Wehman & Schleien, 1980). Often, severely handicapped children or adults have not developed the skills needed to make constructive use of their free time. More often than not, they spend most of their time simply doing nothing. Success in learning leisure time activities can facilitate the development of interpersonal relationships and social skills, and may contribute to success in educational endeavors as well. In a preschool setting, handicapped children who are taught how to play will have more opportunities for social interaction.

Teaching play skills often has a rewarding ripple effect in that it enhances handicapped children's self-concepts; through play with peers, they begin to see themselves as more "like the other kids" and accepted as a member of the group.

The mainstreaming policy assumes that there are benefits to nonhandicapped as well as handicapped children. By being with developmentally limited children early in life, normal children may become more tolerant, understanding, and open to people with problems (Bricker, 1978). Nonhandicapped children who are encouraged to be "teachers" for the handicapped children in their classroom may learn and practice desirable social behavior, thus enhancing their own social development (Fallows et al., 1980).

Preschool children tend to be less inclined than slightly older, primary school children to make inappropriate and hurtful comments, taunt, or exclude handicapped children from their play (Peterson, 1978). Preschoolers *are* curious and will ask questions of both the "different" child and their teachers. Such questions should be answered honestly, without elaborate details. They should be answered when they are asked, not later "after Johnny has gone home." In this way, both the handicapped child and the nonhandicapped child may come to accept physical and mental disabilities as matters of fact, not as mysterious or shameful conditions.

The more familiar nonhandicapped and handicapped children are with one another, the better off both groups will be. Teachers can help emphasize the individual differences and uniqueness of *all* children, thus encouraging interactions on a basis of equality.

CONCLUSION

Each child is born into a family and a culture, and these, in turn, are primary components of the total socializing environment. Each social environment has prescribed behavior patterns to which children must adjust in learning socially acceptable behavior.

Children begin learning social skills in infancy, and the early establishment of positive patterns of social behavior appears to be important for later adjustment. One of the most common reasons parents give for enrolling their children in preschool (when not out of necessity) is to enhance the child's social skills. The ability to interact both verbally and nonverbally, to share, and to cooperate are skills parents value in their children. Kindergarten teachers also frequently put the ability to take turns, to cooperate, and to be able to separate from parents (in other words, to be social) at the top of the list of kindergarten readiness skills. Hartup (1977) has concluded, ". . . it is my contention, and the contention of the Committee on Maternal and Child Health Research (1976) that social competence should receive a much higher priority in our policy deliberations during the next few years than it has received previously" (p. 2).

Social interaction is especially important for handicapped preschoolers. Through social interaction, children observe and imitate available models of appropriate motor, cognitive, and language behavior. Further, social interaction with peers in a preschool setting provides an opportunity for the handicapped child to come into contact with naturally reinforcing events in the environment; in other words, play with peers promotes the continued development of positive social play behavior. Teachers in mainstreaming classrooms may not be able to rely entirely upon the automatic and spontaneous occurrence of social interactions between handicapped and non-handicapped children. To maximize the social development of all children, teachers should try to identify those children who indicate delays in social skill development. Regular development monitoring of social interaction skills of children is important, as is the tailoring of assessment and training procedures to individual settings and children. Because the need for social skills continues through life, it is a job well worth the investment.

REFERENCES

Allen, K.E. *Mainstreaming in early childhood education.* Albany, N.Y.: Delmar Publishers, 1980.

Allen, K.E., Hart, B.M., Buell, J.S., Harris, F.R., & Wolf, M.M. Effects of social reinforcement on isolate behavior of a nursery school child. *Child Development,* 1964, *35,* 511–518.

Allen, K.E., Rieke, J., Dmitriev, V., & Hayden, A.H. Early warning: Observation as a tool for recognizing potential handicaps in young children. *Educational Horizons,* 1972, *50*(2), 43–55.

Asher, S.R., Gottman, J.M., & Oden, S.L. Children's friendships in school setting. In E.M. Hetherington and R.D. Parke (Eds.), *Contemporary readings in child psychology.* New York: McGraw-Hill, 1977.

Ayala, J., Holt, W.J., & LeBlanc, J.M. Effects of training preschool children in the use of reinforcement techniques. Paper presented at the Annual Convention of the American Psychological Association, Montreal, Canada, September 1973.

Bandura, A., & Walters, R.H. *Social learning and personality development.* New York: Holt, Rinehart and Winston, Inc., 1963.

Bates, E. *Language and context: The acquisition of pragmatics.* New York: Academic Press, 1976.

Block, J.H. Conceptions of sex role: Some cross-cultural and longitudinal perspectives. *American Psychologist,* June 1973, 512–526.

Brazelton, T., & Tronick, E. Preverbal communication between mothers and infants. In D. Olson (Ed.), *The social foundations of language and thought.* New York: W.W. Norton & Co., 1980.

Bricker, D.D. A rationale for the integration of handicapped and nonhandicapped preschool children. In M.J. Guralnick (Ed.), *Early intervention and the integration of handicapped and nonhandicapped children.* Baltimore, Md.: University Park Press, 1978, 3–26.

Bronfenbrenner, U. A report on longitudinal evaluations of preschool programs: Is early intervention effective? (Pub. No. (OHD) 75-25) Washington, D.C.: U.S. Department of Health, Education and Welfare, 1974.

Cartledge, G., & Milburn, J.F. (Eds.). *Teaching social skills to children, innovative approaches.* New York: Pergamon Press, 1980.

Coats, B., Pusser, E.H., & Goodman, I. The influences of *Sesame Street* and *Mr. Roger's Neighborhood* on children's social behavior in the preschool. *Child Development,* 1976, *47,* 138–144.

Cooper, A.Y. An experimental analysis of the effects of contingent related teacher attention and special activities for developing cooperative play. Unpublished Masters thesis, University of Kansas, 1972.

Cooper, A.Y. The influence of environmental conditions on play behaviors of preschool children and some procedures for increasing cooperative play. Paper presented at the National Association for the Education of Young Children, Dallas, 1975.

Cooper, A.Y. Promoting social interaction in the classroom. Paper presented at the Native American Preschool Project Early Childhood Conference, Sioux City, Iowa, June 1980.

Cooper, A.Y., Ruggles, T., & LeBlanc, J.M. The development of social skills in handicapped and nonhandicapped preschool children. In B. Gentry (Ed.), *In preparation for tomorrow*. Lawrence, Kan.: University of Kansas Research Institute for Early Childhood Education for the Handicapped, Bureau for the Education of the Handicapped, United States Office of Education 300-77-0308, Departments of Human Development and Special Education, University of Kansas, Lawrence, 1980.

Cooper, A.Y., Ruggles, T., & LeBlanc, J.M. Teaching techniques for increasing the positive social interactions of disruptive children. Paper presented at the Council for Exceptional Children, Dallas, April 1979.

Cooper, A.Y., Schilmoeller, K.J., & LeBlanc, J.M. A comparison of the effects of teacher attention and special activities for increasing cooperative play of a heterogenous group of normative and developmentally limited children. Paper presented at the Biennial Meeting of the Society for Research in Child Development, Denver, Colorado, April 1975.

Darlington, R.B., Royce, J.M., Snipper, A.S., Murray, H.W., & Lazar, I. Preschool programs and latter school competence of children from low-income families. *Science*, 1980, *208*, 202–204.

Eckerman, C.O., Whatley, J.L., & Kutz, S.L. Growth of social play with peers during the second year of life. *Developmental Psychology*, 1975, *11*, 42–49.

Embry, L. H. Analysis, assessment, and development of family support for handicapped preschool children: A review. In J.A. Gallagher (Ed.), *New Directions in Special Education*. San Francisco: Josey-Bass, in press.

Evans, E.D. *Contemporary influences in early childhood education*. New York: Holt, Rinehart & Winston, Inc., 1975.

Fallows, R.P., Cooper, A.Y., Ruggles, T.R., & LeBlanc, J.M. Manipulation of peer behavior and teacher attention as an antecedent stimulus to increase the social interaction of an isolated child. Paper presented at the annual Association for Behavior Analysis, Dearborn, Michigan, May 1980.

Fox, S., & Huston-Stein, A. Television's hidden curriculum. *The National Elementary Principal*, 1977, *56*(3), 62–68.

Gardner, W.I. *Children with learning and behavior problems*. Boston: Allyn and Bacon, 1978.

Goetz, E.M., Domash, M.A., & Allen, K.E. Applied self-control in higher education. In L.E. Fraley & E.A. Vargas (Eds.), *Behavioral research and technology in higher education*. Copies may be obtained from James M. Johnston, Department of Psychology, University of Florida, Gainesville, Florida 32611, 1976, 127–140.

Goetz, E.M., Thomson, C.L., & Etzel, B.C. An analysis of direct and indirect teacher attention and primes in the modification of child social behavior: A case study. *Merrill-Palmer Quarterly*, 1975, *21*(1), 55–65.

Goodman, M.E. *The culture of childhood: Child's eye views of society and culture*. New York: Teachers College Press, 1978.

Guralnick, M.J. Social interactions among preschool children. *Exceptional Children*, 1980, *46*, 248–253.

Hart, B., and Risley, T.R. In vivo language intervention: Unanticipated general effect. *Journal of Applied Behavior Analysis,* Fall 1980, *13*(3), 407–432.

Hartup, W.W. Issues in child development. Peers, play, and pathology. A new look at the social behavior of children. *Society for Research in Child Development, Inc. Newsletter,* Fall 1977.

Hartup, W.W. Peer interaction and social organization. In P. Mussen (Ed.), *Carmichael's manual of child psychology* (Vol. 2). New York: Wiley, 1970.

Horton, P.B., & Hunter, C.L. *Sociology.* New York: McGraw-Hill, 1964.

Kempe, C.H., & Helfer, R.E. *Helping the battered child and his family.* Philadelphia: J.B. Lippincott & Co., 1972.

LeFrancois, G.R. *Of children.* Belmont, Cal.: Wadsworth Publishing Co., Inc., 1977.

Longstreet, W.S. *Aspects of ethnicity: Understanding differences in classrooms.* New York: Teacher's College Press, 1978.

Marion, M. *Guidance of young children.* St. Louis: C.V. Mosby Co., 1981.

Marzollo, J., & Lloyd, J. *Learning through play.* New York: Harper Colophon Books, 1972.

McClure-Porteous, S., Cooper, A.Y., Plummer, S., & LeBlanc, J.M. Increasing social interaction by training children to reinforce peers. Paper presented at the American Psychological Association, Washington, D.C., 1976.

McGhee, P.E., & Fruch, T. Television viewing and the learning of sex-role stereotypes. *Sex Roles,* 1980, *6,* 179–188.

Moerk, E. Changes in verbal child-mother interaction with increasing language skills of the child. *Journal of Psycholinguistic Research,* 1974, *3,* 101–116.

Parten, M.A. Social participation among preschool children. *Journal of Abnormal and Social Psychology,* 1932, *27,* 243–269.

Peterson, N.L. *Peer interaction and their effect upon social behavior, play and learning in integrated classroom environments.* Kansas Research Institute for the Early Childhood Education of the Handicapped: Reviews of Literature, University of Kansas, 1978.

Piaget, J. *The moral judgment of the child.* London: Paul Kegan, 1932.

Pinkston, E.M., Reese, N.M., LeBlanc, J.M., & Baer, D.M. Independent control of a preschool child's aggression and peer interaction by contingent teacher attention. *Journal of Applied Behavior Analysis,* 1973, *6,* 115–124.

Rogers, D. *Child Psychology.* Belmont, Cal.: Wadsworth, 1977, 441–457.

Rubenstein, J., & Howes, C. The effects of peers on toddler interaction with mother and toys. *Child Development,* 1976, *47,* 597–605.

Safford, P.L. *Teaching young children with special needs.* St. Louis: C.V. Mosby Company, 1978.

Schacter, F.F. *Everyday mother talk to toddlers: Early intervention.* New York: Academic Press, 1979.

Warren, S.F., & Rogers-Warren, A.K. Currect perspectives in language remediation. *Education and Treatment of Children,* 1980, *3,* 133–152.

Wehman, P., & Schleien, S. Severely handicapped children: Social skills development through leisure skills programming. In G. Cartledge & J.F. Milburn (Eds.), *Teaching social skills to children: Innovative approaches.* New York: Pergamon Press, 1980.

White, B.L., & Watts, J.C. *Experience and environment: Major influences on the development of the young child* (Vol. 1). Englewood Cliffs, N.J.: Prentice-Hall, 1973.

Chapter 5

Development of Motor Skills and the Management of Common Problems

Mildred E. Copeland

OVERVIEW

Motor development has been defined by Johnston and Magrab (1976) as the step-by-step acquisition of skills that involve movement. Herr and Goodwyn (1978) detail the definition further to include the length of time and speed it takes a child to learn body use and control. The acquisition of motor skills is achieved through multisensory stimuli. Sight, hearing, and touch are key factors in guiding motor action. The central nervous system (CNS) is the coordinating or integrating agent for directing sensory inputs to initiate the appropriate motor response. As the child matures, so does the CNS, enabling a wide range of stimuli to be integrated and interpreted into higher and more complex motor responses. The normal child learns to assimilate, modify, and adapt what has been mastered in a particular situation and to transfer this knowledge to newly learned skills (Fiorentino, 1973).

For many children with motor dysfunctions (cerebral palsy, mental retardation, or orthopedic conditions) the sensori-motor experiences known to them has been limited. Their innate desire to explore and experience their environment via their mobility has been greatly reduced. With such children, early training can increase agility, balance, and strength (Baumgartner, 1971). Studies by Ayres (1972) and Isamil and Gruber (1968) indicate that motor training with a sensori-motor base has a significant effect in academic learning in children with certain types of motor problems. Kephart (1971) concurs by stating that the first encounter between the child and the surrounding world is through motor activity, which in turn lays the foundation for cognitive learning.

If muscular weakness prevents head control, trunk control, or both, a child in a sitting position cannot master stringing beads and cannot maintain a grip on a pencil unless adaptations are made to the equipment and to teaching techniques. Both minor and major motor dysfunctions can be minimized through normal positioning, adaptations of materials or equipment, and employing behavioral management techniques. All of these objectives can be accomplished with materials easily obtained by the teaching staff.

RATIONALE

By the time a child enters kindergarten or the first grade, many motor behaviors have been established and only require refinement or mastery at a higher, more complex level. During the first five to six years of life, the child has been assimilating numerous sensory inputs and integrating (or transferring) this information into meaningful motor actions. Motor development follows a highly predictable sequential and overlapping pattern (Blackhurst & Berdine, 1981; Connor, Williamson, & Siepp, 1978; Illingworth, 1980). The various stages of motor development occur within a predicted age range for most children. Depending on the specific motor skill, the normal range may span a couple of months or extend four to six months (Illingworth, 1980). Whatever the length of time the child requires to master various levels of development, the teachers should keep in mind several basic principles that apply to all motor accomplishments.

One important principle to remember is that the rate of development is closely related to the maturation of the nervous system. Illingworth (1980) indicates that "an important factor which governs the age of sitting and walking is myelination of the appropriate part of the nervous system" (p. 170). All incoming messages are transferred through the sensory system via the nervous system to the appropriate levels of the brain stem and brain. The sensory system includes tactile (touch), visual (seeing), auditory (hearing), proprioception (postural adjustment to muscle and joint changes), vestibular (body changes to gravity), and kinesthetic (combined response to proprioception, vestibular, and visual).

Initially, the motor responses are described as involuntary, primitive, and without definite purpose. The reason for these "haphazard" movements is that muscular maturation occurs from cephalo-caudal (head to feet) as well as in a proximo-distal direction (control of the shoulder area occurs before finger manipulation) (Zaichkowsky, Zaichkowsky, & Martinex, 1980). Therefore, what appears to be the uncontrolled flailing motions of an infant are actually the beginnings of what will become purposefully directed movement. Only when infants are given the opportunity to explore and experiment actively with their own bodies and their immediate environment will they learn to regulate and restrain these "wild" movements. For example, the posture of a full-term newborn is with the extremities generally held close to the body in a flexed position. The baby learns best about the body and the world through the senses and "finds" certain actions as a result of the sensory inputs that bring pleasure, food, love, or even pain and discomfort. Random movements begin to acquire special meaning and purpose; eventually they become an established motor pattern (Dmitriev, 1974). In the growth process, the child continues to reach out into space and to explore surrounding space. Repeated explorations lead to smooth controlled motions, which in turn allow for advanced motor tasks to be explored.

Blackhurst and Berdine (1981) point out that all areas of development are interrelated. Best (1978) also emphasizes that all areas of growth are connected to each other, and one function cannot be trained to the exclusion of another function. The teacher must always consider the total child while assessing and planning the child's individualized educational program (IEP). When there is a delay in one area, language, for example, deficits will usually arise in one or more other areas, such as social, cognitive, or motor.

Copeland, Ford, and Solon (1976) stated that the difference between normal and abnormal motor achievements generally depends on the following three major factors: (1) the *rate* at which handicapped children acquire skills is less; (2) the *level* of performance fluctuates with each chronological age; and (3) there are obvious differences in the *quality* of performance. It is therefore important that teachers of young children have readily available to them not only the normal developmental milestones but also knowledge about how children perform these skills. Motor actions such as climbing, running, or skipping follow a developmental sequence. Teachers who are aware of and able to identify the early "awkward" attempts are better able to interpret them as normal or abnormal. The teacher may wish to focus on the child's motor level in either case, but the approach in achieving the ultimate goal may be quite different.

Developmental delays are often created when primitive reflexes fail to become integrated into higher level voluntary motor responses (Snell, 1978). The child either becomes unable to learn higher level skills or has learned to compensate in an atypical fashion in order to do the motor task. Reflexes refer to involuntary behavior in which each reflex when elicited has a specific cause and effect. Reflexes can be classified according to their ordinal level within the spinal cord and brain (Fiorentino, 1973). Reflexes at the spinal cord level are normally present at birth, are protective in nature, and respond to tactile stimulation. Brain stem reactions respond with changes in muscle tone as a result of head movement. These reflexes are noted within the first six months of life. By four to six months, the midbrain reflexes associated with skills of rolling, sitting, and creeping are responding to the infant's increased activity. At the cortical level (starting at six months and continuing throughout life), reflexes react to subtle changes in the center of gravity within the body. Automatic reactions are a group of reflexes responding to sudden or rapid body movement.

For young toddlers to reach the voluntary independent motor stage, such as walking, many of the earlier reflexes must be "phased out" or integrated in order for higher level reflexes or voluntary movements to take over. Otherwise, each time the child's foot touched the ground, a stimulus would elicit a stepping response, even when standing still. Repeated tumbles would quickly extinguish any interest or motivation for the child to continue exploring the environment. With assistance from therapists (occupational, physical, and developmental), teachers can learn effective ways to position and handle children that will assist and encourage voluntary motor behavior. Table 5–1 shows several selected reflexes and the age of their onset and integration. For a more detailed description of reflex development see Fiorentino (1973) and Bobath and Bobath (1972).

How can teachers learn to identify those children who have minimal as well as major motor problems? The basis for any motor evaluation is a broad knowledge of normal growth and development (Dmitriev, 1974). Understanding the extent of a child's deviations from the norms can be used as a guide in developing individual motor programs. Many developmental checklists derived from standardized research are readily available and easily administered. Generally, the checklist items are designed on a chronological level and require a pass or fail scoring procedure. With minimal adaptation to the test form itself, the teacher can obtain valuable information on the degree of verbal and physical assistance that must be given for the child to complete the task. This additional information serves as a guideline in planning a motor program. There are a number of standardized tests that provide a wide range of motor competency skills. These include the Denver Developmental Screening Test (Frankenburg & Dodds, 1967); the Bayley Scales of Infant Development (Bayley, 1969); the Koontz Child Development Program (Koontz, 1974); and the Brigance Diagnostic Inventory of Early Development (Brigance, 1978).

No matter what type of evaluation tool is used (observation, checklist, or standardized test), the teacher should comment on "how and why" the motor behavior was performed and not just whether the child could or could not perform the task. The information needed should specify what, if any, additional information is needed for the child to complete the task. For example, does the child require physical assistance to master cutting with scissors?

Table 5–1 Appearance and Integration of Selected Reflexes

Reflex Timetable

Responses	Weeks	Months											Years			Source
	1–4	2	3	4	5	6	7	8	9	10	11	12	2–3	3–5	After 5	
Moro	+	+	+	±	±	±	±	±	±	−						Peiper
Asymmetrical TNR	+	±	±	±	±	±	−									Peiper
Symmetrical TNR	+	+	+	+	+	+	−									Fiorentino
Tonic labyrinthine	+	+	+	+	−											Fiorentino
Grasp	+	+	+	±	±	±										Peiper
Neck righting		+	+	±	±	±	±	±	±	±	±	±	±			Bobath
Labyrinthine righting		+	+	+	+	+										Bobath
Optical righting						+	+	+	+	+	+	+	+	+	+	Fiorentino
Body righting on the body							+	+	+	+	+	+	±	±		Bobath
Protective extension of the arms						+	+	+	+	+	+	+	+	+	+	Fiorentino
Equilibrium reactions in																
Prone						+	+	+	+	+	+	+	+	+	+	Bobath
Supine							+	+	+	+	+	+	+	+	+	Bobath
Sitting								+	+	+	+	+	+	+	+	Bobath
Quadrupedal												+	+	+	+	Bobath
Standing												+	+	+	+	Bobath

Source: D.A. Sukiennicki, "Neuromotor Development." In B.S. Banus (Ed.) *The Developmental Therapist.* Thorofare, N.J.: 1971, p. 135.

Vulpe (1977) is an advocate of providing explicit information relating to the child's functional ability. She states that this type of information will indicate the level of "learning style and the teaching approach" best suited for that child (Vulpe, 1977). In addition, teachers should make observational notes on how the child handles the body when engaged in gross and fine motor activities. Does the child's muscular strength and tone hinder these activities? If so, how does the child manage to get from a sitting to a standing position or how is a crayon held in the hand?

Once this information is obtained, teachers have a clearer picture of the functional level of the child and the type of motor goals that need to be initiated. Hayden (1974) stresses that a primary responsibility of teachers is to help and guide students to become as "self-sufficient and independent as possible." Failing to do so only reinforces feelings of worthlessness in the child, thereby increasing dependency on others and retarding the child's motor development even further. Motor failure begets failure in language, social, and academic skills. Motor delays develop a "Catch-22" syndrome with individuals with whom the child has close contact. If the child is confronted with too high expectations or if the child is not praised for minute efforts from parents, peers, or teachers, that child may avoid trying certain skills, thereby easing frustration but prolonging dependence. For this reason, careful assessment of the child's ability and how that child performs is of the upmost importance. Therefore, the teacher should create learning situations that are "appropriate, properly sequenced and interesting to the child" (Hayden, 1974, p. 61).

Through the use of a consistent program that uses positive reinforcement, shaping and chaining steps, and the inclusion of adapted equipment (where it is needed), motor and emotional development can be assured. Teachers must remember that play is a child's work and that toys may be designed to promote gross and fine motor movement. Toys may also be the teachers best tools for stimulating the child's physical development in conjunction with behavioral management techniques.

BASIC PRINCIPLES

Motor skills can be classified into two major categories: gross motor and fine motor. Gross motor activities refer to those skills related to large muscles that control balance, equilibrium, and the postural control required in sitting, standing, walking, running, and climbing.

Gross motor skills also require a concept of where the body is in space and the ability to master newly learned skills and to incorporate these patterns at an unconscious level (Vulpe, 1977).

Fine motor skills include responses requiring the use of small muscles, not just of the hands, but the eyes, mouth, and the combined realtionship of those areas to the hands. Specific movements include grasping, releasing, manipulating, and the dexterity or skill and ease of handling smaller objects. Sucking and blinking are also skills of fine motor ability. Since motor growth develops from general to specific movement (Herr & Goodwyn, 1978; Illingworth, 1980), delays in achieving gross motor skills will certainly impede the acquisition of fine motor manipulation (Vulpe, 1977).

Various ways of looking at the developmental sequence can be found in the current literature. Ayres (1972), de Quiros and Scharager (1978), and Montgomery and Richter (1978) have approached normal development and treatment of abnormal motor behavior by way of the neurophysiological system. Such an approach demands a thorough understanding of the nervous system, the normal functions of the skeletal and muscular system, and the actions of the reflexes; therefore, it is best left to the physical or occupational therapist to evaluate and interpret these aspects of motor development. Teachers and therapists, however, can learn to work together in the classroom and to share the knowledge they have acquired in their own domains. Not only do the children profit, but so does the professional staff.

The works of Frankenburg & Dodds (1967), Gesell and Amatruda (1962), and Griffin, Sandford, and Wilson (1975) lay as their foundation for evaluating motor skills the hierarchy of normal developmental sequences. The evaluations prepared by these individuals and their colleagues are valuable for teachers to use as a measure of the child's ability across several categories. These evaluation instruments may also be used as a refresher course in developmental growth and behavior.

A similar developmental approach will be presented in this chapter, that is, motor growth will be viewed from the general to the specific; stationary (static) balance before locomotive (dynamic) balance; head control prior to feet control; and arm movement before hand manipulation. The breakdown or "pinpoints," as identified by Cohen, Gross, and Haring (1976), and Galka and Fraser (1980), of gross and fine motor development can be listed in the following manner:

Gross Motor

- supine
- rolling
- prone
- half-kneeling
- standing
- walking

Gross Motor *(continued)*

- sitting
- all-fours
- crawling
- kneeling
- skipping

- running
- jumping
- hopping
- climbing

Fine Motor

- generalized hand and arm movement
- reaching
- grasping
- releasing
- coming to center of body
- rotation
- transfers object from one hand to other
- manipulation
- dexterity

All activities, such as writing, reading, dressing, eating, and jogging, contain one or more of these motor components.

Since development is based on a gradual continuum of events, the teaching of new muscular patterns or more complex skills is most effectively accomplished through behavioral management training. A person cannot expect an adult to master the game of golf or tennis until the mechanics have been mastered through repeated training. Similarly, a child who has been confined to a horizontal position cannot be expected to stand up and walk until the earlier prerequisites have been conquered and practiced. The success of both the adult and child depends on their teacher's ability to program the skills for a successful end product. Therefore, the teacher must learn to break down into simple steps (task analysis and problem solving) both motor movements and the activity itself.

Robinson and Robinson (1978) reviewed the following several questions that teachers should ask themselves prior to the start of any training program:

- What reinforces the child?

- Are the response criteria appropriate for a given child?

- Are the instructional objectives appropriate for a given child?

- Are the procedures to evaluate learning appropriate for a given child?

Additional questions might also include the following:

- Is the specific activity a functional task for a given child?

- Are adaptations to materials required for a given child?

By normalizing atypical motor patterns with proper positioning, new motor movements can be added through behavioral management techniques. A child with weak muscles resulting in poor neck control can be helped to strengthen the neck muscles if placed over a wedge or cylinder with arms and hands over and in front of the equipment. Many times this is not sufficient motivation for the child to raise the head, a motor activity that assists in developing neck control. Rewarding the child when looking at a musical toy or reaching for a colorful object held above the child's eye level is just one technique for increasing a desired behavior. Teaching a child to hold on to a spoon can be initiated with physical support by placing the teacher's hand over the child's hand. The teacher may then fade support with first a light touch on the child's hand, then lightly supporting the wrist, moving to the forearm, and finally to the elbow. As the child maintains grasping the spoon for longer periods, physical assistance becomes less and less, thus developing independent grasp. The teacher has not only used positive reinforcement and fading prompts, but has also shaped the child's behavior and broken the task into simple steps (chaining). This process is only one component of the total program designed for independent feeding.

The same basic principles were used by Project FEATT (1976) in teaching walking with assistance. After making sure the child possessed the prerequisites (maintaining a standing posture while holding on), a small chair was placed in front of the child. The instructor knelt on the other side of the chair and moved the chair a few inches away from the child.

Initially, the adult may have to model what is requested by moving the child's feet forward. A doll or toy placed on the seat of the chair can also be used as a functional reason for pushing the chair. Verbal cues and praise often encourage the child to continue moving forward. The number of steps taken or duration of walking (number of seconds or minutes) can be plotted on a graph to ascertain the effectiveness of the program and to determine if the criterion level has been met.

It is not always wise at the start of a program to ignore inappropriate motor behavior while reinforcing appropriate motor behavior. The child may be physically unable to obtain the desired position independently. It is better to establish the proper pattern first so the child understands what is expected.

Determining what task to work on is based on a combined appraisal of normal motor development and the current motor ability of the child. The knowledge of normal development helps the teacher determine what is the next developmental skill the child will need to master.

The questionnaire in Exhibit 5–1 can assist the teacher in observing the child and can be used as a guide in defining current motor ability.

PROBLEM AREAS AND MANAGEMENT

It is not the intention of this chapter to cover all the problems (and the solutions) teachers will encounter in their careers, but rather to provide a few suggestions that might be helpful in encouraging normal movement. Not all of the recommendations will prove successful, as teachers often may encounter an individual child who needs more thorough identification of existing problems. For those children with severe motor delays, an evaluation of reflexes, motor development, and self-help skills should be administered and interpreted by a registered occupational therapist or a registered physical therapist.

Teachers may question why they must take the time to correct a child's position or change his or her mode of movement when the task eventually is accomplished. The following should explain the importance of proper body alignment for the child's total growth. Children who remain on their backs or in one position over time become stiff. Thus, if their movement ability is limited, they become locked into a low developmental level.

Proper positioning and movement ensures the following:

- better body alignment, which in turn diminishes the chances of permanent physical damage (that is, hip dislocation, lateral curvature of the spine, sway back, or hump back);

- an avoidance of pressure sores that can become a health problem;

- an increase in the child's ability to move with greater ease and comfort;

- improved dressing, feeding, and toileting skills;

Exhibit 5–1 Observational Questions to Guide in Defining Current Motor Ability

	Yes	No	Sometimes
Prone			
1. Can child raise head 45 degrees?			
2. Can child raise head 90 degrees?			
3. Is weight supported by forearms?			
4. Is weight supported by hands?			
5. Can child obtain an all-four position?			
6. Can child open hands in all-four position?			
7. Can child reach with one hand while shifting weight to other side of body?			
8. Can child actively obtain an all-four position?			
Supine			
1. Are arm movements observable?			
2. Are arm movements equal?			
3. Is one arm and hand moving more than the other?			
4. Are arms bent most of the time?			
5. Are leg movements equal?			
6. Is one leg moving more than the other?			
7. Are leg movements observable?			
Head			
1. Is head always turned to one side?			
2. When head turns sideways, do arms assume the "fencing position?"			
Rolling			
1. Can child roll from back to side?			
2. Can child roll from back to front?			
3. Can child roll from front to back?			
4. Does child roll as a "log?"			
5. Can child roll segmentally?			
Sitting			
1. Can child attain sitting position from horizontal position?			
2. Can child maintain sitting? How long ___?			
3. Does child "W" sit?			
4. Does child side-sit?			
5. Does child "tailor" sit?			

Exhibit 5–1 continued

Sitting (continued)
6. Does child long-leg sit?
7. Can child maintain posture in a regular chair?

All-Four Position
1. Can child assume this position?
2. Can child maintain this position?
3. Can child crawl once this position is achieved?
4. Can child crawl reciprocally?

Kneeling
1. Can child assume this position?
2. Can child maintain this position?
3. Can child move while kneeling?

Standing
1. Can child actively get to standing?
2. Is weight equally distributed?
3. Can child walk without assistance?
4. Can child balance on one foot? (left_____ or right_____)
5. Can child balance on either foot?
6. Can child stand on uneven surface without losing balance?
7. Can child stand on tiptoes?
8. Can child stand on one foot for five seconds?
9. Can child stand on one foot for ten seconds?
10. Can child walk length of balance board ($2'' \times 4'' \times 6''$)?

Walking
1. Can child walk unassisted?
2. Does child need equipment (walker, crutches, and so on) to walk?
3. Can child walk with a normal gait?
4. Does child lean when walking? If so, how?

Running
1. Does child run stiffly?

Exhibit 5–1 continued

Running (continued)
2. Can child run on tiptoes?
3. Can child run well with few falls?

Climbing
1. Can child climb into adult chair?
2. Can child climb ladders and/or other types of vertical equipment?

Jumping
1. Can child jump in place with step-tap pattern?
2. Can child jump with two feet together?
3. Can child jump over objects? How high? _____
4. Can child broad jump? How far?

Hopping
1. Can child hop on one foot?
2. Can child hop on either foot? How far?

Skipping
1. Can child skip on one foot?
2. Can child skip on either foot?
3. Are skipping movements smooth and coordinated?

Kicking
1. Does child walk into ball to kick?
2. Can child swing leg to kick stationary ball?
3. Can child kick moving ball?

Throwing
1. Can child hurl ball?
2. Can child throw ball overhand?
3. Can child throw ball at large target?
4. When throwing, does child step forward with leg opposite hand throwing ball?

Catching
1. Does child trap ball with body and arms?
2. Does child catch ball with hands?
3. Can child catch small ball with one hand?

Exhibit 5–1 continued

Rolling
1. Does child roll ball using forward motion of arms and hands?
2. Can child roll ball toward adult?

Fine Motor

General hand and arm movements
1. Does child open hands only when body is tilted backwards?
2. Can child open hands voluntarily?
3. Can child touch thumb to each finger?
4. Can child rotate forearm?

Grasping
1. Is child able to maintain grasp?
2. Does child grasp crayon with fist?
3. Does child grasp crayon in adult fashion?
4. Does child grasp small objects using whole hand?
5. Does child grasp objects with neat pincer grasp?
6. Does child grasp with one hand only?

Releasing
1. Does child drop object immediately?
2. Can child voluntarily release object?

Manipulation
1. Is child able to stack blocks? How many? _____
2. Is child able to transfer objects from hand to hand?
3. Is child able to bang objects together?
4. Is child able to complete simple puzzle?
5. Is child able to complete complex puzzle? How many pieces?

- an ability to do more tasks independently, which will increase self-esteem, which in turn affects motivation for learning and interacting with the environment.

During any activity the teacher has planned for a child, there are general guidelines to follow, in addition to behavioral management techniques, that will increase the probability of a successful outcome of the program. Some of these guidelines are presented in Exhibit 5–2.

Prone

The prone position is a prerequisite to higher developmental levels, such as supporting the entire body weight on the hands and knees while creeping, crawling, or kneeling. Head control is best controlled and strengthened in the prone position. Between one to four months, a normally developing infant is able to lift the head up to 90 degrees and to rotate the head from side to side with little difficulty. By six months, the pivot-prone position is well established, and the child is turning 360 degrees on the stomach. The child is also now rolling from back to stomach and vice-versa. Preschool children with moderate to severe motor difficulties may not be able to obtain this position. Placing the child in the prone position while the child is working on academic lessons strengthens the extensor muscles of the neck and back. (See Figure 5–1.)

Exhibit 5–2 Activity Guidelines

Do's	*Don't's*
1. Do explain what you are going to do.	1. Don't allow the child to play or dress while lying on his or her back.
2. Do talk to the child at eye level.	2. Don't allow "W" sitting or bunny hopping.
3. Do provide all types of stimulation (tactile, visual, auditory).	3. Don't make sudden movements that may startle the child.
4. Do allow for frequent position changes.	4. Don't stand over the child while giving instructions.
5. Do encourage bilateral activities at the center line of the body.	5. Don't hurry the child to complete a task.
	6. Don't allow the child to always use the "good" side.

Figure 5–1 The Prone Position

Neck and back muscles are strengthened using wedge. Arms in front of wedge are able to support partial weight of the body.
Source: Genevieve Galka and Beverly A. Fraser. *Gross Motor Management of Severely Multiply Impaired Students.* Volume II Curriculum Model. Baltimore, Md.: University Park Press, 1980, p. 6. Reprinted by permission.

Positioning a child in the prone position can be accomplished by using the following outline:

- Place a child in prone position over a wedge (or cylinder or rolled-up blanket).
- Place both arms in front of the wedge. This allows normal patterning for reaching and grasping.
- Position toys on a small table or stool several inches above the floor to encourage head extension.
- Establish baseline data for duration of lifting head.
- Use a variety of toys that the child likes in order to encourage head control, arm extension, and hand manipulation.

Supine

Placing a young child with motor delays on his or her back is generally discouraged. This is the child's "normal" position, and this locks the child into limited movement. If back positioning must be used, elevate the head and trunk area to increase the visual field and allow for hand manipulation. A large bean bag chair is an effective piece of equipment for this position.

Side-lying

It may be more feasible for a child to be actively involved with an academic program if placed in a side-lying position. This position decreases the influences of primitive reflexes, encourages use of both hands at the midline of the body, encourages proper trunk alignment, and controls random arm and hand movements (Galka & Fraser, 1980). Figure 5–2 shows how a side-lying position can facilitate these objectives. Additional adaptations that can be made to assist the child and teacher are placing materials on a slant board or placing the child on a wedge on the side that elevates the head and trunk area.

Rolling

There are three abnormal ways children get from one horizontal position to another. Rolling over like a log is the most frequently observed method. Other children arch their back and try to push themselves over with their feet and head. A third way has been noted in those children who become caught in a fixed arm position due to the presence of a primitive reflex (asymmetrical tonic neck).

The desired goal toward independent rolling is to turn the body in a sequential order. The head initiates movement with the shoulders moving next, followed by the trunk, with the hips and the legs being the last to follow. With this motion the arms can be pushing upward as the legs are turning over to attain a sitting or all-four position. Normal independent

Figure 5–2 Side-Lying Position

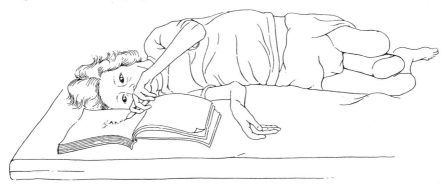

Source: G. Galka and B.A. Fraser. *Gross Motor Management of Severely Multiply Impaired Students.* Baltimore, Md.: University Park Press, 1980, p. 33. Reprinted by permission.

rolling is essential for proper achievement of sitting, all-fours, kneeling, half-kneeling, and standing positions.

Methods for reaching these goals are started by using physical assistance until the child is able to initiate the segmental rolling. Motivation through verbal and physical rewards are prime factors in assisting the child toward this goal. The following seven-step outline describes a program that was designed for a two-year-old boy diagnosed as a mild cerebral palsy child with minimal involvement in the lower extremities and normal muscle tone in the arms and hands.

Independent Rolling Program

1. Child is placed on back.
2. A favorite toy is placed slightly above the child's head on the right side.
3. Adult kneels facing the child's feet.
4. Adult assists in proper placement of child's right arm at shoulder height away from the body.
5. The adult's right arm is placed under child's left leg, and the adult's right hand rests on top of the child's right leg.
6. The child's leg is moved with the movement of the adult's arm over toward the child's right side.
7. When the side-lying position has been reached, active movement is encouraged to complete the roll-over maneuver.

Using the backward chaining procedure, the child is passively rotated up to the seventh step of the program. The child is then encouraged and rewarded for active movement in completing this step. The left arm may or may not be strong enough to work against gravity when reaching for the toy. Children with weak muscle tone and strength can assist only when gravity takes over, which occurs beyond the middle of the rolling process.

When the criterion level of step seven has been met, active movement of the child's left arm is rewarded. The more independent the left hand becomes in reaching the toy on the opposite side of the body, the greater the change of the cephal-caudal process occurring. The next procedure of this program would be a gradual decrease of the physical support to the lower extremities (legs) until just verbal instructions are necessary to have the child roll over. Final independence occurs when the child initiates "when" rolling will take place.

Sitting

One of the most common sitting problems that occurs with both hand-icapped and nonhandicapped children is the "W" or inverted sitting in which the child's buttocks are positioned between the heels of the feet. Most adults have a difficult time maintaining this position for any length of time, but children, being more pliable and flexible, find this a natural posture when sitting on the floor. Generally, children shift from this position to several other postures depending on their play interests and needs. There are other youngsters who find it most uncomfortable to sit in a side position, circle position, tailor position, or a long-leg position. Such discomfort may be because there are muscles or groups of muscles of the lower extremity that are so tight that the only position that provides the child with a stable base of support is the "W" position.

Over time the "W" position can create an abnormal standing posture, that is, standing with both legs internally rotated with the knees touching each other and weight supported on the inside of the feet. In order to maintain this posture, a child must also bend or flex at the waist. Standing or walking is awkward, if not difficult, as are the other gross motor skills, such as running, hopping, or skipping. Other activities, such as ball throwing or catching, require flexibility, endurance, and strength of both extremities, and are greatly limited because of this posture. Trunk mobility is also limited, both in the sitting and standing position, when a child is locked into a "W" sitting pattern. Because of the deleterious effect that the inverted sitting position has on more complex motor skills, other variations of sitting should be encouraged.

Floor activities for preschool children are good motivational techniques to promote academic learning and to encourage social interaction. Described here are several ways of training different sitting patterns that discourage or inhibit a high rate of "W" sitting. With all of the variations described, the teacher must periodically check to see that the child is sitting up straight. If not, the child with poor muscle tone may not be able to maintain that posture. Kneeling behind the child, the teacher only has to pull the child's hip back toward her, thus making sure the child is on the buttocks and not slumped over. These children may have spent months and even years in an abnormal position. Therefore, a consistent behavioral management program may also take time, but eventually it will assist in making this transition to a new sitting position effective and easily obtained.

Following are suggested program steps for three sitting positions:

Side Sitting

- With the child in the "W" position, ask, "_____, how are you supposed to sit?"

- If there is no response, give the command, "_____, sit to the side."

- If the child does not follow through, raise the child's buttocks off the floor, over the right leg, and on the floor to the right of both legs.

Circle (Tailor) Sitting

- With the child in the "W" position, ask, "_____, how are you supposed to sit?"
- If there is no response, give the command, "_____, sit with your legs in a circle."
- If there is no response, repeat the command, and give physical assistance.
- Hold the child at the knee and foot of one leg.
- Lift and turn the leg so the knee is pointing away from the center of the body.
- Repeat with the other leg.
- Place the soles of both feet so they are or are almost touching each other.

If the child has difficulty maintaining circle sitting, it might be better to begin training the child in "long sitting." When greater ranges of mobility have been developed, the circle sitting can be added to the child's repertoire.

Long Sitting

- With the child in "W" position, ask, "_____, how are you supposed to sit?"
- If there is no response, give the command, "_____, sit with your legs out in front of you."
- If there is no response, repeat the command, and give physical assistance.
- Hold the child at the knee and foot of one leg.
- Lift and straighten the leg.
- Repeat the procedure with the other leg.

The teacher should be aware that changing the preferred sitting position to one that is new may be so uncomfortable that the child may soon shift back to "W" sitting (Fallen, 1978). Rewarding the child for continued efforts to remain longer in the new position will assist in achieving the goal of normal sitting posture. This can be done by providing interesting activities. The teacher should also establish specific times for floor activities when data are recorded on the duration of a particular sitting position. The criterion level should be at a minimum and should be gradually increased as the child is able to tolerate this "new" posture. Teachers must also remember that it is good therapy to shift the child to different sitting positions to avoid cutting off circulation or cramping muscles (Fallen, 1978).

Good sitting balance can be obtained while sitting astride a firm bolster. Placement of the legs on either side of the bolster prevents the legs from turning in as happens in the "W" position. This position also increases trunk stability and rotation as the child reaches for toys that are presented for language or cognitive stimulation. Existing equipment or inexpensive materials can be adapted to provide proper trunk support as is shown in Figures 5–3 and 5–4. Cylinders can be purchased or inexpensively made by the teaching staff. Both Levy (1973) and Herr and Goodwyn (1978)

Figure 5–3 Trash Can and Box Seats for Trunk Support

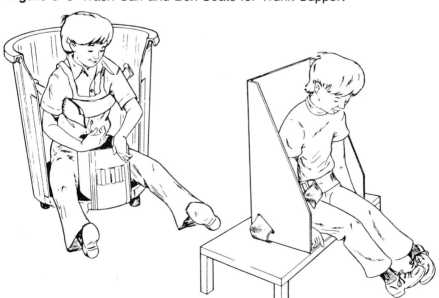

Source: N.H. Fallen and J.E. McGovern. *Young Children with Special Needs* (Columbus, Ohio: Charles E. Merrill Publishing Co., 1978), p. 146.

Figure 5–4 Foam Roll for Trunk Support

Source: N.H. Fallen and J.E. McGovern. *Young Children with Special Needs* (Columbus, Ohio: Charles E. Merrill Publishing Co., 1978), p. 144.

describe how easily and quickly cylinders of different sizes can be put together.

The following case study points out the importance of assessing the child's total motor ability and not just the obvious motor problem. Karen, a three-year-old cerebral palsied child, had good use of the upper extremity, but she was unable to get to a standing position or to walk unassisted. Her means of locomotion was to "bunny hop" and then transfer to a "W" sit. The teacher requested assistance in training Karen to develop normal patterns of walking. Since Karen had not yet developed normal crawling and sitting behavior, these skills were the focus area. Inability to walk unassisted appeared to be the primary problem, but the key to the solution lay in establishing normal sitting and crawling patterns.

Normal developmental sequencing of basic motor behaviors reinforces and establishes proper movement of higher complex motor skills. The data sheet in Figure 5–5 was used to record the child's progress in side sitting over a one-week period and follows the program suggested under side sitting described earlier.

Figure 5–5 Sample Data Sheet To Measure Progress in Occupational Therapy

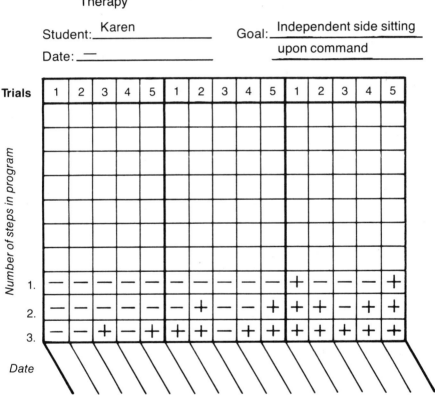

Student: Karen   Goal: Independent side sitting upon command

Date: —

Trials	1	2	3	4	5	1	2	3	4	5	1	2	3	4	5
1.	−	−	−	−	−	−	−	−	−	−	+	−	−	−	+
2.	−	−	−	−	−	−	+	−	−	+	+	+	−	+	+
3.	−	−	+	−	+	+	+	−	+	+	+	+	+	+	+

Number of steps in program

Date

Comments:
1. Completes task when asked how she should sit.
2. Completes task after verbal command.
3. Assists teacher in transferring position.

Code:
− = Did not comply with request.
+ = Did comply with request.

Balance and Equilibrium Skills

Bunker (1978) defines balance as "the ability to maintain equilibrium relative to gravity" (p. 185). Two primary ways in which children demonstrate this ability are when they are engaged in static or dynamic balance. Static balance is noted when an infant is learning to sit, when a toddler is learning to stand, or when a young child is trying to stand on one foot. Static balance is basically an attempt to maintain an upright position while working against gravity in a stationary position.

When a child moves out of a stationary position, that child is engaging in dynamic balance. Motor tasks in this category include walking, running, hopping, and skipping. These skills require a higher level of neurodevelopmental maturity, that is, a better integration of the primitive reflexes and evidence of equilibrium reactions, and protective extension reactions. Essentially, these skills require the child to perform the task of moving through space without falling down.

Walking

Once a child has mastered an upright position, a second component, movement, is soon added. These two ingredients are the basis for initial walking. This type of walking is accomplished by holding on to a parent's hands, couches, coffee tables, or other available supports. Going from one piece of furniture to another is identified as "cruising" or "side stepping" and helps to establish the confidence needed for the child to strike out independently.

Initially, independent walking is attained with feet widely spaced apart, with knees and arms bent, and with an irregular high-stepping pattern. Falls are frequent, especially on uneven terrain. At approximately four years of age, walking has usually developed into a mature rhythmic gait with a narrow base of support, heel-toe progression, and hand-foot opposition. By this age, most children also exhibit confidence and assurance in stepping over and onto objects.

Running

Running has been described by Bunker (1978), Cratty (1979), and Espenschade and Echkert (1967) as an extension and adaptation of the walking pattern with an increase of speed, increase in the length of the stride, increased movement and flexion of the arms, and a forward angle of the body. As with walking, mastery of running skills develops in a sequential fashion. The form of early running is stilted; arms and legs move in unison (left arm with left leg); foot distance above the floor is barely noticeable;

there is more movement in the trunk than with the extremities; and the forward movement from one side of the body with the other is uneven. Maturation develops as the leg stride increases, and as leg and arm angle increase and move in opposition to each other.

Jumping

In order to accomplish jumping skills, the child must be able to maintain suspended balance while exaggerating enough strength and flexibility to propel the body through space and while simultaneously keeping both feet off the ground. Early jumping patterns are characterized by the lack of coordination between upper and lower extremities. Movement of the feet are often separate, with the typical "hop-step" motion noted before development of the final sychronized (bilateral) life of both legs.

Hopping

Balancing on one foot must be achieved before the intricate movements of hopping can be mastered. Basic hopping on one foot for eight to ten steps can be performed by most five year olds (Cratty, 1979). Rhythmic, or two-foot hopping, is difficult for children at this age. Higher levels of hopping incorporate strength, endurance, and speed, which signifies a mature nervous system.

Skipping

A series of alternating hopping steps is called skipping. It has also been defined as a succession of step-hop movements. The child takes a step, hops on the same foot, and quickly follows the same series of movements with the opposite leg. This requires a shifting of weight as the transfer is made from one leg to the other. Most frequently, the early type of skipping is done on the child's dominant side. It is clearly evident that one side of the body is able to coordinate the step-hop pattern, but on the other side the foot appears to slide or drag as the child propels forward (Bunker, 1978).

A classic example of balance and equilibrium problems was noted in Brady, a three-year-old boy. Brady had developed a cerebral brain tumor; following surgery, he displayed both visual and motor problems. Corrective lenses remedied his visual problems, but he needed specific training for dynamic balance and postural reactions, especially on uneven terrain. The initial evaluation indicated a motor age the equivalent of 1½ years in motor tasks such as jumping with both feet, hopping on one foot, catching a large playground ball, and throwing a ball at a specific target. Cognitive skills were well within the normal range for his age. It was decided to incorporate his preacademic skills as a motivating and reinforcing factor to increase his balance. Brady was scheduled for an hour session once a week in addition to his home program.

One of the treatment activities was to have Brady squat and regain standing posture with 80 percent accuracy. Pieces of a puzzle chosen by Brady were placed on the floor. Instructions were given to pick up the pieces by squatting (unassisted) and to place them back in the puzzle board on a nearby table. Initially, Brady required physical support in standing up, but within 16 weeks he had met the criterion level of 80 percent accuracy.

Puzzles were interchanged with other toys to sustain Brady's interest in the therapeutic activities. Primary reinforcers were also a high motivating instrument for this child.

Brady looked forward to what he called his "snack" for completing the specified number of trials. Raisins, cereal, and gum were his favorite snacks. Brady was especially fond of being picked up and swung in circles while being held upside down.

Fine Motor

Early use of fine motor manipulation involves the eyes, mouth, and the hands. As a baby's eyes spot a toy, both hands usually reach out to hit at it in an uncoordinated fashion. Before long, the reaching phase is followed by grasping the object with one or both hands. In addition to the visual and hand exploration of objects, the child generally mouths everything in hand for added sensory input. Gradually the development of fine motor skills begins to take shape. By toddler age, tasting nonedible objects has almost vanished, but the coordination between the eyes and hands strengthens with each new experience.

The child first learns to grasp items using the whole hand (palmer grasp) but with little involvement of the thumb and index finger. Next comes a fisted grip. This is best observed in the early use of a crayon. The crayon is either held with the thumb next to the paper or with the little finger moving across the paper. Refinement of grasping gradually moves toward the thumb and index finger in what is called the scissors or inferior grasp. Objects are held with the side of the finger and the fatty pad of the end of the thumb. The final stage of grasping (at 18 months) is when the child is able to use the tip of the index finger and thumb (Bunker, 1978). Mastery and refinement continue until the age of five to six years.

Other components of fine motor skills in addition to grasping include two-hand coordination, eye-hand coordination and manual strength, and dexterity (Johnson & Werner, 1975). The following activities have been used with a 24-month-old child (Jody) with Down's syndrome who displayed a palmer grasp and poor muscular strength. Two objectives were established: (1) to increase thumb-finger involvement; and (2) to increase muscular strength of the hands and arms. The item chosen for establishing both objectives was the *Mattel Farmer See'N Say* toy. Language, visual, and auditory memory, and cognitive skills also received attention during these sessions. Forward chaining, physical prompts, praise, and fading methods were used in the following fashion:

- Toy was presented to Jody to hold and examine.

- Adult demonstrated mechanics of toy.

- Adult placed child's entire hand around ring and held on to his hand for three trials, releasing child's hand for string to return.

- Adult then placed child's index finger and thumb in and around ring, and helped Jody pull ring out.

- Adult helped Jody to release the ring.

- Adult showed ring to Jody and had child place fingers correctly. Physical assistance was given for pulling and releasing.

- Jody was told to hold and pull ring.

- Adult gave assistance the last half of pull and gave help in releasing.

- Jody was told to pull on ring all the way and was given partial help in releasing.

- Jody was told to pull and release on command.

- Jody was able to manipulate the toy without further verbal or visual assistance.

Verbal and physical praise was given for successful approximations and for correctly completing each step. Since this toy was used at home and was one of Jody's favorite toys, motivational interest assisted in achieving the objective within a four-week period. Toys with similar mechanics are now being used on a random schedule to maintain interest and ability, and to avoid satiation that might occur if only one toy were used.

A similar task analysis program was planned for a four-year-old girl who was having difficulty with eye-hand coordination. A graded program was developed with large blocks, cups, and plastic rings. As the child required less and less assistance, smaller items were introduced. The girl is now in the process of stacking objects of graded dimensions.

Dressing

Handicapped and nonhandicapped children learn to undress themselves before mastering dressing techniques. Normal acquisition of these skills is accomplished during the child's first five years (Table 5–2). Most manipulative skills, such as buttoning, zipping, and shoe tying, are learned by the sixth year of life. Independent dressing skills are best acquired through backward chaining, shaping and reinforcing appropriate skills, and fading of physical prompts. Both forward and backward chaining have been used in teaching dressing skills; Snell (1978), however, states that backward chaining signals the completion of a task, and with it comes a reward. The process of chaining requires that the desired task be broken into a series of steps. Shaping involves pulling these steps back together through reinforcing each step learned. Backward chaining is rewarding the completion of the last step prior to the next to last step until the entire task has been taught.

As with all other self-help skills, an evaluation of the child's current functional level in dressing will indicate specific items to be trained. An

Table 5–2 Order in Which Normal Children Acquire Dressing and Undressing Skills

Age	Dressing and Undressing Skills
12 to 18 months	Child begins to take off hat, socks, and mittens, and cooperates in dressing by extending an arm or leg into his clothing.
2 years	Child removes unlaced shoes, socks, and pants if he has assistance getting them off over his hips. Children at this age enjoy dressing.
2½ years	Child takes off all clothing and can put on socks, shirt, and coat but not always accurately.
3 years	Child undresses rapidly and well, including front and side buttons. He is able to dress except for heavy outer clothing and needs help telling front from back.
4 years	Child dresses and undresses with little assistance, especially if clothes are laid out. He can distinguish front from back, lace shoes, and button front buttons.
5 years	Child dresses and undresses completely except for back buttons and tying shoe laces.

Source: Gesell, A., and F. L. Ilq. *The child from five to ten* (Harper and Row, New York, 1946) p. 89.

informal dressing and undressing checklist in Exhibit 5–3 will help the teacher focus on components of various garments and the type of assistance needed to complete the article.

An effective dressing program is one where the teacher schedules a sufficient amount of time for practice to occur and does it at times during the day when dressing skills are needed (Snell, 1978). Appropriate times can be when the child comes to school and hangs the coat up, goes outside for recess, goes to the bathroom, or takes clothes off prior to nap time. Figure 5–6 shows the various steps that John, a Down's syndrome child, was using to remove his polo shirt via the backward chaining method. Criterion level had been set at five correct responses before the next step was trained. While only one new step was trained at a time, the child was assisted through the entire chaining process. It is important for the child to learn how each chaining step is shaped into a completed task. In this way each succeeding step will have been carried out previously.

The works of Allen (1980), Copeland et al. (1976), Snell (1978), and Finnie (1975) will provide guidance in designing and implementing dressing programs.

Toileting

Until recently, many preschool programs would not accept children into their centers unless they were toilet trained. Even summer camps and some babysitters excluded those children who could not handle their own toileting needs. This requirement limited the chances of these children for independence and for growth in social, recreational, and academic areas. There is no sound reason for children who are not toilet trained to be excluded from school or prevented from partaking in extracurricular activities.

At about 12 months of age, the child begins to develop an awareness of and regularity related to bowel movements. By 18 months, the awareness of and regularity related to bladder control is beginning to be established. When the child reaches five years of age, all toileting needs are completed. Table 5–3 indicates the normal developmental sequences in toileting skills. Blackwell (1979) states that sphincter control depends on maturing of the spinal cord. She further explains that an indication of this maturing is if the child is up walking and remains dry for two hours.

There are other signs indicating toilet-training readiness. Table 5–4 lists several common signs that teachers and parents should check prior to starting a toilet training program. Connor et al. (1978) stresses the following additional questions to be asked:

Exhibit 5–3 Pretest of Dressing Skills Data Sheet

Child's name:
Date:

Pretest of dressing skills	Independent	Verbal assistance	Physical assistance	Description of method child uses to complete the task
Undressing trousers, skirt 1. Pushes garment from waist to ankles 2. Pushes garment off one leg 3. Pushes garment off other leg				
Dressing trousers, skirt 1. Lays trousers in front of self with front side up 2. Inserts one foot into waist opening 3. Inserts other foot into waist opening 4. Pulls garment up to waist				
Undressing socks 1. Pushes sock down off heel 2. Pulls toe of sock pulling sock off foot				

Dressing socks
1. Positions sock correctly with heel-side down
2. Holds sock open at top
3. Inserts toes into sock
4. Pulls sock over heel
5. Pulls sock up

Undressing cardigan
1. Takes dominant arm out of sleeve
2. Gets coat off back
3. Pulls other arm from sleeve

Dressing cardigan flip-over method
1. Lays garment on table or floor in front of self
2. Gets dominant arm into sleeve
3. Other arm into sleeve
4. Positions coat on back

Undressing polo shirt
1. Takes dominant arm out of sleeve
2. Pulls garment over head
3. Pulls other arm from sleeve

Dressing polo shirt 1. Lays garment in front of self 2. Opens bottom of garment and puts arms into sleeves 3. Pulls garment over head 4. Pulls garment down to waist			
Undressing shoes 1. Loosens laces 2. Pulls shoe off heel 3. Pulls front of shoe to pull shoe off of toes			
Dressing shoes 1. Prepares shoe by loosening laces and pulling tongue of shoe out of the way 2. Inserts toes into shoe 3. Pushes shoe on over heel			

Source: M. Copeland, L. Ford, & N. Solon. Occupational Therapy for Mentally Retarded Children (Baltimore, Md.: University Park Press, 1976), p. 95.

Figure 5–6 Activities of Daily Living Data Sheet

Name: Trainer: Session number:

Date: Task: Undressing polo shirt   Trials completed:

Trials

Subtasks	1	2	3	4	5	6	7	8	9	10
1. Grasps left cuff with right hand.										
2. Pulls garment off left arm while pulling arm back and down.										
3. Pulls garment over head by grasping right shoulder seam in left hand, pulling over head.										
4. Grasps cuff of right sleeve.										
5. Pulls garment off right arm.										
6.										
7.										
8.										
9.										
10.										

Code: + = independent;   A = assistance;   − = failed.

Source: M. Copeland, L. Ford, and N. Solon. *Occupational Therapy for Mentally Retarded Children* (Baltimore, Md.: University Park Press, 1976), p. 103.

- Is there any neurological damage that may impair sensations to the bladder and/or bowel control?

- Does the weakness of muscles prevent bladder and/or bowel control?

- Is the child on medication that may have side effects on elimination?

Questions related to persistent wetting due to an urinary tract infection or virus, or embarrassment in using the school bathroom has been suggested

Table 5–3 Developmental Sequence for Toileting in Normal Children

12 months	Regularity of bowel movements
18 to 21 months	Regularity of urination
2 years	Daytime control with occasional accidents
	Must be reminded to go to the bathroom
	Requires assistance
2½ years	Tells someone he or she needs to go to the bathroom
	Requires assistance
3 to 4 years	Goes to the bathroom by himself or herself if his or her clothing is simple
	Needs help in wiping clean
4 to 5 years	Completely independent

Source: M. Copeland, L. Ford, and N. Solon. *Occupational Therapy for Mentally Retarded Children* (Baltimore, Md.: University Park Press, 1976), p. 150.

by Allen (1980). Lohman, Eyman, and Lask (1967) consider dressing and undressing skills, as well as an absence of behavior problems, to be skills that, if present, will facilitate early toilet training.

The first step to a toilet-training program is to collect baseline data. Teachers and parents should work together to record every half-hour the child is awake whether the child is dry (D) or wet (W). Over a period of several days, this record can provide a pattern of elimination from which a program can be initiated.

Foxx and Azrin (1973) have developed a rapid toilet-training method with effective follow-up data. Their program has been successful with non-handicapped (Azrin & Foxx, 1974) and handicapped (Foxx & Azrin, 1973) children. The sequence of this method is outlined in Table 5–5.

Adaptations to any program may be required for children who have difficulty using a regular or child's toilet seat. Footrests may have to be added to a potty chair to provide proper support and to eliminate a feeling of "hanging in space." Additional support may have to be made to prevent

Table 5–4 Toilet Training Pretest

_____ 1. The child stays dry for several hours.

_____ 2. The child indicates he or she is about to urinate by facial or body expression.

_____ 3. The child ambulates sufficiently from one room to another with or without assistance.

_____ 4. The child can follow simple instructions, such as "Point to your nose, eyes," and so on or "Come here."

_____ 5. The child can sit in a chair up to five minutes at a time.

_____ 6. The child dislikes being soiled.

Source: M. Copeland, L. Ford, and N. Solon. *Occupational Therapy for Mentally Retarded Children* (Baltimore, Md.: University Park Press, 1976), p. 150.

Table 5–5 Sequence of Steps in the Bladder Training Procedure (Start exactly on the half-hour)

1. Give as much fluid to the resident as he or she will drink while seated in his or her chair.
   a. Wait about one minute.
2. Direct resident to sit on toilet seat using the minimal possible prompt.
3. Direct resident to pull his or her pants down using the minimal possible prompt.
4. a. When resident voids, give edible and verbal praise while seated, then direct him or her to stand.
   b. If resident does not void within 20 minutes after drinking the fluids, direct him or her to stand.
5. Direct resident to pull up pants using the minimal possible prompt.
   a. If resident voided, direct him or her to flush the toilet using the minimal possible prompt.
6. Direct resident to his or her chair using the minimal possible prompt.
7. After resident has been sitting for five minutes, inspect for dry pants.
   a. If pants are dry, give edible and verbal praise.
   b. If pants are wet, only show the edible and admonish.
8. Check resident for dry pants every five minutes.
9. At the end of 30 minutes, begin the sequence of steps again.

Source: R.M. Foxx and N.H. Azrin. *Toilet Training the Retarded* (Champaign, Ill.: Research Press, 1973), p. 45.

---

leg crossing. This can be done by having the child straddle a specially-made potty chair with a handle to hold on to for stability (Connor et al., 1978). See Figure 5–7 for design of the chair.

Feeding

It is not enough for a school to provide a nutritious lunch for all children; the developmentally delayed or neurologically impaired child may have a number of abnormal eating skills. Types of eating problems range from inability to suck or swallow, to ineptness in using utensils, to inability to handle a cafeteria tray (Wehman & Goodwyn, 1978). It is essential that along with knowledge of normal motor development teachers be cognizant of normal feeding sequences. Milestones of eating skills are in a developmental sequential order (Bunker, 1978; Copeland et al., 1976).

Identification of feeding difficulties are best assessed by one or more of a number of professionals (Holm, 1978). Physicians, physical therapists, speech therapists, occupational therapists, and nutritionists can provide valuable information and suggestions for the teacher to implement that will promote independence in eating and other related table skills. Without a proper feeding program, the process of eating can be a frustrating and exhausting task for both child and adult. Proper feeding patterns can im-

Figure 5–7 Specially Made Potty Chairs for Stability

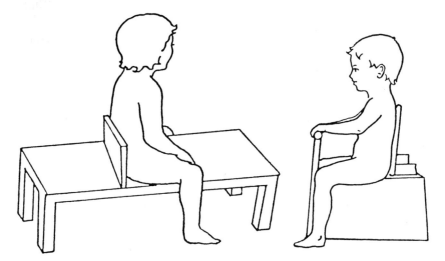

Source: F.P. Connor, G.G. Williamson, and J.M. Siepp. *Program Guide for Infants and Toddlers with Neuromotor and Other Disabilities* (New York, N.Y.: Teachers College Press, 1978), p. 356.

prove the child's attitude toward mealtime, ameliorate health problems, decrease drooling, and improve speech potential (Utley, Holvoet, & Barnes, 1977).

The following questions can cue the teacher of possible eating difficulties and provide a referral basis for further testing in this area:

- Is the child's muscle tone weak or stiff?

- When the child's head turns, are there involuntary movements of the arms?

- Can the child maintain an upright head position? For how long?

- Does the child's head movement appear normal?

- Does the child's head fall forward or to the side?

- Can the child maintain a sitting position without support of the arms?

- Does the child drool? Some of the time? All of the time?

- Can the child handle a regular spoon and bring food to the mouth?

- Does the child gag on liquid or solid food?

- Does the child have difficulty in swallowing liquids or solid foods?

- Does the child remove food or liquids using the teeth rather than the lips?

If a child is having problems with any of these items, further testing may be warranted.

Positioning

Copeland et al. (1976) emphasize that establishing the following body posture as soon as possible will minimize abnormal feeding patterns that are difficult to change as the child grows older:

- Adaptations should be made to the sides and back of chair with foam padding to assist in proper flexion of hips, knees, and ankles.

- The position of the head should be in a slightly downward direction.

- The height of the table should be high enough for arm support if needed.

Swallowing

This is one of the most common feeding difficulties. To aid swallowing, the following steps should be taken:

- Place the child's head in a slightly downward position.
- Initially, use only a small amount of liquid in a glass.
- Place rim of glass on the child's lips; do not allow child to bite down on the glass with the teeth.

Tongue/Jaw Control

Problems encountered while eating include chewing with the mouth open, pushing food out with the tongue (called tongue thrust), gagging as the food is placed on the tongue, and biting down on the spoon before removing food. The following techniques will help decrease abnormal tongue and lip behavior:

- Present small amounts of food on the front half of the spoon (teaspoon or baby spoon) directly in front of the child.

- Sit in front of the child, and place thumb below the child's lower lip, index finger at the side of the jaw, and the third finger under the chin (Finnie, 1975). Jaw movements can be manipulated by opening and closing the mouth in this manner.

- Lip closure is obtained by sitting on the left side of the child and bringing right arm around the child's shoulders. Place thumb at the jaw, index finger on the upper lip, and the middle finger on the lower lip. With this position, removing food with the lips and keeping the tongue inside the mouth can be obtained (Finnie, 1975).

Spoon Feeding

Many children have difficulty maintaining a grasp, scooping food onto the spoon, and bringing the food to the mouth. The objective of independent spoon feeding is easily broken down into training steps as outlined in Table 5–6 (Copeland et al., 1976). A sample data sheet for using a spoon is detailed in Figure 5–8. General guidelines are as follows:

- Adaptations to the spoon make it easier to scoop food onto the spoon.

- Allow the child to decide which hand to use (Wehman & Goodwyn, 1978).

- Food should be removed with the lips and not the teeth.

Any type of feeding problem can be broken down into chaining steps that incorporate physical prompting, fading methods, reinforcing appropriate behavior, and charting changes in the child's current functional level.

DO NOT GIVE UP

Normal motor development follows a gradual but steady sequential growth. The growth pattern of many mentally and physically handicapped children follows a similar line but at a slower rate with limited quantity and quality of those skills that are learned. Without early training at the infant and preschool level, many of these children fall further and further behind in motor skill acquisitions.

As mentioned earlier, delays in motor skills will develop deficiencies in language, social, and academic development. However, the time spent in proper positioning of the child and materials, as well as designing specific

Table 5–6 Training Steps in Spoon-Feeding Program

Trainer	Child
Step A:	
1. Places child's hand around spoon handle.	1.
2. Assists to fill spoon.	2.
3. Guides child's hand to mouth.	3.
4. Inserts food into mouth.	4.
5. May assist.	5. Removes food with lips.
6. Returns spoon to plate.	6.
Step B:	
1. Places child's hand around spoon handle.	1.
2. Assists to fill spoon.	2.
3. Brings food to 3″ of mouth.	3.
4. May assist.	4. Inserts food into mouth.
5.	5. Removes food with lips.
6. Returns spoon to plate.	6.
Step C:	
1. Places child's hand around spoon handle.	1.
2. Assists to fill spoon.	2.
3. Brings food ½ way to 3″ from mouth.	3.
4. May assist.	4. Brings food 3″ from mouth.
5.	5. Inserts food into mouth.
6.	6. Removes food with lips.
7. Returns spoon to plate.	7.
Step D:	
1. Places child's hand around spoon handle.	1.
2. Assists to fill spoon.	2.
3. Brings food ½ way from plate.	3.
4. May assist.	4. Brings food ½ way to mouth.
5.	5. Inserts food into mouth.
6.	6. Removes food with lips.
7. Returns spoon to plate.	7.
Step E:	
1. Places child's hand around spoon handle.	1.
2. Assists to fill spoon.	2.
3. May assist.	3. Brings food from plate to mouth.
4.	4. Inserts food into mouth.
5.	5. Removes food with lips.
6. Returns spoon to plate.	6.
Step F:	
1. Places child's hand around spoon handle.	1.
2. May assist.	2. Fills spoon with food.
3.	3. Brings food from plate to mouth.
4.	4. Inserts food into mouth.
5.	5. Removes food with lips.
6. Returns spoon to plate half way.	6.
7.	7. Returns spoon rest of way.

Table 5–6 continued

Step G:

1. May assist.	1. Places hand around spoon handle.
2.	2. Fills spoon with food.
3.	3. Brings food from plate to mouth.
4.	4. Inserts food into mouth.
5.	5. Removes food with lips.
6. May assist.	6. Returns spoon to plate all the way.

Step H:

1.	1. Places hand around spoon handle.
2.	2. Fills spoon with food.
3.	3. Brings food from plate to mouth.
4.	4. Inserts food into mouth.
5.	5. Removes food with lips.
6. Touch wrists lightly with downward tap.	6.
7.	7. Returns spoon to plate.

Source: M. Copeland, L. Ford, and N. Solon. *Occupational Therapy for Mentally Retarded Children* (Baltimore, Md.: University Park Press, 1976), p. 148.

---

behavioral programs, will assist in decreasing the deficiencies in these other areas also.

Teachers must realize that motor progression for these children takes time, and the increments achieved will be gradual with periodic stages of leveling off. The goals may vary only slightly from one period to another. Therefore, teachers must be careful not to set goals and criterion levels so high that they are never met. Teachers must work closely with parents, not just on academic and social achievements, but on functional skills (dressing, eating, and toileting) as well. In fact, achieving functional skills for their child may be the primary objective of the parents. Training the parents to carry out the same behavioral steps at home can greatly change the motivational attitude of the child, thus improving academic ability.

Flexibility is the key word when setting up any type of motor program. Learning to adapt to the child's moods and to the materials available may be the turning point in increasing the child's motor skills. When in doubt, teachers should seek advice from the therapists within the school district. Above all, they should not give up. The range of the child's independent motor potential lies to a great extent in the ability of the teacher to seek all avenues possible in designing and acquiring an overall successful motor program.

Figure 5–8 Sample Data Sheet for Using a Spoon

Name: Trainer: Session number:

Date: Task: Feeding   Trials completed:

Trials

Subtasks	1	2	3	4	5	6	7	8	9	10
1. Places hand around spoon handle.										
2. Fills spoon with food.										
3. Brings food 3″ from mouth.										
4. Brings food halfway to mouth.										
5. Brings food from plate to mouth.										
6. Inserts food into mouth.										
7. Removes food with lips.										
8. Returns spoon to plate half way.										
9. Returns spoon to plate all the way.										
10.										

Code: + = independent; A = assistance; − = failed.

Source: M. Copeland, L. Ford, and N. Solon. *Occupational Therapy for Mentally Retarded Children* (Baltimore, Md.: University Park Press, 1976), p. 149.

REFERENCES

Allen, K.E. *Mainstreaming in early childhood education.* Albany, N.Y.: Delmar Publisher, 1980.

Ayres, A.J. *Sensory integration and learning disorders.* Los Angeles, Cal.: Western Psychological Services, 1972.

Azrin, N.H., and Foxx, R.M. *Toilet training in less than a day.* New York: Simon & Schuster, 1974.

Baumgartner, B. Goals for self-help and independence. In W.B. Stephens (Ed.), *Training the developmentally young.* New York: John Day, 1971.

Bayley, N. *The Bayley scales of infant development.* New York: Psychological Corporation, 1969.

Best, G.A. *Individuals with physical disabilities.* St. Louis: The C. V. Mosby Company, 1978.

Blackhurst, A.E., and Berdine, W.H. *An introduction to special education.* Boston: Little, Brown and Company, 1981.

Blackwell, M.W. *Care of the mentally retarded.* Boston: Little, Brown and Company, 1979.

Bobath, K., and Bobath, B. Cerebral palsy. In P.H. Pearson and C.E. Williams (Eds.), *Physical therapy services in the developmental disabilities* (fifth printing). Springfield, Ill.: Charles C. Thomas, 1972.

Brigance, A.H. *Brigance diagnostic inventory of early development.* North Billerica, Me.: Curriculum Associates, Inc., 1978.

Bunker, L.K. Motor skills. In M.E. Snell (Ed.), *Systematic instruction of the moderately and severely handicapped.* Columbus, Ohio: Charles E. Merrill Publishing Company, 1978.

Cohen, M.A., Gross, P.J., and Haring, N.G. Development pinpoints. In N.G. Haring and L.J. Brown (Eds.), *Teaching the severely handicapped* (Vol. 1). New York: Grune and Stratton, 1976.

Connor, F.P., Williamson, G.G., and Siepp, J.M. *Program guide for infants and toddlers with neuromotor and other developmental disabilities.* New York: Teachers College Press, 1978.

Copeland, M., Ford, L., and Solon, N. *Occupational therapy for mentally retarded children.* Baltimore, Md.: University Park Press, 1976.

Cratty, B.J. *Perceptual and motor development in infants and children* (2nd ed.). Englewood Cliffs, N.J.: Prentice-Hall, 1979.

Dmitriev, V. Motor and cognitive development in early education. In N.G. Haring (Ed.), *Behavior of exceptional children: An introduction to special education.* Columbus, Ohio: Charles E. Merrill Publishing Company, 1974.

Espenschade, A.S., and Echkert, H.M. *Motor development.* Columbus, Ohio: Charles E. Merrill Publishing Company, 1978.

Fallen, N.H., with McGovern, J.E. *Young children with special needs.* Columbus, Ohio: Charles E. Merrill Publishing Company, 1978.

Fiorentino, M.R. *Normal and abnormal development.* Springfield, Ill.: Charles C. Thomas, 1972.

Fiorentino, M.R. *Reflex testing methods for evaluating c.n.s. development.* Springfield, Ill.: Charles C. Thomas, 1973.

Finnie, N.P. *Handling the young cerebral palsied child at home* (2nd ed.). New York: E.P. Dutton, 1975.

Foxx, R.M., and Azrin, N.H. *Toilet training the retarded.* Champaign, Ill.: Research Press, 1973.

Frankenburg, W.K., and Dodds, J.B. The Denver developmental screening test. *Journal of Pediatrics,* 1967, *71,* 181–191.

Galka, G., and Fraser, B. A. *Gross motor management of severely multiply impaired students.* Baltimore, Md.: University Park Press, 1980.

Gesell, A., and Amatruda, C.S. *Developmental diagnosis.* New York: Paul B. Hoeber, Inc., 1962.

Griffen, P., Sanford, A., and Wilson, D. *Learning accomplishment profile* (diagnostic ed.). Winston-Salem, N.C.: Kaplan School Supply Corporation, 1975.

Herr, D.A., and Goodwyn, R.L. Motor skills. In N.H. Fallen (Ed.), *Young children with special needs.* Columbus, Ohio: Charles E. Merrill Publishing Company, 1978.

Hayden, A.H. Perspectives of early education in special education. In N.G. Haring (Ed.), *Behavior of exceptional children: An introduction to special education.* Columbus, Ohio: Charles E. Merrill Publishing Company, 1974.

Holm, V.A. The pediatrician with a special interest in child development. In K.E. Allen, V.A. Holm, and R.L. Schiefelbusch (Eds.), *Early intervention—A team approach.* Baltimore, Md.: University Park Press, 1978, pp. 147–168.

Illingworth, R.S. *The development of the infant and young child: Abnormal and normal.* New York: Churchill Livingstone Inc., 1980.

Isam, A., and Gruber, J. *Motor aptitude and intellectual performance.* Columbus, Ohio: Charles E. Merrill Publishing Company, 1968.

Johnson, V.M., and Werner, R.A. *A step-by-step learning guide for retarded infants and children.* Syracuse, N.Y.: Syracuse University Press, 1975.

Johnston, R.B., and Magrab, P.R. (Eds.). *Developmental disorders: Assessment, treatment, education.* Baltimore, Md.: University Park Press, 1976.

Kephart, N. C. *The slow learner in the classroom.* Columbus, Ohio: Charles E. Merrill Publishing Company, Second Edition, 1971.

Koontz, C.W. *Koontz child developmental program: Training activities for the first 48 months.* Los Angeles, Cal.: Western Psychological Services, 1974.

Levy, J. *The baby exercise book.* New York: Pantheon Books, 1973.

Lohman, W., Eyman, R., and Lask, E. Toilet training. *American Journal of Mental Deficiency,* 1967, *71,* 551–557.

Montgomery, P., and Richter, E. *Sensorimotor integration for developmentally disabled children: A handbook.* Los Angeles, Cal.: Western Psychological Services, 1978.

Project FEATT. *Next steps together* (video series). Lafayette, Ind.: Purdue University, 1976.

de Quiros, B., and Scharager, O.L. *Neuropsychological fundamentals in learning disabilities.* San Rafael, Cal.: Academic Therapy Publications, 1978.

Robinson, C.C., and Robinson, J.H. Sensorimotor functions and cognitive development. In M.E. Snell (Ed.), *Systematic instruction of the moderately and severely handicapped.* Columbus, Ohio: Charles E. Merrill Publishing Company, 1978.

Snell, M.E. *Systematic instruction of the moderately and severely handicapped.* Columbus, Ohio: Charles E. Merrill Publishing Company, 1978.

Sukiennicki, D.A. Neuromotor development. In B.S. Banus (Ed.), *The developmental therapist.* Thorofare, N.J.: Charles B. Slack, Inc., 1971.

Utley, B., Holvoet, J., and Barnes, K. Handling, positioning and feeding the physically handicapped. In E. Sontag (Ed.), *Educational programing for severely and profoundly handicapped.* Reston, Va.: Division on Mental Retardation, Council for Exceptional Children, 1977.

Vulpe, S.G. *Vulpe assessment battery* (2nd ed.). Toronto, Ontario: Canadian Association for the Mentally Retarded, 1977.

Wehman, P., and Goodwyn, R.L. Self-help skill development. In N.H. Fallen (Ed.), *Young children with special needs.* Columbus, Ohio: Charles E. Merrill Publishing Company, 1978.

Zaichkowsky, L.D., Zaichkowsky, L.B., and Martinex, T.J. *Growth and development: The child and physical activity.* St. Louis: The C. V. Mosby Company, 1980.

Chapter 6

Language Skills in Young Children, and the Management of Common Problems*

Betty Hart

OVERVIEW

There are many language skills young children need to learn. They need to learn pronunciation, grammar, and vocabulary. They need to learn to express ideas, to listen, to tell stories, and to ask and answer questions. By the time most children come to an early childhood setting, they have already learned basic skills in each of these areas. Some children may still have difficulty pronouncing certain sounds, and most children will have limited vocabulary. Story telling may be limited to several sentences describing an event that occurred outside the early childhood setting, but the basics in each of the skill areas are present.

If children have not acquired these basic language skills by the time they come to an early childhood setting, they are likely to need special help. After about age three, children who never talk, who cannot imitate, whose speech is unrelated to ongoing events, or whose words cannot be understood by other than family members usually need some one-to-one training in basic langauge skills. Teachers seldom have the time or the specialized skills required to conduct such training. Instead, in such cases, teachers work with the communication or speech and langauge therapist to help such children practice, in their everyday interactions in the early childhood setting, the skills taught in the special, one-to-one training sessions.

The teacher's basic task is to help all children, each in terms of individual skill level, practice using the skills they have already acquired. To this end, teachers arrange for children to listen to stories; to narrate and describe

*This work was supported by a grant (HD 03144) from the National Institute of Child Health and Human Development to the Bureau of Child Research and the Department of Human Development and Family Life at the University of Kansas.

during show-and-tell; and to increase concept-related vocabulary through counting, naming colors, and describing natural events and objects. In addition, they arrange for language learning to occur throughout the children's day. They provide children with many and varied materials and activities to talk about, and a variety of adults and children with whom to practice using language. Early childhood settings thus provide opportunities for children to practice the skills they already have, not training in basic skills.

RATIONALE

Language use is a social skill. Individuals talk because they have something they want to say to someone else. Only in special circumstances do individuals talk in order to display pronunciation, grammar, or vocabulary; these aspects of language are used in the service of communicating a message to someone else. Individuals use certain words, pronounce them in certain ways, and present them in a certain order so that a hearer can understand a message and respond (Creider, 1979). Different social purposes call for different words, pronounced and arranged in sentences in different ways. Asking for directions when lost, for instance, requires that an individual use a somewhat different kind of language than does casual interaction among friends at a party.

Communication involves a hearer as well as a speaker; what is said and how it is said depends on who the hearer is. Even four year olds, for instance, simplify the language they use to children younger than themselves (Shatz & Gelman, 1973). By the age of three, children are using language not only to express their individuality, but to comment on who they see the hearer to be, to manipulate, and to get something (if only attention) from the hearer, all at the same time (Halliday, 1975). Speakers use language for several purposes at once, often deliberately, so that hearers can choose the meaning they prefer (Streeck, 1980). Speakers often use politeness strategies, for example, in order to give and get simultaneously. Thus, before making a major request, a speaker is likely to prepare the hearer with some expression of interest, friendship, or sympathy (Brown & Levinson, 1978).

Once children have learned basic language skills, it is these sophisticated, socialized uses of language that they need to learn. They need to learn how to use language in order to assert and defend, to make friends and resolve conflicts, to explain, to persuade, and to participate in play and pretending. Equally important, they need to learn how to use language in order to display knowledge, to question and inquire, and to organize and express ideas and experiences so as to attract or compel hearers to respond in ways that lead to increases in knowledge, ideas, and experience.

It is these sophisticated, socialized, uses of language that early childhood settings and teachers are uniquely prepared to teach. The setting provides many different people—peers and adults—and many different materials and activities for children to try out talking to and about. The opportunities available to children in early childhood settings for trying out how language works are more varied than in the children's homes or in the schools the children will attend later. This richness of opportunities is made available to children just at the time when they most need and are most ready to learn sophisticated skills for using language in social interaction. Also, the expertise of early childhood teachers lies expressly in their skills for arranging such opportunities and helping children take advantage of them. Thus, the focus of teaching language skills in early childhood settings is on children's social use of language throughout the day.

BASIC PRINCIPLES

The basic principle in talking is contextual control; individuals must say "the right thing in the right way at the right time and the right place in accordance with the norms of their society" (Ervin-Tripp, 1971, p. 37). If they do not, hearers do not understand. No matter how good the pronunciation, grammar, and vocabulary, for instance, French will not be understood by those who speak English exclusively. At a gas station, individuals can use only a limited set of the vocabulary they know. The language they use has to match the circumstances of use in order to be judged appropriate. Just as speakers have learned appropriate ways of talking, hearers have learned how to respond. When hearers do not know how to respond (for example, to an individual who continually talks about invaders from Mars), institutionalization of the speaker is often the result.

Unless their language is deviant, children who enter early childhood settings have already learned this basic principle. Parents tend to focus in the early stages of language acquisition, not on correct grammar and pronunciation, but on "truth value" (Brown & Hanlon, 1970), the essential match between what is said and what is being talked about. For instance, if a child says, "Dat a dog," a parent is likely to correct the child, not for saying "Dat" instead of "That is," but for saying "Dog" when talking about a cat or a horse. The child's use of "Dat," however mispronounced, is matched to the context of talking about a cat, horse, or dog; only the label for the animal is mismatched.

Since what is said must be matched to the immediate context (what is being talked about), the talk has to change each time the context changes.

Thus, what is said must change with each change in the topic, material, or activity talked about, with each change in hearer, and with each utterance and hearer response. Everything a person says changes the situation in some way—adds information, asks for an answer, directs to action — so that both hearer and speaker have to adjust subsequent talk in terms of that change.

When children enter an early childhood setting, the new context calls for new ways of talking. Children have to learn to talk to new people about new topics and old ones. Some children may have to learn about the "right time" for talking in the new setting, for example, when they must share teacher attention or wait to comment until the story is over. Other children may have to learn about the "right place," for example, that they must learn to talk more (or less) politely in the early childhood setting than at home. The teacher's major task in helping children improve their language skills is helping children learn how to match their talk to the new demands and conditions for talk within the early childhood setting.

The first step in helping children learn is assessment. The teachers should begin by evaluating the levels of skill children already have. To assess children's skill at talking, the teachers should look at the following four aspects of each child's talk: (1) amount, how much and how often the child talks; (2) topic, what the child talks about; (3) cues, who the child talks to, when, and where; and (4) effects, what happens when the child talks. Teachers should isolate problems by looking at these aspects and decide on problem-solving strategies.

Amount

How much a child talks is likely to be the best single indicator of the level of the child's language skill. Highly talkative children have been found to have more sophisticated language skills than children who seldom talk. Highly talkative children use more different words and have larger vocabularies (Hart & Risley, 1980). They also test as significantly superior on measures of articulation, grammar, and receptive syntax (Landon & Sommers, 1979).

Highly talkative children are children who tend to notice and either inquire about or comment on everything that happens. They are children who persist in asking why, and their feelings will be hurt if the teacher or other children do not have time to listen to the complete story of what they did yesterday. These are children who work with language all the time, trying to find out things, to describe, to express, and to influence. Each time they talk, they get feedback. The feedback lets them know whether they chose the correct vocabulary, put the question in the correct way, or described an event of real interest to the hearer. Because they have sophisticated skills, they get frequent positive feedback, so that they can usually accept correction or criticism of their language and profit from it with hardly a pause in their overall rate of talking.

Children who seldom talk tend to be children who use language primarily when there is something they really want or need. They tend not to call attention to themselves and talk little about their personal experiences and ideas. They often wait patiently in silence to be helped or to be included in some activity. When they do talk, it is often about many of the same topics (things they really need or want). Much of their talk, especially to other children, is likely to consist of demands. Because of this, teachers see them as needing to learn social interaction skills, as well as language skills.

Because appropriate language is matched to the context of use, the more things and events children talk about, the more different words they use. The more different relationships children talk about, such as past happenings and future possibilities, the more different sentence structures are needed in order to express those relationships. The more often children compete for hearer attention, the more likely they are to employ clauses in order to pack maximum information into a minimum of utterances. The more often children talk, the more often they explore what language can do.

Topics

What children talk about in an early childhood setting is to a considerable extent determined by what there is to talk about. The richer the variety of materials and activities available in a setting, the richer the language the children use in the setting will be in topics.

Therefore, each setting must be evaluated in terms of what it offers children as topics for talk, and how interesting and compelling to talk the classroom and activities are. Also, the setting must be assessed in terms of its facilitation of talk, that is, who there is to talk to, how available and responsive those hearers are, whether activity areas are arranged to promote face-to-face interaction, whether there are enough materials so that several children can use them cooperatively, and how much free play-time is available for children to choose topics and partners for conversation and pretending.

When the topics in children's talk are restricted, it almost always indicates that the children are restricting their activities and interactions. Even in a classroom rich in attractive materials and activities, there may be children whose participation tends to be hesitant and minimal; such children are often those who also talk little. However, whether the cause of restriction may be attributed to lack of stimulating activities and materials or to lack of child contact to those activities and materials, the topics in children's talk can be made more varied only through getting children interested in more varied things. For some children, it is sufficient merely to introduce new materials for them to explore and talk about. For other children, it may involve long-term teacher efforts to expand the child's interests, both in doing things and in talking about them.

Cues

The more people children talk to, and the more times and places they talk, the more opportunities they have to learn what is the right thing said in the right way at the right time and the right place. Children generalize language skill by trying out how language works in many different places with many different people. They learn, for instance, that different kinds of politeness work better to get the cooperation of adults, that sitting on Santa Claus' knee calls for talk on certain topics, and that indirect threats (such as, "If you do that, you're going to get hurt.") are less likely to be punished than direct ones (such as, "I'm going to hurt you."). Each time children try out language, they get feedback about how well matched that language is to the norms of their society.

When children come into an early childhood setting, they bring with them what they have learned about when, where, and to whom to talk; for some children this may or may not be the right thing for the new place. A cue, such as a teacher question that evokes talk from one child, may, for another child, be a cue for silence because the teacher is still one of the strangers to whom the child has learned not to talk or because the child has learned that adults only ask questions when something is wrong. Some children have learned that "Why?" is a question that adults cannot resist answering. Others have learned that children are much more receptive, interested, and uncritical hearers than adults.

One of the goals in early childhood settings is that children acquire generalized language skill and that they be able to use language effectively with many different people in many different places at many different times. A necessary aspect of generalized language skill is the ability to talk about a variety of topics with those different people and to talk as much or as little as is appropriate. Generalized language skill is the ability to talk about the right topics with the right people in the right amount at the right time and place. What is "right" is defined by the norms of the society. The society is the person, or persons, who respond.

Effects

People (society) define what is right by how they respond. It is the hearers who have already learned the norms of their society who determine how the language of the next generation will work and thus transmit the culture (Halliday, 1978). Hearers tend to respond automatically to language that is right, that is, appropriately matched to the context of use. For instance, when they hear someone say, "Pass the salt," at the dinner table, they usually pass the salt. Saying "Pass the salt," when what the speaker wants is the mustard, is likely to be tolerated only from non-English-speakers and small children.

Because the adults with whom a child lives define what is right by how they respond, all children who enter an early childhood setting must assume that the language that they have learned is right. Highly talkative children, for instance, can be assumed to have learned that talking is right. Children who seldom talk have probably learned that it is right to talk only when they really have something to say. Children whose speech is largely incomprehensible to teachers are often readily understood and responded to by hearers at home.

Teachers also define what is right by how they respond. What is right in the early childhood setting may be somewhat different from what is right at home for some children. Some children may need to talk more or less; some may need to learn to talk to more different people about more different things. To help children learn the new ways of talking that are right in the early childhood setting, teachers cue, guide, and prompt children in what to say when and to whom so that the children can experience how language works in the new setting. Teachers deliberately arrange that different ways of talking work better to get from hearers the kinds of responses the children want.

However, when children have already learned a right way (such as, speaking English), learning a new right way (such as, speaking French) for the new setting can take considerable time. Teachers have to be patient and persistent about prompting and responding to the new right way, rather than to the old. It is relatively easy for young children to learn to speak French, for instance, in settings where no one speaks English. It is made clear to such children every time they speak that French is right, for nothing else works to get a positive response. It takes much longer, usually, to learn to speak French among hearers who understand English. Because hearers understand, they tend to respond automatically; it is difficult to fake true incomprehension.

Teachers in an early childhood setting are likely to be in the position of English-speakers trying to help English-speaking children learn to talk in

French. They are likely to find it difficult to be consistent and to respond only when a child uses a new right way of talking. Teachers often do understand what a nonverbal child or a child with incomprehensible speech is trying to communicate, for it is often apparent from what the child is doing. Even when it is not, teachers have often attended to the child before they realize that the child's words are incomprehensible or that the child has not vocalized. Thus, even while trying to change the language a child is using, teachers tend to continue to respond to the old, inappropriate uses of language in ways that make that language continue to work for the child.

The basic principle in talking is contextual control; talking depends on the immediate situation. Children talk because the setting cues talking; there are a variety of interesting things to talk about, there is time for talking, and there are interested and responsive listeners. How much children talk depends on how receptive they are to the cues for talking. How receptive children are depends on what happens (and has happened in the past) when they talk.

Because talking depends on the immediate situation, teachers can change talking. They can change the immediate situation by changing the cues for talking, introducing more stimulating materials, giving children more time, or becoming more responsive as listeners. As more responsive listeners, they change what happens when children talk.

Assessment

Basic to making a change in how children talk is assessment. Assessment takes several forms. One form of assessment is the routine evaluation teachers make for each child shortly after a period of adaptation to the early childhood setting. This may consist of each teacher rating each child's level of language skill on a list of language behaviors. The language behaviors listed are those that constitute the objectives for language learning in the early childhood setting. They are likely to include the following behaviors:

- uses grammar and vocabulary appropriately

- pronounces words clearly

- talks to both teachers and children

- waits for a turn to speak

- responds to questions

- listens when others talk

- follows directions

- expresses needs, ideas, and feelings.

Since the majority of children develop normally, such early assessment should show that most children have basic skills in each of these language areas and use them most of the time.

If children appear to lack basic skills in one or more of the language areas, additional assessment is needed. Teachers refer the child to a language and communication specialist for the kind of professional assessment described by Reike and Thompson (1978). Teachers do not normally have the special skills and equipment necessary for making a professional assessment. Rather, they depend on the language and communication specialist both to assess the child's current skill levels and to recommend the changes that need to be made within the classroom in order to help the child learn new ways of talking.

A third form of assessment is the impromptu evaluation that teachers normally make every time a child speaks. Teachers need to be aware that, as normal hearers, they are quickly and informally assessing a speaker's language prior to every response that each of us makes. When children's language is appropriate, teachers' responses seem automatic. Teachers answer spontaneously because the child has said the right thing in the right way at the right time and place. Thus teachers can use their own behavior to evaluate a child's language skill. They can talk about how frequently they have to wait for a child and how frequently they have to prompt, repeat a statement, or ask for clarification.

Most of the common problems that teachers encounter with how children talk are assessed in this informal way. Just as teachers recognize normal developmental levels of basic language skill, they recognize common lags in development and learned ways of speaking that have become inappropriate. They recognize that most common problems, such as stammering, refusal to answer, reluctance to speak, or monopolizing a teacher's attention with talk, are problems likely to appear at one time or another, more or less frequently, for all children. These kinds of problems are so commonly encountered that they are considered "normal." They are not seen by teachers as requiring formal assessment procedures or the design of formal remediation strategies. They are the kinds of problems that teachers informally assess in the course of their everyday interactions with children and routinely respond to in ways that result in change and improvement in the children's language.

Making Changes

The basic principle in making change is how the teacher responds. How teachers respond is a matter of what they do before children talk and what they do after. Before children talk, teachers set the stage for talking. They respond to children's skill levels and interests by arranging a classroom full of things the children will want to talk about and people the children will want to talk to. To change the way children talk, the teachers change the setting. They add new materials and activities in order to give children new topics for talk or to reduce arguments over possession of materials in short supply.

They prompt changed ways of talking directly and indirectly. They tell children directly what to say by modeling the correct answer during group instruction before asking the question or by supplying children with appropriate verbalizations for getting things and for keeping them. They prompt indirectly by rearranging the situation. In other words, they give one child some special material in order to increase the likelihood that other children will accept or make contact with that child, or they assign to separate activity groups a bossy child and an overly compliant one.

Teachers respond to inappropriate ways of talking by changing the cues for talking whenever possible. They change materials, combinations of children, and available activities. They then use these changes to prompt, directly and indirectly, more sophisticated ways of talking. Changing the cues for talk challenges teachers to use their ingenuity to make subtle changes that result in more sophisticated child uses of language.

Teachers can also change the ways children talk by what they do after children talk. They can arrange what effects the children's talk produces. What they can arrange to happen after children talk will inevitably be one of the following three types of events: (1) something good (positive reinforcement); (2) something bad (punishment); or (3) nothing (extinction). Before children talk, children can choose what looks "good" among all the prompts and cues for talk that teachers have arranged; they can avoid the "bad" and what has "nothing" of interest for them. After they have talked, however, they no longer can choose what happens; what happens is up to the hearer.

The principles of reinforcement apply to talking in the same way they apply to any other behavior. Positive responses tend to increase talking; punishment tends to decrease it. Ignoring is likely to lead to an initial increase (for example, the speaker begins to nag), followed by a gradual decrease. Also, as with any other behavior, what is a positive or a punishing response to talking can be determined only by looking at the change in a child's rate of talking. What is a positive response for one child, for instance, may be punishing to another. What looks positive to a teacher may actually be punishing to a child.

Often, after a child has already said something, teachers find themselves in a position of trying to distinguish for the child between what was said (the message) and how it was said (the grammar, pronunciation, or vocabulary). For instance, teachers may respond positively to a child's message ("That's good that you said, 'Those are mine,' instead of hitting"), while at the same time responding negatively to its form ("But you need to say, 'Those *cars* are mine'; we both thought you meant the animals, since you're building a zoo"). The distinction between message and form is extremely difficult for children (and even adults) to make after the fact. All speakers always have the choice of whether or not to talk, and a great many speakers, rather than learning to pay attention to how they talk, simply choose to talk as seldom as possible to those hearers who regularly criticize the way they talk.

Teachers have to be careful about punishing children for talking. If talking is punished or ignored too often, children may stop talking, at least to teachers, which leaves teachers with little behavior to work with. It is for this reason that teachers should try never to simply criticize. (For instance, they should never tell children, "Don't say, 'ain't.' ") What they should do is prompt. They should select those times when there is something a child wants, because those are the times when a child is most likely to repeat a message in order to get the hearer's cooperation. Then, before the teacher responds to the child's message (and gives what the child wants), the teacher should prompt. Thus, teachers should correct the form of a child's talk by delaying the effects of the child's talk for just a moment. They should prompt a corrected form so that they can make something positive happen in response to that corrected form. When teachers do not criticize, but instead prompt the correct form and respond positively to it, they tend to increase not only the probability of the child's learning that form, but the child's willingness to repeat and try a better form.

PROBLEM AREAS AND SOLUTIONS

Low Rate of General Talk

One of the language goals for children in early childhood settings is that they talk frequently. Children who talk frequently and appropriately may pretend with other children and respond to nearly everything other children say with some contribution of their own. They may spend a long period in silence as they work a puzzle or draw a picture, but if a teacher comes to attend, they are likely to give a running commentary on everything they do. Frequent users of language tend to learn more sophisticated language skills without any planned or direct teaching. Each time they talk they set the occasion for learning from the feedback others provide. Each time they talk they must adapt their talk to the immediate circumstances of talk, to the hearer, and to what the hearer has said or is likely to want to hear. The more often children practice using language, the more often they practice noticing the social, hearer, and setting cues to which sophisticated language must be adapted.

Low rate of general talk may characterize a group of children or a few children within a group. It should be pointed out that teachers have a problem with the low rate of talk among a group of children if, well into a program, the teachers are talking more than the children. (A high rate of teacher talking is appropriate only during group story or instruction times.) There seems to be a certain ambient noise level in unstructured social settings such as free play; teachers can readily judge whose voices are creating this ambiance by remaining silent for several minutes. If the ambient noise level is not markedly reduced, it may be that only certain children have low rates of talking. Such children are often those who do more watching than participating in play; who often play with materials such as blocks, crayons, or puzzles that can be used alone; and who call teachers' attention to what they do but have little to say when teachers do attend.

Low rate of general talk is a problem that must be dealt with before teachers can plan any other targets for language remediation. Promoting high rates of general talk ensures that children are practicing language and are learning its social uses without direct teacher intervention. This frees teachers to focus on the problems of individual children. With individual children targeted for intervention, teachers also need to get fairly high rates of general talk so that when they reduce the rate of a particular kind of talk, the children still have plenty of talk left to be positively responded to and so that talking as a behavior does not cease.

The first step in promoting high rates of general talk is arranging the setting to cue language use. Teachers should arrange a classroom rich in attractive materials and activities that children will be interested in contacting and talking about. Then teachers should begin making themselves cues for talk. When children are new to a program, teachers should give them a great deal of feedback, letting them know that what they are doing is the "right thing" throughout every program activity. This continuous early feedback not only establishes appropriate patterns of play and participation among the children, but establishes the teachers as people who notice the right thing, and frequently and openly approve.

Once teachers have established themselves as responsive and approving, they can use their attention as a cue. When children are interested in their attention, teachers can begin to let the children know that, though they are generally responsive and approving of all appropriate child activity, they are particularly so when that activity is combined with talking. Thus, teachers should begin to watch children's play with interest, but in silence; if the children do not feel like talking, the teachers should not impose talk on them. However, if a child speaks, a teacher should move immediately to that child. Teachers should show children over and over in this way that the most effective means of getting and holding teacher attention is talking. When teachers go to children who are talking, they should attend without interrupting, showing all the children that they are more interested in hearing children talk than in talking themselves. Rather than modeling what a good speaker does, teachers should focus on modeling for children what a good listener does.

When teachers have established themselves as cues for talking, for example, when they come and attend to a child's play, the child is likely to initiate a comment about the play (such as, about a block building, "This is a house."). Teachers can then begin to use the consequences of talking to increase the overall frequency of talking. They can plan that what happens when children talk is something that leads to more talk. One procedure that is easy and based on what parents of well-developing children naturally do (White, 1978), is incidental teaching (Hart & Risley, 1978). When a child initiates talk for example, by commenting, "This is a house.", the teacher can then take up the child's chosen topic and ask the child to say more. The teacher can say, for instance, "A house? Who lives there?" If the child answers, the teacher can ask for still further information or comment. The teacher's goal should be to explore the topic with the child by asking the kinds of questions that will keep the conversation going. When the child stops talking or changes the subject (perhaps because the teacher's question was one the child did not know how to respond to or was uninterested in responding to), the teacher should accept the child's choice and go along with the change of subject or the choice of silence.

In incidental teaching, teachers focus on being positively responsive to children's talk. Teachers show children that what they are most interested in talking about at any particular moment is whatever the children are most interested in talking about. Teachers also show that they are interested in talking about the topic just as long as the children are. Teachers model what a highly attentive and responsive listener does when a speaker is talking about something the listener is particularly interested in. Teachers give feedback that shows that they are really listening and interested. They frequently, for instance, repeat part of the speaker's statement before adding their own. Seldom do they make vague comments that suggest that they may not have really listened or understood what the speaker said.

When teachers repeatedly let children know that they are interested in hearing the children comment, question, inform, and explain, high rates of talk to teachers result. When children are talking frequently, this creates the conditions for generalization. When teachers are responsive and interested in what children have to say, children begin to tell them more and more both about what they are currently doing and about what happened to them in other places and at other times. Children begin asking questions, both to hold teachers' attention and because they are genuinely curious. As they talk about more different things in more different ways, their language skills improve. Also, the more children talk, the more likely they are to talk to one another, to respond to one another's topics, and to explore common interests found through talk.

The Child Who Won't Answer

Some children may have adequate general rates of talking, and may readily initiate to teachers and carry on a conversation when they have chosen the topic. However, when a teacher initiates to them by asking a question, they do not answer. It is important that children learn to answer direct questions. They need to talk about their problems with other children, for instance, so that teachers can help them learn new ways of handling social interaction. Also, it is crucial to success in later schooling that children be able to display knowledge on request and answer information questions (questions for which there is a single right answer, one that the asker already knows). Teachers often ask information questions in order not only to find out whether a child knows the right answer, but to discover where a child is having difficulty. When teachers can determine the nature of a child's misunderstanding, they are in a better position to help the child learn a right understanding. They depend on children, however, to let them know.

Children who talk freely on their own but fall silent when asked a question are probably children for whom adult questions have in the past set the occasion for something bad to happen. Such children may have learned that whatever they say will be wrong. They may feel that if they are going to be criticized or punished, they may as well be criticized for stubborn silence. Silence may result in punishment and the adult leaving, while answering may result in prolonged interrogation and critical evaluation. Such children are usually selective about when to refuse to answer. They often readily answer social questions where any answer is acceptable. When asked an information question by someone who already knows the answer, however, the pressure is on to get the answer right. Children figure out what the hearer wants them to say. Even when they know (and the teacher knows they know), they are often not sure enough to take the risk of publicly displaying ignorance or receiving even the mildest of teacher disapproval.

Teachers can avoid the problem by not asking children direct questions. In order to find out what children know and determine which areas of knowledge children are having difficulty with, teachers can change the circumstances in which they ask. For instance, when a child calls a teacher to look at all the cars in the garage she has made, the teacher can casually ask the child to display counting skills by asking, "That looks like a lot of cars. How many have you got there?" Similarly, teachers can routinely ask children to name colors as they dispense paint at the easel. When information questions are embedded in a social question (or an incidental teaching) context, teachers are much more likely to get an answer. A particular child has probably not been punished for answering the social question in the past, especially because it is often acceptable for the child not to answer. Also, teachers, in using this social-question context for asking information questions, are willing to accept no answer. They will simply ask again, in a casual way, at another time.

This does not change the cue-value of direct questions for the child, however. It avoids what is often a fairly punishing interaction for both teacher and child, but it does not help prepare the child for handling the kinds of direct questions likely to be encountered on entering public school.

To help children learn to answer direct questions, teachers should begin by removing the risk. Whenever they ask a direct question to a particular child, they should tell the child the right answer first. For instance, a teacher could say, "This is a red car. What color is the car?" Also, teachers could have the child practice the answer first, by asking the child to say "red" and then confirming the rightness of the answer before asking, "What color is this?"

Gradually, teachers can shift to asking another child to say the right answer as a cue. For instance, a teacher could ask another child, who readily answers information questions, "What color is this?" The teacher could repeat the correct answer, confirm its rightness, and then turn to the target child to ask, "What color is this?" Teachers can use this strategy to help children learn to listen to the answers of other children in order to discover what answer the teacher wants to hear.

Solving the problem for children who will not answer is a matter of changing the cue value of teacher questions. To this end, teachers should give such children frequent practice. They should often ask these children obvious questions so that the children can experience getting the answer right and having something good (approval) happen when they answer. They should remain aware, however, that these children are likely to be extremely alert to that subtle change in a teacher's voice that signals a serious question. These children are also likely to learn a distinction between teachers who do not criticize wrong answers and teachers (or parents) who do. Thus, teachers should work on the child's social skills at the same time they are working on language skills. They should encourage appropriate risk taking during free play, and they should try to help the child learn to handle criticism in appropriate ways.

Children with Immature Speech

A teacher's goal should be that all children speak clearly and freely, and that they use correct grammar and vocabulary. Thus, teachers should routinely help children improve immature speech patterns. If necessary, they should consult with the speech and language therapist about whether a particular child's speech patterns are evidence of immaturity or of a lack of a basic language skill. Generally, though, teachers are aware of how language normally develops, and so they recognize normal developmental irregularities, such as stammering, infantilisms, and letter substitutions that usually call for speech therapy only if they persist beyond age six.

Teachers recognize that certain patterns of speech reflect immaturity, rather than, for instance, a language deficit. Chief among such patterns are stammering (children who repeat parts of words or whole words in an attempt to produce an utterance), infantilisms (children who, for instance, say "me" in place of "I"), and letter substitutions (children who lisp or say "goggie" in place of "doggie"). Teachers assess the extent to which such immaturities are likely to be a problem by observing their frequency. Children who always stammer, who never use any pronouns correctly, or who substitute letters within all utterances so that nearly all their speech is incomprehensible are likely to need special help from speech therapy, in addition to teacher help in practicing the skills the speech therapist works on. However, children whose speech is only sometimes immature or who have only some aspects of immature speech can readily be helped within the classroom.

Teachers may assume that immature speech patterns are being responded to by hearers. They may observe their own behavior to see whether they are answering when children stammer, lisp, or say "me" rather than "I." Probably, since teachers tend to respond to the message rather than how the message is formed, the teachers often are in fact answering. The immature forms of speech are thus getting the things the children want; they are having effects on the environment that tend to maintain them. Thus, teachers may recognize that the problem lies as much with their own be-havior, since they are responding to the immature forms.

Solving problems of immature speech involves dealing as much with teachers' responses as with children's ways of talking. Teachers know, for instance, that they cannot consistently ignore immature speech; for ex-ample, they must act first when a child falling from a swing says, "Me fall." Also, they know that after-the-fact criticism tends to be resented. Punishing an individual for not noticing what they are doing tends to encourage pausing, hesitation, and nonspontaneity. When individuals are criticized often for how they talk, they are encouraged to stop talking, at least to the person who criticizes them. This hampers teachers who have to have fairly high rates of talking before they can begin to solve problems.

A teacher's main strategy with children who display immature speech, therefore, should be prompting. Teachers should respond to whatever a child says, but they should delay their response for a moment, during which they should prompt a more mature form. For instance, a child says, "I want pa-uh." The child regularly pronounces the last syllable of words of more than one syllable merely as "uh." The teacher should get the paper for the child, and as she offers it, should say, "Say, pa-*per*." The teacher may need to lift the child's chin so that the child is looking at her mouth. Initially, she may have to show the child what to do by gently compressing the child's lips. This is not only necessary in order to say "per," but cues the child to a general strategy of closing the mouth prior to saying the end of a word.

The teacher should prompt once (at most, twice) and then give the child the paper. If the child says "pa-uh" at the first prompt, the teacher should gently compress the child's lips and prompt again. Whatever the child says after this second prompt, the teacher should give the child the paper. If the child said "pa-per," the teacher should praise enthusiastically. If the child did not pronounce correctly, the teacher should say nothing.

Teachers know that changing a well-established habit of leaving off the ends of words is going to take considerable time and practice. However, they have time, for the child is probably in the setting for three or four hours every weekday. Thus teachers must make sure that the child practices and establishes a new habit of saying the ends of words. Also, teachers can get frequent practice only if the child continues to talk frequently. Therefore, they should not punish talking by criticizing or by making the child try over and over again to say it right. This may make the child lose all interest in getting paper and only want to get away from the teacher's demands. Teachers can actually get the same total amount of practice from the child if they prompt twice relative to paper (rather than ten times), and then prompt again with other words.

With children whose speech is not clear, teachers should also ask naturally for clarification. When teachers do not understand what a child is saying, they should ask the child to repeat. When teachers are genuinely trying to figure out what a child is saying, they may continue to ask for a repeat or an explanation as long as the child will respond. This may actually help the child realize the problems that hearers are having and the necessity for clear pronunciation. The teacher should ask the child to describe what is wanted or to point to it. The teacher should also accept the help of other children, who often are more able to interpret mispronunciations. If the teacher finally succeeds in deciphering what the child wants, the teacher should prompt a clear pronunciation, and give the child what was wanted.

Teachers should establish themselves as interested and responsive listeners who really want to hear and understand what children say. They should convey this attitude in particularly deliberate fashion with children who stammer. Just as all children occasionally mispronounce words and are casually prompted in the correct pronunciation, all children are likely to stammer on occasions when they are tense or anxious while talking.

Occasional stammering is likely to be a normal result of fear. (Like incomprehensible speech, chronic and continuous stammering is referred for consultation with a language and communication specialist.) Children are likely to stammer when they are afraid that they have done something wrong, that they will not be able to talk right, or that the listener will not hear them out or respond if they do not hurry. Teachers should naturally respond on occasions of stammering by listening closely and waiting without comment for the child to finish, exactly the same way they do when the child is not stammering.

Some children, however, may stammer in an effort to hold the teacher's attention. They rarely, though, have control over their stammering; it is not particularly comfortable to stammer on purpose, and hearers usually readily recognize deliberate stammering and interpret it as a game. Rather, children who stammer in an apparent effort to hold an adult's attention may become tense at the slightest sign that an adult may stop listening. Often these children talk so incessantly that adults do stop listening. This only compounds the problem, with the occurrence of just what the child was afraid of, losing the listener.

The problem in this case, therefore, is not so much the stammering as the child's efforts to monopolize the listener with incessant talk. Teachers must, eventually, turn away and thus confirm the child's fear that they will do so. Therefore, teachers should prompt the child ahead of time. For instance, when the child begins to talk, they should put a hand on the child's arm and say, "Now I'm going to listen just to you. But you see Ann and Andy are here too, and we have to share with them. So in a minute it is going to be their turn. I'll take my hand away and that means you have to finish up so they can have a turn." When the teacher removes the hand, the child should be allowed ample time to finish. Then the teacher should turn away even though the child may have begun to stammer. It will take many repetitions for the child to recognize the teacher's cue, but the cue will eventually let the child know that as long as the teacher's touch is present, the teacher will not turn away. This will encourage the child not only to realize that there is no need to hurry or to be afraid of losing the listener, but that the less the stammering, the more talk can be gotten into the time available. Gradually, the teacher should fade the prompt, touching the child without explaining the cue beforehand and signalling withdrawal of the hand by withdrawing eye contact. Once the child is used to this cue, the teacher should begin not touching the child, but just withdraw eye contact as a signal for the child to finish.

Teachers should also prompt in cases of ungrammatical speech. Since teachers are aware of the normal stages in the development of language, they are aware that children gradually learn what constitutes fully grammatical speech. They are also aware that what constitutes grammaticality differs across dialects. What is grammatical in black English, for instance, is not the same as what is grammatical in standard English (Labov, 1970). What is grammatical in formal speech or in writing is not the same as what is grammatical in informal conversation (Ochs, 1979). In a particular program, teachers may decide to teach children to use standard English or to use formal speech. The procedures they would use to do so are essentially the prompting procedures described here. The chief addition would be a plan specifying the special occasions for prompting the new kind of talk. The teachers would plan to have a particular context (snacktime, for instance, or the creative area) cue the use of a different way of talking. This would help the children learn when or where to switch codes (Shuy, 1970). It would also help communicate an extremely important attitude concerning language: there is no form of language that is intrinsically better than any other. There is just a right way at a right time and place, and right changes with every change in time and place and hearer.

The kinds of ungrammatical speech that teachers routinely deal with are those that are merely signs of immaturity. As children acquire language, they devise a succession of rule systems (Chiat, 1981). For instance, they initially devise a rule for the past tense that calls for the addition of *-ed* to the present tense form of a verb; therefore, they apply this newly devised rule to all verbs, and they replace the irregular past tenses (came, ran, took), which they have been using for months with "comed," "runned," and "taked." With time, the past tense rule will be further revised to include rules covering irregular verbs, and the children will again say, "came."

With time, most children develop mature rule systems. In the meantime, if teachers want to help children revise immature rule systems, it may be useful to call the children's attention to particular cases for which the children need new rules. When children are speaking readily and frequently, and their messages are being responded to, they may not attend to the fact that certain aspects of their speech are different from the speech they hear. They may not notice, for instance, that they are saying "comed," while all the adults they know are saying "came." Even if they do notice, the difference may not be important enough for them to revise their current rules. When teachers prompt, however, it points out the difference to the child and suggests that it is important.

Thus, teachers should casually prompt a correct form before they respond to a child's utterance. For instance, when a child says, "Me made a house," the teacher should say, "I made a house." At first, the teacher may have to ask the child to say the corrected utterance. However, with time and teacher consistency in restating the child's utterance, the child will come to repeat after the teacher and then continue almost as though the repeated statement was the one the child had originally said. Then the teacher can begin to reduce the prompt until the teacher is saying only the word that the child needs to correct. For instance, when the child says, "Me want one," the teacher can prompt simply, "I," and the child will restate, "I want one." It is at this point that self-correcting may begin. The child may be heard to sometimes say "Me—I want one." Once the child has recognized that only a certain form of a pronoun can appropriately occur in a certain place in an utterance, the child is ready to revise the rules he or she currently has concerning pronoun use.

Children with immature speech almost always mature, and the immature speech matures with them. Of all the common problems encountered in early childhood settings, immature speech is likely to be one that teachers do not have to be particularly anxious about. Most immature speech patterns correct themselves with time and practice. Thus, encouraging high rates of speech (frequent practice) may help immature speakers more than any direct intervention on the forms of speech. The last thing teachers should do is to criticize or punish children for the way they talk; this could turn a normal developmental irregularity into a habitually inappropriate pattern of speech in need of therapy. Therefore, teachers should prompt corrected speech only when they can do so in a positive way, as a casual introduction to a positive response to a child's talk.

Group Conversation Time

Another language goal should be that children be able to talk before a group and express ideas to a general audience of listeners. Talking before a group involves different language skills than does talking to a single receptive listener. A speaker before a group not only has to be able to handle being the center of attention, but has to adapt content and style of presentation to the interests of a group so as to engage and hold their attention.

The skills for speaking before a group tend to be learned fairly late. The early childhood setting may be children's first opportunity for speaking before a group. Children may feel shy about being the center of attention and so may either hesitate to speak or begin to "perform" in inappropriate ways. Because of inexperience, children usually have little awareness of what topics are likely to interest a group. In addition, children sometimes lack the language (vocabulary and narrative skills) with which to express their ideas.

A teacher's approach to encouraging group conversation should be, as usual, to first arrange a setting that cues casual talk. Children should be seated in a circle so that they can all readily make eye contact, regardless of who is speaking. Speakers should remain seated so that the center of attention can shift easily from one speaker to another, and no one child is put on the spot. The teacher should take the role of a member of the group, sitting within the circle.

To encourage children to talk to one another, the teacher should take as minimal a role as possible. Children are likely to look to the teacher to cue them as to what to say during group conversation time, especially when they are new to the early childhood setting. Teachers thus may find themselves in a position of selecting the topics for group talk, selecting which children will talk, and deciding how long they will talk. The teachers may end up managing and directing the conversation, so that children tend to talk to them rather than to other children and to talk in ways and about topics that teachers approve of. Teachers may find themselves giving feedback (and so determining the topics and expressions of children) because the other children are not involved in the conversation. Meanwhile, the other children are learning to be a passive audience; they are learning the same listening skills that they learn at group storytime, rather than learning to be an active audience participating in shaping the skills of the speaker.

To avoid preempting the roles of the children as participants in group conversation, the teachers must keep adult participation to a minimum and be patient. Usually, the teacher should begin the conversation time with a general question, "Who has something to tell us today?" They should then call on children who speak or raise a hand. The teachers should model the behavior of attentive listeners, nodding, saying "Ahh," and maintaining eye contact. In the early days of conversation time, they should sometimes model a response such as "Then what happened?" or "And what else?"

They should ask only open-ended questions in order to avoid suggesting content. When the child who is speaking falls silent, the teacher should comment, for example, "That was very interesting, thank you for telling us." The teacher should then turn to see whether another child is ready to talk.

Teachers may have to encourage children to talk for at least a month before the children begin spontaneously conversing with one another. The conversation times may last only five minutes or even less, but it is absolutely essential to children's later spontaneity that teachers establish that any topic a child brings up and anything a child says on any topic is acceptable. The children must see by repeated demonstration that the teachers will not determine the topics for talk and will not criticize or correct no matter who is speaking, what is said, or how much is said. Therefore, teachers in the early days of conversation time should not suggest topics to children or ask them to show-and-tell the group about something brought to school. Teachers should establish that group conversation time is truly the children's time to talk.

While children are learning that the teacher's role during group conversation is nondirective, teachers should try to maintain the group in some form of exchange of talk by modeling the listener's behavior and facilitating the sequence of turns at talk. During this time, some child in the group may say something interesting enough for another child to laugh spontaneously or say, "Me too." The teacher should respond immediately to such child-child feedback, smiling and focusing attentively on one speaker and then the other without interrupting. When the speaker finishes talking, the teacher should offer the floor to the child who commented and should ask, for instance, "You saw that too?" If the child does not want to talk, however, the teacher should open the floor to other children.

Thus, the teachers initially encourage children to comment and interrupt other children's talk. As teachers encourage spontaneous comments (by listening and never criticizing), they encourage children to give feedback and to respond to one another. It is this feedback that helps speakers learn to talk about interesting topics in ways that interest other children. Also, the spontaneous commenting of other children encourages even the hesitant children to participate, so that the whole group of children is talking.

Once many children are talking spontaneously, commenting on what one another is saying and interrupting when their interest in the topics carries them away, teachers are at last in a position to help children learn skills for group conversation. Now they can prompt the more hesitant children to talk, by suggesting (before group conversation time begins) that the children bring an object to tell the other children about or describe something at group conversation time that they have spent some time telling just to the teacher during free play. Also, teachers can prompt children in how to deal with interruptions by saying, "Excuse me (I'm not through yet)." If necessary, teachers should call the interrupter's attention to the speaker's signal to wait.

If the rate of spontaneous talk at group conversation time is high, a certain amount of clowning can be ignored. One or two children, who for a short time put their hands over their ears, may be considered to be giving relevant feedback to a speaker, as can children who burst into laughter. Teachers should only have to intervene if the majority of the group begins giving negative feedback to one or more children's talk. Then teachers may devote a group instruction time to discussing and having children practice what good listeners do. At the instruction time, the teacher should model and have children imitate appropriate listener responses, such as nodding, smiling, saying something positive, or adding to the topic, while sitting with hands in laps. Such an instruction time should be held at another time of the day, so as not to insert suddenly even implied criticism and teacher direction into the child-conducted conversation time proper.

Teachers are also likely to have to help children deal with a speaker who tries to keep the floor whenever allowed to speak. Such children are often encouraged by other children initially, for they often can narrate highly creative stories about imaginary or fantastic events. Once amply encouraged, however, these children become repetitive or their stories become so farfetched that their audience loses interest. The teacher should prompt such children to notice loss of audience attentiveness. Also, when the teacher sees children in the audience making eye contact with one another rather than with the speaker, the teacher should interrupt at the next pause, saying, for instance, "Look, Miko seems to want a turn." The teacher may prompt the speaker to ask a question of Miko or the teacher may do so. Teachers can thus use children's appearance of distraction to cue the speaker to stop and to let listeners know that this is an appropriate way to signal disinterest or a desire for a turn at talking.

Teachers can help children learn group conversation skills only if they truly have group conversation among children. First, teachers must wait and accept everything children say until the children are sure that they can talk about anything in any way they want. Then, when they are talking spontaneously, the children tend to give one another feedback in ways that reveal which topics are interesting and what kinds of information they need to be given in order to maintain their interest. When children are talking interestedly and spontaneously, they are likely to be receptive to minimal teacher prompts about how to manage turn taking within a group conversation, how to express interest, and how to ask for more information, for these skills are now relevant to enjoying the full extent of the activity they are creating among themselves.

The Child Who Talks to Adults Rather Than to Peers

One of the primary aims of early childhood teachers is for children to learn to interact with one another in satisfying and appropriate ways. Learning to use language in order to facilitate interaction with peers is an integral part of such social learning.

Children who talk to adults rather than to peers are often children who have well-developed social skills. Usually they can handle social interaction with other children quite adequately. (Children who lack social skills are likely to interact little with either children or adults.) The problem for teachers is that some children prefer to interact with adults, perhaps because adults give more positive feedback than do children. Because of this preference, such children have often learned that particular kinds of talk, on particular topics, are responded to by adults consistently or with particular interest. Many adults cannot resist answering children's questions, reassuring children who express fear, or responding to personal criticism or compliments.

Children who talk to adults rather than to peers have often learned adult styles of talking. Not only can they discuss adult topics, such as marriage, crime, and sickness, but they can mimic adult intonations and expressions. Adults usually find such behavior amusing; the mismatch between the child's expression of knowledge and the child's actual knowledge is delightfully incongruous. The adult's enjoyment is clear, positive (though also often puzzling) to the child, and thus encourages more such talk on the part of the child. Children who talk to adults rather than peers are children whom adults enjoy listening to (whether they realize it, admit it, or not).

Thus, teachers' problems, as usual, lie as much with their own behavior as with the child's. They must first decide that they will not encourage certain kinds of talk from children. When children begin to mimic adult styles of talk (except when role-playing adults in the course of pretending with other children), the teachers should—no matter how interesting or amusing the child's talk—resolutely give only a minimal response and then change the subject. When children criticize or compliment teachers on their personal appearance, teachers should accept the comment matter-of-factly. Teachers should answer children's obvious (purely attention-getting) questions with questions of their own. They should be noncommittal in response to children's repeated expressions of unrealistic fear. (For example, the teacher could say "That's an interesting story," in response to a child's, "I hid under my bed all night because there was a monster in my room playing with my toys.")

As teachers turn away from talk on certain topics in certain styles, they simultaneously prompt talk in appropriate ways on appropriate topics. The more often the child experiences different teacher responses to different styles and topics of talk, the faster the child is likely to learn what kinds of talk teachers prefer to listen to. Thus, a teacher may look away until the child completes an inappropriate utterance and then prompt, "I'd rather hear about (what you did after school, before school, what you are making)."

Sometimes, though, such children are not nearly as skillful at talking about what they are doing or have done, and often the only activity they are engaged in is talking to a teacher. Therefore, teachers should prompt the child to do something else, for example, by saying, "Here's a paper, let me watch you draw." Then the teacher can use the child's activity as a topic for talk and help the child learn skills for talking about current activities. At the same time, the teacher is encouraging the child's interest in activities other than talking to adults.

As the child engages in activities other than talking, the teachers gain opportunities both to model appropriate conversation, as they talk with other children also engaged in that activity, and to prompt the child to talk with other children rather than teachers. Thus, the teacher can prompt the target child to notice what another child is doing, and model a comment or ask what the target child thinks. When the target child responds, the teacher can prompt the other child to respond and interpret the other child's response in such a way that the target child is prompted to respond in turn. Teachers can use the same procedure in reverse, prompting another child to comment on the target child's activity, and interpreting and prompting the target child to respond. Thus, the teacher acts as mediator between two (or more) children's turns in the dialogue, prompting each to say utterances that will encourage the other to respond.

As teachers mediate talk between two children, they provide children with experience in learning which topics are of interest to other children. They interpret other children's responses in words that prompt a hearer in how to respond to keep the conversation going. If necessary, they should model the positive response that will encourage a child to talk more often in appropriate ways, which other children may not, as yet, completely understand. Teachers should devote their skills to encouraging and facilitating conversation, even of the most primitive type, between children. This is perhaps the best way of encouraging children to talk to peers rather than adults, and it has the advantage of increasing the depth and variety of children's language skills at the same time.

SYNTHESIS

Teachers should approach common problems in the area of language skill in the same way they approach other problems children may be having in skill learning. They should recognize the importance of frequent practice and positive feedback for minor improvements in skill. As in all other areas of skill learning, teachers should focus on arranging a classroom setting that will cue appropriate behavior and on prompting children to behave in ways that will draw positive feedback. They should recognize that the essence of their skills and effectiveness as teachers lies in the realm of cueing and prompting improved behaviors that will enable children to get more "good things" (information, experience, interaction) from the environment. They should deal with each child as an individual who has learned certain ways of behaving and certain levels of skill, and who must be helped to improve in terms of those individual levels and ways of behaving. They should recognize that change is slow and mistakes inevitable, and thus should be patient and accepting even when they cannot be positive in their responses.

The basic principles teachers should rely on in dealing with problems in areas of language skill are the same principles they would use in dealing with other problems. They should assess the nature of the problem by looking at the circumstances and consequences of the children's behavior, and relate their observations to their skill-learning goals for particular children. Then they should plan how to rearrange the setting and their behavior to cue and prompt improved or more appropriate behavior from those children. The rearrangements planned should be those that are most likely to enable teachers not only to cue and prompt in natural and spontaneous ways, but to respond automatically with some positive consequence (approval, cooperation, materials) to improved or more appropriate behaviors.

A teacher's goal in language skill learning should be that each child learn to adapt language in more subtle and sophisticated ways: that each child learn to say the right thing in the right way at the right time and the right place in accordance with the norms of the society. To meet this goal, teachers must decide about what constitutes right within the society of the early childhood setting so that the setting and their behavior can be arranged in ways that communicate and encourage whatever they decide is right.

Then teachers should focus on practice. They should promote high rates of talking on the part of children by presenting themselves as responsive and interested listeners who always want to hear more appropriate talk from children. When children are encouraged to talk all the time, about anything and everything, they inevitably encounter the ways in which society naturally regulates the appropriateness of talk. Hearers ask for clarification when they do not understand, and in that way encourage clarity of pronunciation and precision of vocabulary and sentence structure. Hearers respond with interest to interesting conversational topics; they contribute in positive ways and keep conversation going when the talk is appropriately matched to the time and place of talk, and when the speaker's talk is related to what the hearer is saying. For talk to be effective in getting "good things" (materials, cooperation, continued talk), speakers must notice what their hearers do and say. Speakers must watch and listen as well as talk so that they can adapt what they say to make their talk effective.

The more often children talk, the better they get at adapting their talk to when, where, and to whom they are talking, and what they are talking about. Generalized skills are a natural result of high rates of use, for the society of hearers in which language is used automatically responds in ways that let children know when they have got it right. Thus, if children just talk, they will learn appropriate language skills (in the same way their parents and teachers may have done). The unique expertise—and the responsibility—of teachers in early childhood settings lies in facilitating this learning through arranging a setting, and cueing and prompting children so that they can experience success and so discover themselves saying the "right" thing, as perceived in the school setting.

REFERENCES

Brown, R., & Hanlon, C. Derivational complexity and order of acquisition in child speech. In J.R. Hayes (Ed.), *Cognition and the development of language.* New York: Wiley, 1970.

Brown, P., & Levinson, S. Universals in language usage: Politeness phenomena. In E.N. Goody (Ed.), *Questions and politeness.* New York: Cambridge University Press, 1978.

Chiat, S. Context-specificity and generalization in the acquisition of pronominal distinctions. *Journal of Child Language,* 1981, *8,* 75–91.

Creider, C.A. On the explanation of transformations. In T. Givon (Ed.), *Syntax and semantics. Vol. 12: Discourse and syntax.* New York: Academic Press, 1979.

Ervin-Tripp, S. Social backgrounds and verbal skills. In R. Huxley & E. Ingram (Eds.), *Language acquisition: Models and methods.* New York: Academic Press, 1971.

Halliday, M.A.K. *Learning how to mean.* New York: Elsevier, 1975.

Halliday, M.A.K. *Language as social semiotic.* Baltimore, Md.: University Park Press, 1978.

Hart, B., & Risley, T.R. Promoting productive language through incidental teaching. *Education and Urban Society,* 1978, *10,* 407–429.

Hart, B., & Risley, T.R. In vivo language intervention: Unanticipated general effects. *Journal of Applied Behavior Analysis,* 1980, *13,* 407–432.

Labov, W. The logic of nonstandard English. In F. Williams (Ed.), *Language and poverty.* Chicago: Markham, 1970.

200 EARLY CHILDHOOD EDUCATION

Landon, S.J., & Sommers, R.K. Talkativeness and children's linguistic abilities. *Language and Speech*, 1979, *22*, 269–275.

Ochs, E. Planned and unplanned discourse. In T. Givon (Ed.), *Syntax and semantics. Vol. 12: Discourse and syntax.* New York: Academic Press, 1979.

Rieke, J.A., & Thompson, G. The communication specialists: The speech pathologist and audiologist. In K.E. Allen, V.A. Holm, & R.L. Schiefelbusch (Eds.), *Early intervention—a team approach.* Baltimore, Md.: University Park Press, 1978.

Shatz, M., & Gelman, R. The development of communication skills. *Monographs of the Society for Research in Child Development,* 1973, *38,* 1–38.

Shuy, R.W. The sociolinguists and urban language problems. In F. Williams (Ed.), *Language and poverty.* Chicago: Markham, 1970.

Streeck, J. Speech acts in interaction: A critique of Searle. *Discourse Processes,* 1980, *3,* 133–154.

White, B.L. *Experience and environment* (Vol. 2). Englewood Cliffs, N.J.: Prentice-Hall, 1978.

Chapter 7

Preacademic Skills for the Reluctant Learner

Trudylee G. Rowbury

In early childhood classrooms across the nation, children receive opportunities daily to sample learning experiences that facilitate a normal progression of conceptual skills. Most children arrive at preschool already possessing a natural curiosity about their person, the objects around them, and the relationships of objects and events they see as they move through their world. If this natural curiosity is met at school with a range of interesting materials, ample time to engage in manipulative exploration, and an encouraging teacher who has planned carefully across weeks and months, then normal expansion of the requisite conceptual skills will be evidenced in the children across the course of the school year.

When young children are observed in a well-designed early childhood classroom, it is evident that "play is learning, and learning is play." A creative teacher provides materials, settings, and information that stimulate the child's already active curiosity. In this way opportunities to learn are matched to a period of life when the child is most interested in new explorations and mastery. Fortunately, early learning in the majority of children occurs in this way. An active curiosity is fostered and then is maintained by positive support from home and classroom. Learning can be distributed across "natural, informal, and structured settings" as they are encountered in the many environments that constitute the child's world (Charlesworth & Radeloff, 1978).

There are some children, however, who come to their first school experiences and do not exhibit this motivating curiosity. They lack the attentional and exploratory skills and do not make use of the available learning settings, be they natural or structured. When children fail to engage in the spontaneous participation and learning demonstrated by their peers, they appear to be "reluctant learners." Early learning problems may be signaled by a reluctant learner in a variety of ways, such as "exclusive interest," "drifting," "competing disruptive patterns," or "daydreaming" during most ongoing activities. These patterns compete with a child's learning of early preacademic conceptual skills. Often the child will avoid effective contact with activities and materials designed to teach counting (number skills), spatial relations (basic identities), and duplication of patterns (visual discrimination), to name only a few. Yet, this basic conceptual learning is necessary for later school success.

John is an example of "exclusive interest." Each day when he comes to school he plays only with cars and trucks. He either refuses to shift to other conceptual activities when asked, or he slips away from them as soon as possible. Mary is a "drifter." She moves from one area to another of the available learning centers but remains only long enough to pick up a cube, put on a smock, or briefly watch before she moves on. She spends the greater portion of her time wandering in and out of contact with learning materials. Tina has learned that noncompliance and tantrums can compete with conceptual learning. When a teacher requests that she sit with a group doing puzzles, she yells, "No," or throws herself on the carpet, crying. Finally, there is Rod, who will sit with any group when requested, but who merely looks around the room and does not appear to be in contact with any part of the ongoing learning. He responds slowly when his name is called, and he generally appears to be "daydreaming" unless guided by the teacher.

While most three- and four-year-old children have relatively short attention spans and demonstrate occasional bouts of disinterest or opposition, an observant teacher will note that the patterns of "reluctant" learning described earlier persist over several weeks. Whether passive (exclusive interest, drifting, or daydreaming) or active (tantrums or noncompliance), such patterns signal a need for early remediation. The teacher first should arrange for medical, vision, and hearing screening to be sure that the behavior patterns are not related to a physical problem. If these screenings prove negative, then the teacher should begin plans for remedial teaching of the reluctant learners. Through appropriate curriculum structuring, these children can develop into curious, effective learners before they enter public school. In most cases the reluctant learner already is showing delays in one or more basic conceptual or preacademic areas. Remediation is essential during the preschool years because preacademic deficits are cumulative (Gardner, 1978; Bereiter & Engelmann, 1966). At this age, each skill or concept a child learns serves as a foundation for later, more complex understanding and integration.

PLANNING A PROGRESSION FOR REMEDIAL TEACHING

At the most basic level, reluctant learners do not make effective contact with their learning environments. Since learning in preschool is concrete, this means that reluctant learners often are not physically present in the learning setting (the drifter). If they are present, they do not manipulate materials (touching, placing, matching, moving, watching) in a manner that exposes the critical features and relationships. Thus, early remediation for problem learners may have to proceed in the following stages:

- teaching location, basic attention, and brief contact

- expanding basic attention and amount of contact

- teaching independent contact and completion

- expanding to more than one preacademic focus

- programming a normal range of conceptual targets while maintaining individual structure

- expanding individually mastered skills to group practice

- gradually introducing new lessons into group formats

This does not mean that a teacher can or should spend the entire day with a reluctant learner. Instead, the initial focus should be on one or two brief periods of the day, or on a brief time during each major curriculum period, as dictated by the classroom schedule. If the classroom schedule includes one or more periods of preacademic focus when all children are independently occupied with individual preacademic materials (for example, math, duplication of patterns), then this would be a good target for early remediation. In this way, peers increasingly can become models for appropriate attending and completion. One demonstration classroom for children with learning problems (Rowbury & Baer, 1980) structures a work-play alternation for individual preacademic learning. Half of the classroom comes to a designated preacademic "work" area, while the other half continues in free play. When the first group has completed three items from their individually prescribed preacademic tasks, they return to free play. The second group then moves to the preacademic area. In this structure all children have peer models for effective preacademic contact *and* for the more social free-play opportunities.

Every part of a reluctant learner's day cannot be changed or altered at the same time. To do so would invite frustration on the part of the child and the teacher. Instead, changes should be small at first. Both the requirements on the child and the level of learning tasks must be introduced in an orderly progression so that the child and the teacher can be successful from the beginning.

BASIC PRINCIPLES OF SYSTEMATIC SEQUENCING

Remedial teaching of young reluctant learners requires a careful match between characteristics of the child and elements of the curriculum. Certain characteristics are common to many learning delayed children; selected characteristics are described as follows. In addition, a curriculum prescription for reluctant learners may be enhanced if the teacher considers a task analysis or sequencing approach to curriculum organization. Finally, teachers must consider which elements of their teaching repertoire might best promote the "learning to learn" pattern of a given child. Descriptions of the logic of task analysis and selected teacher support strategies are included here as a starting point for teacher planning.

Common Characteristics of Young Children with Learning Delays

These children often avoid contact with preacademic learning materials. When they do make contact it is often in a random, aimless manner or brief in the extreme. A first goal is to help such children initiate productive contact at the request of the teacher.

Delayed learners often respond to teacher input as if it were neutral or even mildly aversive. Some children may never have experienced an interested, encouraging audience for their conceptual endeavors. Others may have experienced audiences that were too demanding, with child-failure the common result. In either case, the teacher will have to help the child accept adult proximity, suggestion, and encouragement as positive events.

Many delayed learners do not know the process for successfully completing a lesson. They do not know where to start, how to continue, or how to determine for themselves when a particular project is completed. Exploration for its own sake is not motivating. For this reason preacademic learning may appear to them to be quite endless rather than stimulating. To promote successful contact by these children, the teacher may want to prescribe initial learning tasks that have visually concrete starts and completions, with periodic cues from the teacher to mark the beginning, continuation, and final product.

As a correlate, many delayed learners do not know how to take pleasure from the products of their contact. Initially the teacher will have to be the one to communicate pleasure and satisfaction at the child's successful solution or completion. Over time the child will begin to use the same or similar positive self-referents, and apply them with pleasure to successfully completed preacademic tasks. One important milestone in "learning to learn" occurs when the child begins to solicit attention and approval from a teacher or peer for some aspect of performance. Comments such as "See, I did it!" or "Listen, I know my _____" mark the beginning of individual satisfaction and motivation toward conceptual learning.

Many delayed learners have poor visual organizing skills. They do not know how to organize a space in which to work. If too many materials are placed randomly in front of them, they will approach them randomly. Often they will become visually distracted before constructive contact is made. Initially the teacher must be prepared to restrict available materials to the necessary minimum and to arrange the work space and the materials visually before the child begins to contact the task.

Delayed learners often become resistive in the presence of novel formats and materials. When novel learning contexts or materials are introduced too suddenly or too frequently, comments such as "I can't" or "I don't know how" or other forms of resistance are common. A skillful teacher will introduce novel elements gradually, provide time for children to practice already mastered lessons, and make it clear to the child that initial assistance will be available when novel elements are added to the learning setting.

Task Analysis: Sequencing Learning Goals

The term "task analysis" refers to a specific logic that can be applied to prescriptions for children's learning. The logic is that of "sequential ordering" of skill acquisition. As development moves from simple to more complex learning, so also should curriculum prescriptions. The logic of task analysis is applied commonly to the following three types of teaching: (1) sequential skill hierarchies; (2) component analysis; and (3) remedial sequencing.

Sequential Skill Hierarchies

In the broadest sense, task analysis involves defining a preacademic content area and then specifying that constellation of skills that taken together constitute complete mastery of that content area. The individual skills within the constellation are then arranged in learning hierarchies to create a sequence of presentation that hypothetically tracks the optimal developmental sequence (Resnick, Wang, & Kaplan, 1973; Cohen & Gross, 1979). Within learning hierarchies, easier skills are listed first, and each skill in order facilitates or is prerequisite to learning of the following skills.

In the task analysis approach to teaching a conceptual content area, task or skill prescriptions proceed in a linear fashion from simple skills to complex. Parallel branches of ordered skills may be introduced, as appropriate, at various points along the continuum. For example, if a teacher selects "color concepts" as a content area, the following six skills, in order, might be written in the early skill hierarchy:

1. Match color object pairs.
2. Match color card pairs.
3. Point to *(blue)* object or card on request (receptive identification).
4. Label color of object or card when asked, "What color is this?" (expressive identification).
5. Match "dark" and "light" objects of a particular color.
6. Proceed through skill hierarchy until child has learned to arrange a shaded series of one color in order from lightest to darkest.

The teacher should introduce teaching of colors with a selected set of color stimuli to minimize child distraction. However, when a child has mastered the third skill, a parallel branch of sequential teaching could be initiated in which the child learns to perform the first three skills with varied objects in the classroom environment. In this example, the child will be learning simultaneously to label a restricted set of color materials (skill 4) *and* to apply skills of matching and receptive identification, in order, to the objects in the classroom (parallel branch).

Resnick, Wang, and Kaplan (1973) have constructed a precise model of task analysis in their hierarchy of early math skills for young children. These authors specified quantity learning from 0–20 as their conceptual content area. They then collected and ordered a series of math skills that, taken together, would constitute mastery of early math-quantity relations. Their sequence consists of eight units, each containing numerous ordered skills or learning objectives. Learning objectives start with rote counting 0–5 and proceed sequentially as far as addition and subtraction with a number line.

While it is desirable to follow a logic of sequential skill acquisition with most children, careful attention to sequence may be critical for children with learning delays. These children may need to start their skill acquisition in each content area at a level long passed by more skillful peers. Thus a teacher must deduce the early prerequisite skills. Many children can tolerate both "potpourri" and "smorgasbord" approaches to learning and create their own order within an age-appropriate range of skills. Learning delayed children who have missed early prerequisites may well need a more orderly guided tour through the menu of preacademic content areas.

In classroom practice, a teacher who wishes to refine the sequential ordering of skills within the target curriculum is advised to proceed with one content area at a time. A partial list of preacademic curriculum areas that might be considered for sequential ordering is included in Table 7–1.

The development of a complete pool of skills related to any one area should involve examining appropriate sections from a variety of curriculum resources. (A partial list of preacademic curriculum resources is available

---

Table 7–1 Partial List of Preacademic Content Areas for Hierarchical Task Analyses

1. Fine motor—manipulative, formfitting, self-help
2. Fine motor—eye-hand coordination leading to pencil control
3. Visual discrimination
   a. matching
   b. sorting
   c. assembling
   d. same versus different
   e. duplication of models and patterns (2-D and 3-D)
4. Basic concept identities (mix of perceptual skills, receptive language, and expressive language)
   a. objects
   b. own name
   c. peers' and teachers' names
   d. color
   e. shape
   f. classification: generic, association, function
   g. first and last name (order and label letters)
   h. spatial relations
5. Language
   a. action words
   b. attribute modifiers
   c. sentence forms
   d. pronoun use
   e. expanded verbal description
   f. creative expression
6. Early math (see Resnick et al., 1973)
7. Advanced identities (stronger language emphasis)
   a. ordering and sequencing events
   b. relational attributes: size, height, weight, length
   c. alphabet letters: upper and lower case
8. Visual memory
9. Auditory discrimination
   a. receptive language identities (often incorporated under units 4, 5, 6, and 7 above)
   b. environmental sounds
   c. verbal instructions
   d. abstract sounds
   e. letter sounds
10. Auditory memory
   a. duplicate sound sequences
   b. sequenced instructions

at the end of this chapter.) It is interesting to note that many curriculum specialists focused their initial efforts on developing preacademic curriculums for populations of children with special learning needs. However, the degree of precision they achieve also will benefit a broad range of young children.

Reading from a variety of sources will help the teacher collect a hierarchy of skills from which learning prescriptions may be made for all children in the class, at each child's level of readiness. Certain basic skills can be found for early learning by delayed children, and advanced skills can be found that could be taught to other children in the group. Jerome Rosner has attempted this type of task analysis in his *Perceptual Skills Curriculum* (1973).

Activities and materials can be selected to match each skill after the teacher has developed a hierarchy of skills within a preacademic area. The teacher should already have a strong base of activities and materials for many skills on the list. Some will have been chosen for early learning, others for independent practice, and others for expansion of the skill to the activities throughout the school day (generalized use of the skill). The materials chosen for early learning should be those that most clearly isolate or focus the skill. Practice materials should be ones the child could complete or explore with minimal teacher support. Expansion activities should be those suitable to groups of children or to incidental teaching at casual intervals throughout the day.

In some cases the teachers may discover a paucity of materials or activities related to a particular skill. When this occurs, the teacher can brainstorm with fellow teachers, consult activity books and commercial catalogs, or look through teacher-constructed material handbooks and resource centers to collect activity ideas. For example, teachers may discover that they have few activities for teaching auditory discrimination. A group might decide to purchase a commercial tape recording of environmental sounds with accompanying pictures. They might decide also to make their own tape of teachers' and children's voices with a poster of photographs of the teachers and children in the classroom. These materials could then be used for lessons related to matching a sound to a picture of the object or person making the sound. Certain skills may be necessary to a given preacademic content area, but the choice of materials and activities for teaching these skills is entirely up to the teacher. Choices should be made that fit the teaching style of the staff, the structure of the classroom, and the available resources. The "name lotto" shown here is one example of a simple teacher-constructed material that can be used to teach children to match the letters in their names, arrange the letters in order, and finally spell their names.

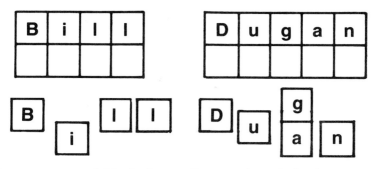

The same sequential logic that applies to task analysis of a content area is also a part of two supplemental teaching strategies that are especially useful with delayed learners. These sequential teaching strategies often are included also under the general title "task analysis" (O'Neil, McLaughlin, & Knapp, 1977). They are component analysis and remedial sequencing. Sequential logic may be applied at all levels of curriculum prescription for delayed learners. These children may require orderly skill hierarchies, component analyses of individual skills, and remedial sequencing within a given task or activity.

Component Analysis

Component analysis is the process of dividing a target behavior, for example, handwashing, into its component parts and of teaching one element at a time in an additive fashion. At the end of the component teaching, the child is performing the entire chain of elements independently to complete the target behavior. Component analysis is most often employed with target behaviors such as self-help skills that consist of a series of discrete responses that are performed in a particular order. However, component analysis also may be applied to preacademic skills, such as assembling puzzles, cutting a straight line, or any other task involving a series of responses leading to a completed product.

In component analysis the first step is to specify the exact behavior to be learned by the child. For example, "dressing" is too general, while "putting on a coat" is specific. The next step is to list, in order, each separate response that is required to complete the target behavior. Finally, the teacher should instruct the child in one response at a time, adding instruction of the next response when the prior one is being performed independently by the child. Responses should be added to the child's chain, one by one, until the child can perform the entire series from start to finish. Learning may be facilitated during component teaching if the child sees all parts of a chain daily, although performing only one or two elements independently during early training.

The teacher may choose either a *forward chaining* or a *backward chaining* procedure for sequencing the child's orderly progression toward a target behavior. In forward chaining the teacher should first instruct the child in the initial element in the chain and then perform the succeeding elements for the child while the child watches. If a backward chaining procedure is chosen, the teacher should initially perform all but the last element while the child watches and then instruct the child in the final steps. Subsequent steps should be added to the child's performance, either from the beginning (forward) or the end (backward), as the child masters the one being taught. Children learn well in both forward and backward chaining procedures. If the easier responses of the chain are in the beginning, a teacher may want to start there (forward) to guarantee early success. If a child appears motivated by finishing a product, a teacher may choose backward chaining, because the child's response will always be followed by a completed product at the end of the chain.

Detailed examples of component analysis are available in sections relating to self-help skills in Copeland, Ford, and Solon's *Occupational Therapy for Mentally Retarded Children* (1976), Johnson and Werner's *Step-by-Step Learning Guide for Retarded Infants and Children* (1975), and Watson's *How to Use Behavior Modification with Retarded and Autistic Children* (1972). From these models it should be possible to create a component analysis teaching strategy for any skill or behavior that involves a series of connected responses. The basic principle of component analysis is teaching a behavior chain in small manageable units. Component analysis is useful when the total unit of behavior is difficult for the child to learn without initial frustration or failure. Many skills that involve difficult motor coordinations for young chilren might be taught effectively through this step-by-step procedure. In fact, teachers have applied component analysis successfully to teach young children to cut with scissors (Thomson, 1979) and to tie shoes (Cooper, 1970).

Remedial Sequencing

Remedial sequencing is the process of refining a skill sequence, redefining a component sequence, or altering a given activity presentation when a child is encountering learning difficulties. In each case the goal is to divide the unit of learning into smaller steps than were originally specified. A teacher may discover that the shift from one skill to another in a hierarchy is too great a jump for certain children. The teacher may revise the skill sequence by adding intermediate steps between the one previously mastered and the one on which difficulty is encountered. These new skills may be retained in the hierarchy if many children encounter similar difficulties.

Most skill hierarchies will undergo a certain period of revision as the teacher collects new information about the content area and watches the progress of the children through the sequence of skills.

In a similar fashion, certain component analyses may require revision, depending on the observed performance of the children. If the child is not learning the initial series of responses, it is useful to reanalyze the chain. Certain responses actually may involve two or three motions that could be separated into smaller learning steps than were originally specified.

Activity or material presentations also may undergo remedial revisions. This is especially true of activities that are prescribed for reluctant learners. Procedures for altering an individual activity can include the addition of extra visual cues to task materials, reduction in the initial response requirements (adjusting criteria), reduction of visual elements that prove distracting during initial contact, or provision of extra prompts and cues by the teacher. Remedial analyses of individual tasks or activities are designed to provide extra support to the child, thus ensuring more easily mastered early learning steps. These supports, whether physical alterations or added adult prompts, are then gradually removed. Eventually the child should be able to participate in the activity as it was originally designed. (That is, a child will learn to use the material or participate in a manner similar to normal peers who are learning the same skill.)

Elements of Teacher Attention

A teacher can use many forms of attention and support during the presentation of a learning activity to a group of young children. The teacher's style or philosophy of education may influence the amount of direct supervision that is provided. Philosophies of "discovery" learning may connote minimal teacher input with maximum independent exploration by the children. A philosophy of "direct teaching" may connote active teacher cueing, instruction, and structuring. In actual practice, a mix of philosophies and teaching styles is found in most early childhood classrooms. Teachers "pull back" to promote child choice and independent exploration on some occasions, and they structure the learning setting with detailed instructions and cues at other times.

Reluctant learners may need more teacher structure and support during the initial phases of "learning to learn." In addition, they may be more responsive to certain elements of teacher attention than to others. This selective response to elements of teacher attention may be correlated with the child's developmental level and with certain prior histories of adult attention. A teacher who works with delayed learners will want to use those elements of teacher attention that will promote the most successful mastery by a child at a given developmental level.

An early approach to developmental research suggested that children first learned to interpret tactile information successfully, then visual information, and finally verbal information (White, 1965). A tentative hierarchy of teacher support strategies might include the modality through which a child is receiving information as a developmental factor, which could influence the degree of support perceived by the child from any one teaching element in a learning segment. If this modality factor is functional, physical cues (tactile) by the teacher might be easiest for the child to interpret; visual cues might be next; and verbal cues would probably be the most difficult for the child to interpret. Thus verbal cues may provide the least degree of perceived support to the child. In practice the teacher who moves the child's hands through the motions of assembling a puzzle (tactile "put through") provides more support than the teacher who says, "First put the ears in . . . now the legs . . . now the head . . ." (verbal instruction).

By the age of three or four, most children have begun to integrate information from all three of the suggested receptive modalities with varying degrees of discrimination. Over time a shift occurs; the visual mode of receiving information predominates over verbal information in young children, but reliance on tactile cues recedes (Eliason & Jenkins, 1977; Hayes & Birnbaum, 1980; White, 1965).

When a teacher attempts to match teaching input to the developmental needs of a child, it may be useful to consider the hierarchy of teaching elements that is presented in Exhibit 7–1. This exhibit of teaching elements is organized hypothetically from most supportive to least supportive, with receptive factors tentatively incorporated. Firm conclusions regarding differential effectiveness of certain elements of teacher attention must await further systematic experimental analyses.

PROVIDING A SEQUENTIAL STRUCTURE FOR RELUCTANT LEARNERS

Patterns of reluctant learning and related learning delays may call for some systematic structuring of a preschool child's early learning experiences. A return to basic patterns of attending and contact may be required. Some children will not deal successfully with the mutlitude of learning opportunities presented daily in the classroom. In fact, the variety of settings, formats, and available materials may prove distracting. Reluctant learners may have difficulty choosing from among freely presented activ-

Exhibit 7–1 Hierarchy of Teaching Elements

Hypothetical Organization

A. Mode of receiving information

easiest	medium	most difficult
physical (tactile)⟶	visual ⟶	verbal

B. Continuum of support

most support   least support

1. physical "put   2 to 10 ⟶   11. verbal informa-
   through" ⟶   tion

Teaching Elements

Physical Cues (tactile)

1. *"Put through"*—The teacher moves the child's hands, arms, and so on through the entire motion being taught.

   Advantages: 1. The child is given the opportunity to experience directly (see, feel, perform) all parts of the response including the final completion and whatever consequences follow from it.
   2. This is a useful technique for promoting a successful initial contact with the learning segment for a child who has difficulty interpreting visual or auditory cues.

   Disadvantages: 1. This technique requires little independent responding on the part of the child.
   2. Certain children may resist tactile contact by the teacher.

2. *Physical prompts*—The teacher starts the child's hand, arm, and so on into the required motion, but performs only part of the motion for the child. Child must continue the motion independently.

   Advantages: This is a tactile suggestion, or reminder, that may help the child initiate the motion and complete it.

   Disadvantages: A teacher must plan to decrease the quantity and frequency of physical support gradually or child dependence will result.

Exhibit 7–1 continued

Visual Cues

3. *Precise arrangement of materials*—A teacher sets out learning materials in such a way that minimum motions by the child will complete a product. (Example: The teacher arranges the pieces of a puzzle on the puzzle frame, touching their respective placement positions. Child has only to slide the pieces into place.)

Advantages:
1. Child has direct experience with successful completion without having to organize materials and actions visually first.
2. The materials directly suggest the learning focus without auditory interpretation.

Disadvantages:
1. Some materials are difficult to structure in this way.
2. The child's response is still an approximation to that of other peers. Independent visual organization must be programmed at a later point.

4. *Visual models*

a. teacher action: The teacher performs the action to be learned while the child watches. The child then duplicates the action.

b. material models: The teacher constructs the exact product to be completed by the child and leaves it as a reference for the child to consult. The child creates a product by referring to the available model.

Advantages:
1. The child receives a "complete picture" of the action or product to be learned. Complete visual information is provided, often in a step-by-step fashion.
2. Auditory interpretation can be kept to a minimum.

Disadvantages:
1. Operating from a visual model does not require independent problem solving, memory, verbal symbols, or creative integration from partial cues. Many advanced preacademic skills will require these processes later.

Exhibit 7–1 continued

5. *Visual prompts* direct the child's attention to some element of the response to be learned.

  a. teacher action: The teacher directs the child's attention to a correct or salient element of the learning segment by pointing to a location, feature, or unit of material. (Example: The teacher points to the correct location for placement while the child is holding a puzzle piece. The child places the piece correctly.) The teacher also may signal a response visually by performing some action previously established as a memory cue.

  b. material prompts: The teacher adds visual cues or supports to the learning materials to focus the child's attention and direct the child's action. (Example: John is having trouble printing the letter "e" from memory. The teacher draws several "e's" lightly with dotted lines for John to trace.)

  Advantages: 1. A visual prompt provides a suggestion to the child without providing a complete model. The child proceeds from partial information and fills in the completed response.
  2. Auditory interpretation is not required.

  Disadvantages: 1. Visual prompts must be gradually removed (faded) to a point where the child is performing without them. Systematic fading may be difficult.
  2. Visual prompts must be selected carefully. Some may actually distract a child away from the criterion concept.

Verbal Cues

Verbal methods of instruction share common advantages and disadvantages.

  Advantages: 1. Verbal cueing through instruction, explanation, and verbal description is by far the most natural way for adults to provide information. Thus verbal methods of teaching are often the most comfortable to a teacher.

Exhibit 7–1 continued

> 2. Children who have learned to interpret verbal cues have reached an advanced level of learning in which the spoken word or invisible sound acts as a symbol for concrete objects, actions, and relations.
> 3. A teacher can use verbal cues at any time or place.
>
> Disadvantages: 1. Many children do not successfully interpret verbal cues as symbols of concrete objects, actions, or relations.
> 2. Excessive verbal teaching can leave the child a passive listener unless provisions for child responses are carefully interspersed.
>
> 6. *Verbal model*—The teacher states the exact word or words the child is to say. The child repeats the verbal pattern. (This procedure is common in language learning.)
>
> 7. *Verbal prompt or partial model*—The teacher vocalizes a partial verbal response for the child. The child either fills in the missing parts or states the entire language chain. (Example: The teacher says, "Then Buffy and Mary went to the _____." The child picks up a sequence card representing a *grocery store,* or the child repeats and extends, "Buffy and Mary went to the *store.*")
>
> 8. *Verbal instruction*—The teacher verbally specifies a single action or a series for the child to complete. (Example: "Find the red circles and put them here.")
>
> 9. *Verbal signal*—The teacher vocalizes an established verbal cue to suggest or remind the child to respond. (Examples: "Shhh" or "It's your turn.")
>
> 10. *Verbal explanation or information*—The teacher describes or explains a concept. Examples: "Circles are round; squares have four sides and four corners (dimensions of shapes)." "Cows, pigs, and sheep all live on the farm (classification)."

ities or sustaining contact if a choice is made. A skillful teacher may want to structure selected elements of this child's learning day. At the same time, this child should continue to have exposure to the less structured free play and group formats for learning. As suggested earlier, peers who are choosing, playing, and exploring may serve as important learning models to the reluctant learner. Teacher structuring of brief parts of the day, plus the child's observation of the classroom peers, should combine to produce enthusiastic participation over time in the reluctant learner.

One goal for delayed learners is to introduce them gradually to elements of preacademic learning in such a way that they: (1) learn prerequisite attending skills; (2) experience initial success; and (3) gradually progress from structured learning to learning in the more flexible formats accepted by their normal peers.

Organizing a Learning Environment

Environmental structuring involves matching the features of the learning environment to the learning characteristics of a particular child. If the child cannot adjust completely to the existing learning opportunities, then parts of the learning setting may be adjusted to match the initial learning needs of the child. It is to be hoped that supplemental structure may be gradually reduced as the child makes learning gains. Thus many elements of environmental structure may be seen as interim remedial tools that are used only for a period of time, and then only for those children who require them. Factors to consider in organizing a remedial learning environment include the location for learning, the selection of learning materials, and the visual presentation of learning materials.

Location for Learning

It may be helpful for the child to have a fixed location where brief preacademic lessons occur daily. This location may be a carpet square in a specific area of the room or an assigned space at a table. Initially the teacher should guide the child to the assigned space and assist in seating so that the child is oriented toward the learning materials. Location, seating, and orientation are three basic elements to early attending.

If the child is provided initially with an assigned location for preacademic lessons, the child will learn a pattern of coming to a specific place at the request of the teacher. This place will then begin to cue attentiveness and other task orientation responses that are prerequisite to learning. An assigned learning location will reduce the distracting choice factors that are present in free choice and learning center environments.

It is not necessary that the child's assigned location for preacademic lessons be totally removed from the activity of other children. If the location is fixed and the teacher is available to guide attentiveness, then most children should learn easily to tolerate potential distractions of other children working in close proximity. In fact, as suggested earlier, the presence of other children working productively and attentively nearby may actually provide an influential model for the reluctant learner.

Selection of Materials

The following is a list of factors to consider when selecting preacademic materials to present to delayed learners:

- Select materials that clearly isolate or represent the concept being taught. Minimize elements that are extraneous to the core concepts. For example, if color recognition is being taught, do not select as the primary teaching material beads that vary in color *and* shape *and* size. Save the multicolored beads for expansion (generalization) learning activities.

- Select materials initially that are "concrete" representations of the concept. A circle that can be touched and manipulated communicates elements of "shape" more concretely than a black and white line drawing of a circle. Many delayed learners have voids of direct experience. They may fail to draw correct deductions from symbolic representations of objects, events, and relations.

- Select materials that provide a maximum of tactile and visual information with a minimum of verbal interpretation required. Verbal interpretation is a developmentally advanced skill that is crucial, but that may have to await later sequential teaching. Most children can learn valuable basic concepts through tactile and visual means before their skills of verbal discrimination have developed completely.

- Select materials that incorporate frequent but easily performed manipulative responses on the part of the child. The child must be an active "doer" to be learning, but the level of manipulative skills may be low initially.

- Select materials whose response requirements and visual complexity can be increased gradually. Many commercial materials incorporate these features. With jumbo pegs, for example, the number of required peg placements can be gradually increased from 1 to 20 or more as the child's attention span increases. Commercial parquetry pattern cards incorporate a sequence in which both the number of pieces to be placed and the visual complexity of the pattern increases gradually. A teacher may alter commercial sequences if their order is not appropriate for certain children.

- Select materials that can be arranged in units and presented to the child as a specific, visible product to be completed. It is helpful to the child to see that there is a fixed beginning and end to early preacademic tasks. The child then can learn, "When I do this much, I am finished." Later the teacher can let the child opt to complete more units if the child wishes. Initially, a minimum visible criterion can facilitate productive attention.

- Select materials that require visible responses on the part of the child. To "see" what the child is learning, in a concrete way, is a crucial ingredient in sequenced task prescription.

Visual Arrangement of Materials

The goal of this element is to present materials to the child in such a way that their physical arrangement cues orderly, efficient child responses. As suggested earlier, reluctant learners may experience difficulty in organizing their own workspace. Thus, the teacher will need to take responsibility for this physical-visual organization. Following are some suggestions that may be helpful:

- Limit available materials only to those that will be needed to complete the task unit.

- Arrange the first task materials on the work surface before the child arrives. A child may lose interest if expected to wait too long for a teacher to find and arrange needed materials.

- Arrange the needed materials directly in front of the child, close enough to minimize unnecessary reaching.

- Look at the materials from the child's eye range. Is there a glare on the materials that masks their detail? (This is often the case with artificial lighting.) Are the child's arms free to manipulate? A table that hits the child at a level higher than the waist may restrict arm movement. A "tall" material such as a form box may require a child to place pieces above the field of vision. In these cases, a taller chair or a shorter table may be simple solutions that will change the light pattern, free arm movements, or return materials to the child's optimum visual field.

- Place loose materials to be used by the child in a "holding container." The holding container will minimize the chance that the child will knock materials to the floor or otherwise lose them. Holding containers that may be used include berry baskets, margarine tubs, and plastic drawer organizers.

- Place parts of the material in front of the child in such a way that they will prompt efficient motions and visual attending patterns. With many materials, the following arrangement is appropriate: (a) place holding container of pieces to the side, close to the table edge, on the child's preferred hand side; and (b) place central material (pattern card, puzzle form, formbox, insets, and so on) directly in front of the child in the center of the work space, close to the edge of the table (or leave this place clear if no central material is required). This arrangement leaves the child a clear visual field in the center on which to work. It also minimizes the number of times the child reaches across the center of attention and work. Excessive reaching across the "product" area may cause the child to brush into already placed pieces, dislodging them. Repeated "fixing" may frustrate the child or make him or her lose interest before completing the unit.

- Attend to the visual order of the material itself. For example, in beginning counting it may be easier for the child first to touch and count a series of poker chips glued to strips of posterboard in a straight row, because the pieces do not move, and the straight row leads to easier remembering of start and finish. Later, the child can learn to point and count disordered (randomly placed) arrays and movable objects.

- Be prepared to add extra physical supports to help the child organize the workspace and task materials. For example, in matching pairs of cards, the child may not know how to *arrange* the ones that go together, even though the child experiences no difficulty *finding* those that go together. In this case, a placement board may be helpful. A lotto (matching) board can be constructed with a cardboard backing and dowels so that two rows of boxes are outlined:

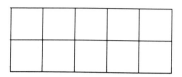

The teacher can arrange sample cards in the top row of boxes, and the child can select and place match cards (from the holding container) in the boxes underneath the sample cards. Once placed, the cards will remain in place because the dowel borders hold them. (They are not easily brushed away by a child reaching across.) Most important, the placement board presents an orderly visual arrangement to the child from start to finish.

The teacher may design other placement boards by simply drawing outlines or rows of boxes on posterboard without the added dowel borders. These location-placement cues may be helpful to children who are learning to place story cards in sequence, count loose objects, arrange letters of their name in order, and so on.

Selection of Initial Learning Goals

A primary goal of learning with reluctant learners should be selecting learning objectives that will gradually build important patterns of attending. In the young child, functional patterns of attending often involve factors of visual scanning (sustained looking) and elaborated manipulation (sustained contact) with preacademic learning materials. Many early learning experiences involve a child's use of stimulus cues across sensory modalities. For example, a child should "look-*and*-touch" while assembling puzzles; a child should "look (scan)-*and*-listen" while learning to identify and label objects, colors, and shapes. Moreover, these early learnings imply some element of duration, that is, increasing a child's "attention span."

Young children with learning delays often show deficits in their patterns of attending. They may manipulate materials only briefly before moving away. They may glance at visual stimuli briefly and fail to pair their looking with their hand movements or with the timing of the teacher's questions or instructions. Examples of these are the following: (1) the child who attempts to assemble puzzles by "scrabbling" pieces in the frame while looking across to another child's activity; and (2) the child who has glanced briefly at a color card but has looked away from it before the teacher can say the color name. In each case the patterns of brief contact or brief glancing compete with the child's acquisition of the concepts being presented. Without effective attending skills children's learning is delayed and inefficient.

Increasing time of contact with materials can be incorporated into many preacademic conceptual areas. Essentially, the teacher should start with a small number of motions to be completed or pieces to place, and gradually increase the response requirements as the child shows proficiency and efficient attending for longer periods of time. Increased contact is best taught when it is tied to specific response requirements rather than to arbitrary units of time. In this way the child is being taught to work productively until finished, but is not constrained by the situation to sit unoccupied while an arbitrary unit of time elapses.

The preacademic area of early fine motor manipulative skills is particularly conducive to teaching basic patterns of sustained contact and visual attending. Pegs and pegboards; formboxes; shape insets; inset cylinders; tong transfers; simple, knobbed wooden puzzles; pop beads; bead stringing; fit-a-space; and many other early learning materials might be included in this area. These materials share the following common features: (1) most require a child to use eye-hand coordination (visual scanning *and* simultaneous manipulation); and (2) most can be broken down into small response units (number of pieces to be placed) that can be increased gradually to produce increases in "attention span."

With these materials and teacher support, the child can learn that placement is "easier" when he or she keeps looking at the material in the hand and that completion of a unit of contact is enthusiastically approved by the teacher. An additional advantage of these materials is that they provide tactile and visual feedback on correctness of placement. When a piece "fits," it stays in place as a tangible product of the child's attention.

In cases of severe attentional deficits, a teacher would be well advised to select early learning units from the fine motor manipulative area. When basic attending and contact patterns have been learned with these materials, they will serve as valuable prerequisites to the attending required in other preacademic conceptual areas. Furthermore, early learning objectives in visual discrimination, basic identities, and early math can be designed to incorporate some of the manipulative attention skills that the child has already mastered. For example, sorting small plastic toys into colored baskets is a "color" skill. However, it incorporates skills of picking up pieces, looking, and placing that have been learned in earlier manipulative lessons.

Visual attending problems are difficult to detect unless a teacher is observing a child closely. In fact, children may have learned good patterns of visual attending in the fine motor area but still have problems in subsequent conceptual areas. These visual attention problems may be especially critical during lessons devoted to basic identities. (For example, color labels may seem especially difficult for some children.) For effective learning to occur, the child should be visually scanning an example of the identity at the same time that the label is heard. In this way the child receives simultaneous visual and auditory pairing that establishes the language identity of the object or attribute in question. (For example, the child should look at a toy car while hearing the word "car." The visual "picture" and the auditory "label" are paired simultaneously.)

In this author's experience, many delays in learning basic identities, especially abstractions (colors) or symbols (numerals) are correlated with a pattern of visual "glancing." The "glancer" often looks *away from* the identity object at the time the verbal label is provided. Thus, the auditory-visual pairing is broken. This pattern of "looking away" can be set up inadvertently by the teacher; many children first look at the object, then look away from the material *to the teacher* who is providing the label.

Patterns of "looking away" must be corrected early in a child's conceptual learning. Some guidelines for teaching more appropriate visual scanning might include the following:

- Sit across from the child, and watch the child's eyes during the presentation of identity materials. Try to time the saying of the verbal label with the time the child is directly looking at the stimulus example (object, flashcard).

- If the child is looking away from the stimulus material, refrain from saying the label. Either wait until the child is again looking at the material or directly prompt this visual scan, and *then* say the label while the child's eyes are on the material.

- If necessary, withdraw the visual material until the child is "ready to look."

- On occasion, a child's "pointing" to the material may cue good "looking." If this is true for a particular child, teach the child to point to the material when it is presented. Say the label while the child is "pointing and looking."

- In some children "tracing" the identity material facilitates more sustained looking and scanning. If this is true for a particular child, have the child look at and trace the stimulus (shape, letter, numeral) while the label is being said.

- If the child is to repeat the label, help the child say the label *while looking* at the stimulus material. A •hild's auditory label should also be paired with simultaneous visual scanning of the identity object. (Often children will look toward the teacher instead of the stimulus while they are naming identities.)

Clearly, not all learning problems are due to lapses in attention. In many cases a child has had inadequate experiences on which to base subsequent learning. However, fleeting contact patterns and "looking away" are attending problems that can compete with efficient learning at any level of curriculum prescription. Thus patterns of attending merit the early and continuous vigilance of the teacher.

Selecting Teaching Strategies

As suggested in Exhibit 7–1, a teacher may choose elements of teaching attention from a continuum of support strategies that range from maximum *physical support* to minimum *verbal information*. Each successive teaching cue on this continuum requires increasing levels of interpretation and independent action on the part of the child. A teacher will want to select teaching cues that match the current development needs of the child within the conceptual area being considered. (A teacher will want to remember, too, that a child may be more advanced in one conceptual area than another. For example, a child may complete fine motor tasks with ease independently but may need a great deal of support during early duplication of patterns activities [visual discrimination].) A teacher undoubtedly will use a variety of teaching cues within any one teaching segment. An effort should be made to start with a majority of those cues most easily interpreted by the child at that time. As the child shows signs of increasing independence, the amount of support may be gradually reduced by shifting to cues further along the support continuum.

Additional guidelines for choosing appropriate teaching strategies are the following:

- Start a teaching activity with a level of support that will help the child be successful immediately, but do not use more support than the child actually needs. One child truly may need physical guidance to ensure initial learning; another child may be successful with efficient visual prompts by the teacher.

- Move from one level of support to another rapidly, but smoothly. The goal is to produce maximum independence by the child as rapidly as possible, but without undue errors and/or frustration.

- Include elements of verbal instruction and verbal information along with physical and visual cueing, unless these prove distracting. While verbal input may be initially neutral as a cue, over time the child will learn to interpret verbal information that has been paired with concrete physical action and visual representation. (However, words should be selected carefully and expressed in a meaningful context.)

- When verbal instruction is being used as a teaching cue, make instructions concise and to the point; then allow a period of time sufficient for the child to initiate or complete the response. Many teachers preempt a child's response by repeating instructions in rapid succession. Some children will need more time than others to hear the instruction, interpret the verbal symbols, and translate the symbols into action.

THE PLEASURE OF TEACHING AND LEARNING

Structuring early learning for the reluctant learner is a continuous process. As suggested earlier, initial lessons in attending and sustained contact should be followed by a gradual progression that includes expanding the child's skills across preacademic areas and then moves the child's lessons gradually into the regular group teaching formats. The teacher should repeatedly add extra attention or physical support, and then withdraw it across all phases of this progression. At each stage the child should become increasingly independent.

Early in this teaching approach, the child and the teacher should start to experience mutual pleasure in the sequential teaching process. The child will be experiencing success and approval for preacademic efforts, perhaps for the first time. Moreover, the child will learn to have confidence in the teacher, who presents skills in steps that can be mastered and who provides positive support as needed. This teacher becomes a desirable companion. The teacher will be rewarded by seeing the child's improvement in attitude toward learning and in skills mastered, perhaps slowly at first, but steadily. Other rewards for the teacher will include the child's smile or comments during the successful completion of a task, the occasional prideful statement of "Oh, this is easy," or the child's use of new concepts, such as color labels during art or snack periods. Parents may also report that a child is using new skills at home, much to their surprise.

Over time, teachers of reluctant learners experience the satisfaction of having intervened successfully at an early stage of problem learning. Their experience with sequential teaching will have shown them that reluctant learners can, indeed, become enthusiastic participants in the early childhood classroom.

REFERENCES

Bereiter, C., & Engelmann, S. *Teaching disadvantaged children in the preschool.* Englewood Cliffs, N.J.: Prentice-Hall, Inc., 1966.

Charlesworth, R., & Radeloff, D.J. *Experiences in math for young children.* Albany, N.Y.: Delmar Publishers, 1978.

Cohen, M.A., & Gross, P.J. *The developmental resource: Behavioral sequences for assessment and program planning* (Vol. I and II). New York: Grune & Stratton, 1979.

Cooper, M. *A shoe is to tie.* Movie produced by Edna A. Hill Child Development Laboratory, Department of Human Developmment, University of Kansas, Lawrence, Kan., 1970.

Copeland, M., Ford, L., & Solon, N. *Occupational therapy for mentally retarded children.* Baltimore, Md.: University Park Press, 1976.

Eliason, C.F., & Jenkins, L.T. *A practical guide to early childhood curriculum.* St. Louis: C.V. Mosby, 1977.

Gardner, W.J. *Children with learning and behavior problems.* Boston: Allyn & Bacon, 1978.

Hayes, D.S., & Birnbaum, D. Preschoolers' retention of televised events: Is a picture worth a thousand words? *Developmental Psychology,* 1980, *15,* 410–416.

Johnson, V.M., & Werner, R.A. *A step-by-step learning guide for retarded infants and children.* Syracuse, N.Y.: Syracuse University Press, 1975.

O'Neil, S.M., McLaughlin, B.N., & Knapp, M.B. *Behavioral approaches to children with developmental delays.* St. Louis, Mo.: C.V. Mosby Co., 1977.

Resnick, L.B., Wang, M.C., & Kaplan, J. Task analysis in curriculum design: A hierarchically sequenced introductory mathematics curriculum. *Journal of Applied Behavior Analysis,* 1973, *6,* 679–710.

Rosner, J. *Preceptual Skills Curriculum.* New York: Walker Educational Corporation, 1973.

Rowbury, T.G., & Baer, D.M. The applied analysis of young children's behavior. In D.S. Glenwick and L.A. Jason (Eds.), *Behavioral community psychology: Progress and prospects.* New York: Praeger, 1980.

Thomson, C.I. Personal communication, 1979.

White, S.H. Evidence for a hierarchial arrangement of learning processes. In L.P. Lipsitt and C.C. Spiker (Eds.), *Advances in child development and behavior,* (Vol. 2). New York: Academic Press, 1965.

Watson, L.S. *How to use behavior modification with mentally retarded and autistic children.* Libertyville, Ill.: Behavior Modification Technology, Inc., 1972.

BIBLIOGRAPHY

Baratta-Lorton, M. *Work jobs.* Menlo Park, Cal.: Addison-Wesley Publishing Co., 1972.

Bluma, S.M., Scherer, M.S., Frohman, A.H., & Hilliard, J.M. *Portage guide to early education.* Cooperative Educational Service Agency #12, Portage, Wisconsin, 1976.

Braga, J., & Braga, L. *Children and adults: Activities for growing together.* Englewood Cliffs, N.J.: Prentice Hall, 1976.

Chapel-Hill Training-Outreach Project. *Learning activities for the handicapped child.* Winston-Salem, N.C.: Kaplan Press, 1976.

Charlesworth, R., & Radeloff, D.J. *Experiences in math for young children.* Albany, N.Y.: Delmar Publishers, 1978.

Cohen, M.A., & Gross, P.J. *The developmental resource: Behavioral sequences for assessment and program planning: Vol. I & II.* New York: Grune and Stratton, 1979.

Copeland, M., Ford, L., & Solon, N. *Occupational therapy for mentally retarded children.* Baltimore, Md.: University Park Press, 1976.

Dubnoff, G., Chambers, I., & Schaefer, F. *Dubnoff School Program, Levels 1–2.* Boston: Teaching Resources Corporation, 1968.

Eliason, C.F., & Jenkins, L.T. *A practical guide to early childhood curriculum.* St. Louis: C.V. Mosby, 1977.

Findlay, J., Miller, P., Pegram, A., Richey, L., Sanford, A., & Semrau, G. *A planning guide to the preschool curriculum.* Winston-Salem, N.C.: Kaplan Press, 1976.

Gray, S., Klaus, R., Miller, J., & Forrester, B. *Before first grade.* Columbia, N.Y.: Teachers College Press, Teachers College, Columbia University, 1966.

Johnson, V.M., & Werner, R.A. *A step-by-step learning guide for retarded infants and children.* Syracuse, N.Y.: Syracuse University Press, 1975.

Karnes, M.B. *Helping young children develop language skills.* Reston, Va.: Council for Exceptional Children, 1973.

Learning activities for threes. Ferguson, Mo.: Parent-Child Education Program, Ferguson-Florissant School District, 1980.

Learning activities for fours. Ferguson, Mo.: Parent-Child Early Education Program, Ferguson-Florissant School District, 1980.

Lillie, D.L. *Early childhood education.* Chicago, Ill.: Science Research Associates, Inc., 1975.

Linderman, C.E. *Teachables from trashables.* St. Paul, Minn.: Toys 'n Things Training and Resource Center, Inc., 1979.

Nimnicht, G., McAfee, O., & Meier, J. *The new nursery school.* Morristown, N.J.: General Learning Press, General Learning Corporation, 1969.

Orem, R.C. *A Montessori handbook.* New York: Capricorn Books, 1966.

Richardson, Jr., L.I., Goodman, K.L., Hartman, N.N., & LePique, H.C. *A mathematics activity curriculum for early childhood and special education.* New York: MacMillan Publishing Co., Inc., 1980.

Robinson, J.I., & Schmitt, B.A. *Vanguard school program, Parts 1–4.* Boston: Teaching Resources Corp., 1970.

Sparling, J., & Lewis, I. *Learning games for the first three years.* New York: Walker and Co., 1979.

Southwest Educational Development Laboratory. *How to fill your toy shelves without emptying your pocketbook.* Reston, Va.: The Council for Exceptional Children, 1976.

Thomson, C. *Skills for young children.* Lawrence, Kan.: Edna A. Hill Child Development Preschool Laboratories, University of Kansas, 1972.

Threshold early learning library: Fostering growth in perceptual and organizing skills (Vol. 1–3). MacMillan Publishing Co., Inc., 1970.

Watson, L.S. *How to use behavior modification with mentally retarded and autistic children.* Libertyville, Ill.: Behavior Modification Technology, Inc., 1972.

Weikart, D.P., Rogers, L., & Adock, C. *The cognitively oriented curriculum.* Urbana, Ill.: An ERIC-NAEYC Publication in Early Childhood Education, University of Illinois, 1971.

White, R., & Rehwald, M. *Mix and match: Activities for classification.* Los Angeles, Cal.: Rhythms Productions, 1976.

Chapter 8

Instructing Difficult-to-Teach Children

Judith M. LeBlanc

Most books and articles dealing with the developing of a curriculum for preschool children emphasize *what* is to be taught and describe *how* to teach it with vague statements such as "remember to praise children when they do well." This failure to provide information on *how* to teach is not unexpected since preschool education was historically and heavily influenced by the stages of development first postulated by Piaget.

In the Piagetian theoretical framework, children are thought not to possess a particular ability until the child has reached the developmental stage incorporating that ability. In the early development of preschool curriculum, therefore, the concepts to be taught at each of the stages, rather than the procedures for teaching, were emphasized. Because these stages of development assumed that certain prerequisite skills emanated from earlier stages, some preschool curriculums were well sequenced, thus providing logical pathways for children to follow in all developmental areas, for example, motor, conceptual, and social.

Until the advent of behavior analysis in preschool settings (Allen, Hart, Buell, Harris, & Wolf, 1964; Hart, Allen, Buell, Harris, & Wolf, 1964), teachers were not only left to their own devices regarding how to control the inappropriate behavior of preschool children, but also how to teach them. In the decade that followed, behavior analysis research repeatedly underlined the potency of teacher attention for dealing with the myriad of behavioral problems with which teachers are faced in the preschool classroom (Allen, Henke, Harris, Baer, & Reynolds, 1967; Brown & Elliot, 1965; Charlesworth & Hart, 1967; Clark, Rowburg, Baer, & Baer, 1973; Hardiman, Goetz, Reuter, & LeBlanc, 1975; Hart, Reynolds, Baer, Brawley, & Harris, 1968; Jonston, Kelley, Harris, & Wolf, 1966; Pinkston, Reese, LeBlanc, & Baer, 1973; Powers, Cheney, & Agostino, 1970; Reynolds & Risley, 1968). Reinforcement procedures other than teacher attention (for example, token systems) were also developed through behavior analysis and were sometimes used in preschool settings (Bushell, Wrobel, & Michaelis, 1968).

In the last decade a growing concern has developed regarding *how* teachers can teach preschool children conceptual, social, and motor skills when these skills do not develop normally. As indicated in Ruggles and LeBlanc (in press), even with the application of the most ideal reinforcement procedures for conceptual productivity and accuracy, some children do not learn. A technology of teaching skills that teachers can use to help preschool children overcome developmental delays is therefore needed. This technology would be expected to be useful not only for children experiencing developmental delays, but also for teaching all children who are learning new behavior.

Reinforcement of desired behaviors is typically a sufficient procedure for teaching children skills that are primarily a combination of previously learned simpler behaviors. For example, if increasingly complex block building is reinforced, creative block building should occur (Goetz & Baer, 1973). The procedure of reinforcing small steps leading to a more complex behavior results in children acquiring the behavior with little of the stress that typically results from incorrect (and thus unreinforced) responses. This procedure of reinforcing increasingly complex behavior can be used to develop many types of complex behaviors, for example, social interaction, climbing, drawing, and so on. There are, however, basic skills to be learned by preschool children that are not composed of small steps leading to a more complex behavior, for example, numeral, shape, letter, and word recognition, in addition to counting, letter writing, and so on. Such basic behaviors require the formation of discriminations that are totally new to the child. They are essentially new concepts that are frequently categorized as academic or preacademic. If reinforcement of correct responding is the procedure used to teach these skills, then some children will make many errors in the learning process. For some, these errors will result in learning incorrect responding that can lead to future academic failure. In fact, errors in children's prior learning history can detrimentally affect later learning on similar tasks even when optimal teaching strategies are incorporated (Schilmoeller, Schilmoeller, Etzel, & LeBlanc, 1977). Preschool is where academic learning begins. It is also where academic failure or enjoyment of learning can also begin. The use of good teaching procedures at the preschool level are necessary to assure early academic success.

Academic learning involves interactions between the following: (1) curriculum materials; (2) the learner's response to those materials; and (3) the events that precede and maintain the learning response. The specific type of interaction between these variables in the learning environment is important for all children, but is especially critical for children experiencing learning difficulties.

Designing learning materials to preclude or greatly reduce errors during the learning process is as important as designing materials to enhance children's enjoyment of the learning process. Most of the emphasis in the development of curriculum materials has, unfortunately, been upon making the materials attractive, and relatively little has been placed upon assuring that learning occurs with few or no errors. This is not surprising, since only recently has there been any published research dealing with the development of errorless learning techniques for use with preschool children (Ruggles & LeBlanc, in press; Etzel & LeBlanc, 1979; Schilmoeller & Etzel, 1977). Teaching children with few or no errors is dealt with in another chapter in this book and thus is only mentioned here as being important because errors escalate to produce failure.

How a child responds to learning materials provides the teacher with an evaluation of the learning materials and teaching procedures being used. If the child is not learning, the arrangement of the learning environment must not be correct for that child. Teachers should thus be sensitive and shift to alternative procedures when children begin to experience failure.

The third category of variables involved in the learning process, that is, the events that precede and maintain learning, is the topic of current discussion. The effectiveness of the total learning environment for enhancing learning can be evaluated by assessing the following four components: (1) the motivational system; (2) the possible presence of child responses that are incompatible with learning; (3) the presence of prerequisite skills; and (4) the effectiveness of teacher instructions, feedback, and other environmental variables in the learning evironment (Etzel & LeBlanc, 1979). As indicated in Etzel and LeBlanc (1979), the simplest procedure is the procedure of choice if it is effective. For example, simply telling children to "hurry up and wash your hands" has been found to result in equally clean hands and faster execution than the more laborious and typical teaching procedure of lining up and washing hands (Wallace, Hatfield, Goetz, & Etzel, 1976).

Following the logic of choosing the simplest procedure, if reinforcement of correct responses with correction of incorrect responses (trial-and-error learning) is sufficient for a child to learn academic tasks, then this would be the procedure of choice because it is simple and effective. When it is not effective, then the teacher should determine whether the reward for responding is sufficiently reinforcing for the child to learn. Reinforcement effectiveness can be easily determined by implementing the reinforcer (for example, teacher attention) for a behavior the teacher knows the child is able to perform. If that behavior increases and maintains, teacher attention is a likely reinforcer. It is important to remember that what is reinforcing or punishing for one child may not be for another. It cannot be assumed, for example, that teacher praise is reinforcing for all children. For many who have not had a good history of adult attention, praise will not be sufficient to initiate or maintain behavior. Thus, identifying a potent reinforcer for each child must precede any attempts to teach children new behaviors. Teaching new academic behaviors is difficult enough without attempting to do so with a less than powerful reinforcer.

Some children might not learn even after motivation has been increased, because they are engaging in behaviors incompatible with learning, that is, the child is not attending to the task but to other variables in the environment. A child, for example, may be watching classroom peers rather than looking at the learning materials, may point with the fist rather than the finger, may push the materials off the table, may lie in the middle of the material, or may engage in a myriad of other nontask behaviors. If such occurs, the specific nontask behaviors should be identified, and a procedure of ignoring these behaviors, and modeling and reinforcing task-related behaviors that are incompatible with the nontask behaviors should be implemented (Winslow & Etzel, 1972).

After a motivational system is established and the child is engaging in work-related behaviors, then the teacher should determine whether or not the child has the necessary prerequisite skills to learn the task to be taught. This can be accomplished through task analysis (Resnick, Wang, & Kaplan, 1973) by dividing the task entry behaviors into simple behavioral subcomponents and assessing whether or not the child is able to engage in each of them.

If the child is motivated, is engaged in task-related behaviors, and possesses the prerequisite skills for the learning task, but still does not readily learn through trial-and-error procedures, a more comprehensive analysis of the learning environment should be undertaken to determine if variables such as instructions, feedback, and/or other teacher-controlled stimuli are enhancing or retarding learning.

INSTRUCTION FOLLOWING

Early in their development, most children are capable of responding to simple commands, such as "Give me the spoon," "No, don't touch," and so on. Instruction following is the earliest measurable form of receptive language development in children. Children's responses to instructions can therefore provide indicators of whether a child's development is optimal or whether intervention programs should be prescribed. Children who expeditiously follow instructions are also those who, at school age, are successful and with whom teachers enjoy working. Children who do not develop this skill at an early age can look forward to difficulties in school. These difficulties will focus teachers' attention on the negative rather than the positive attributes of such children. This emphasis can, in turn, lead to further retardation of their development. Because it has become necessary to educate all children, the ability to follow instructions is no longer a prerequisite for entering school (Spradlin & Spradlin, 1976). A greater promise of academic success in public schools is assured, however, if children can follow instructions. If one goal of preschools is to provide the child with as strong a foundation as possible for public school education, then instruction following should not only be assessed, it should also be a goal of preschool education.

There are at least two major factors that play a role in the development of instruction following in children: (1) the child's visual and auditory perceptual capabilities; and (2) the past history of the child's instruction following. It is sometimes quite difficult to determine whether a young child is not complying with an instruction because of an inability to interpret the meaning of the instruction, because the child does not wish to comply, or both. Children's perceptual capabilities and environmental histories are exceedingly varied, and it is usually impossible to say precisely why a child does not comply with instructions. The essential fact is that the child does not comply. The reasons are superfluous to the ultimate goal of working with a child experiencing this problem. That is, a child must acquire the ability to comply with instructions if that child's educational process is not to be impeded, and this must be accomplished no matter the reason underlying the problem.

The development of an instruction-following technology should therefore result in procedures to evaluate instruction-following responding and to prescribe intervention programs to enhance *all* children's abilities to follow instructions, regardless of their individual capabilities. That is, it is left to procedures emanating from a child's learning environment to assure the development of instruction following, even when the child's perceptual capabilities are not optimal for such development.

WHAT IS AN INSTRUCTION?

Typically, instructions are thought to be verbal statements delivered by a teacher. This is, however, a somewhat narrow definition. Other forms of instructions occur frequently in a child's environment. For example, the teacher might instruct through modeling the response desired of the child, or the teacher might nonverbally indicate what is to be done. The teacher might also deliver an instruction while providing feedback to the child regarding a previously performed response, for example, "Are there more blue objects like the two you put there?" This feedback tells the child the response was correct and should be performed again. Instructions might also be implied through the arrangement or format of the materials the child is to use. In many workbooks, for example, there will be a correct example provided, and the child is to complete other items in a similar manner. In the educational environment, instructions are essentially everywhere, and only the careful arrangement of these environmental instructional variables will lead to successful learning for many children.

INSTRUCTION FOLLOWING AND REINFORCEMENT

Behavior analysis research on instruction following has followed a pattern similar to behavior analysis research in preschool education, that is, the emphasis has been upon how reinforcement can enhance the potency of instructions, rather than upon *how* teachers should instruct. It is known, for example, that instructions without reinforcement for instruction following can be initially effective to control behavior of young children. Instructions will, however, lose this effectiveness unless instruction following is eventually reinforced (Hopkins, 1968; Zeilberger, Sampen, & Sloane, 1968; Zimmerman, Zimmerman, & Russell, 1969) or not following instructions is punished (Ramp, Ulrich, & Dulaney, 1971). It has also been demonstrated that telling children the classroom rules results in little or no behavioral change unless feedback and contingencies for following the rules are applied (Greenwald, Hops, Delquadri, & Guild, 1974).

Although potency of instructions is based on reinforcement, it is also important to remember that instructions themselves can sometimes be reinforcers (Madsen, Becker, Thomas, Koser, & Plager, 1968; Miller, Holmberg, & LeBlanc, 1971). In addition, if instructions are deleted too early in the learning process and only reinforcement remains, children may fail to learn the task (Baron, Kaufman, & Stauber, 1969). Exposing children to punishment for not following instructions is not as effective as providing instructions about the desired behavior and its potential consequences (Baron & Kaufman, 1966; Scobie & Kaufman, 1969). Instruction following in group settings can be accomplished with tokens (Baer, Rowbury, & Baer, 1973) or teacher attention (Goetz, Holmberg, & LeBlanc, 1975).

Social variables in the learning environment have effects on instruction following. If teachers say or inadvertently imply that they do not care what children do, the children will be less inclined to follow classroom procedures even if reinforcement for procedural compliance prevails in the classroom (Goetz et al., 1975; Steinman, 1970a, 1970b). For example, when children indicate they do not desire to engage in a specific task when instructed and the teacher responds by indicating that is all right since the child is perhaps tired, the child learns that, although the teacher requested a particular behavior, it is not important to the teacher that the child respond. Such situations potentially decrease future instruction following because the teacher counterinstructed the original instruction. The teacher, in effect, said it was all right *not* to comply with classroom procedures (Goetz et al., 1975).

Children are more likely to comply with classroom structure and procedures when teachers are present (LeBlanc, Miller, Pinkston, & Busby, 1971; Marholin & Steinman, 1977; Peterson & Whitehurst, 1970). How the child perceives the adult issuing the instructions is also important (Peterson & Whitehurst, 1970). If the person is viewed as one who does not follow through and ensure compliance, the child is less likely to comply.

Although the social variables surrounding the instructor and how to make instructions more potent through reinforcement are important, there is no assurance that even the most potent instructions will successfully teach a child new academic behaviors. Emphasis upon the content and mode of the instructions, rather than upon the behavior of instruction following, is vital in the academic learning process.

CONTENT AND MODE OF INSTRUCTIONS FOR EFFECTING ACADEMIC LEARNING

To examine the effects of content and mode of instructions on academic learning, it is necessary to attend to such factors as what the instructions say, the placement of instructions with respect to the child's responses, the timing of instructions, the combination of verbal and nonverbal instructions, and the ratio of instructions to responding. Information about such factors is, as earlier indicated, limited. There is, however, a beginning technology of teacher instructions from which some helpful ideas can be drawn about what to do when a child is not learning a prescribed task.

As charged in Spradlin and Spradlin (1976), teachers should have as a goal the actual teaching of instruction following to those children for whom the skill is not developed. To reach that goal, effective instructional procedures need to be identified and procedures developed to determine the best fit between individual children and specific types of instructions, as well as between type of task and instructions.

MODELING

Showing children how to perform, that is, modeling, should be used to enhance learning. Instructions that involve only verbal statements are of limited value for teaching young children and children who have learning problems. It is difficult to know the verbal receptive capacity of these children. In addition, research indicates that some children learn better with visual and others with auditory cues (Lovaas, Schreibman, Koegel, & Rehm, 1971). Considering all these facts, the probability of using instructions that include words and/or phrases outside these children's understanding is great. Teachers should therefore routinely use modeling along with instructions and correction procedures, because the combination of modeling and instructions is eminently more powerful than instructions alone (Smith & Lovitt, 1976; Zimmerman & Rosenthal, 1974). Modeling is also quite powerful when used in combination with self-instruction (Borstein & Quevillon, 1976).

Modeling, however, can also be detrimental to the learning process if ineffectively incorporated. For example, if a teacher wishes to teach children how to tie their shoes, the teacher's hands should be positioned so the demonstrations are not hidden (Cooper, LeBlanc, & Etzel, 1968). This is a common error committed by adults when they concentrate on demonstrating the task rather than on the vantage point of the child.

Modeling enhances most learning processes and, when it is coupled with instructions, correction, and self-instruction, it has a potent influence on learning. Thus, modeling should be one trick in the bag of all preschool teachers for use in combination with instructions when learning new academic tasks.

FEEDBACK AND CORRECTION

A child should always be told when responses are correct or incorrect (feedback). The specific procedures to follow in providing feedback are many and varied. There is no doubt that children learn new tasks faster and with greater efficiency when feedback is provided (Woodward, 1974). In addition to feedback, correction procedures should be utilized in the learning process (Reiber & Lockwood, 1969). When a child makes a mistake, the correction of the error should be made as soon thereafter as possible, and, when possible, the verbal correction should be accompanied by a teacher model of the correct response.

Frequently, after teachers correct a child's incorrect response, the child then performs the response correctly. Sometimes this final corrected response is reinforced as if it were an originally correct response. When this occurs, the child may learn that it is not necessary to be initially correct. In fact, a child may learn that it is easier to wait until the teacher provides the correct response and then imitate that response to obtain the reinforcer, rather than to engage in the more difficult task of trying to determine the correct response initially. When such a sequence develops, children do not learn the discriminations involved in the task. Since the children need only to imitate the teacher to obtain reinforcement, the teacher is caught in a trap leading to no learning.

Sometimes correction procedures lead teachers into another undesirable situation, that is, of correction procedures resulting in more, rather than fewer, incorrect responses (Cunningham, Cooper, Plummer, & LeBlanc, 1975). This usually happens when a child already knows the task and realizes that more teacher attention and teacher time can be obtained when incorrect responses are made. Sometimes children do not wish to engage in tasks that are already learned, and they are more reinforced by receiving the extra teacher attention involved in correction procedures than by the consequences programmed for correct responding. Even bright children sometimes engage in incorrect work to obtain more teacher time. This is a trap for the teacher, and the only resolution is to develop procedures that allow teacher time for children who are readily learning that is equal to that provided for children experiencing difficulty in learning.

There is no conclusive evidence that negative statements made by teachers subsequent to incorrect responding enhance or detract from learning (McTague, 1972; Nelson, 1974; Winston & Redd, 1973). Although the use of negative statements can lead to a sense of failure on the part of the child, some reprimands have been demonstrated to function as reinforcement (Hayden, Herbert-Jackson, Pinkston, & LeBlanc, 1972). Thus, it seems best to eliminate all negative statements from the teaching setting; this includes the use of the word "no." "No" is often the first word children learn, and it indicates that what the child did was "bad." Incorrect responding in an academic setting is not "bad," and for this reason the word "no" should be eliminated from that setting. When children are engaged in inappropriate social behavior during academic time, however, a firm "no" is sometimes sufficient to return them to their academic tasks.

When a child makes an incorrect response, feedback should consist of the teacher indicating only the correct choice and not the error the child made. When teachers demonstrate the child's incorrect response, attention is drawn to that response, and an incorrect model that the child can potentially imitate is available. As more attention is paid to the incorrect stimulus, the probability of the child responding to that stimulus is increased (Stella & Etzel, 1978). Thus, correction procedures should include only a model of the correct response. Sometimes teachers spend much time going over a child's completed academic product and indicating to the child why the child's responses were correct. Such rehearsal of what the child did, however, is quite delayed and serves little useful purpose. When the child is correct, praise for doing good work should be sufficient. Rehearsal of the child's original responding merely prolongs the teaching process and disrupts the pace of learning. Instead, a teacher can provide praise and indicate that the child is progressing to even more challenging tasks.

Children should have a sense of overall progress rather than a feeling of static responding to an isolated task. Most preschool learning tasks are arranged in terms of graduated difficulty. This arrangement provides the teacher with an opportunity to set up a system based on the arrangement that allows the child to see learning progress. For example, if there are eight categories in a task, the same type of feedback card can be developed. Each time a child masters a particular step, the card can be shown to the child, and together the child and teacher can mark off the step leading to the ultimate goal of completing all the steps. This not only teaches the child the concept of working toward an overall goal, it also provides reinforcement by praising the child's success for each step leading to the goal. This also introduces the child to the reporting system that will be used in the public schools.

Feedback and correction procedures are vital in the learning process. They must, however, be carefully developed to enhance rather than impede the learning process. Correct responses should be reinforced as quickly as possible. Incorrect responses should be corrected immediately by indicating what the correct response should be and by ignoring what the incorrect response was. Finally, a method should be devised that provides children with a sense of progressing toward a pre-established learning goal.

CONTENT OF VERBAL INSTRUCTIONS

What teachers say while instructing children receives little attention in the development of teaching procedures or curriculum development. The content of instructions, however, can be directly related to whether or not an individual child will learn a task. As indicated earlier, young children and children with learning difficulties have limited verbal capacities. Many children will vocally respond to an instruction with the last word uttered in the teacher's instruction. Thus, the question "What is in the box on the table?" may receive the answer "table." Undeniably, reinforcement history has an effect on learning, but the amount of information involved in an instruction can have an even greater effect (Piper, 1970). It is possible, for example, that too much information or too many verbal statements can be as detrimental to learning as too little or unclear information (Rintoul, Cooper, Schilmoeller, & LeBlanc, 1975). When children are taught simple discriminations such as the difference between the words "dig" and "dog," instructions should be kept to a minimum for optimal performance (Miller & LeBlanc, 1973, 1974). It is better for the teacher to say "This is the word 'dig', point to 'dig', and say 'dig'," than to say "This is the word 'dig'. You dig in the sand. It's fun to dig. Point to 'dig' and say 'dig'." The latter instructions are much too long and complicated, and the statements have nothing whatsoever to do with the essential differences between the words "dig" and "dog."

In addition to amount of instructions, the relationship between what is said and the task to be learned is critical. In the task described earlier, if the longer instructions are altered to draw the child's attention to the critical differences between the words, then they become as effective, if not more so, as the minimal instructions (Hass, Ruggles, & LeBlanc, 1979). Such instructions might be, "This is the word 'dig'. The word dig has an 'i' in the middle. The 'i' looks like a shovel. You dig with a shovel. Point to 'dig', and say 'dig'." Now the instructions indicate where the child is to look and provide a mnemonic device that the child might use to remember the differences between the two words.

Amount of teacher instructions can preclude child responding. If a teacher suggests that a child engage in social interaction with peers and the child remains close to the teacher rather than complying, the teacher can either stay with the child and continue to make unsuccessful suggestions or can make the suggestion and walk away, leaving the child to comply (Miller, Holmberg, & LeBlanc, 1971). If the teacher remains with the child, the child is receiving the desired teacher attention and thus has no reason to comply. However, if the teacher leaves, the message to the child is that only compliance will result in more teacher attention. Such a procedure, of course, is only successful when the teacher returns to attend to the child when the child engages in interaction with a peer.

The more a teacher talks with children to encourage them to interact, the less the children interact with each other (Rintoul, Cooper, Schilmoeller, & LeBlanc, 1975). When the teacher is talking almost continuously, there is little time left for the children to engage in conversation. Thus, the teacher should initiate conversation between peers with few words and then attempt to decrease teacher participation to a minimum.

When teachers praise children, the praise should be descriptive, that is, the child should be told why praise is being given. When teachers praised a three-year-old, cerebral palsied child for standing by saying "Good, Timmy" or other similar statements, standing did not increase. When, however, a description of what was being praised was added to the praise statements, standing did increase. Essentially, the teachers made comments such as, "My, you are standing tall" or "You look so nice when you are standing," and standing occurred for approximately 95 percent of the three-hour preschool day.

Verbal instructions should be kept to a minimum and be related to the task to be learned. When praise is given, it should instruct the child about why praise is forthcoming. Teachers should also attempt to initiate children's behavior and then retire to a place of lesser prominence so the children can engage in the behavior the teachers are attempting to teach.

INSTRUCTIONAL TIMING

The temporal location of instructions play a large role in instructional effectiveness. The instructional variables occurring prior to child responses are typically referred to as instructions. Those variables occurring subsequent to the response are referred to as feedback or corrections. As indicated earlier, what the teacher does at both times is essential to the success of teaching procedures. In addition, the pace of the delivery of the instructions can have a large effect on children's learning.

When children are allowed too much time to respond to an instruction, the probability that responses incompatible with learning will occur increases. This is especially true when working with children in groups. When a teacher allows children a large amount of time to seek the correct response on a task that they know, the learning setting becomes inefficient and frequently disruptive (Busby & LeBlanc, 1972). Placing time limits on children's learning in such situations decreases disruptions to a minimum. Establishing the appropriate time limitations for the task difficulty is, however, an important consideration. There are tasks that are so complex that even several minutes are required to study the several choices from which to select one (Schilmoeller & Etzel, 1977). When such is the case, the child would probably be actively engaged in visually scanning the task and would not be responding to other variables in the environment or engaging in nontask behavior.

The amount of time between instructions, that is, the pace of instructions, is also critical to the learning process. After a child responds to a particular instruction, if too much time elapses before new instructions are provided, nontask behavior is likely to occur. If the child does not respond to the instructions and too much time elapses before the teacher issues another instruction, the child learns that it is not necessary to complete the task efficiently (Plummer, Baer, & LeBlanc, 1977). In situations requiring the child to work hard to learn, children may even refuse to respond. Children who do this are a problem for teachers who become frustrated in their efforts to make the child respond. When such occurs with great frequency, the typical teacher response is to avoid instructing the child to avoid the overall frustrating situation. Such avoidance, however, results in the child avoiding the work tasks and not learning. Thus, the teacher should continue to instruct the child at a reasonable pace until the child learns that responding to teacher instructions is the only way to conclude the learning task. This technique, however, will not work in isolation (Baxter, Aangeenbrug, Kramer, Ruggles, Etzel, & LeBlanc, 1981). Teachers must also be excited about the child's work and praise the child when responding to instructions finally occurs.

Preschool children typically do not have extended attention spans, and it is difficult to keep them working on the same task for long periods of time. This should be considered when planning the instructional period. One way to maintain attention is to keep the pace of the learning setting moving without lag times. For example, if a child has completed a task and the teacher is working with another child, a simple "filler" task should be available so the child can work until the teacher returns to provide the next set of instructions (Baxter et al., 1981). In addition, all materials to be used in the academic time should be close to the learning setting and organized so the teacher can merely place the materials in front of the child and work can immediately begin. There is no place for "downtime" in the academic setting. Such time only provides an obvious opportunity for children to engage in nontask behaviors. Academic periods are a time to work, and other periods of the day are available for social interaction and play. Children should learn this early in their academic career to ensure future school success. This can only be accomplished if there is always something available on which the children can work.

Because of the emphasis upon working and because typically children must sit at one place at a table to engage in academic work, these periods should not be too long. It is better to have two such periods in the day than to expect children to work without becoming restless for long periods of time.

There is one procedure of instructional timing that can result in errorless or near-errorless learning of certain types of tasks, for example, labeling. This is typically referred to as the delayed cue procedure (Radgowski, Allen, Ruggles, & LeBlanc, 1978; Radgowski, Allen, Schilmoeller, Ruggles, & LeBlanc, 1978; Touchette, 1971). In a color labeling task, the teacher might say, "What color is this?" On the first request the teacher would say "red" before the child had an opportunity to respond, and then the child would merely imitate the verbal response "red." On the second request, the teacher would wait one or two seconds before providing the answer to see if the child responds before the teacher says the answer. The length between the teacher instruction and the teacher provision of the answer should be gradually increased until the child eventually "beats" the teacher and provides the answer first. When using this procedure, at least two labels should be simultaneously taught, randomly intermixing the requests for each. This procedure reduces pressure by reducing errors when children are beginning to learn a new concept. Another appealing aspect of the procedure is that it can be used even more efficiently in teaching groups of children than in teaching children individually (Radgowski, Allen, Ruggles, & LeBlanc, 1978). It is an especially useful remedial procedure when a child is experiencing difficulty learning.

The academic teaching situation should be well organized, move at a fast but reasonable pace, be short with short tasks, have material constantly available on which the child can work, and utilize procedures that allow the child to be as successful as possible. Although children should learn that the academic period is a time to work, in this period they also should learn that learning can be fun and fulfilling.

SELF-INSTRUCTION

In order to strengthen responses expected in certain settings, children should be taught to instruct themselves. For example, if a teacher has difficulty getting children to remain seated and pay attention during times when the total preschool class is expected to be participating in the same activity, then children can be provided with small bead bracelets to count whether or not they are participating at intervals specified by some signal such as a randomly generated tone. After the activity is completed, the teacher and children for whom the counting procedure was implemented can privately discuss the child's individual accuracy and progress (Reiber, Schilmoeller, & LeBlanc, 1975).

A way to strengthen academic learning with self-instruction is to use verbal mediation, for example, when a teacher asks a child to identify certain colors, it is better to have the child point to and say the color rather than only point to the color. The child's rehearsing the name of the color results in faster learning than if the label is not repeated by the child (Bybel & Etzel, 1973).

These types of self-instruction place some of the responsibility for learning with the child. Such procedures, therefore, not only teach children good procedures for evaluating their own work and productivity, but also teach independence through self-responsibility.

INSTRUCTING THROUGH ENVIRONMENTAL ARRANGEMENTS

How the environment and materials are arranged can have great impact on the efficiency with which children learn. When teachers are faced with a chaotic setting rather than organized learning, they should pause and examine the environment in which that learning is expected to take place. If, for example, teachers wish for children to learn to dress themselves after playing in a wading pool, they should fold the children's clothes and put them into the children's lockers in a manner that leads to systematic dressing. When the children return from the pool, they will be much more efficient in their independent dressing than if the clothes are merely bunched into their separate lockers (Plummer, Gaines, Grant, & Holmberg, 1973). This may at first seem like a procedure that requires too much teacher time. It is, however, much less time-consuming than dressing all the children.

Sometimes the simple placement of children at the table in the academic setting can seriously affect their learning. Some children tend to be more disruptive and inattentive than others. These are also children who require more immediate and individualized help in their work. Separating such children when there are more than one in a group drastically reduces such disruptions, because the opportunity to disrupt and respond to each other is not readily available (Baxter et al., 1981). Because they need more help, these children should also be placed so the teacher can see them at all times. When they are in the teacher's peripheral vision, the probability that the teacher will not be able to respond immediately to their academic responses, right or wrong, increases.

Sometimes the arrangement of materials teaches children what teachers do not wish them to hear. For example, if materials are sequenced in such a manner that a left (or right) position is always the position in which the correct response occurs, the child learns to point to that position rather than to the item that the teacher is attempting to teach as correct.

While tasks to be learned should not be too complex, teaching only one item at a time in a particular type of task can yield problems (Britten, Ruggles, & LeBlanc, 1979, 1980). If, for example, a teacher wishes to teach a child the names of some shapes, "circle" should not be taught in isolation. Instead, circle and perhaps square should be taught simultaneously. This allows the child to make a comparison between the two pictures and also to learn what a circle is not as well as what it is. If only circle is taught and the child is responding with the word circle to that picture, and then the picture of the square is introduced, the child is quite likely to respond with the word circle to the picture square. This is because the word circle has been reinforced in past learning, and no discrimination between the circle and square was required on the part of the child.

Materials should be used that provide optimal learning conditions for the child. Many times curriculum designers make materials for preschool children quite large because they assume that children can handle larger materials with greater ease and will attend to them more readily. This is not always true. If a teacher wishes for a child to compare several different pictures and categorize them, large pictures could make the comparison more difficult because the child must scan large areas by moving the head, and comparisons are not possible in one glance. Eliminating any sense of failure in the learning process is important. When children are learning new tasks that are potentially difficult for them, previously learned items should be intermixed with the new items to be learned. This provides the child with the opportunity to be readily successful while working on the more difficult task.

INSTRUCTING CHILDREN IN GROUPS

Individually teaching children is not an efficient method for maximizing staff time. In addition, it is often surmised that teaching children individually is the optimal method for the child. For some types of learning and perhaps for some types of children, this might be the appropriate approach. It is not, however, the approach that prepares the child for future education in public schools. In addition, when children learn in isolation, they have no opportunity to learn from each other. Teachers should therefore attempt to incorporate procedures for effectively working with children in groups into their teaching techniques.

Materials designed for individual children can often be used effectively in groups of children who are operating at approximately the same level. This is especially true if each child must listen to the other children's responses in the group in order to be correct (Sabbert, Holt, Nelson, Domash, & Etzel, 1976).

Additionally, children can learn different but related discriminations in groups, and, through observing the other children's responding, they can learn the discriminations taught as well as some that were not directly taught. For example, if two children in a group are taught to choose the picture of a cow when the teacher asks them to point to the picture of the cow, and two other children in the group are taught to choose the printed word "cow" when the teacher says, "Point to the word 'cow'," the children learn what they were directly taught, what the other children in the group were taught, and also an emergent relationship that was not taught to anyone in the group (that is, to match the printed word cow to the picture of the cow) (Ruggles & LeBlanc, 1979). Procedures such as these can also be used to teach children functional concepts, such as grouping fruits and vegetables (Fallows MacDonald, Cooper, Etzel, LeBlanc, & Ruggles, 1980; Fallows MacDonald, Ruggles, & LeBlanc, 1980). When a teacher wishes for children to attend to other children's responses and learn through observation of what the other child does, simple instructions to watch the other children can be initially effective. However, more potent instructions, such as telling one child to watch a specific other child because the teacher is going to see if the first child can remember what the second child did, and reinforcement for attending are frequently required to maintain the attending that is necessary for children to learn through observation (Kramer, Ruggles, & LeBlanc, 1981).

The behavior of children in group learning situations can also be maintained through indirect instructional control. When teachers say to one child in the group, "I like the way you are working," the other children in the group who were not working typically commence to work (Broden, Bruce, Mitchell, Carter, & Hall, 1970; LeBlanc, Miller, Pinkston, and Busby, 1971).

Even when children are working on dissimilar tasks, teachers can, through good organization and pacing, keep all children working at all times during the academic period (Baxter et al., 1980). It does require, however, that the teacher be constantly moving, watching children, and evaluating their responses.

Close attention should be paid to the arrangement of the learning environment and materials. Materials should be arranged so the desired responses are likely to occur and for the appropriate reasons. Materials should also be sequenced to enhance rather than impede or confuse the learning process. Teachers should analyze what children might learn from one another and arrange the learning environment so that such is likely to occur. The placement of a child in the learning environment and instructions used for all children should be examined so that optimal learning conditions can prevail.

INSTRUCTOR CHARACTERISTICS

The final but most important component in instructional control is the teacher. Teachers could precisely implement all the instructional procedures suggested here and still be totally ineffective if their demeanor is ineffective. Demeanor is an exceedingly important variable in the instructional process, but describing the differences between effective and ineffective teacher demeanor is at best quite difficult. Effective *and* ineffective teachers can be smiling or not; they can speak softly or loudly; or they can talk much or little. However, some are more effective than others. Why? Effective teachers are obviously decisive, in control of the situation, confident, and immediate with their praise or with their displeasure, and they operate on the child's level but command respect, and let the child know through the contingent use of behavioral extremes (for example, smiling and frowning) what the child is doing correctly and incorrectly. They know when to be kind and understanding, and when to be firm. The master teacher is to be admired and respected, but not held in awe. The effective behaviors of the master teacher can be taught, and thus the population of master teachers can be increased (Baxter et al., 1981).

One method for increasing the number of master teachers is to teach teachers to use the best of the currently available technology of teaching and to teach them the skills necessary for evaluating child progress. In addition, teachers should be alert to seeking and developing new effective instructional procedures that can be added to those already available in the developing technology of effective instructional control in academic learning. Such an approach to teaching should lead to the ability to prescribe the optimal teaching procedures for each individual child, and, as indicated so aptly in Bijou (1976), each child, no matter the ability level, should have specifically designed programs of teaching. Only then can all children have the opportunity to be successful in academic learning. When such occurs, failure should never again have to enter the learning process.

REFERENCES

Allen, K.E., Hart, B.M., Buell, J.C., Harris, F.R., and Wolf, M.M. Effects of adult social reinforcement on isolate behavior of a nursery school child. *Child Development,* 1964, *35,* 511–518.

Allen, K.E., Henke, L.B., Harris, F.R., Baer, D.M., and Reynolds, N.J. Control of hyperactivity by social reinforcement of attending behavior. *Journal of Educational Psychology,* 1967, *58,* 231–237.

Baer, A.M., Rowbury, T., and Baer, D.M. The development of instructional control over classroom activities of deviant preschool children. *Journal of Applied Behavior Analysis,* 1973, *6,* 289–298.

Baron, A., and Kaufman, A. Human free-operant avoidance of timeout from monetary reinforcement. *Journal of the Experimental Analysis of Behavior,* 1966, *9,* 557–565.

Baron, A., Kaufman, A., and Stauber, K.A. Effects of instructions and reinforcement feedback on human operant behavior maintained by fixed-interval reinforcement. *Journal of the Experimental Analysis of Behavior,* 1969, *12,* 701–712.

Baxter, D., Aangeenbrug, M.H., Kramer, S., Ruggles, T.R., Etzel, B.C., and LeBlanc, J.M. *Manipulation of task size, teacher instructions, and methods of materials presentation to reduce inappropriate behavior of a child in group teaching settings.* Paper presented at the Society for the Advancement of Behavior Analysis, Milwaukee, Wisconsin, May 1981.

Bijou, S.W. *Child development: The basic stage of early childhood.* Englewood Cliffs, N.J.: Prentice-Hall, Inc., 1976, 172.

Borstein, P., and Quevillon, R. The effects of a self-instructional package on overactive preschool boys. *Journal of Applied Behavior Analysis,* 1976, *9*, 179–188.

Britten, K., Ruggles, T.R., and LeBlanc, J.M. *A comparison of masses and intermixed stimulus presentations—I.* Paper presented at the Association for the Advancement of Behavior Therapy, San Francisco, California, December 1979.

Britten, K., Ruggles, T.R., and LeBlanc, J.M. *A comparison of masses and intermixed stimulus presentations—II.* Paper presented at the Association for Behavior Analysis, Dearborn, Michigan, May 1980.

Broden, M., Bruce, C., Mitchell, M.A., Carter, V., and Hall, R.V. Effects of teacher attention on attending behavior of two boys at adjacent desks. *Journal of Applied Behavior Analysis,* 1970, *3*, 199–203.

Brown, P., and Elliot, R. The control of aggression in a nursery school class. *Journal of Experimental Child Psychology,* 1965, *2*, 103–107.

Busby, K.H., and LeBlanc, J.M. *Response latency as a function of reinforcement and temporal consequences.* Paper presented at American Psychological Association, Honolulu, Hawaii, September 1972.

Bushell, D., Wrobel, P.A., and Michaelis, M.L. Applying "group" contingencies to the classroom study behavior of preschool children. *Journal of Applied Behavior Analysis,* 1968, *1*, 55–61.

Bybel, N.W., and Etzel, B.C. *A study of pretraining procedures for establishing cue relevance in the subsequent programming of a conceptual skill.* Paper presented at the Society for Research in Child Development, Philadelphia, Pennsylvania, 1973.

Charlesworth, R., and Hart, W.W. Positive social reinforcement in the nursery school peer group. *Child Development,* 1967, *38*, 993–1002.

Clark, H.B., Rowbury, T., Baer, A.M., and Baer, D.M. Timeout as a punishing stimulus in continuous and intermittent schedules. *Journal of Applied Behavior Analysis,* 1973, *6*, 443–456.

Cooper, M.L., LeBlanc, J.M., and Etzel, B.C. *A shoe is to tie.* 16 mm, color, 10-minute film depicting a programmed sequence for teaching shoe tying to preschool children. Edna A. Hill Child Development Laboratory, Department of Human Development, University of Kansas, Lawrence, Kansas, 1968.

Cunningham, P.J., Cooper, A.Y., Plummer, S., and LeBlanc, J.M. Correction procedure effects upon an already acquired discrimination. Paper presented at the American Psychological Association, Chicago, September 1975.

Etzel, B.C., and LeBlanc, J.M. The simplest treatment alternative: The law of parsimony applied to choosing appropriate instructional control and errorless-learning procedures for the difficult-to-teach child. *Journal of Autism and Developmental Disorders,* 1979, *9*, 361–382.

Fallows, MacDonald, R.P., Cooper, A.Y., Etzel, B.C., LeBlanc, J.M., and Ruggles, T.R. *The use of stimulus equivalency paradigm and observational learning in teaching concepts to preschool children.* Paper presented at the American Psychological Association, Montreal, Quebec, Canada, September 1980.

Fallows MacDonald, R.P., Ruggles, T.R., and LeBlanc, J.M. *Concept training through a combination of stimulus equivalency and observational learning strategies: An analysis of acquisition rates.* Paper presented at the Association for the Advancement of Behavior Therapy, New York, New York, November 1980.

Goetz, E.M., and Baer, D.M. Social control of form diversity and the emergence of new forms in children's blockbuilding. *Journal of Applied Behavior Analysis,* 1973, *6,* 209–218.

Goetz, E.M., Holmberg, M.C., and LeBlanc, J.M. Differential reinforcement of other behavior and noncontingent reinforcement as control procedures during the modifications of a preschooler's compliance. *Journal of Applied Behavior Analysis,* 1975, *8,* 77–82.

Greenwald, C.R., Hops, H., Delquadri, J., and Guild, J. Group contingencies for group consequences in classroom management: A further analysis. *Journal of Applied Behavior Analysis,* 1974, *7,* 413–426.

Hardiman, S.A., Goetz, E.M., Reuter, K.E., and LeBlanc, J.M. Primes, contingent attention, and training: Effects on a child's motor behavior. *Journal of Applied Behavior Analysis,* 1975, *8,* 399–409.

Hart, B.M., Allen, K.E., Buell, J.S., Harris, F.R., and Wolf, M.M. Effects of social reinforcement on operant crying. *Journal of Experimental Child Psychology,* 1964, *1,* 145–153.

Hart, B.M., Reynolds, N.J., Baer, D.M., Brawley, F.R., and Harris, F.R. Effect of contingent and noncontingent social reinforcement on the cooperative play of a preschool child. *Journal of Applied Behavior Analysis,* 1968, *1,* 73–76.

Hass, S.L., Ruggles, T.R., and LeBlanc, J.M. *Minimal vs. criterion-related detailed instructions.* Paper presented at the Society for Research in Child Development, San Francisco, California, March 1979.

Hayden, M.L., Herbert-Jackson, E.W., Pinkston, E.M., and LeBlanc, J.M. *Reinforcing effects of praise and reprimands in settings of opposing contingencies.* Paper presented at the American Psychological Association, Washington, D.C., 1972.

Hopkins, B.L. Effects of candy and social reinforcement, instructions, and reinforcement schedule learning on the modification and maintenance of smiling. *Journal of Applied Behavior Analysis,* 1968, *1,* 121–129.

Johnston, M.K., Kelley, C.S., Harris, F.R., and Wolf, M.M. An application of reinforcement principles to development of motor skills of a young child. *Child Development,* 1966, *37,* 379–387.

Kramer, S.A., Ruggles, T.R., and LeBlanc, J.M. *The effects of probe trial distribution on children's learning a complex matching task through observation.* Paper presented at the Society for the Advancement of Behavior Analysis, Milwaukee, Wisconsin, May 1981.

LeBlanc, J.M., Miller, R.M., Pinkston, E.M., and Busby, K. *"Stay Right in There": Experimental summer tutorial class for primary grade children considered for retention.* Paper presented at Society for Research in Child Development, Minneapolis, Minnesota, April 1971.

Lovaas, O.I., Schreibman, L., Koegel, R.L., and Rehm, R. Selective responding by autistic children to multiple sensory input. *Journal of Abnormal Psychology,* 1971, *77,* 211–222.

Madsen, C.H., Becker, W.C., Thomas, D.R., Koser, L., and Plager, E. An analysis of the reinforcing function of "sit-down" commands. In R. K. Parker (Ed.), *Readings in educational psychology.* Boston: Allyn and Bacon, 1968.

Marholin, D., and Steinman, W.M. Stimulus control in the classroom as a function of the behavior reinforced. *Journal of Applied Behavior Analysis,* 1977, *10,* 465–478.

McTague, K.E. The effect of reproof on young children's performance on tasks differing in complexity. *Dissertation Abstracts International,* 1972, *33,* 18–23.

Miller, R.M., Holmberg, M.C., and LeBlanc, J.M. *Experimental analysis of contingent teacher attention and continuous and discrete teacher primes.* Paper presented at the Society for Research in Child Development, Minneapolis, Minnesota, 1971.

Miller, R.M., and LeBlanc, J.M. *Experimental analysis of the effect of detailed and minimal instructions on the acquisition of preacademic skills.* Paper presented at the American Psychological Association, Montreal, Ontario, Canada, August 1973.

Miller, R.M., and LeBlanc, J.M. *Experimental analysis of detailed and minimal instructions and their effect on acquisition of a word recognition task.* Paper presented at the American Psychological Association, New Orleans, Louisiana, August 1974.

Nelson, R.O. The effect of different types of teaching methods and verbal reinforcers on the performance of beginning readers. *Journal of Reading Behavior,* 1974, *6,* 305–306.

Peterson, R.M., and Whitehurst, G.J. A variable influencing the performance of nonreinforced imitative behaviors. *Journal of Applied Behavior Analysis,* 1970, *4,* 1–9.

Pinkston, E.M., Reese, N.M., LeBlanc, J.M., and Baer, D.M. Independent control of a preschool child's aggression and peer interaction by contingent teacher attention. *Journal of Applied Behavior Analysis,* 1973, *6,* 115–124.

Piper, J.J. The effects of extinction and information on behavior change. *Dissertation Abstracts International,* 1970, *31,* 233.

Plummer, S., Baer, D.M., and LeBlanc, J.M. Functional considerations in the use of procedural timeout and an effective alternative. *Journal of Applied Behavior Analysis,* 1977, *10,* 689–702.

Plummer, S., Gaines, D., Grant, K., and Holmberg, M.L. *Straightening preschool children's clothes: How to get them dressed more efficiently.* Paper presented at the Society for Research in Child Development, Philadelphia, 1973.

Powers, R.B., Cheney, C.D., and Agostino, N.R. Errorless training of a visual discrimination in preschool children. *The Psychological Record,* 1970, *20,* 45–50.

Radgowski, T.A., Allen, K.E., Ruggles, T.R., and LeBlanc, J.M. *Delayed presentation of feedback in preschool group foreign language training.* Paper presented at the American Psychological Association, Toronto, Ontario, Canada, 1978.

Radgowski, T.A., Allen K.E., Schilmoeller, G.L., Ruggles, T.R., and LeBlanc, J.M. *Training of a foreign language to preschool children using a delayed presentation of feedback.* Paper presented at the Midwest Association of Behavior Analysis, Chicago, Illinois, 1978.

Ramp, E.R., Ulrich, R., and Dulaney, S. Delayed timeout as a procedure for reducing disruptive classroom behavior: A case study. *Journal of Applied Behavior Analysis,* 1971, *4,* 235–239.

Reiber, J.L., Schilmoeller, G.L., and LeBlanc, J.M. The use of self-control to maintain attending of preschool children after self-counting procedures. In T.A. Brigham, R.R. Hawkins, J. Scott, and R.F. McLaughlin (Eds.), *Behavior analysis in education* (Vol. V). Dubuque, Iowa: Kendall-Hunt, 1975.

Reiber, M., and Lockwood, D. Effects of correction on double-alternation learning in children. *Journal of Experimental Psychology,* 1969, *79,* 191–192.

Resnick, L.B., Wang, M.C., and Kaplan, J. Task analysis in curriculum design: A hierarchically sequenced introductory mathematics curriculum. *Journal of Applied Behavior Analysis,* 1973, *6,* 679–709.

Reynolds, N.J., and Risley, T.R. The role of social and material reinforcers in increasing talking of a disadvantaged preschool child. *Journal of Applied Behavior Analysis,* 1968, *1,* 253–262.

Rintoul, B.E., Cooper, A.Y., Schilmoeller, K.J., and LeBlanc, J.M. The effects of decreased teacher interaction and social primes on verbal peer interaction in a small group of preschool children. *Child Study Journal,* 1975, *5,* 3–10.

Ruggles, T.R., and LeBlanc, J.M. *Variables which affect the effectiveness of group training procedures designed for children with learning problems.* Paper presented at the Twelfth Annual Gatlinburg Conference on Research in Mental Retardation and Developmental Disabilities, Gulf Shores, Alabama, 1979.

Ruggles, T.R., and LeBlanc, J.M. Behavior analysis procedures in classroom teaching. In A. Bellack, M. Hersen, and A. Kazdin (Eds.), *International handbook of behavior modification.* New York: Plenum Press (In Press).

Sabbert, J.K., Holt, W.J., Nelson, A.L., Domash, M.A., and Etzel, B.C. *Functional analysis of teaching different sizes of groups.* Paper presented at the American Psychological Association, Washington, D.C., 1976.

Schilmoeller, K.J., and Etzel, B.C. An experimental analysis of criterion- and noncriterion-related cues in "errorless" stimulus control procedures. In B.C. Etzel, J.M. LeBlanc, and D.M. Baer (Eds.), *New developments in behavioral research: Theory, methods and applications. In honor of Sidney W. Bijou.* Hillsdale, N.J.: Lawrence Erlbaum Associates, Inc., 1977.

Schilmoeller, G.L., Schilmoeller, K.J., Etzel, B.C., and LeBlanc, J.M. Conditional discrimination responding after errorless and trial-and-error training. *Journal of the Experimental Analysis of Behavior,* 1977, *31,* 405–420.

Scobie, S.R., and Kaufman, A. Intermittent punishment of variable interval and variable ratio responding. *Journal of the Experimental Analysis of Behavior,* 1969, *12,* 137–147.

Smith, D.D., and Lovitt, T.C. The differential effects of reinforcement contingencies on arithmetic performance. *Journal of Learning Disabilities,* 1976, *9,* 32–40.

Spradlin, J.E., and Spradlin, R.R. Developing necessary skills for entry into classroom teaching arrangements. In N.G. Haring and R.L. Schiefelbusch (Eds.), *Teaching special children.* New York: McGraw-Hill Book Company, 1976.

Steinman, W.M. Generalized imitation and the discrimination hypothesis. *Journal of Experimental Child Psychology,* 1970a, *10,* 70–99.

Steinman, W.M. The social control of generalized imitation. *Journal of Applied Behavior Analysis,* 1970b, *3,* 159–167.

Stella, M.E., and Etzel, B.C. *Procedural variables in errorless discrimination learning: Order of S+ and S− manipulation.* Paper presented at the 86th Annual Convention of the American Psychological Association, Toronto, Ontario, Canada, 1978.

Touchette, P.E. Transfer of stimulus control: Measuring the moment of transfer. *Journal of the Experimental Analysis of Behavior,* 1971, *15,* 347–354.

Wallace, M.A., Hatfield, V.L., Goetz, E.M., and Etzel, B.C. Caring efficiently for young children: Controls versus freedom. *School Applications of Learning Theory,* 1976, *8,* 20–31.

Winslow, M.K., and Etzel, B.C. *Assessment of preattending behavior: Procedural comparison and acquisition training.* Paper presented at American Psychological Association, Honolulu, Hawaii, 1972.

Winston, A.S., and Redd, W.H. Relative effectiveness of positive and negative comments in the control of children's choice behavior. *Proceedings of the 81st Annual Convention of the American Psychological Association,* 1973.

Woodward, E.K. Effects of positive and negative feedback on the performance of impulsive children. *Dissertation Abstracts International,* 1974, *34,* (10-B).

Zeilberger, J., Sampen, S.E., and Sloane, Jr., H.N. Modification of child's problem behaviors in the home with the mother as therapist. *Journal of Applied Behavior Analysis,* 1968, *1,* 47–54.

Zimmerman, B.J., and Rosenthal, T.L. Conserving and returning equalities and inequalities through observation and correction. *Developmental Psychology,* 1974, *10,* 260–268.

Zimmerman, E.H., Zimmerman, J., and Russell, C.E. Differential effects of token reinforcement on instruction following in retarded students instructed as a group. *Journal of Applied Behavior Analysis,* 1969, *2,* 101–112.

Chapter 9

Cognitive Skill Deficiencies: Behavioral Assessment and Intervention

Barbara C. Etzel, Mary H. Aangeenbrug,
Annabelle L. Nelson-Burford, Wilma J. Holt,
and M. Elizabeth Stella

INTRODUCTION

Preschool children between the ages of three to five years should routinely have an assessment of their cognitive repertoires. There is almost uniform agreement with this point of view among professionals in the fields of psychology, child development, and special and early childhood education, in spite of a recent antitesting movement. The major area of disagreement is not whether a child's cognitive skills should be evaluated, but *how* they are to be measured.

Preschool Assessment for What Reason?

A commitment to the U.S. philosophy of an education for all should result in declaring that illiteracy (just as polio) must be a thing of the past. This goal, however, is far from being realized as more evidence accumulates demonstrating the failure of the educational system to teach functional reading and writing to all children.

"Formal" education for many children in this country begins at five years of age. Although the kindergarten experience was once regarded as the year to help prepare children for "formal" education, it has not succeeded in this goal due to large, half-day classes, and teachers, who with little help, teach both morning and afternoon groups (which together often total over 50 children). The curriculum of the kindergarten is demanding since most of the prereading, writing, and arithmetic skills are expected to be mastered by the age of six. Some of these skills are quite difficult to teach. For example, letter sounds and beginning blending skills (phonics) have been considered by teachers to be the hardest (and least interesting) skills for many children to acquire. While the majority of children arrive at first grade with these skills, approximately 10 to 25 percent do not. Many of these children will continue not acquiring the skills, and they will become candidates for remedial education immediately. The problem has occurred primarily because the kindergarten teacher did not identify children needing special help, identified them too late, did not know what special help to give these children to keep them current with their peers, or did not have the facilities or time to offer special help.

To solve this problem, kindergarten teachers on the *first* day of school should be aware of a child's potential academic problem areas and have knowledge of what teaching procedures are successful for that child. This information should be accumulated during the preschool years in a child's life. These years, three to five, should be looked on as an opportunity for the continuous assessment of problem areas and the discovery of successful teaching techniques for each child. Normal preschool children between these ages demonstrate complex cognitive skills, although this fact has not been recognized until the past few decades.

It is the obligation of a preschool teacher to review what the child has learned during the first three years of life, to identify when the child has difficulty learning a skill, and to discover what teaching techniques are successful for that child. It is perhaps the only time in the child's life that these questions can be answered in a pressure-free context, over many months, for the important purpose of helping the child successfully start formal schooling. What better reason for preschool assessment?

Different Approaches to Assessment

Since it is not a question of whether children's cognitive skills should be assessed but rather *how*, then a comparison of the traditional psychometric field with a newer behavioral approach should clarify the "how" issues.

Traditional Psychometric Diagnosis

Historically, classification of behavior has usually followed a medical model due to the marriage of the psychoanalytic movement with the medical practitioners in this country. Thus, the term "diagnosis" was used instead of "assessment." The goal of diagnosis was to be able to label a behavioral problem much in the same way an illness (for example, measles) would be labeled. If a diagnosis is one of the goals, then, as in physical illnesses, some cause should be identified. The term "etiology" (also borrowed from the medical field) was then applied to the diagnostic process. It has referred traditionally to the discovery of some underlying cause for a child's difficulties. Bijou (1972) points out that when a person uses the diagnostic/etiology approach to behavioral problems, this leads to proposing that problems such as a child's reading disability be diagnosed (as, for example, primary dyslexia). The problem with such diagnoses (as dyslexia) is that they are hypothetically constructed (not observed but guessed at). What is observed is that the child cannot read, which the teacher and parents already knew. The label adds little.

On the other hand, many researchers have attempted to discover empirically causes of various behavior problems by taking a more complex view of etiology. Several factors, such as lower socioeconomic status, visual or auditory defects, language deficiencies, and so on, are analyzed to determine if they, as a cluster, contribute to poor conceptual functioning.

The problem with the diagnostic/etiology approaches is that they have not worked, since neither prognosis nor treatment is a clear result of the process. In addition, labeling a child's difficulty and searching for causes do not lead to understanding how a child processes information (Lahey, Vosk, & Habif, 1981). The traditional psychometric approach has been questioned by many on both empirical and theoretical grounds (Bijou, 1972). Intelligence tests may be fairly accurate in predicting behavior (for example, obtaining of college degrees) for large groups of people, but not necessarily for each individual within that group. In addition, intelligence testing research is usually directed toward correlating IQ scores with some other behavior. This is similar to the research on the effects of smoking cigarettes. If a person smokes, then cancer of the lungs is statistically more probable. The research does not tell who will actually get cancer or what the cause of lung cancer is.

The issue of seeking causes of conceptual skill deficiencies should be addressed in its own right. Even if a person could determine a cause for a child's problem, does this mean that a teacher or parent can do something to change a child's behavioral *history* that is already a matter of past events? Educators have been so influenced by thinking "medically" that many would look upon curing conceptual skill problems as they would look upon curing an ailing appendix. If the appendix is infected, it is cut out. However, if the child has problems conceptually, does the analogy hold? Knowing a "cause" of conceptual problems does nothing to help a teacher or parent design procedures that help the child overcome the problem. In fact, children who may have been given different diagnoses (slow learner, autistic, brain damaged) are often successfully "treated" by the same procedures. This realization of the uselessness of the diagnostic/etiological approach to the assessment of conceptual skill deficits has led some (for example, Bijou, Note 1) to propose that the most direct and successful plan of action would be to determine first what the problem behavior (or complaint) is and then to move directly to design a program that would remediate the problem. This obviously skips the steps of searching for the cause(s) and engaging in lengthy diagnostic tests so that a label can be applied. Only one group of authors in the recent literature on this topic has been able to suggest even one plausible reason why a diagnostic label might be helpful (Lahey, Vosk, & Habif, 1981). Their reason is for purely administrative or economic facilitations. They suggest that a label might be applied if it would qualify a child for some beneficial service, such as special education or training, that in the current system would not otherwise be open to them. Of course, if problem areas were given behavioral descriptions rather than diagnostic labels, government agencies would have to change their criteria for admittance also.

The traditional diagnostic (labeling) approach has only provided a legal or administrative device for securing services (and could be changed if the method of obtaining the descriptor was changed). Further, the psychometric approach has not reliably distinguished various patterns of deviant behavior in individual children. This means that a child's conceptual skill problem cannot be directly tied to specific information processing deficits that were thought to cause the problem in the first place (Lahey, Vosk, & Habif, 1981). So what may be another possible approach to the necessary process of assessment?

Behavior Assessment

Within the past decade, a group of professionals from many different disciplines (psychology, education, social work, medicine, law, and so on) have turned to a behavioral (observational) orientation to help them in their understanding, prediction, and training of human behavior. Each of these fields has used the discipline of behavioral psychology to move from the information gathering phase to the treatment plan of human behavior problems in a direct, efficient, and potentially more successful manner than has been true of traditional approaches. The characteristics of the behavioral approach are to describe the problems in observable terms, without attention to a presumed cause or etiology. Once a description of the problem has been made, then a program to remedy the problem is prepared. This program is a logical outcome of the analysis of the problem. Thus, behavioral assessment is directly oriented toward remediation procedures (Bijou & Grimm, 1972). The focus of behavioral assessment is therefore in sharp contrast to traditional psychometric measurement. As Lahey, Vosk, and Habif (1981) have stated, if assessment is given for the purpose of treatment, then the behaviors that are to be changed should be measured.

Sidman (1960) pointed out that human behavior should be measured under active, ongoing conditions. He noted that learning can be viewed as a transition in which the organism moves from one "steady state" through the learning process (transition) to another "steady state." The most adequate analysis of any transition is to study the variables and processes that control behavior *during* the transition. Thus, to predict how a child will learn means that the child's behavior should be measured *while* the child is learning. Not only should learning be assessed while it is ongoing, but the tasks and the environment should be identical (if possible) to the tasks and the setting where future prognosis and/or treatment will be made (Torgesen & Goldman, 1977).

The ideal conditions for measuring and predicting future performance of a child's cognitive skills seem to be the following: (1) to do it with the type of tasks the child is and will be solving; (2) to carry it out in the setting where the predictions and/or remediation will take place; and (3) to measure the skill *while* the child is learning since learning is the behavior to be predicted. These requirements suggest that a behavioral assessment and intervention program for cognitive skill deficiencies for children should be carried out in the preschool classroom in a small group (not individual setting), by the teacher, with academic tasks, while the child is learning new skills. This particular specification of where the assessment occurs, who does the assessment, and with what materials the child is assessed would probably be objected to by some traditional psychometricians since some children will be at a disadvantage under more social or noisy conditions. However, if prognosis and possible treatment are the primary aims of the assessment, then how the child learns through *continuous* assessment (not a one time test score) will be the most predictive of how the child will continue to learn under those conditions. Further, if a child has problems learning in such an environment, then the problems need to be observed and remedied in that environment. Why a child is not learning may not be observable in a quiet, sound attenuated testing room where the child has the complete attention of an adult.

THE DEVELOPMENT OF A TEACHER-ADMINISTERED, LEARNING ASSESSMENT MODEL

For the past five years, the authors of this chapter have been developing a learning assessment procedure to be used in a preschool classroom by the teachers of that classroom. The description of this teacher-administered, learning assessment model that follows will be quite detailed, but easy to follow. The description will provide a step-by-step understanding of how to identify and then help difficult-to-teach children learn.

The greatest problem in the development of this procedure was to find a simple method of recording a child's behavior, while the child was learning a task, so that the teacher (who was engaged in the teaching of that child during small group academic time) could record the data. The procedure was also to be applied continuously across months and, in some instances, years. This was necessary since one of the basic tenets of the experimental analysis of behavior is to observe the organism across time and under the changing conditions that occur in any environment. Special educators have described "learning disabled" children as being notoriously variable on tasks that involve sustained attention (Lahey, Vosk, & Habif, 1981) or on tasks that are repeated daily. Since assessment is directly related to a treatment plan, an analysis of the child's approach to problem solving, error patterns, and responses that are inappropriate or incompatible with learning must be identified. This can only be observed across time. In addition, responses measured across time give the teacher a baseline of behavior under conditions that are typical.

If treating a child is to be the responsibility of the teacher, then the responsibility of identifying the problem should lie with the teacher. Actually, the two steps are not really observably distinct since evaluation continues throughout the treatment process (Bijou & Grimm, 1972). The teacher arranges the learning assessment so that initial information is obtained on what the child can actually do and what the problems are when the child cannot perform. With this information and the teacher's valuable knowledge of skill prerequisites, it is possible to fashion a treatment program. All treatment programs are not initially successful, but this too can be considered assessment information. The amount of environmental teaching and material manipulation that is necessary to have a child learn a skill will suggest what intervention may be expected in the future to enable the child to keep up with the peer group (Etzel & LeBlanc, 1979).

After a procedure for recording children's behavior during learning was devised, the authors then proceeded to develop the tasks the children would use during the assessment. Several considerations guided the selections.

Task Selection

In the past few years, educators have written about criterion-referenced tests that are distinguished by the information they yield about a child's skill in a particular task or area (Bijou, 1976). The purpose of administering a particular test is not to compare one child with another, but to be able to specify precisely what a child knows about some specific area or skill. Thus, there could be many criterion-referenced tests to cover many areas. Glaser (1971) indicates that first a class or domain of tasks is specified. Then measurements are taken from this class that are felt to be representative samples. Thus, information obtained from this sample is attributed directly to the class originally identified as being an important skill or area.

Thus, the tasks selected had to reflect a variety of classes that were felt to be part of what might be called preschool cognitive skills. These skills were analyzed at the criterion (or final) level that the authors wanted to see in a preschool child's repertoire before going to kindergarten. Several of the criterion skills from each of the classes were then sampled to determine if these skills would be the most representative of that class. Of course, one of the main limitations of task selection was ease of administration, that is, ease of identifying correct and incorrect responses, simple instructions (since tasks were to be given during small group time), and simple materials that would not require a great deal of space. Finally, to monitor a child's learning during the preschool year, the tasks had to be graded in difficulty so that as the child learned one level of skill, another level could be presented. This was necessary so that the child's responses could be observed as learning progressed over time. The range of difficulty was initially designed to cover preschool children's skills between approximately three to five years of age. As the procedure was developed and studied, both easier and more difficult tasks were added, while some of the middle level were eliminated. The aim of using difficult tasks for children in this age range was to provide material on which the children would be learning, rather than practice on something already learned. On such tasks, the authors could predict current learning problems and then immediately apply treatment procedures. Keogh and Becker (1973) have suggested that long-range prediction of learning problems is probably not wise. Such predictions for individuals is probably not possible, and assessment, such as being proposed here, should probably be carried out throughout a child's formal schooling life. In this way the child would have continuous evaluation while learning and immediate help with problem areas.

The classes of skills selected were designed to be broad. Some evidence has been collected that suggests that some learning problems are often specific to a class and do not permeate across all cognitive skills (Lahey, Vosk, & Habif, 1981). The classes selected were visual discrimination, numbers, language (including memory), and fine motor. While other areas were felt to be just as important, the authors were forced to limit the number of classes of tasks to those on which a teacher could collect continuous data.

General Information Obtained from Assessment Procedure

Motivation and Independence

In addition to information about how a child learns a particular skill, the tasks also should give the teacher information about what type of teacher consequences (verbal praise, tangible reinforcers, and so on) are needed for each child to progress in his or her learning. The recording system also enables teachers to determine how much assistance they are giving an individual child in order to get the child successfully through a day's activities. Children who have been characterized as "dependent," "low energy," "imitative," and so on are also children who are suspected of being able to learn as well as other children; however, they need a great deal of "support." Identifying these children early can result in a treatment program that could be directed toward more independent problem solving.

Prerequisite Skills and Task Difficulty

Likewise, children who have a clear absence of prerequisite skills for a particular task should be discriminated from children who can perform adequately on easy tasks but who immediately stop if the task becomes slightly more difficult. A treatment program for these two types of children would be quite different although, to the casual observer, the children may look quite similar. The recording procedure was designed to aid in the differentiation of these two types of children.

Length of Problem-Solving Chain

Finally, as problems begin to be identified on the learning-assessment procedure by noting that the child does not make progress in some class of skills, then several routine manipulations are automatically put into the teaching situation. These manipulations were simple and potentially time saving. If a child learned the task under easier procedures, then the teacher would not have to plan a more complex treatment program for the children. All tasks were constructed so that *several* responses were required before the task could be considered completed. Therefore, the teacher systematically reduced the number of responses (by one each day) to determine if the child would ultimately be successful when the task requirement was reduced.

If the child is successful at some point when the number of task responses is reduced, then the teacher begins to increase the requirement slowly back to the criterion number. If the child is not able to sustain success under the decrease and increase in task responses, the teacher may manipulate the consequences of successful responding at this point to determine if there is a motivational problem. Some children may not make successful responses on a task that requires several responses before completion, because the consequences for doing that much are not as important to the child as engaging in some other set of responses (such as watching a neighbor or getting out of the chair to look outside). Other children are often found to be unsuccessful when a task requires several responses due to the lack of a problem-solving plan (when many stimuli are present). When only one stimulus is present, no plan may be necessary; only the simple response to the one set of materials is required. This latter problem calls for a different type of treatment program than changing the reinforcer system.

Task Analysis

If changes in the motivational system do not result in successful responding, the next phase of the evaluation is begun. Tasks that were selected to represent a class of skills have undergone a task analysis. The term task analysis has been used by educators for some years and has generally referred to the detailing of all the component responses needed to solve a task at the criterion (final) level. Most educators have approached a task analysis through a sophisticated "guessing" procedure. This does not always result in a complete analysis, but it probably does produce most of the component subsets of skills. Recently, an attempt to arrive at a task analysis by empirical study (Nelson, Holt, & Etzel, Note 2) demonstrated that the guessing procedure is not always complete since other less obvious responses that were overlooked in the prestudy task analysis were found to be essential for final successful performance.

Lahey, Vosk, and Habif (1981) have referred to this practice of task analysis as being similar to a molecular (the smallest physical unit) assessment, as opposed to a molar (pertaining to a body of matter as a whole) approach. The molar level of assessment in the learning assessment procedure is simply an analysis of task success for all children given the routine procedure. It is only when failure to learn a task becomes evident that the molecular level of analysis is made. Thus, individual children's responses are observed with respect to the task analyses to determine which subset of skills the child has and which are not observed. Once this analysis is made, the treatment plan is simply to teach the child the missing skills. The assessment procedure therefore moves directly into an individual treatment program.

Finally, the learning assessment is not complete until the child is again returned to the criterion level task, following treatment, to determine the child's competency at the end of training. This assessment should be repeated several weeks to a month later to determine stability of responding.

Examples of the Learning-Assessment Procedure

Materials

Tables 9–1 and 9–2 summarize the tasks by areas, levels, materials, and required child response. Table 9–1 is for upper division assessment, and

Table 9–1 Upper Division Assessment: Areas, Levels, Materials, and Required Child Responses

Area	Level	Materials	Child Response
Visual Discrimination	Entry & Level 1	Teaching Resources Look-Alike Discrimination Cards *Shapes — 4 sets	Match pictures with small differences.
	Level 2	Sailboats — 4 sets	Match pictures with small differences.
	Level 3	Flowers — 4 sets	Match pictures with small differences.
Numbers	Entry	*Bear Baskets 4 & 5	Count bears pictured on card attached to baskets; count the same number of plastic bears into the basket.
	Level 1	Bear Baskets 5, 8, 10 Teacher-designed	Label number on card attached to basket; count the same number of plastic bears into the basket.
	Level 2	Number Baskets 0, 5, 7, 9 Teacher-designed	
	Level 3	Quantity-Numeral Match to Sample Sheets 0, 4, 6, 8	Count pictured shapes; circle corresponding numeral from choice of four.
Language Arts	Entry	DLM Visual Memory Cards *Card with 3 colored lines	Copy a series of colored lines from a card onto paper.
	Level 1	Cards with 3 & 4 colored lines (copy color cards)	
	Level 2	Cards with 3 & 4 pictured objects (verbalize objects from memory cards)	Verbalize a series of pictured objects; repeat series from memory.
Fine Motors	Entry & Level 1	Number Paths (teacher-designed) *Path 1	Draw lines inside borders of number paths of 3 decreasing widths, starting at one dot & stopping at another.
	Level 2	Path 2	
	Level 3	Path 4	

Table 9–2 Lower Division Assessment: Areas, Levels, Materials, and Required Child Responses

Area	Level	Materials	Child Response
Visual Discrimination	Level 1	Cards with one shape each — 4 sets	Match cards.
	Level 2	Cards with two shapes each — 4 sets	Match cards.
	Level 3	Cards with three shapes each — 4 sets	Match cards.
Numbers	Level 1	Cards with 0–4 pictured bears	Place a plastic bear on top of each pictured bear.
	Level 2	Cards with 0–4 pictured bears	Count bears pictured on card; count the same number of plastic bears & place bears on empty section of lotto board under card.
	Level 3	Bear baskets 1–5	Count bears pictured on card attached to basket; count the same number of plastic bears into the basket.
Language Arts	Level 1	Cards with 3 lines colored with crayon, small paper strips colored with crayon	Place colored strips on paper to match series of colored lines on card.
	Level 2	Cards with 3 lines colored with crayon; crayons with ½ inch strip, colored with crayons, attached	Copy a series of colored lines from a card onto paper.
	Level 3	Cards with 3 lines colored with crayon; crayons with ¼ inch strip, colored with crayons, attached	Copy a series of colored lines from a card onto paper.
Fine Motor	Level 1	Large vertical paths	Draw lines inside borders of paths of 3 decreasing widths; starting at one dot and stopping at another.
	Level 2	Medium vertical paths	
	Level 3	Small vertical paths	

Figure 9–1 Lower Division—Visual Discrimination

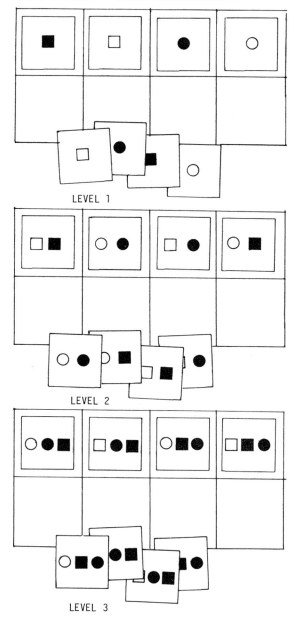

Materials and instructions for the administration of all levels in the visual discrimination class of the lower division assessment. (See Note 2, Teaching Resources Company.)

VISUAL DISCRIMINATION

LEVEL 1: 1 shape
LEVEL 2: 2 shapes
LEVEL 3: 3 shapes

Materials: Shape cards appropriate to level, regular lotto board. Place four sample cards in top sections of lotto board, four cards to be matched (mixed up) in pile below board.

Procedure: "*Find the card on top* (trace across sample cards on lotto board) *that looks just like this card* (point to top card on pile below board). *Put it under the one it looks like.*" Model with one of the cards, point out features that are similar, such as dark square first, light circle.

Error: Incorrect match.

Correction: Praise correct matches and remove. Point out why incorrect ones do not match, have child redo.

Table 9–2 is for lower division (generally younger children) assessment. All children, however, enter the assessment procedure with tasks on Level 1 or entry level of the upper division, which are marked with an asterisk. If the child fails across two days to meet the criterion of responding that is set for any one of the areas at this entry level (criterion was: child solves task with no errors, and no teacher help or instructions except for an initial instruction by the teacher on how to approach the solution), the child is then placed in the lower division assessment. This lower division assessment is only used for those areas failed in the upper division. Hence, a child could be undergoing assessment in both the upper and lower divisions at any one time.

Figures 9–1 through 9–13 illustrate the materials listed in Tables 9–1 and 9–2, and specify the instructions, errors, and correction procedures. Most of the materials were designed by M. H. Aangeenbrug, and some were purchased from the DLM and Teaching Resources companies.[2]

Recording

Children in the learning assessment procedure are grouped around a child-sized table containing approximately four or five children. The teacher also uses this small group time for teaching other skills that the classroom curriculum has dictated, in addition to the learning assessment tasks. Generally, not more than two assessment tasks are ever given during one day's small group time, and the same area (that is, numbers, visual discrimination, and so on) is not immediately repeated the following day. The length of small group time can vary across classrooms depending on the teacher's preference in scheduling activities, but a minimum of 20 minutes seems appropriate if other activities, such as puzzles, are interspersed with the learning assessment tasks. An aid (parent, older child, or assistant teacher) usually monitors the rest of the children in the classroom in various activities while the teacher instructs each small group. Grouping by age or ability is not essential in the small groups since each child is working individually on a task. Some grouping according to number of behavior-problem children in a group is appropriate since only one such child should be included if possible. In addition, the learning assessment procedure should not be started until the group has been composed for several weeks, is under teacher instructional control, has learned to raise their hands for teacher attention, and can work individually on simple materials that the teacher has put in front of them. A cart or an empty bookshelf where the materials have been preselected and placed for easy access is helpful for smooth and efficient operations.

To the right of each child's working area, a piece of masking tape is placed that is stuck to the table with the child's name and task for that

Figure 9–2 Lower Division—Numbers

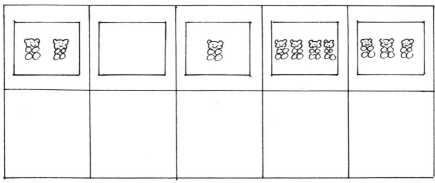

LEVELS 1 and 2

Materials and instructions for the administration of levels 1 and 2 in the numbers class of the lower division assessment.

Level 1

Materials: Special lotto board for vertical cards; cards 0–4; 2 more bears than needed in basket. Place cards in top sections of board, place basket of bears below board.

Procedure: *"Put a bear on top of each bear on all the cards."* Model with card 2 or 3, replace bears used in basket.

Errors: Incorrect number of bears on card.

Correction: Show child that a pictured bear doesn't have a bear on top and/or a card has too many bears on it. Remove correctly done cards and have child redo. If incorrect again, physically put through.

Level 2

Materials: Special lotto board for vertical cards; cards 0–4; 2 more bears than needed in basket. Place cards in top sections of board, place basket of bears below board.

Procedure: *"Count the bears on the card* (point). *Put that many bears from the basket* (point) *in the place* (point to empty lotto section) *under the card."* Model with card 2 or 3 and replace bears in basket. Be sure to count bears on card and count bears from basket audibly, one at a time.

Errors: Incorrect number of bears under card.

Correction: Show child by counting bears on card, then bears under card that there are not the same number of bears under the card. Have child count for you by touching each bear on the card as child counts (physically put child through—point and count if needed).

Figure 9–3 Lower Division—Numbers

LEVEL 3

Materials and instructions for the administration of level 3 in the numbers class of the lower division assessment.

NUMBERS

Level 3

Materials: Special lotto board for vertical cards; bear baskets 1–5, placed out of order in top sections; basket with appropriate number of bears, plus 2 distractors in bottom section of lotto board.

Procedure: "Count the bears on the card *(point to card). Then count that many bears from this basket (point to bears in basket) and put them in the basket with the card."* Model one basket (2 or 3), counting the bears on the card, repeating that number, counting that many bears from the basket, one at a time, into the basket with the card.

Error: Basket with incorrect number of bears in it.

Correction: Show child, by counting the number of bears on the card, then the number of bears in the basket, that there is an error. Have child count bears on card for you, being sure child touches each bear when pointing. Then have the child count from basket. Count with the child if needed and prevent errors.

Figure 9–4 Lower Division—Language Arts

LEVEL 1	LEVEL 2	LEVEL 3
Strips with crayoned colors to match crayoned strips on card; two distractor colors	Red, blue, green, black and orange crayons, each with a ½ in. strip around it, matching the colors on the card.	Same as Level 2—strips are ¼ in.

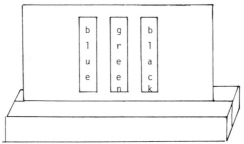

Materials and instructions for the administration of all levels in the language arts class of the lower division assessment. (See Note 2, DLM Company).

LANGUAGE ARTS

Level 1

Materials: Tray with card 3 (black, green, blue colored strips) in stand; black, green, blue, orange, and red strips next to sheet of paper.

Procedure: "*Put these paper strips* (point to strips) *on the paper so that it looks just like the card* (point to card)." Model placing the correct strips, left to right, while naming the colors.

Error: Incorrect colors; colors placed out of order (i.e., black, blue, green).

Correction: Show child which colors are placed incorrectly and have child redo; put through if needed.

Level 2 (3)

Materials: Card 3 (black, green, blue strips) in stand; paper in front of stand; black, green, blue, red and orange crayons with colored strips over ½ (¼) the crayon.

Procedure: "*Make lines with the crayons* (point) *on the paper* (point) *so that it looks just like the lines on the card* (point)." Model, choosing crayons by holding the crayoned paper part up to the lines on the card until the correct one is found. Do not draw the lines.

Error: Incorrect colors; lines placed out of order (i.e., black, blue, green). More than one line of each color.

Correction: Show child incorrect colors, then show child correct colors by holding up crayons to compare with strips.

Figure 9–5 Lower Division—Fine Motor

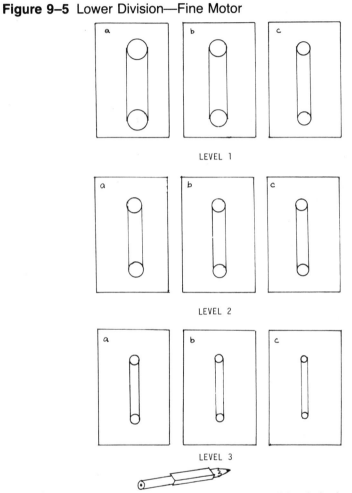

Materials and instructions for the administration of all levels in the fine motor class of the lower division assessment.

FINE MOTOR

Level 1 — Large Paths
Level 2 — Medium Paths
Level 3 — Small Paths

Materials: Paper sheets with number paths a, b and c; pencil with rubber grip.

Procedure: "*Make a line from the top dot* (point) *to the bottom dot* (point). *Remember, start on this dot* (point to top dot) *and stop when your line gets inside this dot* (point to bottom dot). *Stay inside these lines* (point)."

Error: Line not in dot (touching outside of dot acceptable) and/or outside side lines.

Correction: Show child errors. Physically put child through by holding child's hand over marker and drawing line.

Figure 9–6 Upper Division—Visual Discrimination

Shapes

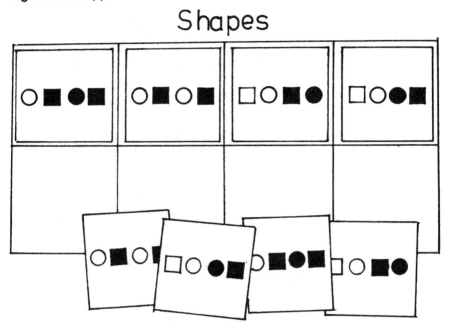

Materials for level 1 and instructions for the administration of all levels in the visual discrimination class of the upper division assessment. (See Note 2, Teaching Resources Company.)

VISUAL DISCRIMINATION

LEVEL 1: Shapes
LEVEL 2: Sailboats   (Look Alike Discrimination Cards—Teaching Resources)
LEVEL 3: Flowers

Materials: Lotto board with 4 sample cards in top sections; 4 matching cards, mixed up, in pile below board.

Instructions: *"Find the card that looks just like this card* (point to first sample card on top). Look at all these cards (point to matching cards below board). *When you find the one with the same (shapes, sailboats, flowers) put it in the empty place below the card it looks like."* (Model, finding matching card, verbalizing why they match—dark square, light circle, stripes on boat, two people, dark flower, etc.; and place in empty section under sample card. Replace in pile before telling child to start task).

Errors: Incorrect match (cards turned the wrong way are not errors as long as the card is under the correct match, but turn so it is placed correctly. Cards not placed in lotto format are errors.)

Correction: Praise child for correct matches and remove them. Point out how to match remaining cards and have child redo. If still not successful, model matching, telling child why they match.

Figure 9–7 Upper Division—Visual Discrimination

Sailboats

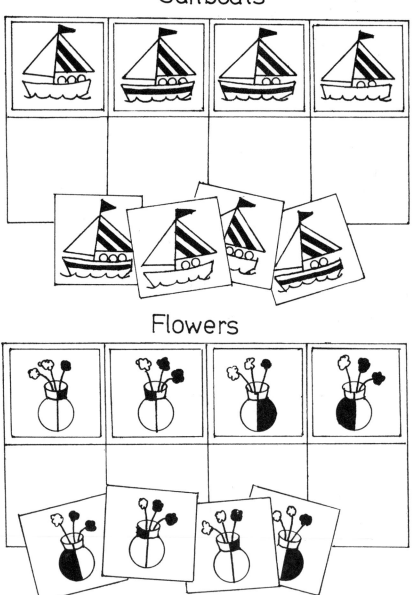

Flowers

Materials for levels 2 and 3 in the visual discrimination class of the upper division assessment. (See Note 2, Teaching Resources Company.)

Figure 9–8 Upper Division—Numbers

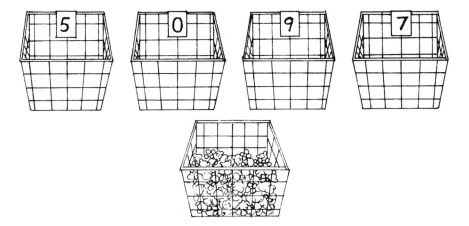

Materials and instructions for the administration of level 1 in the numbers class of the upper division assessment.

NUMBERS

LEVEL 1: Bear Baskets

Materials: Baskets 5, 8, and 10; appropriate number of plastic bears in another basket plus 2 distractors.

Instructions: "Count the bears on the card (point to card on basket). *Then count that many bears from this basket* (point to basket of bears) *and put them into the bear basket* (point again to basket with card)." On first presentation model with one of the baskets, then return plastic bears to other basket.

Errors: Incorrect number of bears, recorded after all baskets are completed.

Correction: Praise and remove correct baskets. Point out baskets with errors and have child recount bears on card (help if needed), then plastic bears into basket (help if needed). Be sure all baskets are done correctly, using physical prompting to ensure correctly done baskets.

All three baskets must be correct with initial instruction on one basket only and no errors.

Figure 9–9 Upper Division—Numbers

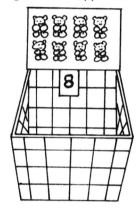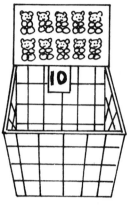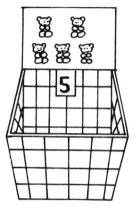

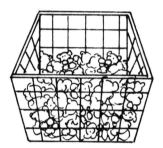

Materials and instructions for the administration of level 2 in the numbers class of the upper division assessment.

NUMBERS

LEVEL 2: Number Baskets

Materials: Baskets 0, 5, 7, and 9; appropriate number of plastic bears in another basket plus 2 distractors.

Instructions: "*Put the same number of bears* (point to plastic bears) *into the basket* (point to basket) *as the number* (point to number)." Do not label numbers for child. Model with any basket but 0, then replace plastic bears to other basket.

Error: Incorrect number of bears, recorded after all baskets are completed.

Correction: Praise and remove correct baskets. Point out baskets with errors, give label of number, and have child redo.

All four baskets must be correct with initial instruction on one basket only and no errors.

Figure 9–10 Upper Division—Numbers

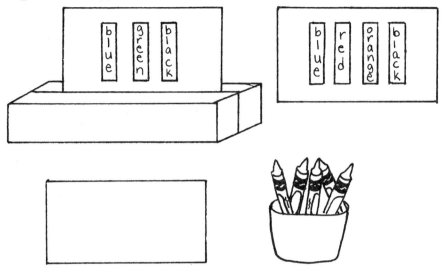

Materials and instructions for the administration of level 3 in the numbers class of the upper division assessment.

NUMBERS

LEVEL 3: Quantity Numeral Match-to-Sample Sheets

Materials: "Count the shapes up here (point to shapes) *and circle the number down here* (trace finger across all numbers) *that tells you how many shapes there are.*" Model on first presentation, not making circle with pencil but tracing circle with finger after counting shapes. Do not model on 0.

Error: Incorrect number circled; no number circled; more than 1 number circled.

Correction: Praise correctly done sheets, remove. Have child count shapes on incorrectly done sheet, using prompts to ensure correct counting. Help child to find that number but do not let child circle the number; tell child to remember to circle that number the next time.

All 4 sheets must be correct with initial instruction on 1 sheet only and no errors.

Figure 9–11 Upper Division—Language Arts

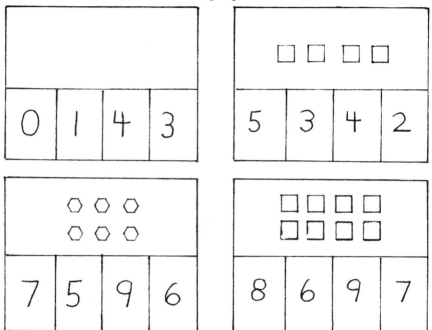

Materials and instructions for the administration of level 1 in the language arts class of the upper division assessment. (See Note 2, DLM Company.)

LANGUAGE ARTS

LEVEL 1: Copy color lines cards (DLM Visual Memory)

Materials: Cards with (3, 4) color lines; wood stands; crayons (colors needed plus 2 more); small strips of paper the size of card.

Instructions: *"There are (3, 4) lines on this card. First I'll point and say the colors* (model, starting on left side of card). *Now you say them with me* (make sure child says each). *Now you say them by yourself.* (Help, if needed.) *Make the same lines* (point to lines on cards) *on the paper* (point to paper) *with the crayons* (point to crayons) *so that the paper looks just like the card."*

Error: Incorrect color, position and/or number of lines.

Correction: Praise correct lines, point out incorrect lines, showing the crayons that should have been used. If more than one line of a color, tell child that only one line should be made. If many errors made, model with other side of paper slowly, telling child to watch how you do it. Child may repeat immediately at discretion of teacher but be sure to record on new ⊦. Do not proceed to 4 lines until 3 lines are correct with initial instruction only and no errors.

Figure 9–12 Upper Division—Language Arts

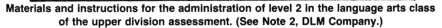

Materials and instructions for the administration of level 2 in the language arts class of the upper division assessment. (See Note 2, DLM Company.)

LANGUAGE ARTS

LEVEL 2: Verbalize objects from memory (DLM Visual Memory)

Materials: Cards with (3, 4) objects

Instructions: *"There are (3, 4) things on this card. First I'll say them* (point from left to right while naming objects). *Now you say them with me. Now you say them by yourself* (help, if needed). (Place card face down on table and ask) *What was on the card?"*

Error: Incorrect label; incorrect order (has to be left to right as on card); not all objects labeled.

Correction: Hold up card again and relabel, stressing labels or order, depending on error. If repeated at teacher's discretion, record on a new ι. Do not proceed to card with 4 objects until 3 objects are correct with initial instruction only and no errors.

Figure 9–13 Upper Division—Fine Motor

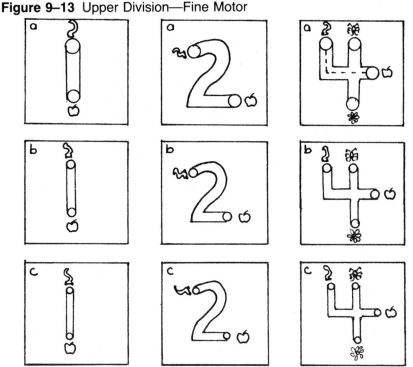

Materials and instructions for the administration of all levels in the fine motor class of the upper division assessment.

FINE MOTOR

LEVEL 1: Number Paths 1 a, b, c
LEVEL 2: Number Paths 2 a, b, c
LEVEL 3: Number Paths 4 a, b, c

Materials: Number Path sheets, pencil.

Instructions: "*Make the worm go to the apple by drawing a line from this dot* (point to top dot) *to that dot* (point to bottom dot). *Keep your pencil inside these lines* (point to border lines)." On Number Path 4, model with pencil on separate copy of level a, stressing starting with worm to apple before picking up pencil to draw line from bug to flower. Tell child not to pick up pencil between dots.

Error: Starting above or below top dot, ending above or below bottom dot (about 1/8 inch leeway allowed at bottom dot to allow for pencil lift); pencil line outside border (touching edge OK); more than one line; visible break in line when child picks up pencil between dots.

Correction: Point out error and tell child to try to keep inside line, start right on the dot, etc. next time.

All levels (a, b, c) must be completely correct (initial instruction only, no errors) in same session. If error on one or two paths, then all three levels must be repeated in another session.

day, written as illustrated in Figure 9–14. Each task's subunits are noted. For example, one of the bear baskets tasks has three subtasks that are noted by the numbers 5, 8, and 10, which are listed horizontally across the tape. Beneath each is an "I" (instruction) on one row and an "E" (error) on the next row. All tapes are made up prior to the small group session. The teacher need only carry a pencil and record a simple tally mark on the left or right side of the I or E. In this recording system, an 'I (with a tally mark on the left) stands for an *initial* instruction, which is defined as any directive to a child that tells the child how to do the task *before* the child begins to work on the task. Initial instructions are always given on the first presentation of a task. Teacher discretion is used on subsequent presentations. That is, if the task format is familiar to the child, the teacher could omit the initial instruction, as the teacher might in regular classroom teaching. If the teacher gives an initial instruction, then the tally mark is placed by the teacher to the left of the I on that task. Once an initial instruction is given (or not given and the child starts work on the task) then any subsequent instructions or corrective instructions are tallied to the right of the I'. A continuing instruction could be requested by the child

---

Figure 9–14 Example of Teacher Recording Tape

Example of Teacher Recording Tape

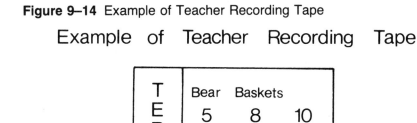

Key

ᴵ = Instruction Prior to Child Working on Task

ᴵ' = Instruction After Task Started, or Correction

Ⓔ = Error After Child Has Indicated Completion of Task

Masking tape, containing the child's name, task, descriptors, and recording code symbols. Tape is placed on the table near each child for easy teacher recording of task related instructions and child errors.

or could be given by the teacher if it is felt that the child needs further instruction to do the task correctly. Instructions to attend to the task or to continue to work are not recorded. Only one tally is recorded for continuing instructions, regardless of how many such instructions are given.

A circle is made by the teacher around the E when an error occurs. An error is defined as an incorrectly completed task at the end of work or an unfinished task, which could include refusal to work on the task. Only one error is recorded, regardless of how many errors occur. Other errors do not have to be recorded because the criterion for successful work on any one task by a child is 0 or 1 initial instruction tallies and *0 errors*. Thus, a tally *after* the I (as well as a circle around the E) means that further work on that task is needed.

Although some teachers often tend to give undue support to children while working on tasks, that support would have to be removed in order for the child to advance to the next level of that task. Following the small group session, the tapes are removed and placed on the sheet in the child's record folder. Later, teachers record the day's data on a learning assessment graph (an example is shown in Figure 9–15).

The learning assessment graph was used in the future planning of the assessment procedure for each child. Both upper division and lower division sheets were used. The example in Figure 9–15 is for the upper division tasks. All four classes of skills are on the sheet, and the first, second, and third levels for each task were included. After each day's data collection, the child's response on that day's task was recorded (following the procedure noted in the key in the upper right-hand corner). For example, the child's behavior illustrated in this graph with visual discrimination tasks shows that in the first session, using the "shapes," the child received a black-filled circle, which indicates the child had no errors, and zero or one initial instructions (see key). The child was then given the boats task on a later day and received an open circle, indicating one or more continuing instructions and/or an error. The boats task was repeated two more days, but errors and/or teacher continuing instructions were recorded. The arrow between sessions four and five notes that an intervention occurred. The type of intervention the teacher planned and the child's responses were recorded on separate forms and filed in the child's folder. After the intervention, the child was given the boats task and, at this time, responded with no errors and no continuing instructions. The flowers task took two sessions for the child to reach criterion. On occasion, several task items were given at the same time, and a box (border) around the items indicates this procedure. This recording system allows the teacher, at a glance, to evaluate the child's progress quickly. For example, this child (Figure 9–15) had immediate success in the language arts class, copying correctly

Figure 9–15 Learning Assessment

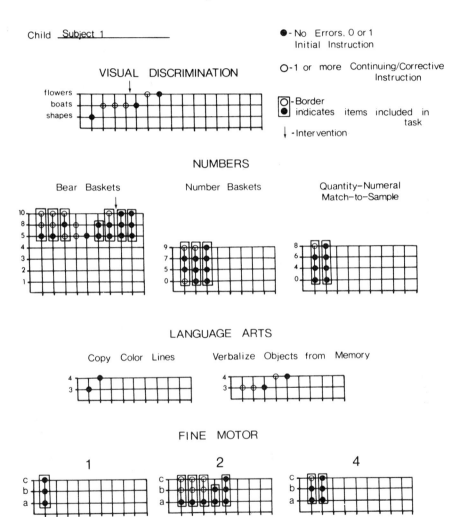

Example of child's responses graphed to reflect degree of correct and unassisted responding (open and closed circles), number of task items presented in a session (border around circles), and where intervention was required (arrows). All levels of each upper division assessment class (e.g., visual discrimination: shapes, boats, flowers) are included on this learning assessment record.

three and four color lines. However, when the child had to remember stimuli (rather than just copy stimuli), difficulty occurred. For example, it took three different days to learn to verbalize three objects from memory and two days to verbalize four objects from memory. An intervention was not necessary since the child met criterion within three sessions. Subject 1's responses on the bear baskets task of the numbers class illustrates several procedures (Figure 9–15). When the child was given 5, 8, and 10 baskets (Figure 9–8), this child encountered some difficulty (three unsuccessful days) and the size (number of baskets) of the task had to be reduced. When the child was still not successful when the number of baskets was increased (Session 7), the child was observed, an error analysis was made on the subset of component responses (made up from a task analysis), and an intervention (noted by the arrow) was made. A separate recording sheet is used for treatment programs and will be illustrated later. After the treatment, the child was again put back on bear baskets 5, 8, and 10, and the child was completely successful. A follow-up (day nine) showed the child continued to be successful. The child then moved to the intermediate level of numbers, and, while some slight difficulty was encountered, the child was generally more successful. Finally, the third level of numbers (Quantity-Numeral Match-to-Sample) was given to the child, and performance was completely correct by the second session.

To summarize, all children were required to complete a task with zero or one initial instructions and no errors. Tasks not successfully completed were repeated with as much teacher help as was felt necessary to train the skill. After three failures at a task, the number of responses (if there was more than one item in a task) was reduced until successful responding occurred, and then the number was gradually increased until the criterion requirement was met. If failure continued at the lower level or if the child was again unsuccessful as the response requirements increased, then motivational intervention was considered if the teacher felt the child had the ability to do the task (from previous observation). This decision, however, was based on data that indicated the child had on several occasions responded for the most part correctly, but was having errors due to lack of care in responding or to distractable behavior.

Task Analysis and Error Analysis

When a decision was made to stop the routine assessment procedure for the class of skills where three failures had occurred, a child was then observed working on the task while the teacher made an error analysis of the component skills used in solving that task. For example, when a task analysis was made for bear baskets (upper division, level 1, numbers, Figure 9–8), it was found that the first skill the child had to demonstrate was (1) to count in a rote manner the bears on the card that was attached to the top of the basket. This skill alone includes a further subset of skills. For example, (2) the child must demonstrate what preschool teachers often describe as one-to-one correspondence. That is, the child points to an object and gives a numeral label for that object at precisely the time of the point. In essence, the mouth and the point must work in unison. Some children will often count faster or slower than the point of the finger. The number arrived at in counting is then different from the number of objects pointed to. A third skill in the counting of the bears is to count in a logical order (usually left to right or top to bottom). Many children who fail to pass this task do not systematically count in some direction and therefore omit objects or count objects more than once. Finally, one other skill that is often taken for granted (but was identified earlier in a research study by Nelson, Holt, & Etzel, 1976) is remembering the number counted for a short period of time. The above five skills are necessary just to count the bears pictured on a card. Once that part of the task has been carried out successfully, the child would still have (6) to reach into the front "holding" basket, count out the number of plastic bears that is the same as the number counted on the card, and then place them in the bear basket. This involves (7) remembering what number the child stopped at when counting the bear pictures and (8) carefully counting either from the holding basket or from a handful of bears drawn from the holding basket. Finally, (9) the child must again remember to stop at the number that had been counted earlier and (10) *not to continue* to count out bears and place them in the bear basket.

It may seem unusual that there are at least 10 subskills (and probably more) that are involved in counting the bears on a card and putting that number in a basket. Each one of those skills have at some time been found to be missing and have resulted in continued errors on the child's part. The important point is that, for most children, teaching these small subsets of skills is not necessary. Normal children, for example, remember how far they have counted and usually remember to stop when they reach that number. Children who do not pick up these skills can be taught them, but only if they are identified as missing. When they are not identified, the child remains at a level, failing to make the appropriate responses, and falls further behind peers, who are moving along acquiring many new skills. This is the main reason for the learning assessment and intervention procedures being described in this chapter.

Recording Error Analyses

Each child who became a candidate for a treatment program that would involve the special materials and instructions (beyond task reduction and/ or motivational assessment) was observed over a period of several days as that child worked on the regular assessment task. A specially developed error analysis chart was used for each task. An example is seen in Figure 9–16, which is a direct outgrowth of the task analysis performed on the bear basket task (upper division numbers, level 1, Figure 9–8). As the child works on the task, the teacher records the following information. The child's name is recorded in the first column, and the date is recorded in the second column. In the third column, the number of bears on the card that the child will count is entered. In the fourth column (1:1 card point and count), the teacher records a plus (+) if the child touched a bear on the card and counted in unison, or a minus (−) if the child gave one bear two counts, skipped counting a bear, counted space between bears, and so on. Column five (1:1 bear to basket count) has similar scoring. A plus is given if a plastic bear is taken from the holding basket and placed in the bear basket as the child counts a number in unison with the transfer of bears from basket to basket. A minus is recorded for counting more bears than exists on the card or not enough bears. Column six (stop at number counted) is scored a plus if the child stops at the number counted on the card or a minus if the child stops before the number counted or continues beyond. Column seven and eight concern the order of the pointing response. The open circles in column eight represent the number and location of bears on the card (the circles with a line through them are marked out by the teacher to indicate they were not on the card on that trial. Then, while the child is pointing, the teacher records the *order* of the points. For example, this subject (Figure 9–16) on the five-bear card started at the top left bear and pointed to it first, and then proceeded from left to right across that row. The same order occurred on the second row for bears 3, 4, and 5. The child received a plus for this response in the "order" column. However, on day 11/21/79, this child's order for counting the eight and ten baskets received a minus because the child counted one bear twice in each task.

Although this child improved on the five-bear basket (from day 11/19/ 79 to 11/21/79), the eight- and ten-basket tasks did not show any clear increases in response success on the various subskills. The skill that was the least successful was the one-to-one, basket-to-bear count that had a total of 17 percent correct responses. The authors' experience with teaching tasks such as this has indicated that continued presentation of these tasks in the same manner would result in continued failure. This suggests that

Figure 9–16 Numbers—Upper Division—Level 1; Bear Basket Error Analysis

Child	Date	Card#	1:1 Card Pt.&Ct.	1:1 B-B Count	Stop at # Counted	Order	
Jenny	11/19/79	5	+	−	−	+	① ② ⊖ ⊖ ⊖ ③ ④ ⑤ ⊖ ⊖
		8	−	−	−	−	ⓃⓄ ◯ ◯ ◯ ◯ ⓇⒺⓈⓅⓄⓃⓈⒺ ◯ ◯
		10	−	−	−	−	ⓃⓄ ◯ ◯ ◯ ◯ ⓇⒺⓈⓅⓄⓃⓈⒺ ◯ ◯
	11/21/79	5	+	+	+	+	④ ⑤ ⊖ ⊖ ⊖ ③ ② ① ⊖ ⊖
		8	−	−	+	−	⑤ ⑥ ⑦ ⑧ ⊖ ④ ③ ② ⑪ ⊖
		10	−	−	−	−	① ③ ⑤ ⑦⑨⑪ ② ④ ⑥ ⑧ ⑩
			2/6 33%	1/6 17%	2/6 33%	2/6 33%	◯ ◯ ◯ ◯ ◯ ◯ ◯ ◯ ◯ ◯
							◯ ◯ ◯ ◯ ◯ ◯ ◯ ◯
							◯ ◯ ◯ ◯ ◯ ◯ ◯ ◯ ◯ ◯

+ = touches & counts each bear − = gives 1 bear 2 #s, skips a bear; counts space between bears; counts between bears.	+ = stops at # counted on card − = stops before # counted; contines beyond #	+ = starts at one end, counts to end of line; on both lines. − = starts in middle of line.

Example of an error analysis used in planning a program to teach a child to successfully complete level 1 (bear baskets) of the numbers class in the upper division assessment. The child's responses to all task items (e.g., card # 5, 8, 10, etc.) were scored as correct (+) or incorrect (−) on component skills required to perform each task item (e.g., pointing and counting simultaneously to each object on a card or 1:1 card pt. & ct.) In addition, the order or sequence in which the child counted the pictured objects was analyzed by numbering the sequence of the child's responses.

the old saying, "practice makes perfect," is not appropriate when a child is not learning. Some change in the teaching procedure must be made immediately and must be designed to the errors the child is making. Research that the authors have conducted (Stella, Hathaway, Villalba, Navarrete, & Etzel, Note 3) has shown that, as children continue to fail to learn, their eye orientations to stimulus materials become more and more infrequent. It appears that the children simply stop looking when the task is not mastered. Not only do children give up, but teachers often avoid giving material to children where the child is having difficulty. Thus, special treatment procedures must be given to children who demonstrate such problems in learning.

Examples of Materials and Teaching Procedures Used in Treatment

One of the skills noted earlier that the child must acquire to be successful on the upper division, level 1 bear baskets (Figure 9–8) is to count the objects in some logical or systematic order. Children who double count or start pointing (and counting) in the middle of the array of objects seldom arrived at the correct total.

Figure 9–17 is an illustration of a program that was used for these children. The circles on the cards are for simplicity of illustration. The actual program had pictures of bears similar to the assessment task (Figure 9–8). Several procedures shoud be noted in this program, which had as its goal the training of a left to right, top to bottom order for counting objects. The starting place was noted by a black dot (upper left object). This was a cue to where the child would put a finger *first* when starting to count. Then the line was to be followed across the objects on the first line, down to the objects on the second line, and then across the lower line. The dot remained as a reminder where to start until the sixth session, when it gradually was faded across the last six cards. The line was slowly shortened starting with the front end.

The authors have found that memory for the direction of visual display (such as letters) is enhanced if the beginning of the display is faded out first while still reminding the child where to start. Several other procedures were also utilized in this program. The number of cards to count was increased from one on session 1, to three by session 4. Since the child had to count three cards on the assessment procedure itself, then it was thought appropriate to increase to this number during the treatment program. Also, each card on the assessment task contained a different number of bears (5, 8, and 10). Therefore, the treatment program used the same numbers, but initially had the child count the small numbers (5 and 8) during the earlier sessions.

Figure 9–17 Upper Division Numbers—Level 1; 1:1 Card Point and Count, Order Program

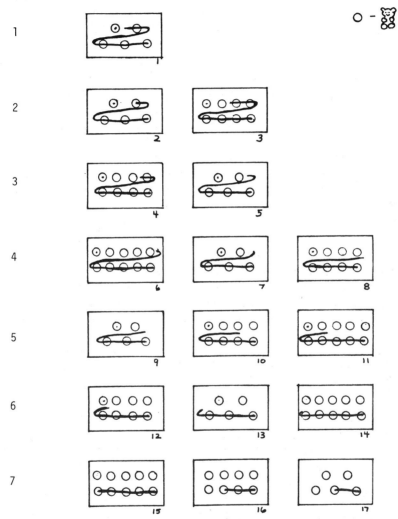

Program intervention cards placed on the bear baskets to teach a systematic counting order and 1:1 counting correspondance. The program consisted of systematic fading of a sequence cue (black line) across trials, increasing the number of items counted across sessions, and fading the dot placed on the bear's stomach that cued the starting point.

This same program was also used to teach children to coordinate the verbal counting with the pointing to the bears. Thus, this one-to-one correspondence of point and count (simultaneously) was taught by teacher instructions to touch the bears that live along the black road. Teacher instructions and prompts, especially to touch each bear carefully, were faded across trials.

Another skill also noted as being absent in some children's repertoire was stopping at a particular number when the counting was over and then remembering the number. This skill was taught by adding a visual cue at the lower right edge of the card where the child counted the bears. This cue, plus a teacher's initial prompt of "How many?" was designed to have the child repeat out loud the *last* number counted so that the number would be remembered. The teacher's cue was faded first. The visual cue consisted of a stick figure with an empty cartoon enclosure, which the child was to supply verbally for the stick figure. It was first determined that the child was familiar with a cartoon's representation of verbalization by showing a comic from a newspaper. The child was told to repeat the last number counted, and this would be the number that the stick figure was saying. Across trials, the stick figure was removed, then the cartoon enclosure was removed. During both of these procedures, the size of the piece of paper was also reduced. Finally, when the paper was removed, the child was instructed to use his or her own hand (the one opposite from the pointing hand) to cue the repeated number. This was done by having the hand cover the basket (below where the visual cue had been located). The child was instructed NOT to begin counting bears into the basket that the hand covered until the number had been repeated (that is, the stick figure was gone). Teacher instructions and prompts to place the hand over the basket were faded across trials as the child continued to repeat the number counted.

Although some children could count bears on a card and arrive at the correct number, some experienced failure when they had to count that number of bears from the holding basket into the bear basket. For these children, a basket-to-basket program was developed. A paper bear, the same size and color as those on the card, was taped to the lower right edge of the basket into which the bears were to be placed. (See Figure 9–18.) The child was instructed to pick up a plastic bear and say the number of that bear (while rote counting), while touching the plastic bear in hand to the paper bear on the edge, before dropping it into the basket. This was designed to prevent errors that resulted from the child not saying a number at all, saying more numbers than bears dropped in, or simply throwing a handful of bears in without counting. The size of the paper bear was reduced across trials and was finally removed, but the child was instructed

Figure 9–18 Intervention: Upper Division Numbers—Level 1; Visual Cue to Touch Side of Basket While Counting

Intervention: Upper Division Numbers–Level 1
Visual Cue to Touch Side of
Basket While Counting
(1:1 Basket to Basket Count)

Session	Trial 1	Trial 2	Trial 3
1			
2			
3			
4			

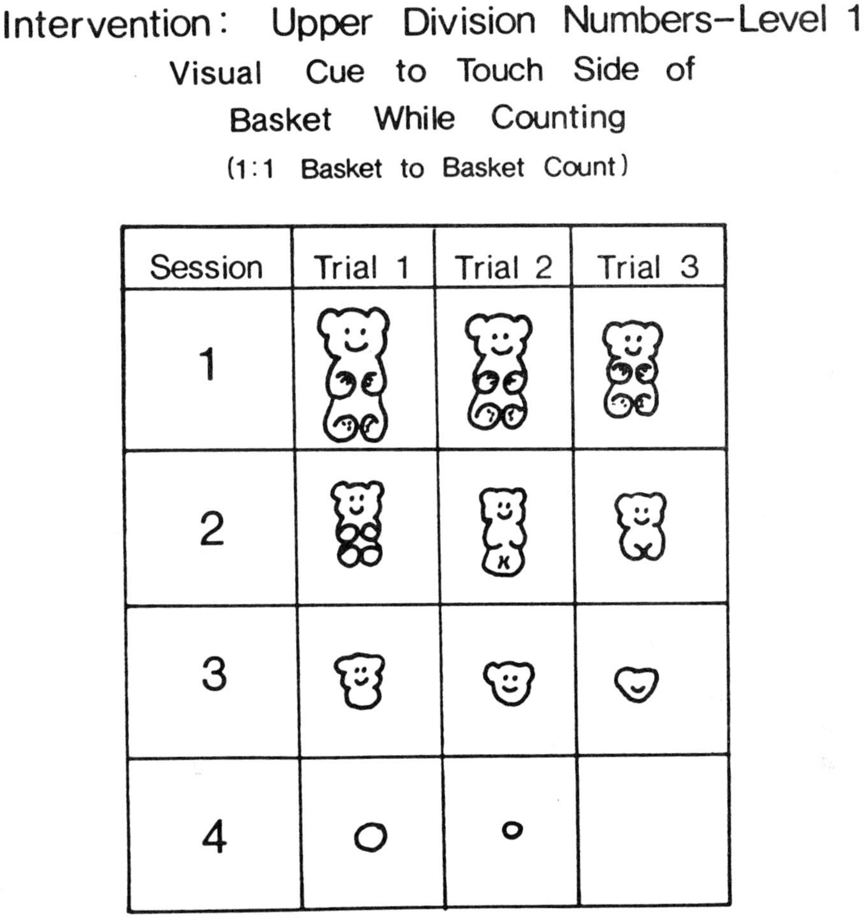

An intervention program designed to train children to transfer the correct number of objects (plastic bears) from one basket to another. The child was taught to touch a picture of a bear (placed on the side of a basket) with each plastic bear (held in the hand). The bear pictures were faded across sessions, leaving the child with a basket tapping response that cued careful 1:1 counting.

to continue to tap the side of the basket where the paper bear had been, while counting.

Another skill that was often missing in some children's responses was the ability to give the verbal label (numeral name) of a numeral. A program was first developed for teaching this skill (Nelson, Holt & Etzel, Note 4) and then extended for the learning assessment research project. (See Figure 9–19.)

Figure 9–19 Number Labeling Program Cues

Number	Number and Superimposed Object	Verbal Response	Motor Response
0		Zip Zero	Pull Up Imaginary Zipper
1		Wiggle One	Wiggle Body
2		Tooth Two	Gnash Teeth
3		Thumb Three	Hold Up Thumb
4		Fishy Four	Wiggle Hands As A Fish Swims
5		Fatty Five	Hold Hands Out As a Fat Stomach
6		Swan Six	Wiggle Hands As If to Paddle
7		Star Seven	Hold Hands Up. Fingers Out As Rays of Star
8		Eggs Eight	Hold Arms Out As Chicken Wings Guarding Eggs
9		Knife Nine	Make Cutting Motion With Side of Hand
10		Train Ten	Pull Imaginary Train Whistle Cord

Number Labeling Program Cues

A program, initially developed by Dr. A. Nelson-Burford and adapted by M. H. Aangeenbrug, was used to teach number labels. Each label was trained by pairing a familiar object and label (zipper and "zip") and a simple motor response (pull up an imaginary zipper) with the unfamiliar number (0) and label (zero).

The program is constructed to resemble a story where a cast of "characters," including the numerals, interact with each other. The child is required to respond only to the numerals with the appropriate name. An errorless stimulus control procedure, referred to as "superimposition," is used to help cue the numeral name. Superimposed over the numeral (Figure 9–19, column 2) was an object with which the child would be familiar. Also, the object started with the same initial sound as the numeral name. This mnemonic procedure, which aids in the remembering of the numeral name, is not new to psychological experimentation. However, the use of superimposition (and, ultimately, the fading of the superimposed object) has been used with retarded and difficult-to-teach children only recently to any great extent (Etzel, LeBlanc, Schilmoeller, & Stella, 1981).

Figure 9–19 illustrates the numeral and superimposed object, and gives the verbal response that the child was taught to use when naming the numeral. Also, in the right column the motor response that child would make as the verbal response was emitted is given.

Prior to the teaching of a program such as this, preschool teachers would include curriculum units in the classroom for the children receiving this training program to assure familiarization with trains, bread knives, chicken and eggs, stars, swans, and other related objects. Although the numeral labeling program as illustrated here does not give enough information as to how it is taught (which is usually with a group of children), the necessary details, as originally programmed by Dr. Nelson-Burford and extended by M. H. Aangeenbrug, are available.[3]

Although most children were able to move from the lower division assessment tasks to the upper division with regular teaching procedures, there were some children who could not make the transition. An example of a program to aid in the transition from counting bears on a card on a lotto board and placing the corresponding number of plastic bears under the card, to a numeral on a card over a bear basket and placing plastic bears in a basket was the following. (See Figure 9–20.)

Ten sessions were used where the child responded to an array of four bear cards on a lotto board and one holding basket. In Figure 9–20, the upper left (session 1) task was similar to the lower division task level 2. (See Figure 9–2.) The child was to count the number of plastic bears from the holding basket that would represent the number on the card on the lotto board above and place these bears directly below in the appropriate square. On trial 2 (top right section of the illustration), the child was told to place the numerals on top of the bear cards after they counted the number of bears on each card. After the child placed the numeral, the child then continued as in session 1 and placed the number of plastic bears in the space below that was the same as the number on the card (and the numeral above the card). By session 3, the empty space below the bear

Figure 9–20 Upper Division Numbers—Level 2; Program for Basket 0

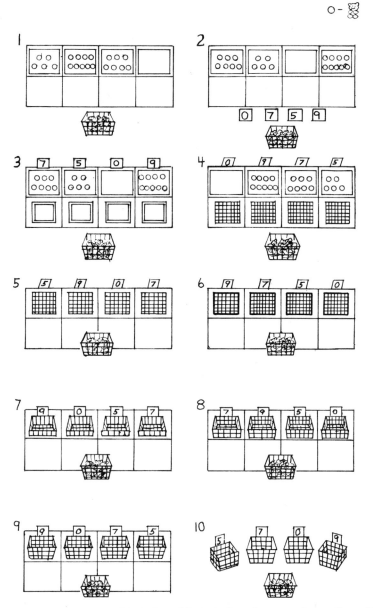

An intervention program used to train subjects to transfer correct counting of bears from a lotto board format to the bear basket format by fading in parts of baskets on the lotto board, across trials.

cards was changed to resemble the top of a basket with the border colored green. The same task was required of the child as in session 2. On session 4, green grids, similar to the green baskets, were added to the space below the bear cards. Again, the task required was to place the number of bears from the holding basket on the grid area as counted from the card directly above. With session 5, the bottom grids from the green plastic baskets were moved up and replaced the bear cards. The task was still to put the number of plastic bears that represented the same numeral on top on the area beneath the grids. On session 6, the top edge of the green plastic basket was added to the grids on the top line of the lotto board. The numerals remained over each grid with its top edge still added. On session 7, the baskets were one-half inch high; by session 8, one inch high; and by session 9, criterion height. The baskets were presented without the lotto board (session 10) resulting in this task being the same as the criterion task in upper division, level 2 number baskets (Figure 9–9). Thus, the transition was made from lotto board and counting bears on a card to identifying a numeral and counting directly into a basket with a numeral located above it.

Most of the illustrations for the treatment or intervention of skill deficiencies in this chapter have been for the number class. Other classes also had treatment procedures, and one example from the visual discrimination class will illustrate how failure to learn some of the subskills was taught. Figure 9–21 illustrates how the criterion assessment task of upper division, level 2 sailboats in the visual discrimination class (Figure 9–7) was taught. Trial 9 of Figure 9–21 is the same as the task illustrated in Figure 9–7. The lotto board was used for this task. The cards that are illustrated on the left side under "sample cards" (Figure 9–21) were placed at the top of the board. The "choice cards," located on the right side of Figure 9–21, were placed in front of the child. The format called for the child to place the choice card directly under the sample card that was exactly the same as the sample card. The teacher then gave one trial a day (or not more than two) of this program to the child. The instructions during the program included counting the number of people in the boat and whether the boat had a line painted on its side. However, in trial 1 only the presence or absence of the painted line was introduced, and the child simply had to match painted line to painted line. The second trial *did not* increase in the number of variables upon which the match was to be made. Only an additional choice card was added. By trial 3 the second basis for matching was added (number of people in the boat). When this occurred, however, the child's number of choice cards was reduced again to one.

In this task, the teacher talks the child through the solution with many short instructions and frequent responding on the child's part, which gives

Figure 9–21 Upper Division Visual Discrimination—Level 2; Sailboats Program

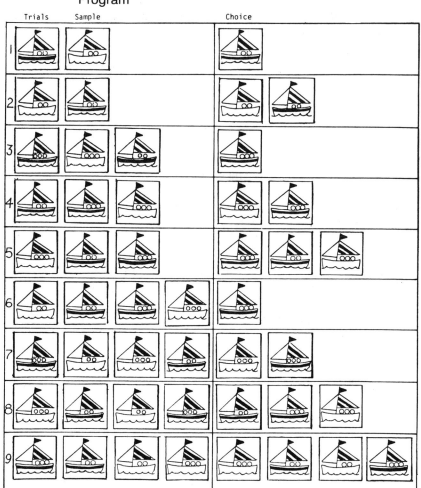

An intervention sequence used to train matching of four choice items (right half of figure) with four sample items (left half of figure), as shown in the last trial (bottom line). This program systematically increased the number of sample items. At each change in the number of sample items presented, the number of choice items was decreased and then systematically increased.

the child a plan for solving the task. For example, for trial 3 the teacher might say the following:

- "Does your boat have a line painted on it?" The child then should look at the choice card and indicate yes.

- "Which boats up here have lines painted on them?" The child should indicate two cards.

- "How many people are in your boat?" The child should count three.

- "Which boat with the line has three people in it?" The child should count people in both boats with lines and point to three-person boat.

- "Put your boat under the picture that has a line and three people."

In trial 6 the number of choice cards is again reduced to one, while the number of sample cards is increased to four, the criterion number in the assessment task. Then, across the next three trials the number of choice cards is also increased to four. Toward the end of this program, the child receives only one trial a day since the task takes quite a bit of sustained attention to solve. Further, the assessment task is only one trial (same as trial 9), and there is no need to train beyond what is needed for success on the assessment task.

Obviously, this program assumes that the child has already developed matching skills. However, children without matching skills would receive the lower division assessment in which matching is taught. Finding out how much and the type of training that would be necessary before the child arrived at the successful solution of the assessment task would give the teacher and parent some understanding of what might be predicted in both kindergarten and first grade.

Those children who needed extensive training were discussed at length with parents with recommendations for an additional year in preschool so that the authors could continue to teach a variety of conceptual skills, in addition to those represented on the assessment task. The authors have found that a one-year delay does not result in a child being too much larger than a one-year younger peer. Also, social behavior often is as "delayed" as the conceptual behavior of such children, so the additional year of preschool aids in this area.

For parents who do not appreciate the value of an additional year in preschool, a compromise is often reached where the child goes to kindergarten for half a day and preschool the other half. This is not the best situation, because the child is usually "completely lost" in kindergarten, yet able to function and learn in preschool. This cannot help but associate failure with formal schooling, since kindergarten teachers seldom identify how much "preacademic" training that particular child should have. However, preschool teachers who have assessed the child in the manner discussed here can serve a useful function of helping the child transfer to the kindergarten by alerting the teacher as to what level and type of instruction will be necessary.

Recording Treatment Data

Although graphing a child's progress may appear to be time consuming, it actually is not, and the benefits of a graph far outweigh the few minutes of daily time spent in this activity. Figure 9–22 is an example of a child who was put in several treatment programs during the school year. Graphs such as this allow the teacher to examine the child's progress and in addition are a helpful way to present material to a parent who would be able to follow even simple explanations of graphed data.

The data graphed in Figure 9–22 were for the numbers class, the upper division assessment of bears baskets 5, 8, and 10, level 1 (Figure 9–8).

Figure 9–22 Numbers—Upper Division, Level 1; Bear Baskets

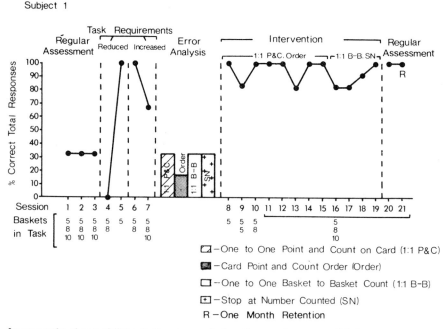

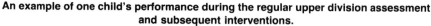

An example of one child's performance during the regular upper division assessment and subsequent interventions.

Subject 1 was given the regular assessment task for three sessions (first three points on graph) and never obtained more than 30 percent correct responses. The task requirements were then reduced by having the child use only the 5 and 8 bear cards (session 4), and then only the 5 card (session 5). Thus, on session 5, with only the 5-bear card to count, the child was 100 percent correct. An increase in the task requirements on session 6 still maintained correct responding. When all three (5, 8, and 10) bear cards had to be counted, errors were again encountered. Next, an error analysis was carried out on the subskills that were considered important responses for this task. This analysis (set of 4 bars) included the following: (1) a one-to-one point and count on card (first bar); (2) an order of counting (second bar); (3) a one-to-one basket-to-basket count (third bar); and (4) stopping at number counted (last bar). The error analysis indicated that none of the skills were more than 33 percent correctly carried out.

An intervention plan was developed for this child that involved a two-step process. The first two skills that were to be taught were one-to-one point and count, and a systematic counting order. Thus, in sessions 8 through 19 the child received a program to teach these two skills, as previously described. (See Figure 9–17.) The solid line and dot represent the child's percent of correct responses on each daily session. The program was quite successful for all days except 9 and 13, where correct responding was at 80 percent. The second treatment program started on session 16 and involved the training of one-to-one, basket-to-basket count and stopping at number. The procedure was similar to that previously described and illustrated in Figure 9–18. By session 19 all of the teacher instructions (prompts) were faded as well as visual cues, and the child was 100 percent successful. A return to the regular assessment material (session 20) and a one-month retention check (session 21) indicated that the child had learned the skill.

Although the teaching materials are altered during a treatment program so that the child is usually successful on each task, it should be noted that teacher prompts are also an important part of most programs.

Observing and recording teacher prompts is not always possible in a classroom where personnel is limited. Obviously, teachers cannot record the number of their own prompts when they are recording the child's errors and teaching the specially designed programs. It was, however, possible to measure one teacher's prompts during a treatment program (with subject 14) since the authors were interested in how prompts interacted with the programs.

Figure 9–23 has teacher prompts noted in open circles and dashed lines during the two parts of the intervention. The scale showing the number of teacher prompts (on the right ordinate) ranges from zero to 10.

Figure 9–23 Numbers—Lower Division, Level 2; Bears Under Card

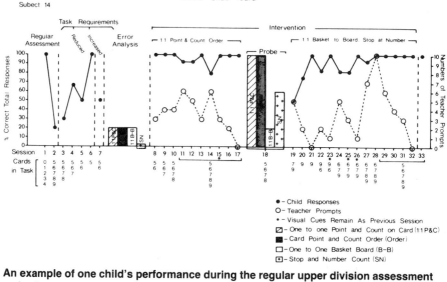

An example of one child's performance during the regular upper division assessment and subsequent interventions. In addition, the number of teacher prompts were graphed, showing that the child was not considered to have reached criterion until the number of teacher prompts was reduced to zero.

When the program was initially introduced, teacher prompts were relatively low (about three or four on sessions 8, 9, and 10) because of the simplicity of the material in the beginning (Figure 9–23). Then, as the program used more material and required more responses, teacher prompts increased, as is seen on days 11 and 12. However, if the child was finally to learn the task, without teacher assistance, then these prompts had to decrease to zero. This was achieved by day 17. Although the child was 100 percent correct for the last three days (days 15, 16, and 17), it was necessary to slowly reduce the teacher prompts before the next treatment plan could begin.

Reducing teacher prompts too quickly on the programmed material can result in errors. It is possible that the first reduction of prompts on days 12 and 13 was too soon for this child and contributed to the 80 percent correct score on day 14. When the prompts were again increased briefly, the child was able to maintain correct responding.

The second part of the intervention (starting with session 19) suggests that there were too few teacher prompts between days 20 and 26. When it became apparent that from session 20 to 26 more than half of the child's correct responses were below 80 percent, a large increase in teacher prompts was made with the programmed materials to help prevent errors. This increase (sessions 27 and 28) in teacher prompts appears to have been helpful. Starting with session 29, teacher prompts were quickly reduced to zero across four days, while 100 percent correct responses for basket-to-basket and stopping (at number counted) continued on the child's part. By session 33, when the assessment task was again measured, the child was now at 100 percent correct.

The important point is that even if teacher prompts can not be recorded, then the teacher should be aware that if the child is not at or above 90 percent correct in such programs, then either teacher prompts should be increased temporarily, the program altered, or both.

Research on this learning assessment procedure has resulted in the elimination of some items (that were clearly too difficult for preschool children of this age range) and the addition of items (for children functioning at a lower level, which were needed for an assessment for designing appropriate treatment programs). In general, however, the authors have found a simple measure to guide in predicting difficulty and concern for a child's future formal schooling.

Determining Future At-Risk Children

The determination of whether a child would progress from one assessment task to the next was based on whether there was an error *and* whether there were any continuing (not an initial) instructions by the teacher for successful responding. The authors then determined how many times a child had a task repeated (up to a standard predetermined number) if zero errors, and zero or 1 initial instructions were *not* obtained. Then the percent of repeated task presentations were calculated for each class of cognitive skills (visual, numbers, language, and fine motor). Also, a total mean for all classes was obtained. This latter score was used as a cutoff score between two groups of children: (1) those who had less than 50 percent repeated task presentations and (2) those who had 50 percent or more repeated task presentations. Although a child may have had one (or more) classes where the task had a repeated task presentation percentage of more than 50 percent, if the *total* of all classes was below 50 percent repeats, then the child was placed in the group with *less* than 50 percent tasks repeated. The formula for arriving at the percentage of repeated task presentations was the following: number of tasks repeated divided by the number of tasks presented. For example, of the three tasks in the upper division of the visual discrimination class that are given (shapes, boats, and flowers), it was necessary to present these three tasks seven times for subject 1 because of failures or continued instructions (Figure 9–15). The number of repeats were four. The percent of repeated task presentations was therefore four divided by seven, which resulted in 57 percent. This would mean that for this child, on visual discrimination, the percent of repeated task presentations is over the 50 percent mark.

When all of the children are grouped into the over or under 50 percent category on the total of all of their classes, it was apparent that few of the children who had their total repeated task presentations under 50 percent ever had a treatment condition, whereas almost all of the children over 50 percent received some form of intervention. The child (subject 1) in Figure 9–15 received two interventions (visual discrimination and numbers). This indicates that this child needed special teacher help and special materials, beyond those used in the normal teaching program, to learn the material at the criterion level. This simple calculation of repeated task presentations appears to predict the performance of the children on later kindergarten experiences, but *not* on IQ differences. (Correlations between IQ and percent of repeated task presentations were not statistically significant.)

Follow-up

The results demonstrated that for those children available for a follow-up assessment in kindergarten and first grade, the authors were accurate in their predictions in 16 out of 20 children. In addition, three of the four children that did not respond on the kindergarten and first-grade assessment tasks as had been predicted had either extensive training or other special handling that would have altered assessment predictions.

The follow-up results available at this time cover a two-year period. Two preschool classes were assessed at the end of their kindergarten experience, and one preschool class was assessed at the end of the first grade. The assessment at the kindergarten and first grade involved a series of paper-and-pencil tasks that reflected the same classes (visual discrimination, numbers, language, and fine motor) assessed at the preschool level. The tasks were teacher administered, in group situations, and consisted of problems appropriate to the level of kindergarten or first grade. The tasks, however, were ones that the child had not seen before, and the child had to follow the directions given by the teacher and apply the instruction to the tasks he or she was to solve. Thus, this assessment also followed an instructional (learning) format. The data were collected during a single school session. On the basis of this assessment, children were then classified as being at-risk or not-at-risk in their current school placement. This classification was carried out independently and without reference to any previous preschool assessment (Aangeenburg & Etzel, Note 5).

Table 9–3 summarizes the kindergarten and first-grade results. Seven kindergarten children (top table) were predicted by the preschool learning assessment *not* to be at-risk, and these seven were found to respond according to predictions. Four kindergarten children were predicted to be at-risk, and three obtained scores that agreed with the prediction. Six first-grade children were predicted *not* to be at-risk, and four agreed with the prediction. Three first-grade children were predicted to *be* at-risk, and two of these children were classified as such on the first-grade follow-up assessment.

The one child in the kindergarten group and the three children in the first-grade group who did not respond as predicted received, except for one, different experiences that may have altered the original prediction.

The one child from the kindergarten group who had been predicted to be below the mean score on the kindergarten task, but who in fact scored above the mean, was a non-English speaking child in the first year of preschool. Although the English improved rapidly, the child had a summer of intensive instruction on kindergarten academic tasks prior to entry into kindergarten. Thus, a language deficiency may have been reflected in the higher number of repeated tasks on the preschool assessment when it was made earlier.

Table 9–3 Kindergarten and First-Grade Results

Kindergarten Follow-up

Preschool Assessment Predicted Child To Be	Number of Children Predicted	Number of Children Agreeing with Prediction	Percent Correct Prediction
Not-at-risk	7	7	100%
At-risk	4	3	75%
(Total	11	10	90%)

First Grade Follow-up

Not-at-risk	6	4	67%
At-risk	3	2	67%
(Total	9	6	67%)

Total Group

Not-at-risk	13	11	85%
At-risk	7	5	71%
(Total	20	16	80%)

Two of the children in the first grade also underwent somewhat different experiences that may have altered the predictions. One child was skipped from preschool to first grade and scored in the at-risk range on the first-grade task. The other child was similar to the kindergarten child and had a summer of intensive work in reading and math skills between the kindergarten and first-grade years.

Only one child who did not have extenuating circumstances associated with school history was predicted to be in the not-at-risk group on the first-grade score but instead scored in the at-risk range. However, this child missed the prediction by only two points.

The greatest concern is not with the predictions of children who were thought to be at-risk but ended up in the not-at-risk group of the kindergarten or first grade. Rather, the concern here is whether all of the at-risk children were identified. Only two children were in this situation: the child who the school system felt could be skipped and the child who missed the not-at-risk group by two points. Neither child would appear to be in much danger of academic failure as the arbitrary grouping of at-risk or not-at-risk would indicate.

Some final considerations about the choice of assessment tasks. This chapter has presented an approach to the assessment of cognitive skill deficiencies that has stressed evaluation *during* learning. Treatment likewise involves specific skills to be learned. The information gained from both will help the teacher prepare both the next teacher the child has and the child's parents as to what teaching approach will be necessary to keep the child current with their peers.

Concerning application of the learning assessment intervention procedures to other settings, the authors do not wish to make any claims for the types of materials used or the tasks that were selected. They found that the tasks they finally used gave information that was helpful in understanding how a child went about learning. Other tasks may be as useful, or even more useful, and they suggest that preschool and special education teachers select their own tasks that fit their subject population and help them observe how a child learns. This chapter should also serve as a model for any teacher, preschool through higher education. Teachers have a specified set of criterion responses they want their pupils to learn. Although workbook and materials change, the goals remain fairly constant. By applying the procedures of learning assessment and intervention during their pupils' acquisition, it should be possible for most students to acquire the behaviors the teachers and society deem important.

For example, one task, which was not included in the scoring of the assessment task but was researched throughout the several years of learning assessment development, yielded a measure of how much information a child was acquiring from that child's peers. Judith LeBlanc has addressed this in the chapter on "Instructing Difficult-to-Teach Children." Children learn many responses that are taught to *other* children, and therefore, they do not need a specific stimulus directed to them to make the appropriate response themselves. It is critical, however, for children to attend while others are learning (that is, from a peers interaction with a teacher).

A procedure for assessing how much children learned from their peers was developed by Etzel, LeBlanc, Aangeenbrug, Holt, and Ruggles (Note 6). The procedure involved a group of four or five children during small-group academic time. The teacher taught five sight words to the group, but each child was taught only one word directly. Each child had the opportunity to observe the other children learning their words as the teacher interacted with each child. Periodically, each child was shown individually all five words and asked to say the word. This gave the teacher a measure of whether the child had acquired his or her own word and which words of the other children's training were also being learned. The words used in this task were "drink," "fruit," "money," "pizza," and "tiger." When it was apparent a child was not learning another child's word, a simple program was applied to the peer's word and presented over an 8-day period. Using superimposition, the first letter of the peer's word had an object such as a child drinking with a straw, placed over (or in place of) the first letter. Then across days, the object was faded out or shaped into the form of the first letter. The treatment that could be used in such a group setting would be to ask the child who had not yet learned the peer's word how he or she knew what the word was. The child would then be reinforced for looking and responding correctly. In this manner, the child could become successful and would be reinforced for looking and learning the peer's word. This same procedure (illustrated in Figure 9–24) was also used with children who did not learn their own word.

The assessment of learning from peers would be important in educational settings where much of the instruction is carried out under group conditions. Also, treatment procedures to help train children to learn to attend to instruction aimed at the peers would be critical if a child were placed in such an educational setting and lacked the appropriate response. The choice of assessment tasks should be based on the type of educational setting, including the teacher's methods of organizing the classroom.

Thus, to suggest that there be specific types of assessment tasks (as is often found in traditional psychometric assessment) that will predict a child's future academic performance is to ignore the issue of in what setting the prediction is being made.

Figure 9–24 Sight Word Program

An intervention program designed to train recognition of a word not learned by stand-ard sight-word trial-and-error training. The program systematically altered or shaped a cue from a familiar or easily recognized picture to the more difficult letter.

SUMMARY

A case is made in this chapter for a different approach to the assessment of young children. The procedures call for measuring the cognitive skills of preschool children while they are learning those skills. The teacher is judged to be the best person to do this, since it should be carried out over a matter of months (even years) and should be directly related to the treatment program that the teacher would develop when deficits are noted. An example of one learning assessment system was presented, and methods for measuring the behavior of the child while learning were described. It is essential that the recording of the assessment be as simple as possible, since the teacher would also be working with the child while simultaneously taking the data. For those children who do not learn, a task analysis on the skill to be taught and an error analysis on each child's individual behavior must be made. Finally, a training program should be developed that uses procedures that eliminate errors, such as programming stimuli and teacher prompts.

Preschool and special education teachers are further encouraged to develop their own tasks within this learning assessment procedure that will help them predict their children's academic behavior successfully toward the child's next classroom experience. This requires the knowledge of where the child will be placed and continuity in planning, with the parents and the teacher for the child's next academic experience.

REFERENCE NOTES

1. Bijou, S.W., & Grimm, J.A. *Behavioral diagnosis and assessment in teaching young hand-icapped children.* Paper presented at the meeting of the International Symposium on Behavior Modification, Minneapolis, October 1972.

2. Nelson, A.L., Holt, W.J., & Etzel, B.C. *Empirical analysis of essential skills in a complex task.* Paper presented at the 84th Annual Convention of the American Psychological Association, Washington, D.C., 1976.

3. Stella, M.E., Hathaway, V., Villalba, D., Navarrete, T., & Etzel, B.C. *Visual attending patterns of normal and atypical children under two training conditions: Trial-and-error compared to criterion-related cue instructions.* Paper presented at the Biennial Meeting of the Society for Research in Child Development, Boston, 1981.

4. Nelson, A.L., Holt, W.J., & Etzel, B.C. *A description of programs to teach beginning math skills.* Invited symposium on preparing atypical preschool children for future academic work, Council on Exceptional Children Annual Convention, Chicago, 1976.

5. Aangeenbrug, M.H., & Etzel, B.C. A two-year follow-up of results on a group administered learning-assessment task for young children. Part of an invited symposium entitled: *Instructional control, learning assessment and observational learning in groups of normal and atypical children.* Paper presented at the Association for Behavior Analysis, Milwaukee, 1981.

6. Etzel, B.C., LeBlanc, J.M., Aangeenbrug, M.H., Holt, W.J., & Ruggles, T.R. *Reading assessment and intervention: Effects of instructional control and incidental learning during group assessment*. Progress Report for the University of Kansas Institute for Research in the Early Childhood Education of the Handicapped, 1980.

REFERENCES

Bijou, S.W. *Child development: The basic stage of early childhood*. New Jersey: Prentice-Hall, Inc., 1976.

Etzel, B.C., & LeBlanc, J.M. The simplest treatment alternative: The law of parsimony applied to choosing appropriate instructional control and errorless-learning procedures for the difficult-to-teach child. *Journal of Autism and Development Disorders*, 1979, *9*, 361–382.

Etzel, B.C., LeBlanc, J.M., Schilmoeller, K.J., & Stella, M.E. Stimulus control procedures in the education of young children. In S.W. Bijou & R. Ruiz (Eds.), *Contributions of behavior modification to education*. Hillsdale, N.J.: Lawrence Erlbaum Associates, 1981. (Also to be printed in Spanish by Editorial Trillas.)

Glaser, R.A. A criterion-referenced test. In W.J. Popham (Ed.), *Criterion-referenced measurement: An introduction*. Englewood Cliffs, N.J.: Educational Technology Publications, 1971.

Lahey, B.B., Vosk, B.N., & Habif, V.L. Behavioral assessment of learning disabled children: A rationale and strategy. *Behavioral Assessment*, 1981, *3*, 3–14.

Sidman, M. *Tactics of scientific research: Evaluating experimental data in psychology*. New York: Basic Books, Inc., 1960.

Torgesen, J., & Goldman, T. Verbal rehearsal and short-term memory in reading-disabled children. *Child Development*, 1977, *48*, 56–60.

NOTES

1. The major source of funding for the development of the contents of this chapter came from the Kansas Research Institute for the Early Childhood Education of the Handicapped, supported by a grant from the Bureau for the Education of the Handicapped, USOE 300–77–0308. In addition, partial support for the conceptualization of the contents of the chapter has come from the University of Kansas General Research Allocation Number 3942; the Kansas Center for Mental Retardation and Human Development, supported by a grant from the National Institute of Child Health and Human Development, HD02528; and the National Institute of Child Health and Human Development, 1 T32 HD07173.

2. Information regarding the commercial materials that were used in this learning-assessment procedure by the DLM and Teaching Resources companies is available by contacting: Developmental Learning Materials (DLM), 1 DLM Park, Allen, Texas 75002; and Teaching Resources, 50 Pond Park Road, Hingham, Massachusetts 02043. The materials from the DLM company are represented in Figure 4 (partially teacher adapted for lower functioning children); Figure 11; and Figure 12. The materials from the Teaching Resources company are represented in Figure 1 (teacher adapted for lower functioning children); Figure 6; and Figure 7.

Details of the teacher-made tasks and individual programs are available at cost of reproduction by writing to: Professor B. C. Etzel, Department of Human Development, University of Kansas, Lawrence, Kansas 66045.

3. Dr. Annabelle L. Nelson-Burford is currently the Director of the Adult Degree Program, Prescott College, Prescott, Arizona 86301.

Chapter 10

Transition from Preschool to Kindergarten for Children with Special Needs

Susan A. Fowler

Five-year-old David has been a student in a preschool class designed for children with learning and behavior problems. He entered the class at the age of three after a local day care center referred him for serious behavior problems, which their staff could not manage. When David joined the special preschool, he was aggressive toward peers, refused to follow many of the teacher's instructions, and was unwilling to try new activities or tasks. As a result of intensive programming and careful planning by the special classroom staff, David has learned to interact pleasantly and constructively with peers and teachers, has acquired new skills, and is often eager to try new activities. David appears ready to leave the special preschool and enter a regular kindergarten.

David's classroom and other preschools enrolling children identified as at-risk for handicapping conditions have prepared many children to enter normal kindergartens. Children who previously did not have the prerequisite skills or conduct for enrollment in a regular class acquire these skills through intensive instruction and the specialized curriculum provided in therapeutic preschool classes (Rowbury, 1980). Even so, the transition into kindergarten can be difficult for some of these youngsters. New friends must be made; new skills must be learned; and new rules must be followed. Some children respond to their new classroom with enthusiasm and excitement. Others respond less positively, showing signs of stress that range from timidness and tears to upset stomachs and tantrums; in extreme cases, school phobia may result. Children with a history of behavior problems are more likely to exhibit conduct and learning problems during their transition into kindergarten than are other children. New behavior problems may appear or former patterns of responding may reemerge. David is a likely candidate for the label of "class problem" unless a coordinated effort is made between the preschool, kindergarten staff, and home to ensure continuity in his educational program.

Guaranteeing a successful transition from preschool to the public school for David and other children like him should be as crucial a goal as the original remediation of the handicapping condition (Anderson-Innman, 1981). Researchers and educators have noted that some children do not consistently generalize the skills and behaviors acquired in the special classes to the regular classes, and that behavior changes that initially transfer do not always maintain (Walker & Hops, 1976; Walker, Hops, & Johnson, 1975; Wildman & Wildman, 1975). Yet little attention has been paid thus far to problems related to transition. Children who do not succeed in the new classroom typically are regarded as "just not ready." They are returned to more specialized environments for further remediation that may or may not facilitate subsequent transition efforts.

How can a preschool staff prepare David and other children like him for kindergarten so that their entry into the public school system is positive and their year successful? No one can guarantee that David will interact pleasantly with *all* classmates and follow *all* teacher instructions; even the best behaved children occasionally present problems. Sufficient planning and training to prepare children for differences between preschool and kindergarten, however, should increase each child's chance for successful adjustment. Such planning should include two goals: (1) training the prerequisite skills needed for a successful kindergarten experience and (2) training for generalization of these skills from preschool to kindergarten. To train effectively for generalization, teachers must be familiar with the future classrooms. Some children's preschool experience may differ from their kindergarten experience in many respects; others may differ in only a few respects. The differences between preschool and kindergarten that interfere with the child's successful adjustment, however, should be identified. These differences can be minimized through adequate planning and communication between the preschool and kindergarten staff. Children can be taught many of the behaviors or skills identified as critical for participation in kindergarten before they enter that program. Additionally, support services can be provided in kindergarten to facilitate the children's acquisition of classroom routines, skills, or behaviors that were not taught in preschool.

The following steps are involved in coordinating a child's successful transition from preschool to kindergarten:

- Identify differences between preschool and kindergarten that may adversely affect a child's adjustment to kindergarten. Differences may be assessed by the preschool teacher through conversations with the kindergarten teacher and other school personnel, and by observations of the kindergarten class.

- Prepare each child for transition by teaching behavior routines and skills during preschool that will facilitate the child's subsequent adjustment to kindergarten. In addition, consider alternative arrangements in kindergarten to accommodate and train needed behaviors and skills not acquired by the child in preschool.

- Establish and maintain communication with the kindergarten before, during, and after each child's transition. The preschool can provide suggestions and information regarding teaching strategies, behavior management, and curriculum activities that were used successfully in the past.

IDENTIFY DIFFERENCES BETWEEN PRESCHOOL AND KINDERGARTEN

Outstanding differences between two classrooms can be assessed by observing both classrooms and comparing them along several dimensions. This information then can be supplemented by interviews with the classroom staff. Many differences are not critical, and some differences may affect one child but not another. Obtaining a composite sketch of the current and future classrooms, and delineating the potentially relevant variations will provide information for decisions regarding individual children's readiness for kindergarten.

The following questionnaire sections were prepared by Fowler (1980) to discriminate differences between preschool, kindergarten, and special education classes.

Classroom Composition

1. How many adults, teachers, aides and volunteers work in the classroom?
2. How many children are in the classroom?
3. Do the numbers of adults and children in kindergarten differ from preschool? (The adult/child ratio is the number of adults to the number of children.) The typical preschool contains 2 or 3 adults and 18 to 20 children. The typical kindergarten contains 1 or 2 adults and 20 to 30 children.
4. Are other children from the special child's preschool likely to attend this kindergarten? (p. 245)

An increase in teacher-child ratio may pose problems for children who learn most readily with individualized instruction or who require close and frequent teacher supervision. A reduced level of teacher attention or availability may adversely influence some children's classroom behavior and learning rate. Thus, an important transition goal for some children will be to prepare them to work independently when teacher access is limited or the teacher is temporarily unavailable (Plummer, 1976). Teaching children to function successfully with fewer teacher instructions, prompts, praise, or attention requires time. However, for older preschool children, the final months of preschool can be used to reduce gradually the frequency of teacher support (Koegel & Rincover, 1974). Teaching children to solicit teacher attention in an appropriate fashion should be another goal. Children should be taught how to request assistance or attention without disrupting the classroom (Bondy & Erickson, 1976; Knapczyk & Livingston, 1974).

The number of new classmates in kindergarten may pose a second concern for some children. Children with less advanced social skills may have a difficult time meeting and befriending their many new classmates. Making friends with one or two classmates before kindergarten begins may ease their transition. Thus, preschool teachers might advsie the parents to acquaint their child with neighborhood children likely to be in the same kindergarten class.

For example, Annie was a language-delayed child who made friends slowly. By the end of her first preschool year, she had several friends with whom she frequently shared activities; nonetheless, she continued to respond in a shy fashion to new children and to children in the other preschool classrooms. The teacher, who was concerned about Annie's social adjustment to kindergarten, discovered that none of Annie's preschool friends would be attending the same school. The teacher thus advised parents to invite one or two neighborhood children who would be in Annie's future class to play at home with Annie before kindergarten began. The parents followed the suggestion, Annie made several new friends, and she entered kindergarten with two familiar companions. The parents reported that she enjoyed her kindergarten experience and eventually developed additional friendships.

Teacher Attention and Reinforcement

1. How frequently do teachers attend to the students with praise, instructions or reprimands? E.g., how frequently do teachers provide praise: every minute, every few minutes, or only at the end of an activity?

2. Do teachers provide special rewards or back-up activities for good behavior? E.g., additional free time, access to the art center, good work certificates, positive home notes.
3. What are the consequences for disruptive or inappropriate behavior? E.g., temporary removal from the activity, loss of recess or free time.

Just as children may behave differently between home and school, so may they behave differently between two classrooms. One way to increase the transfer of desirable performance from preschool to kindergarten is to use similar rules and reinforcement systems (Wehman, Abramson, & Norman, 1977). If rewards were provided for certain behaviors in preschool, then similar rewards initially may be necessary to remind the children to perform the same appropriate behavior in kindergarten.

For example, Jerry responded politely to adult and peer requests in preschool, but he frequently responded unpleasantly to similar requests in kindergarten. In preschool Jerry had received a star on a chart at the end of each activity if he "behaved like a gentleman," that is, complied with teacher requests and used polite forms of speech when responding to such requests. The stars could be exchanged at the end of the day for a period of free-play time. His preschool teacher suggested that a similar chart be introduced temporarily in kindergarten to reduce his disruptive behavior. The suggestion was successful; Jerry's rude behavior quickly disappeared when the chart was reintroduced. Why? Jerry's inappropriate responses may have been an easy way to gain attention in his new class. Introduction of the chart, however, quickly shifted the teacher's attention away from his undesirable behavior to more appropriate behavior. The teacher now ignored Jerry's unpleasantness, but praised and rewarded his politeness. Jerry quickly noticed that his teacher and classmates paid as much or more attention to him when he was pleasant as when he was rude. Finally, the chart also reminded Jerry that polite speech was expected in kindergarten, just as it had been in preschool. Another strategy that might have been tried before transition would have been to reduce gradually the use of stars in the preschool, while maintaining Jerry's appropriate responding with teacher praise.

Researchers and practitioners frequently have noted the importance of reducing reinforcement schedules once a desirable behavior has been developed and an undesirable behavior has been reduced (Allen, 1972; Stokes & Baer, 1977). Simplifying the form of reinforcement (for example, shifting from tokens or stars to praise) once a behavior is established; providing reinforcement on an intermittent, less predictable basis; and gradually delaying reinforcement are three techniques preschool teachers can use to facilitate children's maintenance and generalization of new behaviors (Fowler & Baer, 1981; Jones & Kazdin, 1975; Kazdin & Polster, 1973). If the form of reinforcement can be simplified to praise and the frequency of praise reduced or delayed, then occasional praise from the new teacher is more likely to maintain the child's desirable behavior in the new classroom.

Physical Arrangement

Is the physical arrangement of the kindergarten class different from the preschool? For example:

1. Do children sit on individual mats or on a group rug?
2. Do children work at tables or at desks?
3. Are work and play areas clearly separated?
4. Are play areas visible from work areas?
5. Is the bathroom or drinking fountain adjacent to the classroom or down the hallway?

Although many children adjust as quickly to a new classroom as to the rearrangement of their familiar classroom, some children do not. Their adjustment may be hampered by differences in physical aspects of the new classroom that require new responses or behaviors (Rogers-Warren & Wedel, 1980). For example, the behavioral requirements of sitting on individual mats versus sitting on a large group rug are quite different. Individual mats define a child's space for the child; if the mats are spaced apart, children are spaced apart automatically and thus have few opportunities to touch, tickle, or elbow one another during group instruction. In contrast, when one large rug is used, children often crowd together. If the preschool uses individual mats and the kindergarten uses a group rug, it may be necessary to teach children who are considered distractable or overactive to manage themselves in crowded spaces. Alternatively, the preschool teacher might recommend that the kindergarten teacher initially define space for these children in the new class. Taping X's on the group rug and instructing the students to sit on an X is one simple way to define space. After the children are accustomed to spacing themselves apart, the X's could be removed.

Traffic patterns within the classroom should be considered carefully, too, as they may affect the way in which children participate (Safford, 1978). For example, if children are instructed through a learning center approach, attention should be directed to the boundaries established between centers. If boundaries are not clear (defined either by space, furniture, or movable barriers) then children may be tempted to move materials inappropriately from one center to another, or to change centers before they are instructed to do so. The proximity of certain centers to one another should be considered too. If academic instruction centers are located near play centers, the auditory and visual distractions offered by the play center may compete with the attention of children working in the academic center. Arranging centers so that distractions are minimized is particularly important for children who distract easily, have hearing impairments, or are slow learners.

The effects of new physical arrangements on a child's adjustment are not always easy to anticipate. For example, the location and use of separate toilet facilities affected one child's adjustment to her new kindergarten. The kindergarten class Eve attended did not contain a bathroom; instead, separate boys' rooms and girls' rooms were located in a hallway around the corner from the classroom. Children were allowed to use the bathroom as needed through the day. In preschool, Eve's classmates had used the same bathroom, located within the classroom. Eve, who was not familiar with the practice of separate boys' and girls' facilities, used the boys' room occasionally during the the first week of school. Eve's error evoked teasing from her classmates and a reprimand from her teacher, which upset her. As a result she did not use either bathroom for the remainder of the school year. Her confusion and subsequent embarrassment could have been prevented if her teacher had explained and made sure that Eve understood the use of separate bathrooms and if Eve had been exposed occasionally to the use of different bathrooms before her entry into kindergarten.

Daily Schedule

1. Is the kindergarten in session longer than the preschool?
2. How many minutes do children spend:
   a) in large groups (singing, sharing, listening to stories, having snacks)?
   b) in small groups?
   c) doing academic work and fine motor activities?
   d) in free play activities?
   e) in recess and large motor activities?
   f) in moving from one scheduled activity to another (for example, lining up for recess, waiting to be called from large group to small group)?

The kindergarten schedule may differ from the preschool's schedule. If so, the preschool teacher should consider how it might affect specific children. For example, a preschool teacher who scheduled only one large group activity a day discovered that the kindergarten, which many of the preschoolers would attend, contained three lengthy, large group activities.

The teacher preferred the preschool schedule and did not consider the difference in schedule and teaching style to be important for most of the children. The teacher was concerned about Micky, however, who was distracted easily and who rarely responded to group questions. When he responded, he spoke almost inaudibly. The teacher decided that an important transition goal for Micky would be to increase his participation in the preschool large group. If Micky learned to participate more in the preschool group, he might be able to transfer his participation skills to the kindergarten, despite the difference in the number of large group activities. The teacher's strategy was successful. Micky learned to participate at a more consistent rate in his one large group during preschool. He later successfully transferred these participation skills to the several large groups conducted in kindergarten.

The sequence of activities in one kindergarten schedule appeared to be the factor behind another child's transition difficulties. Tim was an efficient worker during a 20-minute preacademic period in preschool. He worked independently and appeared to enjoy his tasks. In kindergarten, however, he dawdled over many of the same tasks, frequently sought assistance, and appeared to need the allotted 40 minutes to finish his work. The kindergarten teacher considered Tim to be a slow learner and hesitated to give him the extra work that many other class members were completing. What factors were responsible for Tim's poor performance? In preschool, Tim could leave the worktable when he finished his tasks and return to a free-choice activity in the play area. In contrast, during kindergarten the only other activities available were additional tasks or books. The children went to recess after the 40-minute work period if they had finished their assigned tasks. Tim's work rate had slowed to fill the available time. However, an increase in the selection of optional activities available when the children finished their work and praise for efficient work completion once again increased Tim's attentiveness and productivity. As a result, the teacher was able to increase the number of academic tasks that Tim finished each day.

Classroom Rules and Routines

1. Are children required to raise their hands? If so when?
   a) for permission to speak
   b) when they have finished a task
   c) to seek assistance
2. Do children speak out? If so when? (e.g., volunteering answers in large group)

3. During what activities can children talk to their classmates and move about the room?
4. Do children have free or limited access to the bathroom, water fountain, pencil sharpener, supplies?
5. Do children manage all or some of their own materials (e.g., crayons, paper, paste) or do they use community materials? What materials do they manage?
6. Do children walk in line single-file or double-file? Do they hold hands?

Differences in a few classroom rules can cause confusion and produce oppositional behavior during the initial sessions of kindergarten. Unfortunately, this may set up a series of undesirable teacher-child interactions that in a few cases could affect future interactions. Common differences between preschool and kindergarten often involve rules regarding classroom conversation, movement around the room, and hand raising (Plummer, 1976). Many preschools do not emphasize classroom rules, such as hand raising, walking single-file, working quietly; such rules run contrary to a philosophy that preschool is a time for children to explore, to gain autonomy, and to socialize with one another. Occasionally, however, introducing more structure to the preschool may facilitate the children's later transition into more structured kindergartens. A study conducted by Carden-Smith and Fowler (in press) on the kindergarten adjustment of children with special needs suggests that 60 percent of the children's behavior that was viewed by teachers as noncompliant were rule infractions. Yet many of these rules did not exist in the children's preschool. A frequent complaint reported by Fowler (1976) focused on the children's conduct while walking in line. One child, Tina, walked appropriately only if the teacher held her hand or if she walked in the front of the line. At other times, Tina grabbed her classmates' hands or walked out of line. Tina had never walked in a single-file line before kindergarten; in her preschool, children never formed a line to go outdoors, but always walked in small groups, holding a partner's hand or the teacher's hand. Tina was maintaining this routine, albeit inappropriately. Occasional line walking in preschool might have made the routine more familiar to her and facilitated her compliance with such an expectation.

A second common difference between preschool and kindergarten involves the child's management of personal materials (Brackman, 1976). Frequently, crayons, scissors, and glue are community property in preschool. In kindergarten, children often are expected to care for their own materials and keep them in lockers. Allowing older preschoolers to manage and store certain classroom materials in their bin or locker may prepare them for management of gym clothes, library books, workbooks, school papers, and other materials introduced in kindergarten.

Academics

1. Are there minimum competency levels? Is there a kindergarten readiness checklist?
2. What academic subjects are taught?
3. What curriculum materials most typically are used? For example, are math concepts taught through manipulative materials, such as cuisennaire rods, through worksheets, or both?
4. Are lessons taught in large or small groups?
5. How do children respond during instruction?
   a) Do children recite answers? For what subjects? (e.g., alphabet, numbers)
   b) How often and for what subjects do children reply as a group to teacher questions?
   c) How often and for what subjects do children respond individually to teacher questions?
   d) How often and for what subjects do children produce written responses?
      1) What response formats are used? Do children circle the right answer, color in the right answer, mark (X) the right answer, mark (X) the wrong answer?

To ensure continuity in a child's educational program, differences between the preschool and kindergarten instruction and assessment methods should be determined. Such differences may prevent some children from demonstrating the information or skills they have acquired previously. Furthermore, some children may experience difficulty acquiring new information and skills (Rincover & Koegel, 1977). For example, children accustomed to individual instruction may not learn as quickly under group instruction. As members of a large group they are likely to receive fewer individual prompts and may have fewer opportunities to respond. In addition, group-delivered instruction usually is paced according to the group learning rate and not according to the individual child's rate. Thus, it may be necessary to teach the slow learners to attend to instructions and to respond in a group situation before they are expected to acquire new information through group instruction (Koegel & Rincover, 1974).

Children also may not transfer some specific skills across different curriculum materials. For example, in preschool Stan easily and accurately counted groups of blocks, ranging in number from 1 to 10. In kindergarten, however, he could not count groups of five or more objects when the objects were depicted on a worksheet. Stan always touched and then moved the blocks as he counted them, as a way of remembering what was counted and what was left to count. He could not move the pictures on the worksheet. Stan's kindergarten teacher at first thought that Stan was not working hard enough, as Stan's report from preschool indicated he could count objects up through ten. Several days and worksheets later, Stan still was making errors with large numbers. The kindergarten teacher decided that the preschool report was inaccurate, disregarded the other information contained in it, and assigned Stan to another math group.

A similar misunderstanding occurred with Dana, a child who exhibited some emotional problems. She had learned to classify common objects on a worksheet in preschool by placing an X on the objects that were the same. Her kindergarten worksheet instructions were different: she was told to mark with an X the objects that did not belong. Dana was confused by the change in instructions. For several days she marked her worksheet inaccurately and finally scribbled on it. The teacher responded by placing her in a group well below her skill level. Exposing Dana to several different ways of answering (for example, circle the same, draw a line between answers) in preschool might have lessened her confusion and made transfer to another new response format (X the wrong answer) easier.

Alternatively, Dana and Stan's preschool report could have specified the exact conditions under which the children exhibited their skill. Stan's new teacher probably would have recognized that the ability to count concrete, maneuverable objects is less advanced than the skill of counting objects depicted on a worksheet. Likewise, Dana's kindergarten teacher might have explained the workbook instructions more carefully and frequently, and thus minimized Dana's confusion.

Self-Help Skills

What self-help skills do most children demonstrate?

1. dressing independently for outdoors?
2. shoe-tying?
3. drinking milk through a straw?
4. hand washing? nose care?

Training self-help skills should be a transition goal for all preschoolers. Children who do not demonstrate basic-help skills will stand out as markedly different from their classmates. This distinction may create further differences. In addition, their lack of skill may be viewed as an inconvenience for an already busy teacher (Allen, 1980).

The reaction of Max's kindergarten teacher may be typical of other teachers: "I don't mind scheduling extra tutorial time with Max to help him with his printing and math, but I do mind asking the class to wait for him when he needs help putting on his outdoor clothes. The other children become very impatient with him, and so do I. I shouldn't have to worry about his self-help skills." A lack of self-help skills made Max, a child with learning problems, appear different to the other children and was the one deficit that almost compromised his teacher's willingness to accommodate Max in the classroom. If the kindergarten teacher places a high value on independence, then these skills could become goals in preschool and at home. In addition, the kindergarten teacher might consider asking children in the classroom to tutor or assist one another in certain skill areas. Self-help skills seem to be an excellent target for peer tutoring (LeBlanc, Etzel & Domash, 1978).

Support Systems

1. What support services are available to the classroom? E.g.:
   a) resource room assistance
   b) speech therapy
   c) adaptive physical education
   d) physical therapy
   c) paraprofessional aide
2. Do parents work as aides? cooperate in home reward systems?
3. Do older students or classmates tutor children with special needs?

Some classrooms have access to many support systems, and some have access to few such services. If a child is likely to need support services, the available ones should be identified and additional ones requested prior to the child's first day in kindergarten. Advance notification may be necessary to ensure that the child has sufficient access to special services. Some teachers are also willing to develop other support systems that might facilitate a child's adjustment to kindergarten. For instance, parents can provide an important source of support to the child and teacher. If home reward systems have been established in preschool, then transferring the home reward system to kindergarten may facilitate the transfer of many desirable behaviors from preschool to kindergarten.

For example, in preschool Heather received a good report when she completed her preacademic tasks without complaining or disturbing her peers. Her parents provided small rewards at home for each positive report.

These rewards typically consisted of a special activity (reading a favorite story, having her hair braided, watching a favorite TV program). When Heather began kindergarten, home reports and rewards were no longer provided. Many of Heather's maladaptive behaviors reappeared: she was disruptive during learning centers, rarely completed her assignments, and frequently complained that her work was too hard. Her parents suggested that the home report be reinstated. Heather's school behavior immediately improved and her parents maintained an active interest in her school performance throughout the year.

Likewise, some parents can supplement certain academic lessons with home tutoring. A simple home tutoring procedure was combined with storyreading by Wedel and Fowler (1981) for use with kindergarten children who needed extra assistance to learn the alphabet and basic sight words. The parents taught two to four letters or words each week while reading their child a story. During the story, the parent stopped occasionally (a total of 10 or 15 times) to ask the child to identify a letter or word. At the end of each week, the teacher tested the children to determine which of the assigned letters or words had been learned. The parents then were provided with a revised list for the next week. Both children and parents reported that they enjoyed the procedure, and the children successfully learned the alphabet or basic sight words over a three- to four-month period.

PREPARE CHILDREN FOR TRANSITION

Differences between preschool and kindergarten that are identified through the classroom assessments and through conversations between the respective teachers suggest what preparations are needed for a child's adjustment to kindergarten. As indicated in the previous section, many of these preparations can be made before the child begins kindergarten; others can be made only after the child enters kindergarten. The preschool preparations are not intended to turn the preschool into an early kindergarten; rather, much of the transition training can be accomplished in the context of typical preschool activities. For example, preschools can prepare their older children for the increased independence of kindergarten in the following ways:

- by gradually decreasing and delaying teacher attention and praise;

- by gradually reducing teacher instructions and prompts;

- by asking the older children to state or repeat the classroom rules at the beginning of class.

Teachers can prepare children for increased responsibilities by assigning roles, such as clean-up leader or line leader, or by designating the care of certain classroom materials to different children

Children's attention spans can be increased gradually to meet the demands of longer lesson periods in kindergarten in the following ways:

- by gradually increasing the amount of time children are expected to stay at a free-choice center or remain in large groups;

- by teaching the children to find appropriate alternative uses for materials when children still have time left in an activity (for example, sort, label, count colored blocks when the child is "tired" of building);

- by encouraging children to repeat a task with new materials (for example, trade puzzles with a friend when the first puzzle is finished).

When preschool children lack some of the skills expected of incoming kindergarteners, these skills can be incorporated into the preschool curriculum. Many of the kindergarten readiness skills do not need to be introduced in academic situations, however; they can be practiced within the normal routines and activities of preschool. For example, if children are expected to cut with scissors, hold a pencil properly, draw simple shapes, label colors, and count to ten, then these skills and concepts can be introduced first during supervised free-play and art time. During the final months of preschool, teachers can arrange academic activities, similar to activities in kindergarten, to ensure that the children will exhibit these skills in the context of a structured lesson or with curriculum materials typical of kindergarten. Most children are eager to "practice school" and welcome such academic activities.

ADAPT THE KINDERGARTEN TO ACCOMMODATE SPECIAL NEEDS

To minimize the differences between preschool and kindergarten, and to accommodate the needs of special children, changes can be made in the kindergarten class during the first weeks of school as well. Several examples of accommodations made by kindergarten teachers to facilitate the adjustment of children are described here.

Behavior Programs Initially Developed and Implemented in the Preschool

If the preschool used a daily home report and reward system for promoting appropriate classroom behavior (for example, task completion), then it should be reimplemented for a short time in kindergarten. A familiar set of rules and rewards will prompt the child to behave appropriately in the new setting and reinforce such behavior. Furthermore, the familiar system will focus the child's attention on good behavior, and will provide the child with little opportunity or incentive to slip back to former behaviors that were inappropriate but so effective at gaining teacher attention. Such a system may also serve as a prompt to the teacher to reward the child for good performance, thus initiating a cycle of positive interactions between teacher and child.

Familiar Preschool Curriculum as Supplements to the Kindergarten Curriculum

The presence of a few familiar activities or tasks can be important to many children in providing continuity between their preschool and kindergarten experiences. Singing familiar songs or findng a few favorite books, puzzles, or toys in the kindergarten room can reassure a child who has just entered a new class. Preschools and kindergartens often contain many similar materials and games. Using those familiar activities during the first weeks of kindergarten may ensure the child's participation and ease the child's anxieties about the newness of kindergarten.

Grouping Children According to Their Ability

Most kindergarten teachers teach their students in groups rather than as a whole class. Grouping arrangements can be critical to a slow learner's participation and success in school. Instructions can be paced more closely to each child's performance, if children are grouped systematically according to their skill level rather than randomly. Skill deficits and learning problems are more likely to be identified quickly and remedial teaching begun under such a system.

Introducing Parents or High School and College Students as Aides

The addition of one or two adults to a classroom will facilitate individualized instruction and the application of more systematic and contingent reinforcement systems. Such attention and planning may be essential to ensure that a child with learning and behavior problems learns the new rules and routines of the classroom, and transfers the many behaviors and skills that have been developed so carefully during preschool. As the child adjusts and behaves in a desirable manner, this support can be reduced.

An example of this procedure was described recently in a study conducted by Russo and Keogel (1977). In brief, they provided an autistic child with a therapist during the first weeks of kindergarten so that intensive support could be available while the child adjusted to the new classroom. The therapist used a token system with the child to systematically shape and reinforce her desirable classroom behavior (that is, appropriate social interaction, responses to the teacher, and the absence of self-stimulation). When the child had demonstrated acceptable levels of appropriate behavior, the therapist began transferring the token procedure to the teacher. First, the therapist systematically reduced the frequency of token reinforcement by giving tokens on an intermittent basis. Second, the therapist provided instructions and training to the teacher on the use of the token system. Finally, the therapist transferred the token procedure to the teacher. During the first week in which the teacher conducted the token program, the therapist took charge of the classroom during parts of the school day so that the teacher would have more time to spend with the autistic child. In addition, throughout the week, the therapist provided feedback to the teacher regarding the effectiveness of the teacher's interaction with the child. In the weeks that followed, the therapist maintained regular phone contact with the teacher to monitor the child's progress. The teacher was able to reduce the number of tokens awarded to the child until the child was receiving only two tokens a day. Interestingly, the child did not generalize appropriate classroom behaviors to the first grade; reimplementation of the token procedure by the first-grade teacher was necessary to produce the desired school behavior again.

This example is another demonstration of the need to consider differences in classroom environments (preschool, kindergarten, and subsequent grades) and to provide training prior to or following a child's transition, if initial differences presented by the new classrooms are to be minimized and successful integration assured.

Establishing and Maintaining Communication with the New Classroom

Before Transition

Maintaining interaction between the classroom staffs before, during, and after the child's transition can assist the child's adjustment to the new class and the new teacher's adjustment to the child (Grosnick, 1971). Thus, one or more meetings between the preschool, and the public school staff and the parents should be scheduled to discuss the child's transition before it occurs. At these meetings the class placement most appropriate for the child should be assessed and, if needed, special services determined. Other topics for discussion should include the following:

- a summary report of the child's current social and academic skills

- an estimate of the child's future needs

- the teacher's interest and willingness to have the child attend the classroom

- arrangements for parent and child visits to the kindergarten

- the exchange of teacher visits between the preschool and kindergarten (if such visits have not occurred yet)

- the frequency and form of future contact between the preschool and kindergarten

A report from the preschool that summarizes the child's performance can be helpful and informative for the parents and for the future teaching staff. A comprehensive report should detail a child's current academic skills and the conditions under which they can be performed (for example, the curriculum materials used, the degree of teacher guidance required). A list of the child's most recent tasks and descriptions or samples of the tasks may be valuable for the next teacher, who may wish to include some of these familiar tasks during the first days of school. Examples of tasks that the child can master may assist the teacher in determining the child's next sequence of tasks. Suggestions of future tasks by the preschool teacher also may be of assistance in determining this sequence. A list of preferred activities, both academic and play, can be useful for both parents and teachers. These activities often can be used as rewards after the child has attempted a new or difficult task, either at home or at school. In addition to an academic focus, the report should describe the child's current social skills; for instance, the child's ability to initiate social contacts with unfamiliar as well as with familiar children and to maintain the interaction. If the child experiences difficulty in certain social situations, these difficulties should be discussed. Similarly, descriptions of other problem behaviors and ways to manage them can benefit both teachers and parents. The information will provide them with a strategy, proven useful in preschool, that they also may employ. In summary, the report should focus on the child's skills and abilities, since these will serve as the building blocks for the acquisition of future skills and learning. Problem behaviors should be discussed when relevant, and suggestions for managing the problems also should be provided. Appendix 10–A is an example of a report sent to a kindergarten teacher in Lawrence, Kansas.

After the child's current performance has been discussed thoroughly, an individualized education plan (IEP) for the child's first semester in kindergarten should be prepared, either at the initial staff meeting or during a subsequent meeting. The preschool staff's summary report supplied information about the child's current abilities and typical learning rate; the kindergarten staff can report the expectations and goals typically established for kindergarteners. By combining this information, along with goals requested by the parents, a reasonable and systematic education plan can be developed for the child.

If teachers from the two classrooms have not exchanged visits to one another's classrooms, the development of the IEP should be postponed until such visits have taken place. Information acquired from the observations is sure to be useful in producing a comprehensive plan. As part of the IEP, the teachers should discuss the frequency of future contact between the preschool and kindergarten after the child's transition. Regularly scheduled phone calls between the old and new staff can be an important and inexpensive form of insurance for the child, guaranteeing continuity between the child's two school placements.

Finally, a visit to the kindergarten by the parent and child should be arranged at the meeting. This visit will provide them with an opportunity to see what kindergarten is like and how it differs from preschool. In addition, the visit may ease fears that some children (and parents) experience when moving to a new school (Klein, 1975).

During Transition

Most children begin kindergarten on the first day of school and remain in the class for the full half-day session. Many children with handicaps or special problems will begin kindergarten in the same fashion. However, alternative arrangements should be considered if the parents and teachers are concerned about the child's ability to manage a full session. Flexible scheduling may facilitate the child's active participation and adjustment. Thus, some children might attend kindergarten for only part of the session each day during the first week or two. In this way the number of activities introduced to the child may be increased gradually from day to day. Such a gradual introduction will allow the child with special needs to master participation in each new activity, before beginning the next activity. Within a few weeks, the child can be attending the entire session and will be familiar with the routines and schedule of the classroom. This gradual introduction may be advisable for children with little or no previous school experience, or for children with serious handicaps. It is also advisable for classrooms where an adult is not available throughout the session to introduce a special child to each new activity and prompt successful participation in the activity. A teacher with 20 or more new children may have time only to assist the special child through one new activity a day.

Alternatively, the child might begin kindergarten for the full session with the aid of an adult, who can provide extra assistance, as needed, during the first week of school (Russo & Koegel, 1977). When the child masters the new routines and becomes familiar with the activities, the adult support can be withdrawn gradually. The assisting adult might be a member of the special services team, a member of the child's former preschool staff, or a parent volunteer.

Finally, some children might begin kindergarten while maintaining half-day enrollment in the preschool. If a full-day school experience is advisable, then the preschool can supplement and support the child's kindergarten experience. In addition, part of the child's school world will remain familiar and stable through continued participation in the familiar preschool. Maintaining a child's coenrollment in preschool may facilitate an exchange of information between the preschool and kindergarten. The teachers can discuss the activities and concepts being introduced in each classroom. Futhermore, a child's ability to demonstrate skills and concepts newly acquired in one classroom can be assessed in the other classroom. Skills and concepts that do not generalize to the other classroom subsequently can be practiced and reinforced in that classroom. This exchange of information should maintain educational continuity between preschool and kindergarten as well as enhance the child's daily educational program.

After Transition

Regularly scheduled meetings or phone calls between the new and former teaching staff will assist the new teacher's efforts in creating a successful school experience for the child. Such contacts might be weekly at the beginning of school, but decrease to biweekly or monthly as the child progresses through the year of kindergarten. The purpose of such contacts by the preschool staff is threefold:

1. to exchange information regarding the child
2. to convey concern regarding problems that may arise and recommendations for their solutions
3. to offer enthusiastic support for the child's (and teacher's) success.

Former teachers can appreciate the excitement that a new teacher may experience when a handicapped child masters yet another skill in the new classroom after several days of careful planning and instruction. The former teacher can offer support and enthusiasm for the child's progress, and understanding if progress in some areas becomes slow and frustrating. Likewise, suggestions based on past teaching history with the child can be provided as well as encouragement for the occasional discouraging day that all teachers face. Finally, these contacts can provide much needed opportunities for both teachers to express the frustrations as well as rewards of working with a special child.

SUMMARY

In summary, David, the child from a special preschool class, soon will be one of many kindergarten students. David's chances for success are high, *if* his preschool has prepared him for the entry skills and routines of kindergarten, *if* the two classrooms have cooperated in planning his admission to kindergarten, and *if* they continue their contacts during David's adjustment to kindergarten. With this planning and the combined efforts of preschool and kindergarten professionals, David and other children like him can look forward to a successful early education and to a comfortable and successful future in the mainstream of the public school.

REFERENCES

Allen, K.E. Behavior modification: What teachers of young exceptional children can do. *Teaching Exceptional Children*, 1972, *4*, 119–127.

Allen, K.E. The early childhood education specialist (ECES). In K.E. Allen, V.A. Holm, and R.L. Schiefelbusch (Eds.), *Early intervention: A team approach*. Baltimore, Md.: University Park Press, 1978, 287–306.

Allen, K.E. *Mainstreaming in early childhood education*. Albany, N.Y.: Delmar Publishers, 1980.

Anderson-Innman, L. *Transenvironmental programming: Strategies for promoting success in the regular class by maximizing the effect of resource room instruction*. Paper presented at the Association for Behavior Analysis, Milwaukee, May 1981.

Bondy, A.S., & Erickson, M.T. Comparison of modelling and reinforcement procedures in increasing question-asking of mildly retarded children. *Journal of Applied Behavior Analysis*, 1976, *9*, 108.

Brackman, B., & Peterson, N. Environmental development and environmental changes. In *Developing a functional program for the transition of young children in integrated public school classrooms*. Symposium presented at the Council for Exceptional Children, Chicago, April 1976.

Carden-Smith, L., & Fowler, S.A. An assessment of student and teacher behavior in treatment and mainstreamed classes for preschool and kindergarten. *Analysis and Intervention in Developmental Disabilities* (in press).

Fowler, S.A. Support and follow-up services provided for special problem children one year after preschool. In *Developing a functional program for the transition of young children to integrated public school classrooms*. Symposium presented at the Council for Exceptional Children, Chicago, April 1976.

Fowler, S.A. Transition to public school. In K.E. Allen, *Mainstreaming in early childhood education*. Albany, N.Y.: Delmar Publishers, 1980, 242–254.

Fowler, S.A., & Baer, D.M. "Do I have to be good all day?" The timing of delayed reinforcement as a factor in generalization. *Journal of Applied Behavior Analysis*, 1981, *14*, 13–24.

Grosnick, J.K. Integration of exceptional children into regular classes: Research and procedure. *Focus on Exceptional Children*, 1971, *3*, 1–9.

Jones, R.T., & Kazdin, A.E. Programming response maintenance after withdrawing token reinforcement. *Behavior Therapy*, 1975, *6*, 153–164.

Kazdin, A.E., & Polster, R. Intermittent token reinforcement and response maintenance in extinction. *Behavior Therapy*, 1973, *4*, 386–391.

Klein, J.W. Mainstreaming the preschooler. *Young Children*, 1975, *5*, 317–326.

Knapczyk, D.R., & Livingston, G. The effects of prompting question-asking upon on-task behavior and reading comprehension. *Journal of Applied Behavior Analysis*. 1974, *7*, 115–121.

Koegel, R.L., & Rincover, A. Treatment of psychotic children in a classroom environment: I. Learning in a large group. *Journal of Applied Behavior Analysis*, 1974, *7*, 45–59.

LeBlanc, J.M., Etzel, B.C., & Domash, M.A. A functional curriculum for early intervention. In K.E. Allen, V.A. Holm, and R.L. Schiefelbusch, (Eds.), *Early intervention: A team approach*. Baltimore, Md.: University Park Press, 1978, 331–381.

Plummer, S. Program problems and a system for diagnosis. In *Developing a functional program for the transition of young children to integrated public school classrooms*. Symposium presented at the Council for Exceptional Children, Chicago, April 1976.

Rincover, A., & Koegel, R.L. Classroom treatment of autistic children: II. Individualized instruction in a group. *Journal of Abnormal Child Psychology*, 1977, *5*, 113–127.

Rogers-Warren, A., & Wedel, J.W. The ecology of preschool classrooms for the handicapped. *New Directions for Exceptional Children*, 1980, *1*, 1–24.

Rowbury, T.G., & Baer, D.M. Applied analysis of preschool children's behavior. In D. Glenwide and L. Jason (Eds.), *Behavioral community psychology*. New York: Praeger, 1980.

Russo, D.C., & Koegel, R.L. A method for integrating an autistic child into a normal public school classroom. *Journal of Applied Behavior Analysis*, 1977, *10*, 579–590.

Safford, P.L. *Teaching young children with special needs*. St. Louis, Mo.: The C.V. Mosby Company, 1978.

Stokes, T.F., & Baer, D.M. An implicit technology of generalization. *Journal of Applied Behavior Analysis*, 1977, *10*, 349–367.

Walker, H.M., & Hops, H. Use of normative peer data as a standard for evaluating classroom treatment effects. *Journal of Applied Behavior Analysis*, 1976, *9*, 159–168.

Walker, H.M., Hops, H., & Johnson, S.M. Generalization and maintenance of classroom treatment effects. *Behavior Therapy*, 1975, *6*, 188–200.

Wedel, J.W., & Fowler, S.A. *"Read me a story, Mom."* Using storytime to remediate academic deficits. Paper presented at the Association for Behavior Analysis, Milwaukee, May 1981.

Wehman, P., Abramson, M., & Norman, C. Transfer of training in behavior modification programs: An evaluation review. *Journal of Special Education*, 1977, *11*, 217–231.

Wildman, II, R.W., & Wildman, R.W. The generalization of behavior modification procedures: A review—with special emphasis on classroom applications. *Psychology in the Schools*,
   1975, *12*, 432–448.

Summary Report: David Smith

Birthdate: 4/18/75

From: Susan Fowler
Edna A. Hill Child Development Laboratory
Haworth Hall
University of Kansas

Date of Report: 5/1/82

Referral: David was referred in October 1980 by the Children's Center Preschool for disruptive and aggressive behavior, such as tantrumming, hitting, and kicking. The staff stated that the behavior occurred two to three times a day and appeared to be accelerating. They found it difficult to manage him in a group containing younger or smaller children.

Current Classroom Behavior: When David entered the Special Preschool in November 1980, he had not yet acquired a variety of skills necessary to learn from the classroom activities. He needed reminders to sit in a chair to be ready to work, to listen to instructions, to finish his work, to play appropriately with other children, and to follow classroom rules and the daily routine. At the beginning of December, he had an irregular pattern of good and bad days, demonstrating that he could participate appropriately sometimes.

By the end of the spring semester, David's days were consistently better. He approached the classroom routine with more assurance and was successful in the work and play periods. He learned to sit properly and to work quickly in the preacademic work period. He played well with the other children and earned privileges, such as helping the teachers prepare snack and calling children for snacks. He provided assistance during field trips by helping the younger children stay with the group.

David rarely exhibits any of the disruptive testing behaviors that we first saw after he was referred. He is, in fact, working on more sophisticated behavior, such as waiting turns quietly, working carefully at an appropriate pace, refraining from talking during work, and requesting help only when he actually needs it. David earns checkmarks for such appropriate "young man" behaviors during each of the eight periods of the day. It is clear that

David understands the rules of this system, since he is noticeably upset when he does not earn all his checkmarks for the day.

In summary, David seems to enjoy the classroom and has developed good interaction skills. He is well liked by both the other children and the teachers. He is an active participant in all of the classroom activities such as art activities, table toys, puzzles, and building with blocks. He also enjoys large motor activities, such as climbing and jumping. On the playground, he likes to run and climb, and he often asks other children to join him.

Academic Skills to Date:

Visual-Motor Skills: David has progressed greatly during the last nine months. He has completed the DLM plastic puzzles, the large parquetry designs, and the bead sequence, and he is currently working on the cube duplication and small parquetry and is almost finished with the puzzle sequence. The paper-and-pencil tasks that David has completed include tracing horizontal, vertical, and diagonal lines and a variety of shapes including squares, rectangles, and triangles.

Math Skills: David has worked extensively with numerals one through five and been exposed to numerals through ten. He can complete numeral-object correspondence tasks accurately through five, but he often makes errors with higher numbers. He can rote count to ten. David has worked primarily with manipulative math materials: counting blocks into bins labeled with a numeral, counting chips glued to strips of paper, using the Montessori number sorter.

David's mother requested that we teach him to recognize and print his first name, so a name lotto task was introduced in December 1981. He learned the placement of the letters of his first and last name. Then he began to write his name in name boxes. He is practicing the following letters this semester; a,c,b,r,e,s, and j. He has mastered the first three, but he is still working on the others. David recently began printing on kindergarten-style paper.

Language Concepts: David has made great strides in this area. He has completed the object lotto, color lotto, shape lotto, play scenes lotto, and DLM-motor expressive cards. He can identify the missing part on a variety of paired association cards. He finished the opposite concepts sequence, which included the concepts hot/cold, on/off, over/under, in/out, happy/sad, dirty/clean, and up/down.

We had some difficulty understanding David's sentence structure and articulation at the beginning of school. Because of this, we first worked on play scene lottos to help him use complete sentences and we introduced the sequenced picture cards that included face washing, showering, toothbrushing, dressing, bike riding, going to school, and the routine of the preschool day. He completed these sequences quickly. At the end of spring semester, David was presented with a new picture each day and was asked to explain what the picture was about. His descriptions have increased in length and spontaneity. David usually fills two minutes describing details in the picture.

Other Current Tasks:

In group times, David is working on labeling letters of the alphabet, identifying numerals 1 to 10, and rote counting. Following instructions and taking turns was an important goal in a variety of activities and games. Go Fish, pegboards, and parquetry puzzles were used in this manner.

Favorite Toys and Activities:

David enjoys a variety of toys and activities. He plays with the climbing and jumping toys when they are available. He also enjoys building with the unit blocks and working with playdough. He likes to run, play chase, and engage in group activities during outdoor times.

Future Task Suggestions:

We suggested that David continue to work on the tasks sequences that he is currently following. Special emphasis should be placed on his math and number tasks, as this is his greatest area of difficulty.

Also David should continue to receive praise and feedback for his classroom behavior. Discussions of classroom rules are still important.

Social Skills—Peers:

David works and plays well with the other children. In many activities he is a leader and a good model for the other children. On occasion David teases other children, but this has not been a severe problem.

Social Skills—Teachers:

David is friendly and polite to adults. He enjoys talking with them about a variety of subjects. He sits quietly during book-reading times with teachers, though he sometimes tries to control group activities and needs to be reminded to follow the teacher's directions.

Problem Behaviors and How to Deal With Them:

David rarely displays the aggressive and disruptive behaviors for which he was referred. His current problems are perhaps a result of higher expectations by the classroom staff. He sometimes works too fast and is consequently careless, talks while working, or tattles on other children. A "young man" program was developed for these behaviors. He earns a checkmark for each of the periods of the day in which he acts in a pleasant and polite manner. If he misses no more than one checkmark in a day, he is allowed to choose a special outdoor activity or large group activity. He seems to respond well to clearly specified rules and guidelines for appropriate behavior.

Current Impressions:

We have been very pleased with David's adaptation to our classroom routines, expectations, and classroom structure. He seems to respond well when expectations are clearly laid out for him and followed up with praise and other positive feedback.

Recommendations:

Should David have difficulty with social or conduct behaviors in the future, we recommend the following routine:

- Inform him what the appropriate behaviors are, and specify behaviors he cannot do.

- Set up regular check periods, and give yes-no feedback (checkmarks, stickers) at the end of each period.

- Tell David at the end of the day if he has earned enough checks.

- Minimize negative feedback if he misses, emphasize, instead, that he can try again tomorrow.

Index

H

I

About the Authors

K. EILEEN ALLEN is a supervisor in the Edna A. Hill Child Development Laboratory Preschools and a professor in the Department of Human Development and Family Life at the University of Kansas, Lawrence. For the past 25 years, Professor Allen has been engaged in a variety of professional activities related to early childhood development and education. Her work, conducted first at the University of Washington in Seattle and then at the University of Kansas, includes extensive research activities, course work for graduates and undergraduates, and teacher training in both laboratory and community settings.

Professor Allen has published numerous articles and a variety of films and textbooks related to child development and early childhood education for both normally developing and atypical children. She has held major offices in a variety of national organizations and has been an invited presenter and keynote speaker for a large number of conferences and conventions at both the national and international level. A number of honors have also been awarded Professor Allen, most recently a year-long appointment in Washington, D.C., as a Congressional Science Fellow. She was selected for this post by the American Association for the Advancement of Science and the Society for Research in Child Development.

ELIZABETH M. GOETZ, coauthor of this book, is an associate professor in the Department of Human Development and Family Life at the University of Kansas. In addition, Dr. Goetz is Director of the Edna A. Hill Child Development Laboratory Preschools, which serve approximately 150 young children. Her research experiences with young children are reflected in her publications, which have covered such areas as self-control, creativity, comprehension, incidental teaching, prereading, social interaction, and ethical issues. Recently, she presented a paper on behavior analysis for the whole child at an international symposium on applied behavior analysis in education in Mexico City. Her service to the profession includes serving as associate editor on a research journal for the education and treatment of children and as president of the board of a day care center. Currently, she teaches undergraduate and graduate students in research and the education of young children both in the classroom and the applied setting of the preschool.